Advancing Aboriginal Claims

ADVANCING ABORIGINAL CLAIMS

VISIONS ▪ STRATEGIES ▪ DIRECTIONS

Edited by Kerry Wilkins

Purich Publishing Ltd.
Saskatoon, Saskatchewan
Canada

Published in association with the
Centre for Constitutional Studies
University of Alberta
Edmonton, Alberta, Canada

Copyright © 2004 Centre for Constitutional Studies, University of Alberta
Copyright of individual papers remains with the authors

All rights reserved. No part of this publication may be reproduced or transmitted in any form or by any means without permission in writing from the publisher, except by a reviewer, who may quote brief passages in a review, or in the case of photocopying or other reprographic copying, a license from ACCESS (Canadian Copyright Licensing Agency) in Toronto. All inquiries and orders regarding this publication should be addressed to:

Purich Publishing Ltd.
Box 23032, Market Mall Post Office
Saskatoon, SK Canada S7J 5H3
Phone: (306) 373–5311   Fax: (306) 373–5315
Email: purich@sasktel.net
Website: www.purichpublishing.com

Library and Archives Canada Cataloguing in Publication

Advancing Aboriginal claims : visions, strategies, directions /
edited by
Kerry Wilkins.

(Purich's aboriginal issues series)
"Published in association with the Centre for Constitutional Studies,
University of Alberta".
Includes index.
ISBN 1-895830-24-9

1. Native peoples—Legal status, laws, etc.—Canada. 2. Native
peoples—Canada—Claims. I. Wilkins, Kerry, 1946- II. University of Alberta.
Centre for Constitutional Studies III. Series.

KE7709.A83 2004   342.7108'72   C2004-906556-4
KF8205.A83 2004

Series design by NEXT Communications Inc., Saskatoon, Saskatchewan.

Cover design by Duncan Campbell, Regina, Saskatchewan.

Copy-editing, design, and layout by Roberta Mitchell Coulter, Saskatoon, Saskatchewan.

Printed in Canada by Houghton-Boston, Saskatoon, Saskatchewan, on acid-free paper.

Published in association with the Centre for Constitutional Studies, University of Alberta, Edmonton, Alberta, Canada.

The publisher acknowledges the financial assistance of the Government of Saskatchewan through the Cultural Industries Development Fund towards the publication of this book.

Readers will note that words like Aboriginal, Native, and Indigenous have been capitalized in this book except in some quoted material. In recent years, many Aboriginal people have argued that such words should be capitalized when referring to specific people, in the same manner that European and American are capitalized. We agree.
The Publishers

CONTENTS

Contributors   7

Acknowledgements   10

Introduction   11
Kerry Wilkins

PART I
VALIDATING ABORIGINAL EXPERIENCE

Aboriginal Paradigms: Implications for Relationships to Land
and Treaty Making   26
Leroy Little Bear

The Right of Inclusion: Aboriginal Rights and/or Aboriginal Women?   39
Patricia A. Monture

Aboriginal Jurisprudence and Rights   67
James (Sákéj) Youngblood Henderson

PART II
SUBSTANTIVE ARGUMENTS

Indigenous Rights and the *Lex Loci* in British Imperial Law   91
Russel Lawrence Barsh

Continuity of Aboriginal Rights   127
Kent McNeil

Métis Aboriginal Title in Canada: Achieving Equality in
Aboriginal Rights Doctrine   151
Larry N. Chartrand

PART III
PRACTICAL CONSEQUENCES AND CHOICES

Fear, Hope, and Misunderstanding: Unintended Consequences
and the *Marshall* Decision   190
Christopher P. Manfredi

"Let Us Face It, We Are All Here to Stay"
But Do We Negotiate or Litigate?   202
Leonard I. Rotman

Aboriginal Resource Rights After *Delgamuukw* and *Marshall*   241
Gordon Christie

First Nations–Crown Relations in British Columbia
in the Post-*Delgamuukw* Era   271
Gurston Dacks

Conclusion: Judicial Aesthetics and Aboriginal Claims   288
Kerry Wilkins

Index   313

CONTRIBUTORS

Russel Barsh gained an interest in British imperial law at Harvard Law School. He has taught at the University of Washington, University of Lethbridge, and New York University. His areas of specialization include international law, traditional ecological knowledge, and issues of intellectual and cultural property. He has been involved with the international movement of Indigenous peoples at the United Nations, as well as the World Intellectual Property Organization and the World Trade Organization. In 2002, he returned to his intellectual roots in paleontology and ecology as founding director of the Center for the Study of Coast Salish Environments, a program in marine ecology sponsored by the Samish Indian Nation.

Larry Chartrand is currently director of the Aboriginal Self-Governance Program at the University of Winnipeg. Prior to this appointment, he was an associate professor of Law at the University of Ottawa. His main research efforts are in the field of Aboriginal rights, including self-government, treaty rights, Métis rights, Aboriginal health issues, and international human rights as they pertain to Indigenous peoples. He obtained his B.Ed. from the University of Alberta in 1986 and his LL.B from York University in 1989, was called to the Bar of Upper Canada in 1990, and obtained his LL.M from Queen's University in 2001. He is the past president of the Indigenous Bar Association and an arbitrator for the Sahtu Dene and Métis Land Claim Agreement.

Gordon Christie is a professor of Law at the University of British Columbia, teaching in the areas of tort law, jurisprudence, and Aboriginal law, and conducting research primarily in the field of Aboriginal law. He has taught at a number of institutions in Canada and the United States, in both faculties of Law and departments of Philosophy. He is Inuvialuit.

Gurston Dacks received his B.A. from the University of Toronto and his Ph.D. from Princeton University. He is professor of Political Science and associate dean of Arts (Research) at the University of Alberta, on whose faculty he has served since 1971. For the past twenty-five years, he has studied the political development of the Canadian North and in particular constitutional issues, division of the Northwest Territories, and Aboriginal claims and self-government. More recently, his research has broadened to examine issues related to Aboriginal rights and governance in southern as well as northern Canada.

Born to the Bear Clan of the Chickasaw Nation and Cheyenne Tribe in Oklahoma in 1944, **James (Sákéj) Youngblood Henderson** is married to Marie Battiste, a

Míkmaw educator. They have three children. In 1974, he received a Juris doctorate in law from Harvard Law School and became a law professor who created litigation strategies to restore Aboriginal culture, institutions, and rights. During the constitutional process (1978–1993) in Canada, he served as a constitutional advisor for the Míkmaw nation and the National Indian Brotherhood–Assembly of First Nations. He is now working at the Native Law Centre of Canada, College of Law, University of Saskatchewan. His latest books are *Aboriginal Tenure in the Constitution of Canada* (2000), *Protecting Indigenous Knowledge and Heritage* (2000), and the forthcoming *Indigenous Jurisprudence and Aboriginal Rights* and *Treaty Rights in the Constitution of Canada*.

Leroy Little Bear is a member of the Small Robes Band of the Blood Indian Tribe of the Blackfoot Confederacy. After graduating from the University of Utah with a Juris Doctor degree in 1975, he was a professor in the Native American Studies department at the University of Lethbridge. After his retirement in 1997, he was director of the Harvard University Native American Program until 1999. He has served as a consultant and as a member of various committees, commissions, and boards, including the Task Force on the Criminal Justice and Its Impact on the Indian and Metis Peoples of Alberta in 1990–91. He is the author of many articles, including "A Concept of Native Title," which has been cited in a Supreme Court of Canada decision, and has coauthored books including *Pathways to Self-Determination, The Quest for Justice,* and *Governments in Conflict* with Dr. Menno Boldt and Dr. Anthony Long. His current interests include North American Indian science and Western physics and exploring Blackfoot knowledge expressed in songs, stories, and landscape.

Christopher P. Manfredi, Ph.D., is professor of Political Science at McGill University, specializing in Canadian public law and comparative legal systems. He is the author of *Feminist Activism in the Supreme Court: Legal Mobilization and the Women's Legal Education and Action Fund* (2004), *Judicial Power and the Charter: Canada and the Paradox of Liberal Constitutionalism* (2d ed., 2001), and *The Supreme Court and Juvenile Justice* (1997). His research on constitutional and legal issues has been published in many prestigious journals.

Kent McNeil teaches at Osgoode Hall Law School in Toronto. He specializes in Indigenous rights in Canada, Australia, and the United States. He is the author of numerous works on this subject, including *Common Law Aboriginal Title* (1989) and *Emerging Justice? Essays on Indigenous Rights in Canada and Australia* (2001). He advises First Nations on Aboriginal land claims, treaty negotiations, and fiduciary obligations.

Patricia A. Monture is Mohawk from Grand River Territory. Her legal education was completed at Queen's University and Osgoode Hall Law School. She is also a graduate of the University of Western Ontario. At present, she is a full professor in the department of Sociology at the University of Saskatchewan. Her academic interests are varied and include issues of constitutional law and Aboriginal peoples, the rights of women, critical race theory, and other issues of social justice, including the rights of prisoners.

Leonard Rotman, B.A. (Toronto) (With Distinction), LL.B. (Queen's), LL.M. (Osgoode Hall), S.J.D. (Toronto), of the Ontario Bar, is a professor at the Faculty of Law, University of Windsor. He is the author of *Parallel Paths: Fiduciary Doctrine and the Crown-Native Relationship in Canada* (1996), co-editor of *Aboriginal Legal Issues: Cases, Materials & Commentary* (1998) and *Canadian Corporate Law: Cases, Notes & Materials* (second edition, 2001), author of "Remedies" (with J. Berryman) and "Fiduciary Law" in F. Woodman and M. Gillen, eds., *The Law of Trusts: A Contextual Approach* (2000), and author of numerous law review articles covering topics in the Aboriginal law, fiduciary law, trusts, and corporate law fields. An inaugural recipient of the University of Windsor Award for Excellence in Scholarship and Research, he has received awards and grants from the Social Science Federation of Canada, the Foundation for Legal Research, the Centre for Innovation Law and Policy, and the Law Societies of Alberta and Ontario. He has been cited by broadcast and print media, by various courts, including the Supreme Court of Canada, acts as a peer reviewer for a variety of law and law-related journals and book publishers, and serves as a consultant to the private bar and government.

Kerry Wilkins is a Toronto lawyer and sometime adjunct professor of law at the University of Toronto, whose practice has focused in recent years principally on constitutional issues arising from the Canadian law about Aboriginal peoples. He has published articles on legal education, the division of federal-provincial powers, section 88 of the *Indian Act*, inherent rights of Aboriginal self-government, and the relationship between provincial capacity under the constitution and treaty and Aboriginal rights, and book reviews on a wider range of legal subjects.

ACKNOWLEDGEMENTS

This book is the culmination of a research project initiated and supervised by the Centre for Constitutional Studies at the University of Alberta, with the generous (and indispensable) financial support of the Alberta Law Foundation. It could not have come to fruition without the inspiration, industry, and commitment of a series of executive directors at the Centre, each of whom made a distinctive contribution. David Schneiderman conceived of the project and laid the initial groundwork for its realization, hiring James Guest as project director. It was James who recruited the authors and commissioned the papers that appear in this volume and who first attracted interest in the project from the distinguished publishing house that accepted the book for publication. David's successor, Tsvi Kahana, recruited me to edit the collection. Most recently, Janna Promislow, the incumbent, has brought fresh and welcome energy to the project; her dedication and supervision have expedited its completion substantially. I am grateful to them all for this opportunity.

I am equally grateful to Don Purich and Karen Bolstad, who are Purich Publishing Ltd., whose unwavering support for the project, and commitment to it, kept it alive. I hope that the book in published form rewards their confidence in it. I am sure that they and the Centre will join me in thanking Roberta Mitchell Coulter, whose meticulous copy editing improved the text in several places, and the several students at the University of Alberta who took part in checking the citations, cross-references, and quotations. Among the latter, Lorne Randa's thorough and efficient work was particularly valuable.

I owe personal thanks to innumerable friends and relatives (who know who they are) for remaining my friends and relatives despite the attention, cheerfulness, time, and energy of which my work on the book for the past three years has too often deprived them.

Above all, though, I owe gratitude to the authors whose papers appear in this book—Russel Barsh, Larry Chartrand, Gordon Christie, Gurston Dacks, James (Sákéj) Youngblood Henderson, Leroy Little Bear, Kent McNeil, Christopher Manfredi, Patricia Monture, and Leonard Rotman—for their truly remarkable patience, cooperation, and courtesy with a rather demanding editor throughout this vicissitudinous process. I hope our paths cross again another time.

Kerry Wilkins

INTRODUCTION

There is no shortage of legal and other scholarly writing today about Canadian law and the rights of Aboriginal peoples. One would like to hope that all this academic industry is doing something useful to improve the plight of the Indigenous communities still trying to preserve and keep fresh "the way to live most nicely together"[1] in the midst of the settler regime that still presumes to dominate their traditional territories. One might forgive at least some of those communities for preferring instead, as Elvis Presley once famously did, a little less conversation, a little more action. When there are so many other ways in which we could use our time and resources to help address more immediately Aboriginal peoples' predicaments, those of us who persist in contributing to this literature bear some real obligation to earn the time, and the attention, of an audience.

When the Centre for Constitutional Studies embarked on the project that has become this book, they undertook to select featured authors whose work could satisfy that exacting standard. Those efforts yielded work that is thought-provoking, committed, timely, topical, and wise.[1a] My task is to demonstrate how their works fit together to make a distinctive collective contribution that is worthy of particular attention.

To me, the single greatest virtue of this collection is its thematic focus on the matter of strategy. Readers of the recent academic literature will have little trouble finding elsewhere closely reasoned doctrinal analyses of the relevant law, insightful theoretical writings featuring normative frameworks from which to address Aboriginal issues, and critical commentary on particular judicial decisions affecting Aboriginal peoples, especially decisions from the Supreme Court of Canada. Largely missing, however, from the deliberation to date has been sustained reflection on the choices real Aboriginal peoples and communities face in dealing with a dominant legal and political system developed by others without any special regard for their deeper rhythms. How, and to what extent, can such a community today take advantage of the still fairly recent constitutional changes that offer new protection to treaty and Aboriginal rights without incurring serious risk of compromising the texture of relationships and responsibilities that continue to constitute and give purpose to life within it? What can Aboriginal peoples realistically hope to achieve from negotiations with the Crown or with private non-Aboriginal interests? When, if ever, is litigation a necessary, or even sensible, recourse, having regard, among other things, to the doubts that some academics—and even Supreme Court judges, as one contributor here points out—have entertained about the courts' suitability to address the profoundly difficult issues that flow from the imperative to be fair in contemporary terms to the Aboriginal presence in Canada? Is it sensible even to try to deal with these sorts of choices abstractly, or does too much depend on particularities?

It does not speak especially well of contemporary Canada that the Aboriginal nations—whose willingness to accommodate the increasing presence of foreigners facilitated the process of peaceful settlement that we take for granted today—now face so many soul-tearing choices in their efforts to maintain sufficient space and resources to be themselves. But there it is. This book is in no sense the last—and surely ought not to be the only—word on the subject of strategic thinking in and on behalf of Aboriginal communities. Its value, at this place and time, is to do what it can to initiate rigorous exploration of these practical questions.

Three requirements, at a minimum, structure such exploration: a deepening understanding of the unifying and the distinguishing features within Aboriginal experience, as shared by Aboriginal people speaking from the depths of their own traditions; a familiarity with, ideally to the point of mastery of, the lines of doctrinal argumentation from the dominant mainstream tradition that offer real, trustworthy support to Aboriginal legal positions; and specific attention, framed and informed by both of these other sources, to the relative merits of the legal and other strategic options practical for particular communities in particular circumstances.

This collection is in three parts, each addressed primarily to one of these three imperatives. It would be a mistake, however, to suppose that the papers featured here contribute usefully only to discussion of one or another of these different requirements. Many deal insightfully with more than one and could have held their own, more or less, if placed instead in another part of the book. Patricia Monture, for example, offers some pointed suggestions about the conduct of litigation in the course of her thorough discussion of the significance of gender, traditionally and today, in Aboriginal communities. Larry Chartrand, whose principal aim here is to identify the best doctrinal foundation for Métis Aboriginal title, notes that certain lines of argument would operate, if adopted, to undercut the Métis sense of autonomy. Gordon Christie explicitly considers, from a strategic perspective, the impact of current Aboriginal rights and title jurisprudence on Aboriginal peoples' conceptions, traditional and contemporary, of their relationships to the land. I could go on. Surprisingly often, these authors seem to be in conversation with one another, shedding crosslight on each other's themes, within and across the book's different parts.

Part I, "Validating Aboriginal Experience," features thinkers from three different Aboriginal nations and language groups, writing independently. Each of their papers undertakes, for somewhat different reasons and in different degrees of detail, to communicate to readers of English, whose expectations of nature, order, and fairness derive predominantly from European paradigms, something of what it means to experience the world from within the categories and relationships endemic to the authors' home communities. This is not an easy thing to do. The ways of organizing experience that emerge most naturally from regular use of the English language and Canadian jurisprudence are by no means the same as those that emerge from the languages and teachings that developed independently in the Indigenous nations of North America. It might well be surprising if they were.

Not having grown up within an Aboriginal language or community, I come to their writings from a certain distance. From this distance, what catch my attention particularly are the overlaps: the features common to their characterizations of Indigenous experience. Each of them calls attention to the magnitude of the qualitative difference between the mainstream Canadian way of waging experience and the flavour and texture of life traditional to his or her home community. Each reports that, from this latter perspective, human beings and their communities subsist, first and foremost, in relationship, not only within and among themselves but indeed with everything else that is part of creation. These relationship networks, which make life and experience possible, inspire respect and reverence and require active ongoing maintenance through performance, observance, and ceremony. At or near the centre of this orientation is the land itself. Considered generically, the land is at once the stage on which the drama of relational existence plays out and the source of all that is needed to nourish and sustain it. In its specificity, particular land has its own unique features and its own sacred sites. The different animals, plants, and earthen materials that it provides and supports in different localities prescribe the kinds of livelihoods and relationships considered appropriate there.

It is in Leroy Little Bear's lead essay, "Aboriginal Paradigms," that these themes receive their most extended development. To him, a culture is, in effect, a collective agreement among the members of a group or society about the nature of reality. It includes philosophy (the theoretical part), customs (which operationalize the philosophy), and values (which register, in relation to the philosophy, which kinds of beliefs and conduct are acceptable and which are not). Writing principally from a Plains Indian perspective, he enumerates the key features of Aboriginal philosophy: holism; equality among all things because all things have spirit; the primacy of spatial relationships; an underlying chaos that, in the absence of vigilance, can overtake and jeopardize the whole, or any part, of creation at any time; and a concomitant shared responsibility, faced with this ongoing threat of chaos, to maintain and renew the patterns and relationships on which our existence depends. These commitments bespeak a respectful, reciprocal relationship with the land, and a recognition that the land has significance of its own, over and above the material and spiritual sustenance it provides. For centuries, First Nations, operating within this shared paradigm, have made treaties and alliances with one another in the interest of extending still further their effective relational networks and facilitating fulfilment of their stewardship obligations to the land and to the Creator. They assumed they could and would do the same with the Europeans. Imagine their surprise to discover—too late—that the settlers took the cosmic relational network entirely for granted, focused on the boundaries between things instead of the linkages among them, and treated the land as little more than just another fungible commodity that could be chunked out, owned, and traded around. Imagine their incredulity at the very idea that someone could think that he could extinguish their responsibilities to, and relationship with, the land by purchase, by military conquest, or just by showing up.

For Patricia Monture, the missing piece in the Canadian jurisprudence on Aboriginal issues, and in much current Aboriginal thinking—including, she candidly acknowledges, much of her own—on issues of self-determination and litigation strategy is an understanding of the importance of gender in Aboriginal communities. In a wide-ranging essay, written in the spirit of her Mohawk storytelling tradition, she articulates some of the ways in which various Aboriginal societies acknowledge and constitute gender, the differences that gender makes in organizing life and experience in those societies, and the ways in which traditional mainstream attitudes toward women and the litigation of Aboriginal issues in Canadian courts have operated to compromise the situation of Aboriginal women in their own communities. Traditionally, she reports, gender was not a problem in First Nation societies. It was simply understood prereflectively that men and women had different contributions to make in the society and had gendered teachings and "knowledges" that accompanied their roles; that their roles, though different, were complementary; and that there was no need for hierarchy among the roles or the genders themselves. They were functioning parts of the much larger relational network of responsibilities; to overlook or interfere with them was to disturb the balance of things. Today, by contrast, First Nations' societies must address the impact that colonial notions of patriarchy and gender hierarchy have had upon their internal arrangements. They must be cognizant, too, of the ways in which their legal relations with settler courts and governments have obscured the significance of their women's contributions and the particular precariousness of the women's present situation. Treaty negotiations, for instance, rarely gave the same primacy to gathering and growing, for which the women were responsible, as they gave to hunting and fishing, which typically came within male authority. So far, Aboriginal rights litigation has dealt disproportionately, in her view, with hunting and fishing prosecutions, and has been shaped in part by traditional colonial prejudices about women. It has all but ignored the women, and the significance of gender, in contemplating what is integral to distinctive Aboriginal cultures, even when First Nations women have themselves been among the litigants. This phenomenon, Monture suggests, reflects in part traditional colonial prejudices about women and the disproportionate prevalence in such litigation of hunting and fishing prosecutions. In this sense, litigation has potential to mask the diversity of the First Nations' cultures. As a result, First Nations face a difficult choice in litigation. Do they—must they?—choose to suppress issues of gender difference for the sake of increasing the odds of securing recognition of their claims, even though gender has always itself been integral to the very cultural practices they are seeking to protect?

James (Sákéj) Youngblood Henderson, of Chickasaw and Cheyenne descent, begins his contribution from the somewhat novel premise that the Supreme Court of Canada got something important right in its explication of the constitutional protection now accorded to existing Aboriginal and treaty rights.[2] The decisive judicial insight, he argues, is that such rights are, by their nature, embedded in distinctive Aboriginal cultures and social practices. To him, this acknowledgement bespeaks acceptance of the existence of, and a willingness to be guided by, the teachings that constitute the pre-existing systems of law and governance—the "jurisprudences"—of the various Aboriginal peoples, from which the constitutionally protected rights derive and take their coloration. This development is fully consistent with the Supreme Court's recent articulation and enforcement in other contexts of unwritten constitutional principles; it also continues appropriately the protection that the pre-existing Aboriginal orders were accorded by imperial law and practice. Even so, he suggests, it is nothing less than a transformation of Canadian common law and constitutional jurisprudence.

The difficulty, in Henderson's view, is that the mainstream courts, despite their professed sensitivity to the Aboriginal perspective, have not yet done what is required to fulfil the promise that these commitments entail. The courts know little about the teachings of the various Aboriginal communities whose rights claims are before them; in their ignorance, they make key mistakes about the character and scope of the rights it is their business to protect. Aboriginal jurisprudences developed before and apart from exposure to European legal and conceptual paradigms and reflect fundamentally different orientations: substantively, imperatives of sacredness, holism, and ecological integrity; adjectivally, reliance on performance, ceremony, and oral tradition in preference to written records and political assemblies. They form complete, self-consistent knowledge systems that can be fully learned and understood only by means of the pedagogy—and, strictly speaking, only in the languages—traditionally employed by Aboriginal peoples themselves. Yet so far, courts and lawyers have ignored Aboriginal jurisprudences; they have not, for instance, issued respectful invitations to Aboriginal Elders or law-keepers to appear as expert witnesses and introduce them to the essential teachings. Instead, they have presumed to identify Aboriginal rights by means of external Anglo-Canadian techniques of analysis. In doing so, they have failed in their constitutional responsibility to accord proper respect and dignity to Aboriginal jurisprudences. It will take cooperation on both sides, Henderson concludes, to inculcate and incorporate a real understanding of the essential Aboriginal teachings, but nothing less will suffice to achieve the reconciliation promised by the constitutional reforms of 1982.

The papers in Part II, "Substantive Arguments," use the idiom, doctrine, and style of analysis characteristic of principled Anglo-Canadian jurisprudence to recognize the legitimacy and facilitate accreditation within the mainstream framework of Aboriginal interests in land, traditional practice, and governance. No strategic agenda for Aboriginal peoples in Canada can be complete or fully informed without a deep understanding of the dominant legal tradition—the tradition whose criteria will be used in polite encounters to appraise the merits of Aboriginal claims and arguments—or without a grasp of the potential for effective doctrinal advocacy within it. The three papers comprising this part each substantiate, in the course of their different but complementary preoccupations, Henderson's observation that the founding principles of English and imperial law leave room for and protect Aboriginal legal arrangements and interests.

It is Russel Barsh whose paper undertakes this task most explicitly. His argument, briefly stated, is that legal pluralism—an institutionalized respect for the laws, traditions, and customs of the foreign lands that have come at various times under Crown control—has been an accepted feature of English domestic and colonial law since Tudor, Norman, and even Roman times. The true anomaly, he suggests, has been the failure, until very recently, of Canadian (and Australian and New Zealand) law to begin to acknowledge and accommodate to that reality. The tension between the central authority and the pre-existing legal arrangements of the peoples already occupying lands over which the Crown assumed dominion has been thematic from the earliest days of the Crown's expanding hegemony. In a series of judicial decisions from the late sixteenth through the late eighteenth century, British courts clarified that English laws applied routinely to the affairs of settlers only in territories that were otherwise uninhabited at the time of settlement. In settlements acquired by treaty, cession, or military force, the king had the power (pending establishment of a local legislature) to impose the English law, but except when and as he did so in an unmistakable way, the pre-existing arrangements continued to govern unless they were contrary to English law, were repugnant in themselves, or were, in a relevant circumstance, just silent. This was the pattern carefully followed in the British settlements in Africa and India, where colonial courts routinely respected, discerned, and applied the local customary laws, sometimes (as in polygamy cases) even when they seemed irreconcilable with contemporary British social norms. Given that North America was hardly uninhabited at the time of British settlement (a fact attested by the British practice of entering treaties with the locals from the earliest times), one would have expected similar patterns here. I have long wondered why the legal practice in North America developed so differently from the practice elsewhere in the empire; Barsh's thoughtful discussion of this issue is the first that I have seen. For me, it is among the highlights of his rigorous and carefully documented presentation.

Kent McNeil has spent much of his professional career investigating and explicating Canadian and Commonwealth law of Aboriginal rights and title. "Continuity of Aboriginal Rights," his paper in this collection, continues that exploration. According to the leading cases on Aboriginal rights and title, communities asserting such rights must demonstrate to a court's satisfaction that a certain state of affairs was in place as of a much earlier date in history. To prove an Aboriginal right, they must prove that the relevant custom, tradition, or practice was integral to the community's distinctive culture at the time of first contact with Europeans.[3] To prove Aboriginal title to a given tract of land, they must prove that they had exclusive occupation of that territory at the moment of Crown sovereignty over it.[4] Communities relying for this purpose on evidence dating from times subsequent to contact (or to sovereignty) must demonstrate, in addition, a continuity between the pre- and post-contact custom, tradition, or practice (or the pre- and post-sovereignty occupation of the relevant land). But must they prove continuity even where they have sufficient independent evidence of the pre-contact practice (or the pre-sovereignty occupation)? And where the law requires them to demonstrate continuity, how far back does the evidence of continuity have to reach?

These are the questions on which McNeil focuses here. His answer to the first question is in the negative. Proof of continuity is not, he says, an independent requirement to establish an Aboriginal right or Aboriginal title; it is an alternative way of proving what needs to be proved about the state of affairs before contact or sovereignty. Its introduction, McNeil asserts, was meant to ease the burden of proof for claimant communities that could not provide sufficient affirmative relevant evidence from before the moment of contact or sovereignty, now hundreds of years ago. In answer to the second question, he draws upon the ancient English law of customary rights. According to that law, proof that a given custom has been in place for as long as living memory creates a rebuttable presumption that the custom has existed since time immemorial. The same presumption, in his view, should operate in respect of customs, practices, or traditions asserted as Aboriginal rights. Like the customs recognized and enforced in English law, Aboriginal customs should be understood, once established, not to be susceptible to loss by abandonment. As for rights to land, it has long been true in English law that present occupation of land creates a presumption of title, shifting to those contesting the title the burden of proving otherwise. Communities asserting Aboriginal title to the lands they currently occupy should, in McNeil's view, be entitled to the benefit of the same presumption.

Larry Chartrand's paper addresses in detail the challenges Métis people faced in proving Aboriginal rights, and still face in proving Aboriginal title. Requiring, as the Supreme Court of Canada did in *Van der Peet*,[5] that Aboriginal rights be authenticated as of the moment of European contact risked precluding altogether valid Métis claims of Aboriginal right. This conclusion, however, seemed incompatible with the inclusion of the Métis among the "aboriginal peoples of Canada" whose Aboriginal rights are now entitled to constitutional protection.[6] The Supreme Court's decision in *Delgamuukw*[7] to authenticate claims of Aboriginal title as of the moment of Crown sovereignty in the relevant area leaves some room for the establishment of Métis Aboriginal title, but still has potential to subject the title claims of the Métis to a form of jeopardy not faced by First Nations title claims.

The question Chartrand considers is how best, from a doctrinal standpoint, to deal with the unfairness of this. One option, which he calls the "trace theory," proposes that Métis rights and title be derived—and that Métis have only such Aboriginal rights and title as can be derived—from the rights and title belonging to their ancestral First Nations communities. In the *Powley* decision,[8] the Supreme Court rejected the trace theory and, in Chartrand's view, was correct to do so. For one thing, the theory has numerous doctrinal, practical, and evidentiary drawbacks; not all the members of established Métis communities, for instance, share ancestry from the same First Nations. More important, however, he argues, is the fact that the Métis could not consistently insist upon their autonomy as a separate Aboriginal people if they sought to trace their special rights exclusively from the rights of their First Nations ancestors. A second option is to scrutinize Métis claims of right or title against a standard different from the one used for First Nations claims, substituting for Métis claims a different, more recent reference date—the date of effective Crown control—for the date of contact or sovereignty. This is what the Supreme Court of Canada chose to do in *Powley*[9] to make room for Métis Aboriginal rights. The disadvantage of this approach, Chartrand argues, is that it differentiates invidiously between Métis and other Aboriginal peoples, holding First Nations claims to a stricter standard than Métis claims. The unfortunate part, in his view, is that it was not necessary for the court to resort to such differentiation to leave room for valid Métis claims. It was possible before *Powley* in the law of Aboriginal rights, and is still possible today in the law of Aboriginal title, to accommodate valid Métis claims within a single standard applicable to the claims of all Aboriginal peoples. The way to do this, he suggests, is to adopt a richer understanding of the notions of "contact" and "sovereignty": one that recognizes, in accordance with international law and Privy Council jurisprudence, that the date of sovereignty cannot precede the date of effective control, because effective control of a territory is a necessary step in perfecting any claim of sovereignty over Indigenous inhabitants.

It is in Part III, "Practical Consequences and Choices," that this collection turns to the pragmatic dimension of the inquiry into strategy. The four papers comprising this part take a step away from doctrine to contemplate two principal issues: the relative efficacy of negotiation and litigation as means of protecting and advancing Aboriginal interests (or, from another perspective, as means of managing Aboriginal disputes), and the impact on Aboriginal relationships with land and resources of the developing Canadian jurisprudence on Aboriginal rights and title.

Few can forget, even today, the circumstances surrounding the Supreme Court of Canada's 1999 decision in *Marshall*.[10] There, the court held that a provision in a treaty from the early 1760s between the imperial Crown and Mi'kmaq communities conferred on those communities today, by implication, a constitutionally protected right to carry on traditional harvesting activities for commercial purposes, to the extent required to sustain a moderate livelihood. Governments, therefore, have to justify any regulations or other restrictions they seek to impose on this right; in the *Marshall* case, they had not done so. The decision provoked a reaction of unprecedented hostility from non-Aboriginal fishers and their communities in Atlantic Canada. Two months later, the court unexpectedly issued a second judgment,[11] designed, at least in part, to "clarify"— i.e., in some respects, to narrow the doctrinal reach of—its earlier decision and to moderate the expectations its earlier ruling had engendered in affected Mi'kmaq communities.

Christopher Manfredi's paper, "Fear, Hope, and Misunderstanding," reflects on these events and their significance. It identifies striking parallels between the *Marshall* scenario and what had happened some years earlier, when the Supreme Court's decision in *Askov*[12] (on accused persons' *Charter*[13] right to be tried within a reasonable time)[14] resulted in the dismissal and abandonment of thousands of criminal charges. Each instance, Manfredi points out, featured questionable use of expert evidence, confident but inaccurate predictions of limited impact, denial of judicial responsibility for the consequences, and a follow-up judgment designed to clarify and to improve things. Each, in his view, reflects a miscalculation on the part of the Court and raises larger issues about the competence of courts as such to deal with complex, multifaceted issues of social policy. The temptation to address some such issues arises from courts' propensity to see themselves as guardians and enforcers of our "basic constitutional values," but the very character and orientation of litigation—its emphasis on rights and duties over costs and benefits, for instance, and its necessary focus on the static historical events that give rise to specific private disputes—limit judges' capacity to make constructive, well-considered policy. The *Marshall* experience, Manfredi reports, has prompted a seemly caution since then in the Supreme Court of Canada's approach to Aboriginal issues. Perhaps, he suggests, it ought also to prompt some reflection about the consequences of the regime of rights-based judicial review that resulted from the constitutional amendments of 1982.

The wisdom of resort to the courts to vindicate Aboriginal claims concerns Leonard Rotman, as well. His concern, however, has different sources and arises within a somewhat different context. In his contribution to this collection, Rotman appraises the relative merits for Aboriginal peoples of litigation and negotiation as means of achieving binding results that vindicate their claims. Negotiation, as he observes, is intuitively the more palatable option for Aboriginal peoples, not least because it is more in keeping with traditional Aboriginal notions of good relationship. Traditionally, however, the Crown has been unwilling to negotiate Aboriginal issues—and to abandon hard-line positions in negotiations—except when compelled to do so by the threat, or the reality, of unfavourable litigation results. It was only after the *Calder* decision[15] held, in 1973, that Aboriginal title is a justiciable right in Canadian law that the federal Crown agreed to negotiate First Nations' land claims; it was only after the *Sparrow* decision[16] in 1990 gave meaningful effect to the constitutional guarantee of existing treaty and Aboriginal rights[17] that the Crown took an active interest in facilitating such negotiations. Today, there are approved procedures in place for resolving First Nations' claims consensually, through negotiation, but those procedures, despite some recent attempts at improvement, remain, in Rotman's judgment, deeply imperfect and unfair in important ways to Aboriginal participants. As a result, he argues, Aboriginal peoples still often require the leverage available, in principle, to them from pursuit of their claims through litigation. In recent years, however, there has been growing reason to doubt the efficacy of litigation as a means of vindicating Aboriginal claims. For one thing, several court decisions have seemed to dilute the robust protection that the *Sparrow* decision appeared to promise to treaty and Aboriginal rights. For another, incidents involving two Supreme Court judges—Justice Bastarache's remarks some years ago in newspaper interviews, which received nation-wide circulation, and Justice Binnie's participation in the *Wewaykum* decision,[18] despite having given advice on the claim while serving, during the mid-1980s, as federal associate deputy minister of Justice—have, in Rotman's view, led some to question the Court's capacity to entertain their claims impartially. Given the courts' explicit interest in facilitating the negotiated resolution of Aboriginal claims, it seems essential that judges recognize the role they can't help playing in prescribing the context, and the climate, within which such negotiations must take place. If Aboriginal peoples come to perceive that neither litigation nor negotiation affords them a fair, accessible way of resolving their just claims, he argues, it will hardly be surprising if their impatience and discontent with the injustices they have suffered grows.

The current climate in Canada for Aboriginal claims and aspirations is the product of the Supreme Court's jurisprudence to date on issues of treaty and Aboriginal right. The two final featured contributors each reflect in some depth on what it means to dwell and to try to function—to negotiate and, as need be, to litigate—within that climate.

Gordon Christie's principal focus here is on the practical impact of this jurisprudence on Aboriginal peoples' rights to use and harvest natural resources. To Christie, the Court's decisions, considered in aggregate, display a concern to ensure that the exercise of Aboriginal peoples' resource rights not interfere with, let alone preclude, non-Aboriginal people's land-use and resource-exploitation opportunities. He cites as evidence the Supreme Court's relative willingness to accredit limited harvesting rights that address exclusively Aboriginal peoples' personal, social, ceremonial, and subsistence needs, its much greater reluctance to accredit rights to harvest resources for trade, and the much more diluted forms of protection accorded to commercial harvesting rights when the court is prepared to accredit them. One might have supposed that the *Delgamuukw* decision,[19] which characterized Aboriginal title as an exclusive collective right to occupy the land and to determine how it will be used, would have been enough to guarantee Aboriginal peoples the right to harvest resources on their own traditional lands. As Christie points out, however, this doctrine offers communities no protection unless and until they succeed in court in proving their title to the lands: an expensive and uncertain undertaking. And once a community does succeed in proving its Aboriginal title, its exercise of that right remains subject to any and all justifiable forms of government regulation. The burden is on the community to challenge such regulations; the standard of justification for breaches of Aboriginal title is the less onerous one applied to limits on rights to engage in commercial harvesting activity. This standard does require the Crown to involve the title-holding community in its decision-making processes when they affect community lands, but rarely requires the Crown to defer altogether to the community's rights. One startling consequence of this arrangement, Christie points out, is that traditional Aboriginal harvesting for subsistence is actually better protected by free-standing Aboriginal rights than it is when engaged in pursuant to a community's Aboriginal title.

Consider now the incentives that emerge from this arrangement. A community concerned to use and care for its land and resources in a traditional spirit of stewardship, conservation, and reciprocity will meet with resistance in the rights regime the Supreme Court jurisprudence has called into being. Such an orientation requires capacity to exclude, capacity to protect the resource from disrespectful use, in the interest of preserving and promoting the mutually supportive relationship the community has with the land. Such capacities, Christie argues, are exactly the kind of thing the Crown and the courts will be most concerned to oppose, because they conflict with the Crown's own interest in controlling resource allocation and development and with the wealth-creation aspirations of private concerns. On the other hand, a community willing to regard the resource as just another source of wealth available for exploitation can reasonably expect to do rather well in this regime. The prevailing standard of justification requires that the community's right to the resource be given some priority. This fact gives such a community some additional bargaining power in its dealings with the Crown about access to the resource and to a fair share of the revenue.

The conclusions Gurston Dacks has reached are in some ways surprisingly similar. He directs his attention to the situation in mainland British Columbia, where very little of the land mass and very few of the numerous Aboriginal communities are subject to treaties with the Crown. For over ten years now, a formal treaty process, involving both federal and provincial Crowns and many, but not all, of the Aboriginal communities with territories in the province, has been underway, but it still has yet to produce a single treaty. This is so, Dacks argues, for several reasons: there are deep differences over amount and computation of quantum; Aboriginal communities perceive the Crown's insistence on certainty as an unwelcome attempt to domesticate their historic rights; some areas are subject simultaneously to competing claims from different First Nations; and the First Nations involved have not received sufficient funding for timely, fully informed participation in the negotiations. If anything, Dacks suggests, the Supreme Court's decision on the Aboriginal title issue in *Delgamuukw*[20] aggravated the tensions already present within this process. The Aboriginal parties inferred from the Court's description of Aboriginal title—as an exclusive interest in land that entitles its holders to engage in a wide range of economic activities and to be compensated for infringements—an increase in the economic value of the lands they claim; they expected a commensurate increase in the generosity of the governments' offers in negotiations. The governments, for their part, perceived those elevated expectations to be unacceptably costly and declined to increase the value of their settlement offers, pointing out (correctly) that no court has yet accepted any Aboriginal title claim as valid. The governments' intransigence, however, has damaged the credibility of the Aboriginal leaders who led their communities into the treaty process, thereby limiting their room to negotiate.

This impasse, and the interest all parties (including the private resource developers) have in maintaining good relations and avoiding litigation, has created a need for measures that deal in the meantime with the day-to-day issues. At present, such measures include consultations with affected First Nations and with resource developers whenever a proposed initiative seems to pose a meaningful risk to Aboriginal rights, and specific "interim measures" arrangements with First Nations in the treaty process aimed at facilitating, while negotiations continue, cooperative management of resources in the area in dispute. Such measures, though still small in scale, give those First Nations added incentive to remain in the treaty process, meanwhile increasing their stake in the mainstream economy and redirecting their focus onto their interests from their rights. These developments, Dacks observes, dismay some First Nations traditionalists, but they have the advantage, in his view, of giving resource developers a greater understanding of First Nations' needs and interests and of giving participating First Nations greater clout than before in the policy process. Such advantages cannot help but seem attractive.

The concluding essay is my contribution to the conversation here about strategy. In preparing it, I learned a great deal from this book's featured contributors, even those whose work it does not acknowledge expressly. I share the view that litigation is going to remain an essential component of any prudent strategy for protecting treaty and Aboriginal rights in and from mainstream Canada and offer some strategic suggestions aimed at increasing the likelihood of success in litigation for claims of treaty and Aboriginal right.

Kerry Wilkins

NOTES

[1] See Patricia Monture-OKanee, "Thinking About Aboriginal Justice: Myths and Revolution" in Richard Gosse, James Youngblood Henderson & Roger Carter, eds., *Continuing Poundmaker and Riel's Quest* (Saskatoon: Purich, 1994) 222 at 227. She reports (*ibid.*) that this phrase is the most accurate English rendering of the Mohawk expression for "law," and that "[l]iving nicely together is an onerous standard."

[1a] With one unavoidable exception. Just as this book was going to press, the Supreme Court of Canada released its long-awaited decisions in *Haida Nation v. British Columbia (Minister of Forests)*, 2004 SCC 73, and *Taku River Tlingit First Nation v. British Columbia (Project Assessment Director)*, 2004 SCC 74. By then, it was too late in the process for most of our authors to take any—and for any of our authors to take sufficient—account of these two decisions in their papers. One should keep this in mind when reading and citing the papers in this collection.

[2] See *Constitution Act, 1982*, being Schedule B of the *Canada Act 1982* (U.K.), c. 11, s. 35.

[3] See principally *R. v. Van der Peet*, [1986] 2 S.C.R. 507 [*Van der Peet*].

[4] See principally *Delgamuukw v. British Columbia*, [1997] 3 S.C.R. 1010 [*Delgamuukw*].

[5] *Supra* note 3.

[6] See *Constitution Act, 1982, supra* note 2, s. 35(2).

[7] *Supra* note 4.

[8] *R. v. Powley*, [2003] 2 S.C.R. 207, 2003 SCC 43 [*Powley*].

[9] *Ibid.*

[10] *R. v. Marshall*, [1999] 3 S.C.R. 456 [*Marshall*].
[11] *R. v. Marshall*, [1999] 3 S.C.R. 533.
[12] *R. v. Askov*, [1990] 2 S.C.R. 1199 [*Askov*].
[13] The *Canadian Charter of Rights and Freedoms* [*Charter*] is Part I of the *Constitution Act, 1982*, *supra* note 2.
[14] *Charter, ibid.*, s. 11(b).
[15] *Calder v. B.C.(A.G.)*, [1973] S.C.R. 313 [*Calder*].
[16] *R. v. Sparrow*, [1990] 1 S.C.R. 1075 [*Sparrow*].
[17] *Constitution Act, 1982, supra* note 2, s. 35.
[18] *Wewaykum Indian Band v. Canada*, [2002] 4 S.C.R. 245, 2002 SCC 79 [*Wewaykum*].
[19] *Supra* note 4.
[20] *Ibid.*

PART 1

Validating Aboriginal Experience

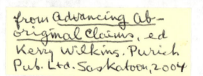
from *Advancing Aboriginal Claims*, ed Kerry Wilkins, Purich Pub. Ltd. Saskatoon, 2004

ABORIGINAL PARADIGMS

Implications for Relationships to Land and Treaty Making

Leroy Little Bear

The primary purpose and goal of this paper is to articulate, in a general overview manner, Aboriginal paradigms to assist the reader in understanding the worldview of Aboriginal peoples and the consequent relational expectations arising from those paradigms. Worldview is important because it is the filter system behind the beliefs, behaviour, and actions of people. It is the tacit infrastructure people use for their beliefs, behaviour, and relationships. Two persons with differing worldviews can look at or experience the same event and come away with very different interpretations. Expectations arising out of differing worldviews can also be very different. The "Indian Problem" for Euro-Canadians is a good example. Questions such as "Why can't they be just like us?" are manifestations of frustration arising out of a different worldview.

The author will write primarily, but not exclusively, from a Plains Indian perspective. Where appropriate, Blackfoot and Cree experience will be used for illustration purposes. The paper begins with a definition of culture, then examines three basic aspects of culture—philosophy, customs, and values—showing how they ground Plains Indians' relational expectations. It then examines Aboriginal relationships to land. It concludes with an explication of the relational expectations arising out of the Aboriginal paradigms as applied to treaty making.

CULTURE

Culture at its most fundamental is a collective agreement of the members of a society, linguistic group, and/or nation-state regarding the nature of reality. It includes prescriptions and circumscriptions about what is acceptable and what is not. It includes beliefs, customs, values, and sanctions. It may be said that culture says, "This is how we are going to run and operate our society." Clyde Kluckhohn defines culture as follows:

> Each different way of life makes its own assumptions about the ends and purposes of human existence, about ways by which knowledge may be obtained, about the organization of the pigeon-holes in which each . . . sense datum is filed, about what human beings have a right to expect from each other and the gods, about what constitutes fulfillment or frustration. Some of these assumptions are made explicit

in the lore of the folk; others are tacit premises which the observer must infer by finding consistent trends in word and deed.[1]

According to the Task Force on the Criminal Justice System and Its Impact on the Indian and Métis Peoples of Alberta ("Alberta Task Force"):

> Every society has a way of life which sets forth patterns of belief and actions based on premises and categories that are linked and make for an interdependent, coherent whole. This wholeness we call culture.[2]

Culture includes philosophy, customs, and values. Philosophy is, more or less, the theoretical (and sometimes rather esoteric) part of culture. Customs and ways of doing things are the functional and practical applications of the philosophy, belief system, and ways of thought. Values are those mechanisms a society builds into its culture that say, in essence, to the members of the society, "If you subscribe to and pursue these values, you will be rewarded, recognized, and given prestige. But if you do not, you may be the object of criticism, ostracism, jokes, and the like."

Philosophy

Aboriginal philosophy consists of and includes the ideas that there is constant motion/flux, that all creation consists of energy waves, that everything is animate, that all of creation is interrelated, that reality requires renewal, and that space is a major referent. Gary Witherspoon observes:

> The assumption that underlies this dualistic aspect of all being and existence is that the world is in motion, that things are constantly undergoing processes of transformation, deformation, and restoration, and that the essence of life and being is movement.[3]

As regards interrelations, the Alberta Task Force states:

> The wholistic view leads to an implicit assumption that everything is inter-related. Inter-relatedness leads to an implicit idea of equality among all creation. Equality is brought about by the implicit belief that everything—humans, animals, plants, and inorganic matter—has a spirit. Anthropomorphic factors are not important because metamorphosis readily occurs. The common denominator is the spirit.[4]

Aboriginal philosophy incorporates the idea of renewal. There is a tacit assumption that, in the cosmic flux, there exists a particular combination of energy waves that allows for our continuing existence. If this particular combination of energy waves dissolves, this particular reality we are in will disappear into the flux. Cajete, writing about Native science, observes:

> Chaos is both movement and evolution. It is the process through which everything in the universe becomes manifest and then returns to the chaos field. The flux, or ebb and flow, of chaos appears in everything and envelops us at all times and in all places. From the evolving universe to the mountain to the human brain, chaos is the field from which all things come into being. No wonder Native science envisions the

spirit of the natural world alive with disorder becoming order and all the mystery of mirrored relationships.[5]

Consequently, Aboriginal people have a large number of ceremonies revolving around renewal: sweatlodge, sundance, medicine bundle ceremonies, and the like.

Space is a very important referent in the minds of Aboriginal peoples. Certain events, patterns, cycles, and happenings—animal migrations, cycles of plant life, seasonal rounds, and so on—are readily observable on and from the land. The cosmos is also observable, its patterns detected from particular spatial locations. According to Vine Deloria, Jr.:

> In shifting from temporal concepts to spatial terms, we find that a revelation is not so much the period of time in which it occurs as the place it may occur. Revelation becomes a particular experience at a particular place, no universal truth emerging but an awareness arising that certain places have a qualitative holiness over and above other places. The universality of truth then becomes the relevance of the experience for a community of people, not its continual adjustment to evolving scientific and philosophical conceptions of the universe.
>
> Holy places are well known in what have been classified as primitive religions. The vast majority of Indian tribal religions have a center at a particular place, be it river, mountain, plateau, valley, or other natural feature.[6]

Examples of Blackfoot holy places, for instance, include Chief Mountain on the Blackfeet Reservation in Montana, the Belly Buttes on the Blood Indian Reserve in Alberta, and the hot springs in Banff National Park.

It is interesting to compare and contrast Western thought with Aboriginal thought. In the minds of Aboriginal peoples, space is a major referent. The notion of constant flux results in an holistic and repetitive view. If everything is forever moving and changing, one has to look at the whole to begin to discern developing patterns. It is a way of thinking that looks at the forest and not the trees. The holistic view, in turn, gives rise to values that regard the group as more important than the individual. It values a generalist more than a specialist.

For Westerners, on the other hand, time is a major referent. Time is a good example of the Western way of thinking.

> Time is conceptualized as a straight line. If a Nacirema ["American" spelled backwards] attempted to picture "time" in his mind, he would see something like a river flowing toward and on past him. What is behind would be the past. What is immediately around him would be the present. The future would be upstream, but he would not be able to see very far upstream because of a waterfall, the waterfall symbolizing the barrier to knowing the future. This line of time is conceptualized as quantity, especially as lengths made of units. A length of time is envisioned as a row of similar units. . . . A logical and inherent characteristic of the concept of time is that once a unit of the river of time flows past a Nacirema it never returns—it

is gone forever. This characteristic lends itself to other concepts such as "wasting time," "making up time," "buying time," "being on time," which are unique to the Nacirema.

Another characteristic is that each unit of time is totally different and independent of similar units. Consequently, for the Nacirema, each day is considered a different unit, and thus a different day; every year, a new year. From this the reader can readily understand why there is a need among the Nacirema to have names for days and months and numbers for years.[7]

For Aboriginal people, time just is. Benjamin Whorf, writing about the Hopi concept of time, states:

> [Time] is the realm of expectancy, of desire and purpose, of vitalizing life, of efficient causes, of thought thinking itself out from an inner realm (the Hopian heart) into manifestation. It is in a dynamic state, yet not a state of motion—it is not advancing toward us out of a future, but already with us in vital and mental form, and its dynamism is at work in the field of eventuating or manifesting, i.e. evolving without motion from the subjective by degrees to a result which is the objective.[8]

Plains Indians such as the Blackfoot have time concepts similar to this. Blackfoot think of time in two-day operational increments. There is "now," "tomorrow," and "day-after-tomorrow," and backwards "now," "yesterday," and "day-before-yesterday." Beyond the two-day limit, forward or backward, past and present amalgamate and become one and the same. Plains Indians are not incapable of talking or thinking of the distant future or past, but it is always done with the "constant flux" in mind. One of the implications arising out of this notion of time is that the ancestors are always only two days away. The stories, the songs, the ceremonies, and the teachings are never more than two days old in the memory of the people. This is quite different from Pierre Elliott Trudeau's suggestion, typical of the Euro-Canadian worldview, to the effect that "these treaties are not worth the paper they are written on." In other words, what is past is past; it is gone forever. The only thing that matters is the future.

While discussing philosophy, it is important to make a few observations about language. It can be generally said that Euro-languages such as English are very noun-oriented. English is a good language for dichotomies, categorizations, and reductionist-specificity. In its dichotomy mode, it manifests polarized, binary thinking: good and bad; saint and sinner; black and white; old and new; and so on. Aboriginal languages, generally, can be said to be action-oriented. Everything is about process, actions, happenings. It can be said that constant flux manifests itself in the language. The noun-orientation of English and the action-orientation of Aboriginal languages have led to different relational expectations, especially as regards relationships to land and treaty making, which the author will develop later in the paper.

Constant flux results in a "spider web" network of relations, out of which arises a very important part of Aboriginal philosophy: interrelationships. Because of the constant motion and flux, everything mixes, combines, and recombines with everything else. The flux gives rise to the belief that all of creation is made of energy waves. If all is animate, then all must be somewhat like humans: awarenesses with energy forces that we call spirit. If all have spirit, then all of creation—including animals, rocks, the earth, the sun, the moon, and so forth—are "all my relations."

Another important outcome of the notion of constant flux is the idea of transformation. Again, the flux results in constant mixing, combining, and recombining of energy waves resulting in new combinations. These new combinations may very well be other awarenesses coming into existence. Consequently, outer physical form is not a boundary in Plains Indian belief systems because metamorphosis readily occurs. Dr. David Peat, a physicist, neatly captures Aboriginal and Western philosophies:

> Native American philosophy and metaphysics is profound and far-reaching. Moreover, its traditional knowledge is holistic, exhibiting no fragmentation between science and spirituality, medicine and law, social order and ecological balance. Thus, the Circle, Sacred Hoop, and Medicine Wheel are found throughout North America as an image of completion, return, and renewal. The circle also expresses the nature of time and, through the rotation of its spokes or Sacred Directions, the transformation of form; for whatever is created moves from its birth toward maturity, death, and eventual renewal. Thus, all aspects of life are constantly moving and seeking balance, the one giving way to the other. . . .
>
> The metaphysics of the Algonquin peoples, for example (the Blackfoot, Cree, Cheyenne, Micmac, Ojibway, Naskapi, etc.) refers to a world of process and animation; a world in which energies, spirits, and powers enter into alliances with each other and with human beings. Indeed, the Algonquin languages, with their verbal base, rhythms, and sonic vibrations, are themselves both an expression of and a manifestation within such a world. How far this reality of process seems from our own noun- and object-based world, with its linear time and physical causality. Yet how close the Algonquin worldview appears to the process philosophy of A. N. Whitehead, the holomovement and implicate order of David Bohm, and the discoveries of quantum theory. . . .
>
> In a world in which rocks, trees, plants, animals, and stars are all animate, the cosmos becomes inseparable from us, for we are all part of this whole and within each of these parts is enfolded the whole. In a world of flux, change becomes inevitable. Yet, within the circle of time, there is also a possibility for renewal and return. Thus an indigenous society enters into relationship with the animating principles and energy flows of the cosmos and accepts its obligations for the ceremonies of renewal that must be carried out and the acts that must be performed to ensure harmony and balance.[9]

All of the above lead one to articulate Aboriginal philosophy as holistic, cyclical, linked to place, repetitive, generalist, and process-oriented.

Values

A social value is

> [a]n abstract, generalized principle of behaviour to which the members of a group feel a strong, emotionally toned positive commitment and which provides a standard for judging specific acts and goals. . . . Values provide essential organizing principles for the integration of individuals and group goals.[10]

Values, as stated above, are those mechanisms a society builds into its culture that, more or less, say to the members of a society: "If you subscribe to and pursue these values, you will be rewarded, recognized, and given prestige; if you do not, you may be the object of criticism, ostracism, jokes, and the like." It is difficult to articulate values within any culture, but it is possible if one has a philosophical base from which to work. What are the basic values one would find in Plains Indian cultures? The value of wholeness or totality arises from the concept of constant motion and flux, the cyclical and repetitive patterns and phases. Wholeness incorporates within it the values of strength, sharing, honesty, and kindness. This foursome of values results in beauty, harmony, and balance. Witherspoon states:

> The emphasis on balance in the daily life of the Navajo is found in their avoidance of excess in any area and in their patterns of moderation in all things. The Navajo compulsion for order is found in the numerous and frequent rites they perform and participate in to maintain and restore order. Their avoidance of conflict and confrontation in interpersonal relations and their lack of superlatives and extremism in conversation seem designed to maintain and enhance social order. . . . If a Navajo is to be truly happy and healthy, beauty must dominate his thought and speech, and harmony must permeate his environment.[11]

Beauty, harmony, and balance are cultural goals of most North American Indian tribes.

James Dumont, in "Justice and Aboriginal People,"[12] lists kindness, honesty, sharing, and strength as the four foundational values of North American Indians. For him, kindness means harmony in interpersonal relations joined to the capacity for caring; the resulting behaviour is friendship, caring, amiability, mildness, and acquiescence. It results in a preference for peaceful resolution rather than confrontation. Honesty, Dumont suggests, means truthfulness and integrity conditioned by respect. This results in tolerance and equanimity, respect for others, and a highly internalized conscience and sense of trustworthiness, honour, and loyalty. Sharing means generosity, cooperativeness, and collective well-being, which leads, in his view, to a balance between the assertion of one's freedom and autonomy and a responsibility to ensure harmony and collective well-being. Strength, according to Dumont, means strength of character, self-mastery, fortitude, peace, harmony, and well-being in oneself and others.

Customs

Customs are accepted ways of doing things. Theodorson and Theodorson define "custom" as

> [a] Folkway, or form of social behavior, that, having persisted for a long period of time, is well established in a society, has become traditional, and has received some degree of formal recognition.[13]

Customs, like any other aspects of culture, aim at the preservation of the culture and the survival of the society. For instance, the custom of collective decision-making is utilized with regard to tribal territory, external relations, utilization of resources, movement within the tribal territory, and societal order within the tribe.

ABORIGINAL RELATIONSHIPS TO AND USE OF THE LAND

The relationship to and use of the land manifests itself through a complex interrelational network with all of creation: one that sees humans as simply a part of creation, not above it, and has balance and harmony as its goal. This goal, in turn, is accomplished through ceremonial renewal of the relationships to the land, the animals, the plants, and the cosmos. To appreciate readily the relationships to land, one has to have some knowledge of Plains Indians' land use.

Most, if not all, Plains Indian tribes were big-game hunters; their staff of life was big-game animals indigenous to the plains, the buffalo being the most important. They hunted the buffalo in different ways. Before the appearance of the horse on the plains, they most often used the surround or buffalo jump, but sometimes also chased the buffalo into sloughs and muddy lake beds to get them stuck in the mud. After the appearance of the horse, hot pursuit of the buffalo out on the open plains became the preferred method.

The buffalo, besides providing food, supplied Plains Indians' other needs, including clothing, coverings for tipis, containers such as bags and parfleches, sinew for sewing, and rawhide ropes for all kinds of needs. Even the brain of the animal was used in the tanning process, to whiten and soften the hide. Many parts of the buffalo, such as buffalo tongues, were used for ceremonial purposes.

In spite of the importance of the buffalo, Plains Indians hunted and made use of many other animals and birds for food and other purposes, including elk, deer, moose, antelope, mountain sheep, bear, and porcupine. Birds hunted included prairie chicken, geese, duck, pigeon, and eagle. The eagle was considered very sacred. Its feathers were and continue to be used in many tribal ceremonies.

Plains Indians made use of a large number of plants within their territories for food, medicine, and religious purposes. Plants used for purification purposes, for instance, include, but are not limited to, sage, sweet grass, alpine fir, and tobacco. Plants used for food include many different types of berries, among them saskatoon and chokecherry, as well as wild turnip and the roots of many different plants. Plants used for medicinal purposes are too numerous to be done any justice by an abbreviated list.

Plains Indians, even though out on the bald prairie, did trap small fur-bearing animals such as beaver, otter, muskrat, and weasel. These animals, like the big-game animals, were utilized for different purposes, such as religion, clothing, decoration, and trade.

Last but not least in this brief overview is the land itself. The land is considered "mother": the giver of life. On the land were many sacred places and sites where religious ceremonies, both tribal and individual, were conducted. The land, in addition to the plant and animal life it supported, provided sites for vision quests, burials, and places to plant and harvest special types of plants, such as tobacco, that were very important in the religious life of Plains Indians. The land also provided other materials, such as ochre, used in painting and religious ceremonies. It provided the sacred rocks for medicine wheels and sweatlodges. It provided ammunition (arrow tips) for hunting and warfare.

Despite what missionaries and social scientists often suggest, Plains Indians did not move about their territory at random. In fact, their seasonal rounds were largely synchronized with the movements of the buffalo and other game animals, and with the ripening of plants for food and medicine. It was common for them to move out onto the plains during the summer to follow the buffalo and other game animals, then back to sheltered places for the winter. Plains Indians, all in all, made full use of their territories. These uses and relationships continue even today, although somewhat restricted by present-day boundaries and by privately owned land. But hunting still takes place and plants are still harvested for food, medicine, and religious purposes.

One thing that cannot be overlooked is the role religion plays. Over and above the extended families, the band, and the tribe are many different religious societies whose memberships transcend the above social organizational layers. Each of these societies has its own customs and laws, totems, plant use customs, and sacred sites. Medicine bundles are associated with most, if not all, of these societies. These bundles are regularly transferred to new members. As a consequence, their totems, plant use customs, and sacred sites slowly but surely make their rounds throughout the extended families, bands, tribes, and territories.

RELATIONAL EXPECTATIONS ARISING OUT OF THE ABORIGINAL AND WESTERN PARADIGMS

Pursuant to British, Canadian, and American laws, land is not much different from any chattel or movable property. It can be the subject of use, disposal, or transfer to another for value. In fact, one can say that the estate fee system is set up to facilitate transfers from one person to another. "Title" evidences an exclusive interest in the land. Previous titleholders can be traced back to the original grantor: the state or the sovereign. All this is in keeping with the linear, dichotomous nature of the Western paradigm with its "either/or" characteristic. As a consequence, the expectation of the British when they met North American Indians was one of purchase of land and extinguishment of Aboriginal title. This was accomplished (from the British standpoint) through treaties, claims of ownership through discovery, military conquest, and other theories. One such theory denied non-Christians capacity to own land; another denied Aboriginal peoples' interests in lands that they were said not to be using productively. These concepts of title acquisition (and the mind set that goes with them) continue to this day; witness the fact that extinguishment of Aboriginal title is still the primary goal of the Canadian government in its settlement of First Nations' land claims. However, according to Thomas Berger:

> No one has ever advanced a sound legal theory to justify the taking of Native land from the Natives of the New World, whether by the Spanish, the Portuguese, the French, the English, the Dutch, the Americans, or—in Alaska—by the Russians.[14]

Canadian law features many theories about the relational bases between First Nations and Canada. Some of these are based on the Royal Proclamation of 1763, some on extinguishing documents such as treaties (as interpreted by Canada), some on the goodwill of the sovereign (*St. Catherine's Milling and Lumber Co.*).[15] All in all, the view expressed in *St. Catherine's* is still the view taken by Canada. It is firmly established in the mind of the Canadian legal establishment. Its pith and substance is that: (1) land, like any other object, is ownable; (2) the locus of ownership is in the Crown; and (3) the Crown may transfer possession and use to individual citizens, and they, in turn, may transfer these to others.

First Nations' interests in their Aboriginal lands are subjected to this view. Their interests get lost in the myriad of other interests in the Canadian estate fee system. But this point of view runs into a problem when considered with reference to recent Supreme Court of Canada decisions such as *Calder* and *Guerin*.[16] These cases take the view that Aboriginal title does not derive from the Crown: it arises out of occupation and use of the land since time immemorial. The Supreme Court of Canada has recently attempted to reconcile these conflicting views. Chief Justice Lamer, in *R. v. Van der Peet,* states:

> [W]hat s. 35(1) does is provide the constitutional framework through which the fact that aboriginals lived on the land in distinctive societies, with their own practices, traditions and cultures, is acknowledged and reconciled with the sovereignty of the

Crown. The substantive rights which fall within the provision must be defined in light of this purpose; the aboriginal rights recognized and affirmed by s. 35(1) must be directed towards the reconciliation of the pre-existence of aboriginal societies with the sovereignty of the Crown.[17]

The reconciliation that Lamer C.J.C. refers to has really not been realized yet. But the *St. Catherine's* view comes as a surprise to most First Nations. Keeping in mind the discussion above of Aboriginal philosophies—which feature notions of constant flux, everything being animate, everything being made of energy waves, everything being interrelated, creation requiring renewal, and space as a primary referent[18]—and Dumont's explanation of Aboriginal values,[19] it should be clear that First Nations' relational expectations are totally different from those of Britain and Canada.

For Plains Indians, land (space) is a primary referent because that is where the "spider web" relational network operates in human experience. It is the place for "all my relations." "All my relations" includes, but is not limited to, animals, plants, inorganic matter such as rocks, and the land itself. In other words, "all my relations" also have an interest in the land, just as humans do. Relating is what maintains the continuity of creation. If the relational network with "all my relations" ceases or is interfered with, imbalances will occur or creation may come to a halt.

How is the relational network maintained? It is maintained through renewal of the stories, songs, and ceremonies on and with the land spread throughout the territory. The connection with the land through these songs, stories, and ceremonies is like a marriage of the people with the land. They are the evidence of title to the land. Suzuki and Knudtson make the following observations about the Gitksan:

> Each Gitksan house is the proud heir and owner of an *ada'ox*. This is a body of orally transmitted songs and stories that acts as the house's sacred archives and as its living, millennia-long memory of important events of the past. This irreplaceable verbal repository of knowledge consists in part of sacred songs believed to have arisen, *literally from the breath of the ancestors*. Far more than musical representations of history, these songs serve as vital time-traversing vehicles. They can transport members across the immense reaches of space and time into the dim mythic past of Gitksan creation *by the very quality of their music and the emotions they convey*. . . . In fact, so vital is the relationship between each house and the lands allotted to it for fishing, hunting and food-gathering that the *daxgyet*, or spirit power, of each house and the land that sustains it are one. . . . *For us*, states Delgam Uukw, *the ownership of a territory is a marriage of the Chief and the land. Each Chief has an ancestor who encountered and acknowledged the life of the land. From such encounters come power. The land, the animals and the people all have spirit—they all must be shown respect. That is the basis of our law.*[20]

When Europeans came to Plains Indian country, First Nations such as the

Blackfoot and Cree assumed that these were people who had similar values of wholeness, strength, sharing, kindness, and honesty. The assumption was that these newcomers would fit into the overall "spider web" relational network and become part of the renewal process through the songs, stories, and ceremonies.

THE APPLICATION OF THE ABORIGINAL PARADIGM TO TREATY MAKING

The idea of making treaty was not new or strange to Plains Indians. First Nations had engaged for years in treaty making as a means of entering into peaceful relations with neighbouring tribes before they engaged in treaty making with Europeans. *Innaisstsisini* is a Blackfoot word that captures the idea of *treaty* in English. The meaning of the word is "making peace." In 1870, near present-day Lethbridge, the last great battle between the Crees and Blackfoot took place. "The following year the Crees sent tobacco to the Blackfeet and in the fall a formal treaty of peace was made between the two nations on the Red Deer River."[21] Hugh Dempsey gives an account of a treaty signed between the Bloods and the Gros Ventres and Assiniboines in Montana in June 1887.[22] Walter Hildebrandt and Brian Hubner also note that there was an alliance between the Crees and Blackfoot in 1670.[23]

Treaty making is aimed at peaceful relationships. Red Crow, for instance, said that in the treaty with the Gros Ventres and Assiniboines, "We have made a treaty and we will smoke a pipe. It is good for us to meet as brothers and not be afraid."[24] Treaty making is not aimed at land surrender. But the Aboriginal concept of land ownership, i.e., maintaining and renewing the "spider web" network of relationships with "all my relations," is certainly not inconsistent with a sharing of the land arising out of the Aboriginal paradigm. So when the European newcomers came out on the plains to sign treaties, the expectation of Plains Indians was that these were new people with whom to have good and peaceful relations. The assumption was that the newcomers were going to participate in the goals of beauty, harmony, and balance. Menno Boldt, for instance, states:

> But, to apprehend the treaties in terms of the sum of the specific provisions is to miss entirely the chiefs' spirit and intent when they negotiated the treaties. The chiefs who marked the treaties profoundly believed themselves to be entrusted by the Creator with the protection of their tribal cultures—the Creator's blueprint for their survival and well-being. When they participated in the treaty-making process they did so from a conviction that they were honouring this sacred trust. In their minds, the treaty was an instrument for fulfilling this sacred obligation to the Creator, to their ancestors, and to generations yet to come. Another implicit understanding of the chiefs who marked the treaties was that they were autonomous peoples, and that the treaties affirmed the continuity of their autonomy. They marked the treaties in the spirit of coexistence, mutual obligation, sharing, and benefit, and as an agreement between themselves and the newcomers not to interfere with each

other's way of life. They assumed the treaties would enshrine this intent and spirit as a permanent and living legacy. Thus, as a frame of reference for justice, the treaties provide a paradigm of high idealism.[25]

In other words, the treaties were to be instruments guaranteeing the continuity of the Indian way of life.

CONCLUSION

Philosophy, customs, and values are inextricably linked together. They form the basis of the everyday habitual thought of a society. Philosophy, customs, and values form the basis of the worldview of a people. The worldview, for our purpose, in turn forms the basis for beliefs about relationships to land and to other societies. Aboriginal philosophy consists of the notions that all is in constant flux, that all creation consists of energy waves, that everything is animate, that all creation is interrelated, that reality requires renewal, and that space is a major referent. This philosophy results in notions of wholeness, harmony, beauty, and balance. It results in viewing land as a place for relating to "all my relations." The relational expectation arising out of this philosophy is that strangers who come into the territory of a Plains Indian tribe will respect the relational network in place in the territory. In contrast, Europeans, with their linear, dichotomous ways of thinking, used the British Crown as their referent, believing that it was the source of title for lands in the Americas: that the Indians' interest in their traditional territories was simply personal and beneficial at the goodwill of the British sovereign. From that point of view, extinguishment of title was easily achievable; all one need do was purchase the Indians' interest through treaty agreements. For the Indians, land is not purchasable, but it can be shared. Land cannot be purchased because "all my relations" have interests in the land, as humans do. So treaties were, for Plains Indians, both a means to guarantee that the relational network would not be interfered with when newcomers or strangers came into their territories and a way of maintaining good relations with other nations.

NOTES

[1] Clyde Kluckhohn, "The Philosophy of the Navaho Indians" in F.S.C. Northrop, ed., *Ideological Differences and World Order* (New Haven, Conn.: Yale University Press, 1949) 356 at 358–59.
[2] *Justice on Trial, Report of the Task Force on the Criminal Justice System and Its Impact on the Indian and Métis Peoples of Alberta*, vol. 1 (Edmonton: Government of Alberta, 1991) at 9-1 [Alberta Task Force].
[3] Gary Witherspoon, *Language and Art in the Navajo Universe* (Ann Arbor, Mich.: University of Michigan Press, 1977) at 48.
[4] Alberta Task Force, *supra* note 2 at 9-3.
[5] Gregory Cajete, *Native Science: Natural Laws of Interdependence* (Santa Fe, N. Mex.: Clear Light Publishers, 2000) at 16.
[6] Vine Deloria, Jr., *God Is Red* (New York: Grosset & Dunlap, 1973) at 80–81.

[7] Leroy P. Little Bear, "Dispute Settlement Among the Nacirema" (1975) 1 J. Contemp. L. 331 at 337–38.
[8] Benjamin Lee Whorf, "An American Indian Model of the Universe" in John B. Carroll, ed., *Language, Thought and Reality: Selected Writings of Benjamin Lee Whorf* (Cambridge, Mass.: M.I.T. Press, 1956) 57 at 60.
[9] David Peat, *The Indigenous American—Western Circle: An Occasional Paper of the Fetzer Institute* (Kalamazoo, Mich.: Fetzer Institute, 1993) at 3.
[10] George A. Theodorson & Achilles A. Theodorson, *Modern Dictionary of Sociology* (New York: Thomas Y. Crowell, 1969) at 455–56.
[11] Witherspoon, *supra* note 3 at 188, 191.
[12] See James Dumont, "Justice and Aboriginal People" in Canada, Royal Commission on Aboriginal Peoples, *Aboriginal Peoples and the Justice System, Report of the National Round Table on Aboriginal Justice Issues* (Ottawa: Supply and Services Canada, 1993) 42 at 64.
[13] Theodorson & Theodorson, *supra* note 10 at 101.
[14] Thomas R. Berger, *Village Journey: The Report of the Alaska Native Review Commission* (New York: Hill and Wang, 1985) at 138.
[15] *St. Catherine's Milling and Lumber Co. v. The Queen* (1888), 14 App. Cas. 46 (P.C.) at 54 [*St. Catherine's*].
[16] *Calder v. British Columbia (A.G.)*, [1973] S.C.R. 313 [*Calder*]; *Guerin v. The Queen*, [1984] 2 S.C.R. 335 [*Guerin*]. According to Thomas Isaac,

> *Calder* affirmed that Aboriginal rights to land exist, that they are not solely dependent upon the *Royal Proclamation* for their existence but rather flow from Aboriginal peoples' traditional use and occupancy of the land, thereby rejecting the notion that the *Royal Proclamation* was the source of Aboriginal rights, as held in *St. Catherine's*:

Aboriginal Law: Cases, Materials, and Commentary, 2d ed. (Saskatoon, Sask.: Purich, 1999) at 29. See *ibid.* at 41 for similar commentary in respect of *Guerin, ibid.*
[17] *R. v. Van der Peet*, [1996] 2 S.C.R. 507 at para. 31.
[18] See *supra* notes 3–9 and accompanying text.
[19] See *supra* note 12 and accompanying text.
[20] Peter Knudtson & David Suzuki, *Wisdom of the Elders* (Toronto: Stoddard Publishing, 1992) at 128 [emphasis in original].
[21] Dr. George A. Kennedy, "Kennedy's Account" in Carlton R. Stewart, ed., *The Last Great (Intertribal) Indian Battle*, Occasional Paper No. 30 (Lethbridge, Alta.: Lethbridge Historical Society, 1997) 10 at 13.
[22] Hugh A. Dempsey, "Final Treaty of Peace" (1962) 10 Alberta Historical Review 8.
[23] Walter Hildebrandt & Brian Hubner, *The Cypress Hills: The Land and Its People* (Saskatoon, Sask.: Purich, 1994) at 31.
[24] Dempsey, *supra* note 22 at 12.
[25] Menno Boldt, *Surviving As Indians: The Challenge of Self-Government* (Toronto: University of Toronto Press, 1993) at 41.

THE RIGHT OF INCLUSION

Aboriginal Rights and/or Aboriginal Women?

Patricia A. Monture

The passage of the *Canadian Bill of Rights*[1] in 1960 was the result of a global trend after the Second World War that focused world attention on civil liberties and the rights of individuals. The discovery of the extent of wartime atrocities had shocked the democratic world. In 1948, the United Nations adopted the *Universal Declaration of Human Rights*. Peter Hogg, a noted constitutional law scholar, has observed that the omission of a bill of rights from Canada's first constitution (1867) was not "regretted until after the second world war."[2] Thus commenced the era of civil liberties and individual rights.[3] Since 1960, respect for the individual rights and freedoms of the people living in the territory now known as Canada has remained a central concern; it prompted entrenchment in the constitution of the rights in the *Charter*[4] in 1982 and informed the legal framework into which the constitutional guarantees of Aboriginal rights (including treaty rights) were deposited in that same year.

Apart from the *Lavell* and *Bedard* decision[5] in 1974 and the 1992 case of the *Native Women's Association of Canada*,[6] however, "Indian"[7] women have not often been active participants in the rights litigation heard by the high court. Since the rendering of the *Sparrow*[8] decision in 1990, the first to delineate the "new" constitutional rights of Aboriginal people contained in section 35(1) of the *Constitution Act, 1982*,[9] more than a decade of Supreme Court of Canada activity has occurred. The Court has handed down more than twenty-five Aboriginal or treaty rights decisions during that period.[10] Although women have sometimes been parties to this litigation,[11] gender has not been a central or articulated component of the Aboriginal and treaty rights debates taking place in the courts.[12] And in the few instances when Aboriginal women have been involved in court challenges unrelated to section 35, their race and culture have most frequently been ignored.[13]

Despite the acknowledgement that gender discrimination is experienced differently across cultures and legal systems, this fact has not had a fundamental impact on the literature discussing the meaning of section 35 of the *Constitution Act, 1982*. Neither is the diversity of First Nations' traditions regarding gender sufficiently understood. Unlike *Charter* analysis, which sometimes entertains discussions of intersectionality, Aboriginal rights analysis is still silent on any potential gendering influence. Given that section 35(4) of the *Constitution Act, 1982* guarantees Aboriginal and treaty rights equally to male and female persons, this omission in the academic literature is fascinating. The literature, when women are mentioned, considers only the impact of the *Charter* on the "rights"[14] of Aboriginal women.[15]

Writing on the *Charter* is equally inattentive to the concerns of Aboriginal women, despite the fact that the *Lavell* decision[16] significantly influenced the way in which *Charter* section 15 differs from the anti-discrimination provision in the *Canadian Bill of Rights*.[17] That decision examined former section 12(1)(b) of the *Indian Act*,[18] which stripped Indian[19] women—but not Indian men—who married non-Indians of their entitlement to registration as Indians. As I have said many times, the Court's reasoning looked at all women as a group and found only Indian women discriminated against and looked at all Indians as a group and found only women discriminated against. The result was to deny the women's claim as either gender or race discrimination. This is what results from failing to recognize that discriminations affect people in ways that intersect. This is the first lesson resulting from scrutiny of the *Lavell* and *Bedard* decision.

The Supreme Court held in that case that the words "equality before the law" in the *Canadian Bill of Rights* did not protect the rights of Indian women. Because of the result in *Lavell* and *Bedard*, section 15 of the *Charter* now protects not only "equality before the law"—the phrase that had not assisted Ms. Lavell or Ms. Bedard—but also "equality under the law." Noting the irony in the outcome of the women's lobby, which succeeded in including four anti-discrimination prohibitions[20] in the *Charter*, I wrote:

> The *Lavell* case fundamentally influenced the women's lobby around the entrenchment of women's rights in the *Charter of Rights and Freedoms*, such that both equality before the law and equality under the law are now protected by section 15 of the 1982 rights document. The legal advancement of the position of all women in Canada has been based on the struggle advanced by Indian women for Indian women. The result of the struggle advanced by Indian women is the betterment of the legal position for all women. Indian women, however, walked away with nothing tangible. Indian women still had section 12(1)(b).[21]

The exclusions are not really surprising; as Sherene Razack has noted, women are frequently forced to "separate their gender from all other aspects of their being."[22] It is clear from the early judicial decisions that, for Indian women, this separation continues.

In a parallel way, Aboriginal women, as such, continue to be disappeared from the developing law on Aboriginal and treaty rights. This disappearance of Aboriginal women reflects problems within the judicial process: with the way in which cases are presented to the courts, and with the way in which litigation strategies have been developed (for Aboriginal peoples and for the Crown). This concern with parties' litigation strategies may or may not reflect or be influenced by community attitudes toward women.

The degree, therefore, to which this new era of individual rights protection has benefited Aboriginal women is open to question. In this discussion, I attempt to put the women first, albeit somewhat artificially, before any concerns for the inherent rights of Aboriginal peoples.[23] This attempt is part of the broader challenge brought by Aboriginal legal scholars who are seeing the law itself as part of the problem faced by Aboriginal peoples in Canada.[24] My goal is to venture into the gender silence that exists in the articulation of Aboriginal and treaty rights despite the express constitutional wording in section 35(4):[25] to begin the task of articulating a space for First Nations women in First Nations' present legal struggles. This focus on gender (male and female)[26] is intended to center women and to begin to examine the way that gender specificity differs in First Nation social, political, and legal structures. As well, it is intended as an introductory discussion that looks at the complexity of those positions across the diversity of First Nations. Gendered responsibilities in First Nations' traditions are not part of a hierarchical ordering such that women's history is a history or experience of disadvantage.

THE NWAC CHALLENGE AND THE AFN

In the early 1990s, the Native Women's Association of Canada (NWAC) invoked the *Charter* to challenge the federal negotiation process that resulted in the Charlottetown Accord. Central to NWAC's argument was the assertion that the "big four" Aboriginal organizations, but particularly the Assembly of First Nations (AFN), were "male-dominated"[27] organizations and therefore did not speak for Aboriginal women. Nor was it likely, in NWAC's view, that these organizations would agree with NWAC that constitutionally protected Aboriginal self-government rights should be subject to the *Charter*.[28]

The irony in this litigation is that it is not clear that NWAC represents all Aboriginal women. The organization does not allow individual membership; it consists of provincial or territorial associations. Those associations most often have "locals": groups organized in smaller geographic areas, often cities and less frequently reserves. Individual women can belong only to these locals.[29] Like organizations of chiefs, NWAC is also non-democratic: only provincial and territorial associations may vote for the national leader. NWAC is not structured, any more than AFN is, on the western democratic principle of one person, one vote. Rather, the structures of both organizations are one chief or one member organization, one vote.

Although I support fully activities that draw attention to the unique circumstances of Aboriginal women's lives, including discrimination against us,[30] I remain skeptical about the net benefits of the NWAC litigation. Certainly (in my experience) this case strained the relationship between AFN and NWAC. As NWAC's membership is significantly urban, this leaves Aboriginal women whose lives are centered in and on First Nation communities in an uncomfortable situation. The national organization publicly understood to represent all Aboriginal women really does not. And the AFN is indeed male dominated (if a count of the gender of the chiefs is sufficient measure of male domination).

The similarities between the AFN and NWAC, as national Aboriginal political organizations, are what is most striking for me. Elsewhere I noted:

> Because the NWAC and the AFN are modelled on the colonizers' ways of political organization, neither can fully give voice to tradition and therefore they are not necessarily about fully reaching out to the goals of emancipation, freedom and independence. These cases are derailed from the outset because of what they do not and likely cannot incorporate in their positions. Therefore, the cases do not hold transformative potential but rather seek only to access the colonizers' way of distributing power.[31]

All national organizations of First Nations or Aboriginal peoples face this representation conundrum. To be recognized by state governments, they must comply with provincial or federal laws of incorporation. But this has the effect of collapsing the diversity of First Nations or Aboriginal peoples, particularly for those viewing from the outside, into a single large "brown blob."

More importantly, the public perception, after both the membership struggle and the *Charter* application controversies, often emphasizes this rift between AFN ("the men") and NWAC ("the women"). This is troubling because it both mischaracterizes the reality and under-defines the experience of discrimination that most Aboriginal women face. It narrowly focuses the issue on the exclusionary membership provisions of the *Indian Act* imposed on us not by First Nations but by the Crown. Registration under the *Indian Act* is not the sole issue of concern to Aboriginal women (nor for some of us was it ever the most important issue). Multiple forms of social, economic, legal, and political exclusion remain issues for many Aboriginal women. The breadth of the experiences of exclusion needs acknowledgement. Often the narrow acknowledgement of exclusions focuses the discussion on state action, including the judiciary, where organizations such as AFN and NWAC really occupy only an intermediary position. Therefore, the goal must be to uncover and name colonialism and its remaining impacts. Honest efforts toward decolonization must take account of the fact that organizations of chiefs are all *Indian Act* based and that there is nothing particularly "Indian" about that piece of legislation.

UNDERSTANDING GENDER FROM WITHIN FIRST NATIONS' TRADITIONS

Honesty[32] also requires that I acknowledge the degree to which I have been complicit in the disappearing of gender specificity in the debate about self-determination. Upon completion of the manuscript *Journeying Forward: Dreaming First Nations Independence*,[33] I reflected on the knowledge that gender did not figure overtly even in my own analysis. This realization arose on the book tour and at the receptions hosted by women's organizations, including bookstores. During those events, questions arose about gender, questions I had not really contemplated. Gender is constantly there between the lines in the book, in that I cannot be anything but a woman.[34] And when I write in a manner that acknowledges the storyteller tradition (an integral component of Indigenous knowledges), I am writing from a gendered position.[35]

As I wrote the book, I had three goals in mind: to examine the law as a venue for securing just resolution of First Nations'[36] claims; to examine the meaning of "self-government," and to search within my experience of community for other pathways to secure well-being in First Nation communities. One chapter of *Journeying*, in fact, deals with the cases that NWAC brought forward; it obviously must lean up against the idea of gender. Even there, however, gendered analysis does not figure prominently. Since this uncomfortable realization in the fall of 1999 (how can one talk of self-governing relationships without fundamentally examining the present reality of gender exclusion and omission?), I have been reflecting on the discomfort I initially felt with my own and with others' writing. This discomfort (or contradiction) is generally an indicator of something that I need to spend more time thinking about.[37] Since then, I have been watching for gender more carefully in my reading and writing.[38]

Understanding my approach in *Journeying* (I am writing as woman) has identified for me that both gender relationships and gender politics unfold differently in First Nations' cultures and traditions. Gender within and across First Nation cultures is exceedingly varied; the diversity of First Nations women must be acknowledged. The second realization is that the way that gender affects our relationships must become explicit. My last book required me to think through issues of political change (often called self-government) generally.[39] It forced me to consider both the framework issues and principles. Difficult as it was for me to write that book, a work that was really a decade in the making, I now see how preliminary it was. I am interested in continuing to advance that framework; my deliberations about gender are just such an advancement, albeit themselves also preliminary. Indigenous knowledge(s), including the way in which it is gendered, cannot exist without community. It is not knowledge when it remains the pondering of one individual.

A word on methodology[40] is probably essential. I have long been committed to following the ways of my people, the Haudenosaunee. We are storytelling people, as are other First Nations. It is the tradition of story that I attempt to bring to my academic writing. There are many different kinds of stories. Some stories are sacred and can only be told by certain people, in certain ways, and at certain times. There are stories that are told for entertainment. There are stories that contain our history. We each hold our own personal stories, which are often shared as a way of teaching life's lessons. I have attempted to inform my academic writing with the understanding that comes from the traditions and stories of my people. This paper is my personal story on the road to being a self-determined individual who is a Kanyen'kehaka (Mohawk) woman.

Self-reflection is one of the basic premises in the methods of sharing Indigenous knowledge(s). Gordon Christie (Inuvialuit) says this:

> There is an intellectual tradition to the cultures of Aboriginal peoples that places value in the ability to think clearly and carefully, but it is not privileged as it came to be in the West, for the intellectual tradition is seen as intermingled with spiritual traditions, emotional traditions and physical traditions.[41]

Thinking clearly is a general responsibility of all citizens.

Gender specificity is also a simple but complex part of these knowledge traditions. There are men's teachings and women's teachings. And there are teachings about gender that belong to everyone, as they are foundational to how social systems are organized amongst many First Nations. We are aunties or uncles, grandpas and grannies, mother or father, brother and sister. Reporting on her interview with the Dakota/Anishnabe artist Lita Fontaine, Rosanna Deerchild (Cree) writes:

> Most Aboriginal cultures have been matriarchal. Although the female was not recognized as being the head of the family, state and church, she was most certainly the root of the family. Therefore, it was the woman who was the true leader of the nation. The basis for that comes from the certainty that the Earth is our original mother. All life comes from the Earth. She feeds us, clothes us and shelters us and, in turn, we give her the highest respect. She is where we are born and where our bodies return when we die. This Mother Earth principle has survived, and there remains a deep respect and connection to the Earth. Many philosophies, values and ceremonies continue to revolve around this principle. An example of this is the Sweat Lodge ceremony. The round lodge symbolizes the Earth's womb and by returning there we are in a sense reborn. Even in the more social activity of the powwow, Mother Earth is present when we dance to her heartbeat. From this basis grows the knowledge that women, like Mother Earth, give us life and feed, clothe and shelter us. Women, too, must be highly respected.[42]

The idea that Indigenous knowledge is gendered is not often expressly acknowledged, either in our own communities or beyond. In part, this is because culture is lived, not analyzed. It is the often unarticulated and unacknowledged way we are. Not recognizing the gendered nature of being, including knowledge sharing, is also the result of colonialism and the forcing of patriarchal relations onto First Nations. As Kim Anderson (Cree/Métis) explains:

> Our ceremonies help us to remember the need for balance between the male and female. Some Aboriginal ceremonies are gender specific, and most mixed ceremonies involve gender divided tasks and responsibilities. So many of our ceremonies include fire and water, and in these ceremonies we usually require men to tend the fire and women to keep the water. In reclaiming the ceremonies, we can reclaim our traditional respect and balance with one another.[43]

Those who live Indigenous knowledge traditions understand that the teachings women speak are often women's teachings (and the same holds true for the knowledge of men). Knowledge is complete only when the complementary stories of women and men have both been told and understood.

Understanding the gendered nature of First Nations knowledges means understanding one reason why First Nations knowledges[44] (and understanding of those knowledges) must be built within the community. External gender hierarchies, including patriarchy, have disrupted (not destroyed) the fundamental gender balance that is an essential foundation to First Nations knowledges. It must be built by involving both (all) genders. To remind us of that balance is often the function of ceremony. Understanding the teachings means being able to internalize them and live them. When I go to my aunties for help or understanding, there have been times when they have sent me to the men. This is true of my teachers who are Haudenosaunee and of those who are Anishnabe. My lived experience (which is greater than mere anecdote because of the requirement that we each be responsible to the teachings) confirms that men's and women's teachings are complementary. Each are necessary parts of the whole.[45]

A simple story from the writing of Linda Hogan, Chickasaw poet and author, demonstrates the operation of gender amongst her people:

> She, the corn, is called our grandmother. She's the woman who rubbed her palms against her body, and the seeds fell out of her skin. That is, they fell from her body until her sons discovered her secrets. Before she left the world, she told them how to plant. She said, plant the beans and corn together, plant their little sister, squash, between them. This, from an oral tradition, came to be rediscovered hundreds of years later, almost too late, by agriculturists in their research on how to maintain the richness of farm soil.[46]

Gender balance is woven through this story of agricultural practices. The corn is female and grandmother (acknowledging her as a teacher). But it is only with the help of her sons that the gift of corn flourishes in this world. This is an example of gender complementarity. The passage also demonstrates that the degree to which Aboriginal traditions have been denigrated as myth requires careful reconsideration.

THEORIZING FIRST NATIONS WOMEN'S EQUALITY

One of the reasons why I think gender is not as visible in Indigenous knowledge practices is that gender has not always been a problematic construct for First Peoples. Although different, the roles of men and women were and are complementary and were at least historically without hierarchy.[47] This does not mean that a romanticized return to tradition is a full solution to the gender discrimination Aboriginal women face in our communities. Patriarchy is now an issue we must deal with. Indeed, I am pointing here to the problem of gender hierarchy, essential to the imposition of patriarchy that predetermines much of the discrimination women currently face. This hierarchy exists clearly in European-based knowledge traditions. Women were seen as inferior and the rights of men (often described as the rights of people) were often dependent on the subordination of women (and others, most often racialized persons).[48] One of the reasons why I continue to believe that feminism cannot fully solve the struggles of First Nations women today is that feminism is a response to systems of hierarchy that are not essential choices of social organization. The struggle with feminism involves more than including women of many races while understanding that the ideology that has resulted in feminism is predominately western, urban, white, and middle-class. It is more than that because often those characteristics are viewed as the desirable ones. None of these outcomes is a universal function of social organization.[49]

Feminism still operates at a distance from my experiences as a Haudenosaunee woman domiciled on a land mass now known as Canada. Equality with men is still understood to be feminism's central goal. In part this is because a determination of legal equality requires by its very nature a comparison to other groups.[50] This influence can be clearly traced in feminist legal discourse, although this is not my goal here. As Mary Jane Mossman notes of the decision in *Bliss*,[51] differences based on sex, such as pregnancy, are not natural, as the court asserted, but socially constructed.[52] This, then, seems to require the conclusion that different social systems construct gender differently. Law, however, binds through precedent. This captures First Nations women, who are just beginning to litigate their gendered realities, to a social construction of women that is already judicially determined, ill fitted, and potentially a new site of colonial imposition.

Identifying and then understanding how hierarchy is legitimized and protected is a central element in the process of deconstructing legal results that are felt[53] not to do justice to First Nations concerns and people. In her analysis of the "spaces" in the trial of two white men for the murder of Pamela George, a young Saulteaux mother in Regina in 1995, Sherene Razack also notes how courts (and states) use "naturalization" to mask their complicity in racialized/gendered outcomes:

> I want to denaturalize the spaces and bodies described in the trial in an effort to uncover the hierarchies that are protected and the violence that is hidden when we believe such spatial relations and subjects to be naturally occurring. To unmap one must historicize, a process that begins by asking about the relationship between identity and space.[54]

The need to reconsider feminism is not just a simple matter of taking account of race and rejecting notions of the universal woman.[55] The problem, as I see it, is much larger than women's denigration; it rests with all social structures that rely on hierarchy, oppression, and/or domination to secure validation. These systems are not always gendered or gendered first. Where feminism assists and informs my analysis, I will turn to it. When it does not, I will turn my gaze to other analytical tools, including Indigenous knowledge traditions. The burgeoning feminist literature does give voice and comfort to my gendered experiences. I often draw strength from these writings. Often it brings to me the courage to continue to speak that which might make me academically unpopular.[56] Feminism does provide a circle of academic comfort for me.

I aspire to a theoretical framework that takes equally into account the multiple sites of privilege and often the corresponding abuse of that privilege. Privilege and the resultant ability to control are constructed in complex and interdependent ways.[57] The examination of relationships based on domination exposes patterns of exclusion. It is my desire that in freeing Aboriginal people(s)—and law is just one part of this strategy—we do not further oppress or denigrate the women. As Lina Sunseri (Oneida) has documented, "once the post-colonial nation is formed, the position of women has not improved much and, in some cases, it has even regressed."[58] This is an issue that we must retain in our consciousness.

It is not my intention to dismiss feminist theory and practice, but merely to note that it is a movement in which I continue to choose not to be fully immersed.[59] Lina Sunseri, self-identifying as a mixed-blood author,[60] locates herself within feminism with this qualification:

> If we all come to understand feminism as a theory and movement that wants to fight *all* forms of oppression, including racism and colonialism, then we could see it as a struggle for *unity* among all oppressed women and men. It is this meaning of feminism that I accept, and therefore I can call myself a feminist without reservation.[61]

While respecting the rights of all women, including Aboriginal women to choose the location that sits well with them, I wish to point out the paradox in this position. The paradox is structural and not of any individual's making. The problem as I see it is that fighting to change feminism from within is a misdirection of our limited resources because feminism is not where the majority of the power is vested. The structural changes that need to occur to abolish First Nations exclusion and oppression require the state to change. In many ways, I also believe that both the state and courts are (and choose to be) isolated from the feminist agenda. For these many reasons, I choose to continue to stand first with the nation, although often within a circle of women.

By defining the analysis presented here as gendered, I mean to distinguish it from what is referred to as feminist analysis, while recognizing that this might be a meaningless distinction.[62] Feminist analysis has far too often been "e-raced" analysis. My hope is that the treatment of gender here situates it in the appropriate colonial, cultural, and racialized contexts.[63] In addition, I am interested in looking at what is happening to the women without embracing the imposed boundaries that arise within academic traditions. My interest is in understanding gender in a culturally[64] honest and respectful way.[65] In my own way, I introduce myself as mother, sister, auntie, and teacher. In societies where relations[66] form the basic social structure, gender is embedded in my introduction—mother, sister, auntie—but it is not explicit. In societies where public/private dichotomies do not prevail, and consequently where family is not solely a woman's domain, identifiers such as these do not indicate any form of subordination. In fact, these terms define the relationships and the set of reciprocal obligations that exist among my people. In societies where the roles of women and men are hierarchical and one is subordinate, the discussion of gender roles and relationships must be express with the oppression named. In turning my mind to gender and the decisions of the Supreme Court of Canada in the last decade, several cases and several observations were obvious.

One of the questions that must be addressed is the degree to which legal remedies that developed in a social system that relies on the public/private dichotomy—another hierarchy—as a basic form of ordering gender relations can offer a solution for individual litigants whose cultural community does not embrace the same ideas. (Remembering, of course, that litigants can come from a people who value a different construction of gender.) This general question is of particular importance for First Nations women. I believe the gender hierarchy created and reinforced by the public/private dichotomy, which orders Canadian society, partially explains legal outcomes such as those in *Lavell* and *Bedard*. Without understanding that women's "place" is not defined by the husband (even after divorce) or that "place" is not an isolated private one, the Court could not fully contemplate the situation of these two women.

Home means a place amongst one's own people. The fact that the decision did not address any of these kinds of questions or acknowledge this context should inform our understandings and strategies today. Issues that are fundamental problems for First Nations, such as the imposition of membership rules (including rules that required that the woman be transferred on marriage to the husband's band list) that imposed foreign constructs of gender, are not acknowledged. Equally frustrating is the lack of acknowledgement that to be a woman and the object of imposed membership provisions affects us concurrently: that it is impossible to separate our identity as First Nations from the fact we are women. This raises a number of questions and issues.

What is the result when law comes into direct contact with societies that seek to reclaim and decolonize governance structures and practices that do not rely on such hierarchical ordering? Are meaningful legal gains being made for First Nations cultures and our different gender structures in legal terms? The simple answer is that gains have not been achieved because gender has not yet been introduced in any rigorous way in the discussions of what Aboriginal rights mean. The subsequent question, has harm occurred because of the failure to turn our attention to gender, invites a more complicated answer. The harm I am most concerned about is continued colonial intrusion, an intrusion often attached to gender.[67]

Experiencing the world as I do through the eyes, thoughts, and feelings of a woman (for my experiences can never be anything else), I have also noticed that little respect has been given in the writings on treaty to either gender or women's roles in those negotiations.[68] More scholarly attention has been paid to this issue in recent years. Gunlög Fur writes:

> "Indian history" has largely painted images of forests peopled only by men, momentous councils visited only by white and red males, or battles in which warriors performed feats of courage. This is barely more historically justifiable than an older tradition of "Indian history" in which every event had a European or white American originator. We know now that the sources are one-sided and formed in a European patriarchal perspective and that this is a major reason why women are invisible. But it is not sufficient to note that. The theoretical question must be, somewhat flippantly, What did women do when men made history? Women were somewhere and they were decidedly active; they did not exist suspended in a timeless vacuum awaiting the return of the men with the meat and the treaty. . . .[69]

Perhaps, as the traditional role of men in many First Nations was that of spokesperson, the women's role in treaty negotiations was not public in forums with the Europeans and, therefore, has been dismissed (or merely missed). This is a frequent problem in the historical record. It is, in part, also the result of the position of women in non-Aboriginal societies more than a hundred years ago. Treaty commissioners and others who left historical accounts were blinded by their own culture, its beliefs, and the inherent gender biases. Although some scholars, including historians,[70] have started to write about Aboriginal women, the record remains incomplete. As Laura Klein and Lillian Ackerman conclude, the discussion of First Nations women in the historical record is superficial.[71] As noted, there are numerous reasons for this historical silence.

Understanding that the structures on which ordered societies (including First Nations, of course) are based are not universal has been a struggle for some academics. Theory is based on the presumption that the world is capable of being generalized and that we can continue to accumulate knowledge and to refine our generalizations. When Aboriginal social structures did not (and do not) fit the generalization, scholars, rather than questioning their own theoretical presumptions, assumed that the "problem" was within the societies studied. This led to the primitivization of Aboriginal nations and of their social, legal, and political structures. This is still a myth that must be disturbed. Equally, the European-dominated social definition of gender roles influenced what scholars chose to study and what remained unexamined, including the stereotypes of "women's place." Klein and Ackerman detail the consequences:

> There is a truism in ethnography, commonly traced to Max Gluckman, that societal rules become clear in times of dispute. The appropriate role of women has been in public dispute in Western culture for at least the last century, and the question of power and gender is, therefore, an issue. In societies where no such dispute is prominent, silence would be expected. The tendency to fill in this silence with powerlessness is the Western bias. In fact, the silence tells us nothing but the lack of dispute.[72]

Today, scholars are beginning to come to terms with the kinds of difficulties caused by generalization as a form of knowledge collection. Equally important, some scholars are now beginning to examine the degree to which scholars generally are responsible for repairing damaging conclusions now apparent in earlier works.[73]

FIRST NATIONS WOMEN AND SECTION 35

Understanding and acknowledging the different ways gender is constructed across cultures is a necessary step in understanding the gaps that now exist for First Nations women in Canadian law. In tracking gender through the case law on Aboriginal rights, some fairly conspicuous observations can be made. Despite the fact that the *Delgamuukw*[74] decision considers the right of "self-government"[75] and the contours of Aboriginal title protected under section 35(1) of Canada's 1982 constitution, gender is not visible in this decision. Candice Metallic and I prepared a long paper for the *Delgamuukw* National Review (an arm's-length project of the Assembly of First Nations between 1998 and 2001) which analyzed *Delgamuukw* from the standpoint of a First Nations understanding. In this paper, we do not mention women as a category of analysis, despite the fact that we are both women centered on being women.[76] The degree to which the present challenges of governance within First Nations communities must expressly contain reflections on the position of women had fallen beyond what even we had chosen to write. Identifying this gap in my own work and thinking has led to this paper.

With considerations of gender significantly in mind, a review of the case law brings forward another recognition. There is a plethora of cases on matters involving hunting and fishing rights. These are generally reactive decisions brought to defend against individual charges laid under provincial or federal wildlife or fishing regimes. However, the category "hunting and fishing" is incomplete. Gathering and agriculture were also central components of First Nations "sustenance"[77] practices (to borrow a phrase from the courts), even before contact. Contrary to popular belief, agriculture is not something the white man brought. And in many nations, it was women who possessed the authority to gather and grow.[78] Sarah Carter has documented the importance of plants in the diet of the Plains peoples:

> The plant food gathered varied according to terrain. The river and creek valleys provided a variety of wild fruit every spring, including saskatoons, raspberries, strawberries, black currants, and chokecherries. The fruit was dried or sold fresh by the pail. Kinnikinnick, a tobacco substitute, was gathered. Wild rhubarb was a favorite in soups. In early spring sap was gathered from maple and birch trees, boiled down, and, according to Dion, "carefully stored away as a treat and soother for grandmother's pets later on." Roots such as wild turnip were collected, peeled, and dried. There was a market for seneca root, an ingredient in patent medicines, and for wild hops. Women cleaned and smoked fish that came up the creeks in the spring and also caught fish through holes in the ice in winter. They snared small animals and birds such as prairie chicken. During moulting season wild fowl were killed in great numbers and women assisted in this. Much of the game was dried, smoked, and stored for winter. In the fall the more northerly Cree women gathered muskeg tea and quantities of moss, which they dried to make moss bags for babies.[79]

Women's responsibilities were essential for the prairie nations' survival; these contributions must be taken into account in the rights that First Nations try to protect today. In reclaiming legal recognition of the centrality of hunting and fishing practices, our view must be extended to include all sustenance practices of the First Nations, including those responsibilities belonging to the women.[80] It must not be only the women, but also our men, who bring forward this knowledge. Political organizations representing First Nations must also do their part in acknowledging the importance of women's responsibility to community sustenance. The inclusive phrase we must embrace is the right to hunt, fish, gather, and grow.

It is, therefore, highly problematic not to recognize the gendered way in which litigation strategies and court decisions have affected First Nations. The experience and responsibilities of First Nations men (hunting and fishing, although these were and are not exclusively male roles)[81] have gained a legal prominence, while women's pursuits have remained invisible and unconsidered as legal rights. Because the Crown is actively involved in imposing a legal regime that operates to limit hunting and fishing rights, its actions must also be seen as a blunt tool with specific gender consequences. The preoccupation with male pursuits is also reflected in the numbered treaties, where only the predominantly male practices of hunting and fishing are dealt with expressly in the text. It is clear that respect for the entirety of First Nations traditional sustenance practices, as they have become known, means considering hunting, fishing, growing, and gathering rights and responsibilities. By disputing Aboriginal claims to hunting and fishing rights, the Crown consumes First Nations resources, leaving them little energy to focus on women and the responsibilities in their realm. This example demonstrates the degree to which colonial impositions still affect the struggle for recognition of First Nations rights.

Gendered omission is just one of the patterns that confront Aboriginal litigants. In one recent Supreme Court of Canada fishing rights decision, the accused was a woman, Dorothy Marie Van der Peet. This fact was insufficient to ensure that the court conducted a gendered analysis. There is only a single reference to women in the case, a simple acknowledgement by McLachlin J., dissenting, that the Métis are a people descended from European traders and Aboriginal women.[82] In the majority judgment, Lamer C.J. summarizes the trial court findings:

> Finally, Scarlett Prov. Ct. J. found that the Sto:lo were at a band level of social organization rather than at a tribal level. As noted by the various experts, one of the central distinctions between a band society and a tribal society relates to specialization and division of labour. In a tribal society there tends to be specialization of labour—for example, specialization in the gathering and trade of fish—whereas in a band society division of labour tends to occur only on the basis of gender or age. The absence of specialization in the exploitation of the fishery is suggestive, in the same way that the absence of regularized trade or a market is suggestive, that the exchange of fish was not a central part of Sto:lo culture.[83]

This is the essence of the decision. The Sto:lo, merely because their division of labour was gendered, were not a tribal society. As a band society (read: less advanced), the Sto:lo could not hold significant rights to trade in fish. The argument they advanced to protect a commercial right to fish failed. And gender hierarchy, applied by academic experts and judges to Sto:lo society, is at the center of those reasons. This is indeed gendered backlash; it occurs despite the promise of protection of equality contained in section 35(4) of the *Constitution Act, 1982*. To be a member of a gender-ordered society means to be less civilized.

Women in some First Nations' traditions, including my own, were the "owners" of the fields.[84] Yet an Aboriginal title decision such as *Delgamuukw* mentions woman only once[85] (and gender not at all). The court did not note whether both men and women were hereditary chiefs.[86] There is no comment about the significance of the fact that both men and women hold title (although I assume the Gitksan and Wet'suwet'en are well aware of its significance). The fact that gender is not a principal focus in *Delgamuukw* now sits uncomfortably with me. As I have already explained, women among some First Nations had particular relationships with the land, including, at least, gathering and agriculture. For some First Nations, land relationships are gendered.

The legal system of Canada is now coming into increased contact with First Nations. Yet the Canadian legal system constructs gender in a very different way; in it, gendered exclusions are not unusual. In my view, the failure to take account of gender in litigating First Nations land or governance issues leaves us vulnerable to another round of colonial intrusions, this time at the hands of the judiciary. This outcome will be harmful to all First Nations citizens, not just the women.

The generalizations we make about First Nations' societies and social structures cause me concern. Not all First Nations will order gender relations in the same way. I do not understand, because understanding requires detail, the degree to which land holding among the Gitksan and Wet'suwet'en is gendered.[87] Nor is this information available in *Delgamuukw*. This is, in fact, my point. It is compounded by the fact that Supreme Court decisions such as *Delgamuukw* serve as precedent. The structure of Canadian law, therefore, masks the specificities of First Nations' cultures, particularly when that structure relies on gendering, and creates a pressure toward homogenized and unitary understandings. Litigation collapses the diversity of First Nations, including gender constructions, into a single concept: Aboriginal. It therefore appears that choosing to litigate First Nations claims courts a danger that gender structures will be unwittingly superimposed (when the diversity of gendered ordering is not considered).

This exposes an interesting dilemma for First Nations. It is common knowledge among the people of the First Nations that women were not respected in western traditions of law. Over time, western views of women have negatively influenced First Nations' social, governance, and legal structures. It is commonly understood that gender relations across western and First Nations' cultures are different, perhaps radically different. When your goal is protecting Aboriginal and treaty rights in a legal system that is not your own, do you choose to silence issues of gender difference if giving voice to your gendered cultural differences might further jeopardize (as in *Van der Peet*) your claim to Aboriginal and treaty rights? Do you ignore the place of your women for the sake of securing recognition of your claims to governance and land (as in *Delgamuukw*)? These apparently conflicting objectives, protecting rights versus respecting gender, must be seen as a structural obstacle superimposed from outside First Nations' social, cultural, governance, and legal structures. They are a consequence of colonial imposition and state sanction. This recognition points to the need to think in a different way of the breadth of the negative consequences that litigation can pose. Gender is, after all, integral to the cultural practices we seek to protect.

There is another place in *Delgamuukw* where the lack of acknowledgement of gender-based understandings, including the voice of women, causes me concern. The Court articulates in strong language the Crown's responsibility to consult with First Nations when First Nations rights are being interfered with. Compliance with the duty to consult is a precondition to permissible Crown interference with Aboriginal rights; as such, it becomes a central (if not backwards) element of Aboriginal rights.[88] Lamer C.J. comments:

> There is always a duty of consultation. Whether the aboriginal group has been consulted is relevant to determining whether the infringement of aboriginal title is justified, in the same way that the Crown's failure to consult an aboriginal group with respect to the terms by which reserve land is leased may breach its fiduciary duty at common law: *Guerin*. The nature and scope of the duty of consultation will vary with the circumstances. In occasional cases, when the breach is less serious or relatively minor, it will be no more than a duty to discuss important decisions that will be taken with respect to lands held pursuant to aboriginal title. Of course, even in these rare cases when the minimum acceptable standard is consultation, this consultation must be in good faith, and with the intention of substantially addressing the concerns of the aboriginal peoples whose lands are at issue. In most cases, it will be significantly deeper than mere consultation. Some cases may even require the full consent of an aboriginal nation, particularly when provinces enact hunting and fishing regulations in relation to aboriginal lands.[89]

In particular, the duty to consult in good faith seems to me to require a contextualized process of consultation[90] that takes into account the historic exclusions of women. Further, given the assault on women's place by the *Indian Act* system of governance, it seems essential that this duty to consult be a gendered duty. It is not just Band Councils that must have a voice; methods of consultation must ensure that gender exclusions are not unwittingly perpetuated. In addition, the state must resist using gender as a divide-and-conquer strategy to interfere in matters of band and tribal governance. It must recognize the impact of the *Indian Act* prohibitions that disallowed women from holding political office until 1951.[91] Consultation could, in fact, be an opportunity to correct gendered oppression and impositions. This would require that the Canadian government establish protocols—yes, relationships—with First Nation entities other than Band Councils.

This brief and specialized analysis of the elements of *Delgamuukw* demonstrates the consequences of not taking gender into account in decisions that focus on First Nations governance and land relationships. It demonstrates that gendered omission can re-impose colonial power relations. This is not, however, the only way in which courts can and do impose gendered difficulties. The consequences of not fully addressing gender are prominent in two further Supreme Court decisions that I believe deserve special mention: *Gladue* and *Corbiere*.

GLADUE AND *CORBIERE*

In *R. v. Gladue*,[92] the issue was the application of the *Criminal Code*, section 718.2(e). In recognition of the Canadian tendency to rely too heavily on incarceration as the sentencing solution, this section provides that sentencing judges should consider alternatives to imprisonment for all offenders, "with particular attention to the circumstances of aboriginal offenders."[93] The problem in *Gladue* was the silencing of gender when the facts disclosed that the accused, who killed her common-law partner, was, more than likely at least, a psychologically battered woman. Consider the description provided by the Court:

> The appellant and Beaver returned separately to their townhouse and they started to quarrel. During the argument, the appellant confronted him with his infidelity and he told her that she was fat and ugly and not as good as the others. A neighbour, Mr. Gretchin, who lived next door was awakened by some banging and shouting and a female voice saying "I'm sick and tired of you fooling around with other women." The disturbance was becoming very loud and he decided to ask his neighbours to calm down. He heard the front door of the appellant's residence slam. As he opened his own front door, he saw the appellant come running out of her suite. He also saw Reuben Beaver banging with both hands at Tara Chalifoux's door down the hall saying, "Let me in. Let me in."[94]

Domestic violence is overwhelmingly directed by men at women. The facts in this case, a woman accused of killing her partner, were insufficient to trigger a gendered context for the decision.

Whether or not the accused was a battered woman is not essential to the issue I wish to raise. That possibility merely increases the gravity of the Court's omission of gender. After all, the experiences of race, culture, and gender impact on Aboriginal people. Taking into account our realities means taking account of gender specificity in all instances. Throughout the remainder of the case, the accused is discussed as an Aboriginal person, rather than an Aboriginal woman.[95] As has already been noted, women are frequently forced to "separate their gender from all other aspects of their being."[96] This is becoming a persistent and troubling aspect of the high court's decision making in cases that involve Aboriginal women.

In a decision rendered on 20 May 1999, the Supreme Court of Canada considered whether the residency of "registered Indians" may be used as a ground for distinguishing those who can vote in band council elections.[97] It is arguable that the decision in *Corbiere* has had greater effect on First Nations communities than other decisions of the Supreme Court of Canada. Decisions such as *Delgamuukw* do go some distance in affirming First Nations views of our legal rights to land (although the result in that case was only to order a new trial). *Corbiere*, ironically, introduces new causes for concern amongst First Nations about the intrusion of non–First Nations ideas of governance into our internal political and community relations. I am not suggesting that the decision in *Corbiere* was wrong. Because I understand that we come from territories and not reserves, I think the inclusion of so-called off-reserve band members is sound in principle. It is, first, the fact that the inclusion results from judicial imposition that causes me concern. Judicial imposition, as much as political imposition, is still imposition.

In *Corbiere*, four band members—John Corbiere, Charlotte Syrette, Claire Robinson, and Frank Nolan—sued on their own behalf and on the behalf of all non-resident band members of the Batchewana First Nation.[98] These individuals claimed that section 77(1) of the *Indian Act*, which defines who is eligible to vote in band council elections, violated section 15(1) of the *Canadian Charter of Rights and Freedoms*. Section 77(1) requires band members to reside on reserve to be "eligible electors." It was argued that reserve residency was an analogous ground[99] of discrimination prohibited by the *Charter*. It is clear, in my view, that the *Charter* does not apply to Aboriginal governments when they are exercising their inherent authority.[100] Otherwise, section 25 of the *Charter*[101] has no purpose. *Corbiere*, however, is a case about the application of the *Charter* to the *Indian Act*. That *Act* does not owe its origins to First Nations' inherent authority, but to Canadian law. The application of the *Charter* to *Indian Act* provisions could concurrently affect First Nations' inherent jurisdiction. Interference with First Nations' inherent authority, prohibited through statutory means since 1982, must not be countenanced collaterally through the *Charter*. For this reason, courts must be careful when considering issues of general *Charter* jurisdiction and applicability to First Nations. Thus far, they have been silent on the intricacies of this matter.

All nine justices of the Supreme Court took part in the decision in *Corbiere*. McLachlin and Bastarache JJ. wrote the majority judgment. They held that section 77(1) and the residency requirement infringed unjustifiably section 15(1) of the *Charter*. L'Heureux-Dubé J., who wrote separately for three other judges, concurred in this result, but for different reasons. The Crown's appeal was dismissed unanimously. The principal difference between the two judgments is that the majority believed the case could be decided on simpler grounds than those espoused by Justice L'Heureux-Dubé. As McLachlin and Bastarache JJ. express:

> If it is the intention of L'Heureux-Dubé J.'s reasons to affirm contextual dependency of the enumerated and analogous grounds, we must respectfully disagree. If "Aboriginality-residence" is to be an analogous ground (and we agree with L'Heureux-Dubé J. that it should), then it must always stand as a constant marker of potential legislative discrimination, whether the challenge is to a governmental tax credit, a voting right, or a pension scheme.[102]

This distinction matters to First Nations communities because the *Indian Act* regime is centered around the on-/off-reserve distinction as the basis for "Indian" entitlements. If distinctions on the basis of reserve residency are repeatedly found unconstitutional, the legal scheme of the *Indian Act* will fail. This was the outcome that the courts took great pains to avoid in the early *Canadian Bill of Rights* case of *Lavell* and *Bedard*.[103] Will the rights of "Indians" on reserve be diminished in an effort to ensure equality? Or will the rights of off-reserve "Indians" be increased? Given its possible implications, the finding in *Corbiere* can be viewed as a new threat to the relationship between First Nations and Canada.[104]

Although it is not heralded as a case about women's rights, the *Corbiere* decision is an interesting example of courts' failure to engage in appropriate gender-specific analysis. L'Heureux-Dubé J., significantly, acknowledged the gendered impact of the *Indian Act*:[105]

> Many of those affected are women, and the descendants of women, who lost their Indian status because they married men who did not have Indian status. . . . Aboriginal women who married outside their band became members of their husband's band. . . . Legislation depriving Aboriginal women of status has a long history. The involuntary loss of status by Aboriginal women and children began in Upper and Lower Canada with the passage of *An Act to encourage the gradual Civilization of the Indian Tribes in the Province, and to amend the Laws respecting Indians*. . . . A woman whose husband "enfranchised" had her status removed along with his. This legislation introduced patriarchal concepts into many Aboriginal societies which did not exist before. . . .[106]

Unfortunately, beyond recognizing that men and women were affected differently by the *Indian Act*'s membership provisions, the case does not fully take account of gender or of all the hardships women faced because of the legislation. For example, until 1985, women were involuntarily transferred to the bands of their husbands, thus prohibiting them from participating further in the politics of their own communities. This fact is equally important in contextualizing the experiences of "Indian" women. The *Indian Act*—which must be recognized as a Canadian, not an Indian, masterpiece—is a significant source of the political isolation of First Nations women. Simply put, the federal Crown bears a substantial share of the responsibility for the gender isolation. Unfortunately, it cannot correct its error except by amending existing legislation (which in itself can be a new form of imposition). To do more would be a further imposition and likely a further travesty to culture.

This points to a difficulty that arises in resolving First Nations' claims in courts of foreign jurisdiction. This is not so much a matter of jurisdiction as it is a culture- and knowledge-based concern that requires an understanding of the political realities in First Nations communities. Contextualization is not a unitary matter; it varies according to a community's and nation's history, circumstance, and experience. The unnecessary linkage between the challenge to the voting provisions and the Bill C-31 amendments is one of the evidentiary bases of L'Heureux-Dubé J.'s concurring judgment. The Court has thereby forced women to the forefront. This puts First Nations women (and other so-called Bill C-31 Indians) in the community at risk of blame for the result in *Corbiere*, creating new potential for the Crown to threaten and interfere with First Nations solidarity. Interference with our solidarity increases the Crown's ability to impose its power over us and to limit the exercise of our rights. This is dangerous and unnecessary; the problem is not really about *who* is excluded but *how* they are excluded. The on-/off-reserve distinction[107] is at the heart of the matter, not the women who married out. As the number of off-reserve "Indians" continues to increase (some nineteen years after marriage out became possible without loss of Indian status), it is obvious that the membership provisions of the *Indian Act* are not the sole cause of the difficulty with voting rights.[108] Inappropriately raising gender concerns can be just as problematic as making them invisible.

L'Heureux-Dubé J. has noted the importance of contextualizing the process judges use to reach decisions:

> When analysing a claim that involves possibly conflicting interests of minority groups, one must be especially sensitive to their realities and experiences, and to their values, history, and identity. This is inherent in the nature of a subjective-objective analysis, since a court is required to consider the perspective of someone possessed of similar characteristics to the claimant. Thus, in the case of equality rights affecting Aboriginal people and communities, the legislation in question must be evaluated with special attention to the rights of Aboriginal peoples, the protection of Aboriginal and treaty rights guaranteed in the Constitution, the history of Aboriginal people in Canada, and with respect for and consideration of the cultural attachment and background of all Aboriginal women and men.[109]

The problem is not with the standard that L'Heureux-Dubé J. proposed but with the Court's ability to analyze, fully and easily, the legislation's impact on "Indian" women. Contextual analysis cannot proceed without a knowledge of the lived experience that is the context. This is also a difficulty with the way the cases are presented to courts.

CONCLUSION

I suspect that the dearth of academic literature examining the full breadth of discrimination against "Indian" women—the totality of our experience in our communities, not just issues of status under former section 12(1)(b)—likely contributes to judicial results such as those discussed above. Former section 12(1)(b) is not the only issue Indian women have struggled against. There is an overlap between the public, academic, and judicial discourses, an overlap most frequently characterized by women's invisibility. This is the trap, identified at the beginning of the paper, that I myself have fallen into when thinking I am writing on issues, such as governance, of general applicability to First Nations.[110]

Although I still believe the 1982 inclusion of the Aboriginal and treaty rights provision in Canada's constitution created new opportunities for validation and redress of First Nations' claims, I remain concerned about the potential for continued impacts whose consequences may be as devastating as the early colonial encounters. These concerns do not lead me to wish to prescribe solutions, but rather to cause ripples that prompt us to think carefully about our actions as they affect future generations. I understand that the assignment of gender roles and responsibilities, our values and beliefs, as well as our involvement with particular legal structures, do influence our ability to ensure that space remains for First Nations to be First Nations in Canada. This, in my view, means needing to reclaim our ability to acknowledge traditional gendered relationships respectfully. This is not just for the women (or the men), but for the nation(s). It is, therefore, important to note that the problem is not solely within courts or the judiciary but in the structure of both Canadian law and politics.[111]

Often the discourse of *Charter* rights and the flowing rhetoric of Aboriginal rights is attractive to us. Ideas such as "[h]uman dignity means that an individual or group feels self-respect and self-worth"[112] are not contrary to the values of the vast majority of people domiciled in Canada. The real challenge seems to be living up to these standards in a way that guarantees them equally to female and male persons. This is a particular challenge in the area of Aboriginal rights, where colonial efforts have interfered with gender representation. This is a matter of extreme importance to peoples whose culture, social structures, and laws are tied to gender responsibilities. Failure to take account of gender in our efforts to reclaim our ways means that First Nations can succeed only partially in stepping beyond colonial impositions.

NOTES

[1] S.C. 1960, c. 44, reprinted in R.S.C. 1985, App. III.

[2] Peter W. Hogg, *Constitutional Law of Canada*, looseleaf (Toronto: Carswell, 1997) at 32-1.

[3] For some of us, the alleged shift feels more the "same" than it does "new." Consider that Indigenous history on this land is over ten thousand years old, whereas "Newcomer" history is less than a thousand.

[4] *Canadian Charter of Rights and Freedoms*, Part I of the *Constitution Act, 1982*, being Schedule B of the *Canada Act 1982* (U.K.), 1982, c. 11 [*Charter* and *Constitution Act, 1982*, respectively].

[5] *Canada (A.G.) v. Lavell; Isaac v. Bedard* [1974] 1 S.C.R. 1349 [*Lavell*, or *Lavell* and *Bedard*].

[6] *Native Women's Association of Canada (NWAC) v. Canada*, [1994] 3 S.C.R. 627 [*NWAC*].

[7] A word on terminology is important. "Indian" is a legal word, defined in s. 2(1) of the *Indian Act*, R.S.C. 1985, c. I-6, as amended, and is appropriately used to describe those individuals who are registered or entitled to be registered under the *Indian Act*. "First Nations" is intended here to refer to people who are Indian (that is, Mohawk, Cree, Maliseet, and so on), whether or not they maintain

registration under the *Indian Act*. "Aboriginal" is defined in the constitution as the "Indian, Inuit and Métis." I will defer to the constitutional usage when appropriate. I am often asked what is the proper word to use when referring to Aboriginal people(s). Each of the labels causes concern (and animated response) in some circles. This is likely a reflection of the fact that all the labels are externally applied (that is, colonial).

[8] *R. v. Sparrow*, [1990] 1 S.C.R. 1075 [*Sparrow*].

[9] Section 35(1) of the *Constitution Act, 1982, supra* note 4, reads:
> The existing aboriginal and treaty rights of the aboriginal peoples of Canada are hereby recognized and affirmed.

[10] See John Borrows, "Uncertain Citizens: Aboriginal Peoples and the Supreme Court" (2001) 80 *Can. Bar Rev.* 15 at 18–19.

[11] See for example *Corbiere v. Canada (Minister of Indian and Northern Affairs)*, [1999] 2 S.C.R. 203 [*Corbiere*] and *R. v. Van der Peet*, [1996] 2 S.C.R. 507 [*Van der Peet*].

[12] For a comprehensive and technical discussion of the *Charter*'s application to First Nations governments, see Kent McNeil, "Aboriginal Governments and the *Canadian Charter of Rights and Freedoms*" in Kent McNeil, *Emerging Justice? Essays on Indigenous Rights in Canada and Australia* (Saskatoon: University of Saskatchewan, Native Law Centre, 2001) 215. See also *Twinn v. Canada* [1997], 2 F.C. 450 (F.C.T.D.).

[13] See *R. v. Lavallee*, [1990] 1 S.C.R. 852. The fact that the accused is a woman of Métis ancestry emerges in the appellate court decision ((1988), 52 Man. R. (2d) 274 (C.A.)), where the statement of Angelique Lyn Lavallee appears as Appendix 1.

[14] From a First Nations standpoint, "responsibilities" is a better articulation of the nature of legal relationships than "rights."

[15] See for example John Borrows, "Contemporary Traditional Equality: The Effect of the *Charter* on First Nations Politics" (1994) 43 U.N.B.L.J. 19; Teressa Nahanee, "Dancing with a Gorilla: Aboriginal Women, Justice and the Charter" in Canada, Royal Commission on Aboriginal Peoples, *Aboriginal Peoples and the Justice System: Report of the National Round Table on Aboriginal Justice Issues* (Ottawa: Supply and Services Canada, 1993) 359; and Mary Ellen Turpel, "Aboriginal Peoples and the Canadian Charter: Interpretive Monopolies and Cultural Differences" (1989–1990) 6 Can. Hum. Rts. Y.B. 3.

[16] *Supra* note 5.

[17] *Supra* note 1. For a full discussion, see Patricia Monture-Angus, "A First Journey in Decolonized Thought: Aboriginal Women and the Application of the Canadian Charter" in Patricia Monture-Angus, *Thunder in My Soul: A Mohawk Woman Speaks* (Halifax: Fernwood, 1995) 131 at 137.

[18] R.S.C. 1970, c. I-5, s. 12(1)(b), repealed by R.S.C. 1985, c. 32 (1st Supp.), s. 4.

[19] This is the correct legal usage of the term "Indian," as it is a reference to only those individuals entitled to be registered under the *Indian Act*. Elsewhere, the term appears in quotation marks when the usage is not legally correct. This is an attempt to reflect the unacceptability of the imposition of names on Indigenous peoples.

[20] *Bliss v. Canada (A.G.)*, [1979] 1 S.C.R. 183 [*Bliss*] did not involve intersecting claims, but did hold that a woman fired because she was pregnant and would not lift heavy boxes was not protected by the guarantee of "equal protection under the law." Subsequently, "equal benefit of the law" was added to section 15 of the *Charter*.

[21] Monture-Angus, *supra* note 17 at 137.

[22] Sherene Razack, "Domestic Violence as Gender Persecution: Policing the Borders of Nation, Race, and Gender" (1995) 8 Can. J. Women & L. 45 at 50.

[23] I am not suggesting a change in my political stance or in my belief that gender and culture are inseparable. I am thinking about a gap I have identified in both political discourse and academic scholarship.

[24] See for example the discussion in Gordon Christie, "Law, Theory and Aboriginal Peoples" (2003) 2 Indigenous L.J. 67 at 68–70.

[25] Section 35(4) was added to the *Constitution Act, 1982, supra* note 4, by consent of the four major

national Aboriginal groups (including NWAC) at the First Ministers' Conference in 1983. It simply reads:

> 35(4) Notwithstanding any other provision of this Act, the aboriginal and treaty rights referred to in subsection (1) are guaranteed equally to male and female persons.

[26] I am not asserting that there are only two genders. For a full discussion, see Kim Anderson, *A Recognition of Being: Reconstructing Native Womanhood* (Toronto: Second Story Press, 2000) at 90–91, and Martin Cannon, "The Regulation of First Nations Sexuality" (1998) 18 Can. J. Native Stud., 1 at 5.

[27] *NWAC, supra* note 6 at 649–51. See also the discussion of these cases in my earlier work "Lessons in Rights Discourse: Charter Challenges and Aboriginal Sovereignty" in Patricia Monture-Angus, *Journeying Forward: Dreaming First Nations' Independence* (Halifax: Fernwood, 1999) 135.

[28] *NWAC*, ibid.

[29] The author was first vice-president of the Ontario Native Women's Association during the 1988–89 term.

[30] For example, it is the efforts of NWAC that have exposed the discrimination that women domiciled on Indian reserves continue to face with respect to matrimonial property. See also the Supreme Court of Canada decisions in *Derrickson v. Derrickson*, [1986] 1 S.C.R. 285 and *Paul v. Paul*, [1986] 1 S.C.R. 306.

[31] See Monture-Angus, *supra* note 27 at 148.

[32] Honesty is one of the traditional values essential to Indigenous knowledge methodologies.

[33] See Monture-Angus, *supra* note 27.

[34] And this I believe is a window into the knowledge that gender is constructed very differently in my own Haudenosaunee traditions.

[35] The style of this paper is not conventional as most academics would understand it. My comments here should not be seen as saying this is not academic work. Nor am I very happy with the label "different." First, there is not a developed body of literature that considers Aboriginal women and s. 35. This alone means that conventional styles of citation and argumentation are not possible. Second, as gender has been invisible as a topic in the academic discourse pertaining to s. 35, my own thoughts remain preliminary and challenging. The opportunity to think in the second legal tradition in which I have been trained remains elusive. Third, academic convention demands an objectivity that is in direct confrontation with my first training in Aboriginal legal traditions. This tradition demands self-reflexivity and a community of thinking and thinkers.

Other Indigenous scholars—such as John Borrows, whose work in his first book, *Recovering Canada: The Resurgence of Indigenous Law* (Toronto: University of Toronto Press, 2002) is a prime example—attempt to bring Anishnabe (Ojibway) knowledge into the form and structure of western academic legal analysis. My goal is to bring western academics to the forms and structures of Indigenous knowledge(s). The need to balance legal traditions, first articulated by the Supreme Court of Canada in *R. v. Gladstone*, [1996] 2 S.C.R. 723, will likely remain elusive if the distance to be travelled in the act of balancing is traversed only by First Nations citizens. The burden of reconciliation must be shared or the journey becomes merely another form of domination and oppression. Reconciliation transforms into colonization if one collective only crosses the distance.

[36] I do mean "First Nations" to refer exclusively to those the law and government would label "status" and "non-status Indians." After a decade on the prairies, I am fully convinced that there is little similarity remaining between First Nations and the majority of Métis, despite their shared origins. Each face unique situations of disempowerment, oppression, and disenfranchisement. I do not believe the solutions, political arguments, and so on should be collapsed into a single "Aboriginal" dialogue. I am suggesting here that the new container "Aboriginal" creates a pattern of falsehood and disguises the diversity that exists between First Nations and Métis.

[37] It is this duty to reflect that is an essential responsibility in Indigenous methodologies and "rules" about living as a "good Indian."

[38] Professor Mari Matsuda calls for a re-examination of how we rely on colleagues' work (and how very narrow that circle can be):

This proposal suggests specific action to end apartheid in legal knowledge. Apartheid is evident in the books shelved, in the journals read, and in the sources considered in the process of legal scholarship. Recurring citations in prestigious legal writing, particularly in theoretical writing, are largely segregated, as Richard Delgado noted in his article, *The Imperial Scholar*. This segregation results in legal knowledge uninformed by the rich and provocative knowledge of outsiders.

"Affirmative Action and Legal Knowledge: Planting Seeds in Plowed-Up Ground" (1988) 11 Harv. Women's L.J. 1 at 2–3.

[39] Gerald R. Alfred also had this difficulty of gender in his first book, *Heeding the Voices of Our Ancestors: Kahnawake Mohawk Politics and the Rise of Native Nationalism* (Don Mills: Oxford University Press Canada, 1995).

[40] To some, this may seem an odd use of the concept "methodology." Although I am trained as both lawyer and sociologist, my research is shaped more by the methods by which knowledge is shared in Indigenous traditions. Although academics have both ignored and shunned these methods over the decades, my choice remains to honour the knowledge traditions of my people and of other First Nations. For a fuller discussion of issues of research in Indigenous communities, see Linda Tuhiwai Smith, *Decolonizing Methodologies: Research and Indigenous Peoples* (London: Zed, 1999).

[41] Christie, *supra* note 24 at 107–8.

[42] Rosanna Deerchild, "Tribal Feminism is a Drum Song" in Kim Anderson & Bonita Lawrence, eds., *Strong Women Stories: Native Vision and Community Survival* (Toronto: Sumach Press, 2003) 97 at 100–101.

[43] Anderson, *supra* note 26 at 175.

[44] Although the plural of "knowledge" is not a recognized English word, it reflects the diversity of knowledge systems, including those belonging to First Nations.

[45] Feminism seeks to expose and then confront social, economic, and political power when it is unfairly distributed according to gender. The methodology I am advocating seeks to understand when and how gender is a foundational concept amongst Indigenous nations. It is only then that feminism can be fully considered in its application to the struggles of First Nations, which may not be centered on unequal distributions of power based on gender.

[46] Linda Hogan, "A Different Yield" in Marie Battiste, ed., *Reclaiming Indigenous Voice and Vision* (Vancouver: University of British Columbia Press, 2000) 115 at 122.

[47] Laura F. Klein & Lillian A. Ackerman, "Introduction" in Laura F. Klein & Lillian A. Ackerman, eds., *Women and Power in Native North America* (Norman: University of Oklahoma Press, 1995) 3 at 14.

[48] Kathleen A. Lahey, "Legal 'Persons' and the Charter of Rights: Gender, Race, and Sexuality in Canada" (1998) 77 Can. Bar Rev. 402.

[49] See bell hooks, *Feminism Is for Everybody: Passionate Politics* (Cambridge: South End Press, 2000) at 4–6.

[50] *Corbiere*, *supra* note 11 at paras. 19, 47–69.

[51] *Bliss*, *supra* note 20.

[52] Mary Jane Mossman, "Feminism and the Law: Challenges and Choices" (1998) 10 Can. J. Women & L. 1 at 5–6.

[53] In the tradition of my people, it is not enough to think. We are taught to "double understand." Knowledge must be carried in both the head and the heart. Hence, my deference to the emotional half.

[54] Sherene H. Razack, "Gendered Racial Violence and Spatialized Justice: The Murder of Pamela George" (2000) 15:2 Can. J. L. & Soc. 91 at 95–96.

[55] The problem with feminism's universal woman is that it creates a binary in which Aboriginal women and women of colour are "othered." Patricia Hill Collins writes:

> [E]ach term in the binaries white/black, male/female, reason/emotion, culture/nature, fact/opinion, mind/body, and subject/object gains meaning only in *relation* to its counterpart.
>
> Another basic idea concerns how binary thinking shapes understandings of human difference. In such thinking, difference is defined in oppositional terms. One part is not simply

different from its counterpart; it is inherently opposed to its "other". Whites and blacks, males and females, thought and feeling are not complementary counterparts—they are fundamentally different entities related only through their definition as opposites. Feeling cannot be incorporated into thought or even function in conjunction with it because binary oppositional thinking, feeling retards thought and values obscure facts.

Black Feminist Thought: Knowledge, Consciousness, and the Politics of Empowerment, 2d ed. (New York: Routledge, 2000) at 70 [emphasis in original].

[56] See also Aileen Moreton-Robinson, *Talkin' Up to the White Woman: Aboriginal Women and Feminism* (St. Lucia: University of Queensland Press, 2000).

[57] Dr. Razack's work on immigration laws, cited *supra* at note 22, is an excellent example of how these processes operate.

[58] Lina Sunseri, "Moving Beyond the Feminism Versus Nationalism Dichotomy: An Anti-Colonial Feminist Perspective on Aboriginal Liberation Struggles" (2000) 20:2 Canadian Woman Studies 143 at 143.

[59] See the discussion in Marlyn Kane (Osennontion) & Sylvia Maracle (Skonaganleh:rá), "Our World: According to Osennontion and Skonaganleh:rá" (1989) 10:2 & 3 Canadian Woman Studies 7.

[60] Ms. Sunseri identifies herself as Oneida of the Turtle Clan and of "an Italian ethno-cultural heritage": *supra* note 58 at 147.

[61] *Ibid.* at 144 [emphasis in original].

[62] Largely as a result of the controversy about the amendments repealing section 12(1)(b)—the gendered "marrying-out" provision—of the *Indian Act, supra* note 18, and the case launched by NWAC in 1994, many Indian men will respond negatively to scholarship that is self-proclaimed as feminist. There is therefore a very fine line I walk in my communities. In part, I am being pragmatic, as my desire is to speak first to other First Nations people, both the men and the women. This is not intended as a criticism of feminism.

[63] See for example Sherene H. Razack, *Looking White People in the Eye: Gender, Race, and Culture in Courtrooms and Classrooms* (Toronto: University of Toronto Press, 1998).

[64] Not only are there many meanings of the word "culture"—I use it to mean the practices, values, and beliefs of First Peoples—it can also become a dangerous concept. Sherene Razack explains (*ibid.* at 58):

> When women from non-dominant groups talk about culture, we are often heard to be articulating a false dichotomy between culture and gender; in articulating our difference, we inadvertently also confirm our relegation to the margins. Culture talk is clearly a double-edged sword. It packages difference as inferiority and obscures both gender-based and racial domination, yet cultural considerations are important for contextualzing oppressed groups' claims for justice, for improving their access to services, and for requiring dominant groups to examine the invisible cultural advantages they enjoy.

Gordon Christie, *supra* note 24, also writes (at 84–85) of the high court's view of culture:

> In relation to Aboriginal resource rights what primarily minimizes tension between collective Aboriginal rights and the individualized rights of non-Aboriginals is the remarkably thin conception of culture the Supreme Court has deployed. While the Court has spoken as if it were attempting to protect "Aboriginality"—the core of Aboriginal identity—by defining culture in terms of pre-contact activities and customs the law has effectively isolated culture from identity.

[65] Using a reference from one of my early works, Janet Mancini Billson notes appropriately that "Iroquois" women are the keepers of "culture, the faith, and the home." She then states: "But the outside world has changed around her, as has life on the reserve." See "Clan Mothers and Sky Walkers: Iroquois Women of the Six Nations, Oshweken, Ontario" in Janet Mancini Billson, *Keepers of the Culture: The Power of Tradition in Women's Lives* (New York: Lexington, 1995) 11 at 23.

Her last sentence is not anything that I would say, write, or feel. Nor do I understand it as the way women in my community feel. We have not stood still (or been frozen in time), allowing the world to slip by us. Billson's statement embeds several unfortunate stereotypes—"Indians as inferior" and "Indians as belonging to the past"—although, I presume, unintentionally. I give this example hoping that careful attention will be paid to what is written about us or how what we have written is used.

[66] Anthropologists would describe this as kinship, but that is perhaps an incomplete term.

[67] Former section 12(1)(b) of the *Indian Act, supra* note 18, the race-specific prostitution provisions and the 1921 attempt to make it a crime for a white man to sleep with an Indian woman (see Canada, *House of Commons Debates* (26 May 1921) at 3906–10) are some examples of ways in which colonialism has been a gendered strategy.

[68] In *Bounty and Benevolence: A History of the Saskatchewan Treaties* (Montreal: McGill–Queen's University Press, 2000), a recent book prepared for the Treaty Commissioner of Saskatchewan by Arthur J. Ray, Jim Miller, and Frank J. Tough, women do not form a significant part of their analysis. For example, a scan through the index indicates a listing for "wolves" but not for "women" (and I mean no disrespect to the wolves as a category of spirit being).

[69] Gunlög Fur, "'Some Women Are Wiser than Some Men': Gender and Native American History" in Nancy Shoemaker, ed., *Clearing a Path: Theorizing the Past in Native American Studies* (New York: Routledge, 2002) 75 at 76 [references omitted].

[70] See for example: Sarah Carter, *Capturing Women: The Manipulation of Cultural Imagery in Canada's Prairie West* (Montreal: McGill–Queen's University Press, 1997); Sylvia Van Kirk, *Many Tender Ties: Women in Fur-Trade Society, 1670–1870* (Winnipeg: Watson & Dwyer, 1999); Julia V. Emberley, *Thresholds of Difference: Feminist Critique, Native Women's Writings, Postcolonial Theory* (Toronto: University of Toronto Press, 1993). These women are all "white" women. Another important academic source is Christine Miller & Patricia Chuchryk, eds., *Women of the First Nations: Power, Wisdom and Strength* (Winnipeg: University of Manitoba Press, 1996).

[71] Klein & Ackerman, *supra* note 47 at 3.

[72] *Ibid.* at 4.

[73] *Ibid.*

[74] *Delgamuukw v. British Columbia*, [1997] 3 S.C.R. 1010 [*Delgamuukw*].

[75] The *Delgamuukw* case, *ibid.*, was originally brought on the footing of jurisdiction and ownership of the land. After trial, the claim was altered so that "Aboriginal title" replaced "ownership" and "self-government" replaced "jurisdiction." A third alteration proved fatal to the appeal. The individual claims brought on behalf of the fifty-one houses of the Gitksan and Wet'suwet'en were collapsed into two collective claims, one on behalf of each nation. This was accomplished without providing an amendment to the pleadings. The Supreme Court held that this caused the Crown "some prejudice" and ordered a new trial: *ibid.* at paras. 76–77.

[76] Women are mentioned at several points in the paper. In our discussion of equality, gender is present in the discussion and in our writing style (for example, we write "men and women," rather than "people"). It is present in our discussion of intersectionality. We also mention the denial of matrimonial property rights to women domiciled on the reserve (an issue that does not apply just to "Indian" women).

[77] This word diminishes the fact that First Nation societies were complex and included integrated and interdependent practices that ensured the survival both within and amongst groups, including other First Nations. First Nations did have complex webs of trading relations that in today's language would be called commercial practices.

[78] See Sarah Carter, *Lost Harvests: Prairie Indian Reserve Farmers and Government Policy* (Montreal: McGill–Queen's Press, 1990) at 28, 176–80, and Laura Peers, "Subsistence, Secondary Literature, and Gender Bias: The Saulteaux" in Miller & Chuchryk, *supra* note 70, 39.

[79] Carter, *ibid.* at 177.

[80] Gender is disappeared because women's traditional responsibilities (gathering and growing) are not as highly regulated by the state. Men's responsibilities, hunting and fishing, have gained prominence in part because of the state's gaze on these activities.

[81] See the discussion in Beatrice Medicine, "'Warrior Women'—Sex Role Alternatives for Plains Indian Women" in Patricia Albers & Beatrice Medicine, eds., *The Hidden Half: Studies of Plains Indian Women* (Lanham: University Press of America, 1983) 267 at 268–69.

[82] *Van der Peet, supra* note 11 at para. 248.

[83] *Ibid.* at para. 90.

[84] Reference to the relationship between Iroquois women and the land can be found in Ann Eastlack Shafer, "The Status of Iroquois Women" in W.G. Spittal, ed., *Iroquois Women: An Anthology* (Ohsweken: Iroqrafts, 1990) 71 at 79, and Judith K. Brown, "Economic Organization and the Position of Women Among the Iroquois" in Spittal, *ibid.,* 182 at 188. See also the discussion of the Newhouse version of the Iroquois constitution in Joy Bilharz, "First Among Equals? The Changing Status of Seneca Women" in Klein & Ackerman, *supra* note 47, 101 at 106.

[85] *Delgamuukw, supra* note 74 at para. 12.

[86] *Ibid.*

[87] I am not assuming that "mainstream" gendered constructs will fully illuminate ways in which gender is constructed in First Nations societies.

[88] *Delgamuukw, supra* note 74 at para. 168.

[89] *Ibid.*

[90] I am not suggesting that I am happy with the Court's conceptualization of consultation. It does not cure colonial evil, past or present.

[91] *Indian Act,* R.S.C. 1927, c. 98, ss. 157, 163. Section 157 reads:
> At the election of a chief or chiefs, or at the granting of any ordinary consent required of a band under this Part, those entitled to vote at the council or meeting thereof shall be the male members of the band. . . .

[92] *R. v. Gladue,* [1999] 1 S.C.R. 688 [*Gladue*].

[93] *Criminal Code,* R.S.C. 1985, c. C-46, as amended, s. 718.2(e).

[94] *Gladue, supra* note 92 at para. 5.

[95] Later in the case, *ibid.* at paras. 58–65, there are statistics about the over-representation of Aboriginal women in the incarcerated population. These comments appear in a general quote on over-representation, not one provided because of its gender specificity.

[96] Razack, *supra* note 22 at 50.

[97] *Corbiere, supra* note 11.

[98] The case attracted significant attention. Interveners included Aboriginal Legal Services of Toronto, the Congress of Aboriginal People, the Lesser Slave Lake Regional Council, the Native Women's Association of Canada, and the United Native Nations Society of British Columbia.

[99] Section 15(1) of the *Charter* expressly prohibits discrimination on the basis of any of several "enumerated grounds." But because the section is open-ended, the courts have held that it also prohibits discrimination on the basis of other grounds analogous to those enumerated. See *e.g. Andrews v. Law Society of British Columbia,* [1989] 1 S.C.R. 143; *Law v. Canada (Minister of Employment & Immigration),* [1999] 1 S.C.R. 497 [*Law*].

[100] See McNeil, *supra* note 12 at 231–40. For a full discussion of the diversity of views and arguments, see Kerry Wilkins, ". . . But We Need the Eggs: The Royal Commission, The Charter of Rights and the Inherent Right of Aboriginal Self-Government" (1999) 49 U.T.L.J. 53.

[101] Section 25 of the *Charter* reads:
> The guarantee in this Charter of certain rights and freedoms shall not be construed so as to abrogate or derogate from any aboriginal, treaty or other rights or freedoms that pertain to the aboriginal peoples of Canada including
> (a) any rights or freedoms that have been recognized by the Royal Proclamation of October 7, 1763; and
> (b) any rights or freedoms that now exist by way of land claims agreements or may be so acquired.

[102] *Corbiere, supra* note 11 at para. 10.

[103] *Supra* note 5.

[104] In argument in *Lavell* and *Bedard, ibid.*, the National Indian Brotherhood (now known as the Assembly of First Nations) observed that the *Indian Act* is the only source of some rights held by Indians and expressed the concern that striking down one section of it would make the entire Act vulnerable to attack. This current threat to the rights contained in the *Indian Act* is, in my view, no different.

[105] McLachlin and Bastarache JJ. also mention the impact of Bill C-31 (as *An Act to amend the Indian*

Act, R.S.C. 1985, c. 32 (1st Supp.) continues to be called), but decline comment on the obvious gender overlays. For example, they say that "[a]ll parties have accepted . . . persons who have been forced to leave the reserve reluctantly because of economic and social considerations . . ." (*Corbiere*, *supra* note 11 at para. 19), but decline to mention that some of these are women who have been forced to leave because of the violence. This oversight typifies the degree to which the analysis and inclusion of gender remains both secondary and incomplete in the court decision.

[106] *Corbiere, ibid.* at para. 86, L'Heureux-Dubé J. (for Gonthier, Iacobucci, & Binnie JJ.) concurring in the majority result.

[107] It is important to remember that the creation of reserves was a colonial act. Living on versus living off reserve is a distinction because the state continues to develop law and policy that emphasizes it. It is frequently used to limit the "rights" of Indians living off reserve. Living off reserve (often while remaining in one's own territory) is not a measure of loss of "authenticity" that arises from the false distinction between on and off reserve.

[108] In *Corbiere, supra* note 11 at para. 72, the Court assumes (in the third factor it addresses about off-reserve experience) that there is a connection between the percentage of people living off reserve and legislative exclusion (and thus, an impact on women). This is a fact that should have been more carefully and fully examined. People leave reserves for many reasons, including seeking greater access to economic resources (education and employment), fleeing violence, and disenfranchisement.

[109] *Ibid.* at para. 67, L'Heureux-Dubé J. (concurring in the majority result).

[110] Perhaps this is connected to my training in the law and to the fact that commitment to that training required a separation from my community.

[111] See Monture-Angus, *supra* note 17.

[112] *Corbiere, supra* note 11 at para. 59, citing *Law, supra* note 99 at para. 53, Iacobucci J.

ABORIGINAL JURISPRUDENCE AND RIGHTS

James (Sákéj) Youngblood Henderson

> Section 35(1), it is true, recognizes and affirms existing aboriginal rights, but it must not be forgotten that the rights it recognizes and affirms are aboriginal. . . . Aboriginal rights cannot, however, be defined on the basis of the philosophical precepts of the liberal enlightenment. Although equal in importance and significance to the rights enshrined in the Charter, aboriginal rights must be viewed differently from Charter rights because they are rights held only by aboriginal members of Canadian society. They arise from the fact that aboriginal people are aboriginal. . . . The task of this Court is to define aboriginal rights in a manner which recognizes that aboriginal rights are rights but which does so without losing sight of the fact that they are rights held by aboriginal people because they are aboriginal. The Court must neither lose sight of the generalized constitutional status of what s. 35(1) protects, nor can it ignore the necessary specificity which comes from granting special constitutional protection to one part of Canadian society. The Court must define the scope of s. 35(1) in a way which captures both the aboriginal and the rights in aboriginal rights.
>
> Lamer C.J.C.[1]

In *R. v. Van der Peet*, the Supreme Court of Canada explained why the diverse legal orders[2] of Aboriginal confederacies, nations, tribes, peoples, societies, cultures, communities, families, and bands received explicit recognition in s. 35(1) of the *Constitution Act, 1982*.[3] It was

> because of one simple fact: when Europeans arrived in North America, aboriginal peoples were already here, living in communities on the land, and participating in distinctive cultures, as they had done for centuries. It is this fact, and this fact above all others, which separates aboriginal peoples from all other minority groups in Canadian society and which mandates their special legal, and now constitutional, status.[4]

This premise triggered development of the jurisprudential framework[5] that has extended the constitution's protection to the rights that characterize Aboriginal peoples' cultures and societies.[6] It is more than mere historical description; it articulates a basic norm[7]—a rule of recognition for Aboriginal rights[8]—that, taken seriously, disrupts the ordinary context-preserving function of the Canadian judiciary. In so doing, it revises constitutional theory and the idea of "mainstream" judicial review. The Supreme Court's reaffirmation in

Delgamuukw of this framework and this premise continues an exceptional and extraordinary transformation in Canadian judicial consciousness. At its heart is a recognition that ordinary Canadian legal analysis and reasoning have not been appropriate to the task of understanding Aboriginal rights or their proper place in Confederation: that what is needed instead is a truly *sui generis* analysis[9] that honours their uniqueness and their anchorage in Aboriginal forms of order and jurisprudence. Aboriginal rights derive from pre-contact Aboriginal legal teachings that structure and inform the jurisprudence in the distinctive legal orders from which they emerge. It is from these same sources, which promote reliance on consensual agreements to bring about change,[10] that the rights in treaties with the British sovereign also derive their force.

Although the Court has not yet had the opportunity to articulate and organize, in a single judicial decision,[11] the principles that inform and orient this new approach, it is possible to begin to discern them from the constitutional cases to date in which it has had to consider questions of Aboriginal right. Its respect for the "simple fact" that distinctive Aboriginal cultures were here first, and that they persist,[12] has impelled the Court to take several steps to create and sustain sufficient "constitutional space for aboriginal peoples to be aboriginal."[13] Such steps include determination of the historic rights of Aboriginal peoples, giving Aboriginal rights constitutional force to protect them against legislative powers,[14] precluding mainstream governments from extinguishing Aboriginal peoples' rights,[15] sanctioning challenges to the social and economic policy objectives embodied in legislation when and as that legislation affects Aboriginal rights,[16] undertaking reconciliation between the sovereignty of the Crown and the rights and interests that emerge from these distinctive societies,[17] and providing a solid constitutional base for fair recognition of Aboriginal rights and for negotiation and settlement of Aboriginal claims.[18] These developments all reflect the constitutional interpretive principle that courts and governments must give Aboriginal rights a generous and liberal interpretation in favour of Aboriginal peoples.[19] This has been judicially interpreted to mean that any doubt or ambiguity as regards what falls within the scope and definition of Aboriginal rights is to be resolved in favour of the Aboriginal peoples.[20] The Court has linked these interpretive principles with the Crown's fiduciary obligation toward Aboriginal peoples.[21] It has held, as well, that the honour of the Crown is always involved in dealings between the government and Aboriginal peoples.[22]

This article will examine the Supreme Court's affirmation of the *sui generis* constitutional framework that situates Aboriginal rights and the innovations in constitutional theory that result from it. My approach is not concerned with reiteration of the Court's pronouncements as informed by the adjudicative traditions of legal positivism. Instead, it focuses on the unarticulated underlying principles of Aboriginal jurisprudence embedded in Aboriginal rights, and on how they operate to protect such rights and to generate *sui generis* constitutional theory.

IMPLICIT PRINCIPLES IN CONSTITUTIONAL ANALYSIS

Section 35(1) of the *Constitution Act, 1982* makes no explicit provision for Aboriginal jurisprudence, orders, or title; all it does is give recognition and affirmation to Aboriginal peoples' rights. These manifestations derive their constitutional importance from judicial interpretation, and in particular from the Supreme Court's adoption as its basic norm of the fact that Aboriginal peoples, even before Europeans arrived in North America, were living on the land in distinct societies and communities and were participating in distinctive cultures.[23] From this foundation arose the special constitutional framework that pertains to the Aboriginal peoples of Canada.[24] That framework prescribes their special legal, and now constitutional, status. *Delgamuukw*, for example, has explicated what it has meant to the Canadian constitutional order to give full effect to Aboriginal rights. It has demonstrated how the term "Aboriginal rights" implicitly constitutionalized Aboriginal title, a right to the land itself, in its full form.[25] It has recognized the significance to the law of Aboriginal title of the pre-existing systems of Aboriginal law and land tenure that belong to the various Aboriginal nations, societies, or orders.[26] And it has affirmed that Aboriginal peoples' laws, practices, and traditions must be given meaningful content beyond the existing common law definitions.[27] These fruits of judicial interpretation reinvigorate Aboriginal peoples' knowledge, heritage, and law.[28]

But this was not the only occasion in recent Canadian jurisprudence on which implicit constitutional principles figured importantly. In 1998, the *Quebec Secession Reference*[29] endorsed an analogous approach to the imperial Acts that delegate power and rights to non-Aboriginal peoples in the constitutional framework. Although the Court acknowledged the primacy of the text of the imperial instruments in determining constitutional questions, it emphasized that the text is not exhaustive.[30] Supplementing the text are certain unwritten, implicit principles derived from the internal architecture of the constitution itself.[31] These principles operate symbiotically with one another and with the text, yielding dynamic interpretive frameworks that link and generate the meaning of the constitution as a whole.[32] Together they are the measure used to evaluate the constitutionality of elected governments' exercise of executive and legislative powers. The Court's theory of constitutionalism[33] displaces much of the older colonial doctrine of parliamentary supremacy.[34] It affirms the idea that the constitutional order itself, which provides for shared jurisdictions, is the supreme law in Canada, rather than legislation or executive rule. The judiciary bears the critical interpretive task of supervising governments' compliance with the constitution.

In the following year, in *Marshall*,[35] the Supreme Court found still another context in which to identify and apply implicit, underlying legal principles. At issue there were the 1760–61 treaties made between the British sovereign and the Mi'kmaw leaders shortly after the British acquired jurisdiction in their war with the French.[36] These treaties reconciled the Mi'kmaw order with British sovereignty. In the English text of the treaty, the Mi'kmaq had promised not to

> traffick, barter or Exchange any Commodities in any manner but with such persons or the managers of such Truck houses as shall be appointed or Established by His Majesty's Governor.[37]

Having regard to the shared intentions and objectives of the treaty parties and the extrinsic evidence about the context in which the treaty emerged, the majority held that this provision implied a constitutional right

> to continue to provide for their own sustenance by taking the products of their hunting, fishing and other gathering activities, and trading for what in 1760 was termed "necessaries."[38]

Justice Binnie, who wrote for the majority, acknowledged that this right was not explicitly embodied in either the written memorandum of the treaty prepared by the British or the oral promises made during treaty negotiations.[39] It was instead implicit in the internal architecture of the entire treaty negotiations and in the principles underlying them. In the words of a Crown witness, Dr. Patterson,

> in recognizing the Micmac by treaty, the British were recognizing them as the people they were. They understood how they lived and that that meant that those people had a *right* to live in Nova Scotia in their traditional ways.[40]

The Court's invocation of implicit principles in the constitutional order takes it outside the familiar positivist understanding of constitutional interpretation and rules.[41] These decisions affirm that constitutionalism, not politics, now governs the constitutional order of Canada. Constitutionalism serves as a corrective to the prejudices and flaws that have infected colonial politics, and to the laws that tend to taint democratic politics. It is this paradigm with which governmental and administrative actions are now required to be consistent.

ABORIGINAL JURISPRUDENCES ESTABLISH ABORIGINAL RIGHTS

Aboriginal jurisprudences existed before the imperial Crown asserted and enforced its sovereignty: prior even to contact between Aboriginal and European societies. They are the source of Aboriginal rights.[42] This fact accounts for and reinforces their *sui generis* distinctiveness.[43] Aboriginal civilizations developed their laws without any knowledge of European jurisprudence.[44] Unlike the jurisprudence in the Euro-Christian tradition, *sui generis* Aboriginal jurisprudences retain their sacredness and their ecological integrity; they have not had to struggle with the Judeo-Christian separation of humans from God's Paradise or with the consequential task of generating artificial human cultures, laws, and governments distinct from nature.

This distinction between Eurocentric and Aboriginal jurisprudence is crucial. Aboriginal jurisprudences rely on performance and oral traditions rather than on political assemblies, written words, and documents. They stress the principle of totality and the importance of using a variety of means to disclose the teachings and to display the immanent legal order. They have always been consensual, interactive, and cumulative. They are intimately embedded in Aboriginal heritages, knowledges, and languages. They are intertwined and interpenetrated with worldviews, spirituality, ceremonies, and stories, and with the structure and style of Aboriginal music and art.[45] They reveal robust and diverse legal orders based on a performance culture, a shared kinship stressing human dignity, and an ecological integrity that demonstrates how Aboriginal peoples deliberately and communally resolved recurring problems.[46] *Sui generis* Aboriginal orders constitutionalize Aboriginal peoples' own understandings of their relationships to the land and to their surrounding ecosystems. They are, in every sense, part of the ancient law of the land. They do not require a sovereign, the will of a political state, or the affirmation of outsiders to be legitimate.

These legal systems have always operated of their own force on Aboriginal peoples. They are conceptually self-sustaining and dynamically self-generating. They symbolize a form of order that is simultaneously heard, seen, felt, and savoured through holistic ceremonies and performances. It can be described as analogous to the "synesthetic" tradition of early Greek and Hebrew societies.[47] Through dynamic synthesis, Aboriginal jurisprudences and laws exist not as things or nouns or rules, but rather as overlapping and interpenetrating processes or activities that represent teachings, customs, and agreements. Within them, many different perspectives—many complementary visions of good relationship—can coexist and nurture one another. Aboriginal peoples understand their jurisprudence as a liquid force that lives through conduct, rather than as something that has to be written or produced by specialized thought and reasoning. It is more a matter of dynamic processes than a matter of logic, causality, or structural theory. Aboriginal teachings have been described as

> a cumulative body of knowledge and beliefs, handed down through generations by cultural transmission, about the relationship of living beings (including humans) with one another and their environment.[48]

They form "a complete knowledge system with its own concepts of epistemology, philosophy, and scientific and logical validity"[49] that "can only be fully learned or understood by means of the pedagogy traditionally employed by these peoples themselves, including apprenticeship, ceremonies and practices."[50]

Aboriginal jurisprudences, therefore, reflect a characteristic vision of how to live well with the land and with other peoples.[51] They are integral to Aboriginal consciousness and its understanding of Aboriginal humanity, and to Aboriginal peoples' legal and political orders. They reveal who Aboriginal peoples are, what they believe, what their experiences have been, and how they act. They disclose Aboriginal humanity's belief in responsible freedoms and order. It is they, and the teachings on which they are based, that prescribe the constitutional content, both substantive and procedural, of Aboriginal and even treaty rights.

In this, they are not wholly different from Eurocentric constitutional traditions.[52] Consider law professor Robert Cover's description of the deep thematic structures of the latter:

> A legal tradition ... includes not only a *corpus juris*, but also a language and a mythos—narratives in which the *corpus juris* is located by those whose wills act upon it. These myths establish the paradigms for behavior. They build relations between the normative and the material universe, between the constraints of reality and the demands of an ethic. These myths establish a repertoire of moves—a lexicon of normative action—that may be combined into meaningful patterns culled from meaningful patterns of the past.[53]

There are, as well, instructive analogies between aspects of the British classical customary law tradition and some *sui generis* legal traditions constitutive of Aboriginal rights.[54] The rights and liberties featured and protected by the British constitutional tradition derive from the cultural identity of the British peoples, structured over time by a set of attitudes, customs, principles, and precedents, and by the liberty interests that those peoples have thought important.[55] That tradition has always spoken through the meticulous craft of the common lawyer, searching in the practices and customs of the society for the ordering principles implicit in British governance and collective identity.[56]

The Supreme Court has acknowledged that distinctive Aboriginal teachings and jurisprudences inhere in Aboriginal societies:[57] that Aboriginal peoples themselves have generated and organized the structures, the themes, and the media that underlie their rights.[58] It has recognized that their *sui generis* constitutional framework and the Aboriginal rights that flow from that framework take neither their origins nor their bearings from British, French, or Canadian sovereignty or jurisprudence.[59] It has declared that these rights are essentially different from, but equal in status to, the rights of the liberal enlightenment that are codified and construed in the *Charter*;[60] it has doubted that traditional notions from French or British law are adequate to express them;[61] and it has affirmed that these rights need not conform to the doctrinal categories, rules, rights, and distinctions familiar from French or British jurisprudence.[62]

The Supreme Court, in other words, has been decisive on what Aboriginal jurisprudences and rights are not, but rather uneducated, so far at least, about what they are. To its credit, the Court has recognized the importance of "sensitiv[ity] to the aboriginal perspective itself on the meaning of the rights at stake"[63] when considering Aboriginal rights under section 35(1) of the *Constitution Act, 1982*, the constitutional significance, at least in the abstract, of traditional Aboriginal laws, and the fact that Aboriginal perspectives can be "gleaned, in part, but not exclusively, from" these traditional laws.[64] And it has acknowledged, again at a fairly high level of generality, that Aboriginal jurisprudences derive, most typically in the form of oral histories and traditions, from the pre-existing legal teachings, heritages, and customs of the Aboriginal peoples.[65] To go any deeper, however, the Court must appreciate the critical importance of comparative, transnational jurisprudential analysis and Aboriginal languages. In the words of a recent Chief Judge of the Maori Land Court in New Zealand, "one culture cannot be judged by the norms of another and each must be seen in its own terms."[66]

Aboriginal jurisprudences are best studied in the context of Aboriginal languages. Aboriginal vocabularies, stories, methods of communication, and styles of performance and discourse all encode values and frame understanding. Aboriginal-speaking Elders and designated persons are primary sources for and authorities on *sui generis* Aboriginal jurisprudences.[67] The integrated methods of knowing cover all aspects of stored heritage as revealed through Aboriginal languages, memories, stories, and ceremonies, and as learned and expressed through Aboriginal peoples' oral and symbolic traditions and teachings.

If there is to be meaningful progress toward a comparative jurisprudence, non-Aboriginal scholars and judges will have to learn Aboriginal languages and jurisprudences. Conscientious non-Aboriginal scholars have always been welcome to study Aboriginal heritage and jurisprudence, but so far have chosen, for the most part, to conduct their examinations from the external perspective, speaking abstractly about a *sui generis* legal realm, about an ideational order of reality,[68] about a distinctive cognitive orientation, or about ethno-metaphysical and primitive laws.[69] But only those who have been taught within the system itself and in its language can really comprehend it.

THE PROTECTION OF ABORIGINAL RIGHTS

Recent Supreme Court decisions confirm that the Canadian constitutional framework protects pre-existing Aboriginal nationhood. In *Van der Peet*, the Court looked to the United States Supreme Court's decision in *Worcester v. Georgia* for help in identifying the underlying interests that s. 35(1) of the *Constitution Act, 1982* was intended to protect:

> America, separated from Europe by a wide ocean, was inhabited by a distinct people, divided into separate nations, independent of each other and of the rest of the world, having institutions of their own, and governing themselves by their own laws. . . . The Indian nations had always been considered as distinct, independent political communities, retaining their original natural rights, as the undisputed possessors of the soil, from time immemorial, with the single exception of that imposed by irresistible power, which excluded them from intercourse with any other European potentate than the first discoverer of the coast of the particular region claimed.[70]

According to Justice L'Heureux-Dubé, dissenting in *Van der Peet* on other grounds:

> it is fair to say that prior to the first contact with the Europeans, the native people of North America were independent nations, occupying and controlling their own territories, with a distinctive culture and their own practices, traditions and customs.[71]

In *Delgamuukw*, the Court affirmed that assertion of British sovereignty over Aboriginal lands did not displace the pre-existing Aboriginal orders,[72] but protected them:[73] that neither the imperial nor the common law replaced Aboriginal jurisprudences.[74] If Aboriginal nations or people were "present in some form" on the land when the Crown asserted sovereignty,[75] their pre-existing regime in respect of that land "crystallized" in British law as *sui generis* Aboriginal title and rights.[76] Together, the Aboriginal jurisprudence and the imperial law governed and limited the reception and introduction in the North American colonies of British statutory and common law,[77] even after the establishment, by prerogative authority, of the local colonial assemblies.[78] The principles and instruments of "imperial constitutional law" protected the forms of authority inherent in the pre-existing Aboriginal order and jurisprudence.[79] In the words of Justice McLachlin, who had also dissented in *Van der Peet*, "the recognition by the common law of the ancestral laws and customs of the aboriginal peoples who occupied the land prior to European settlement" was the "golden thread" of British legal history in the foreign colonies.[80] She identified two fundamental principles in the common law protecting Aboriginal rights:

> The first was the general principle that the Crown took subject to existing aboriginal interests in the lands they traditionally occupied and their adjacent waters, even though those interests might not be of a type recognized by British law. The second, which may be viewed as an application of the first, is that the interests which aboriginal peoples had in using the land and adjacent waters for their sustenance were to be removed only by solemn treaty with due compensation to the people and its descendants. This right to use the land and adjacent waters as the people had traditionally done for its sustenance may be seen as a fundamental aboriginal

right. It is supported by the common law and by the history of this country. It may safely be said to be enshrined in s. 35(1) of the *Constitution Act, 1982*.[81]

Subsequent treaties between the British sovereign and Aboriginal nations affirmed the Aboriginal orders, reconciled them consensually with the Crown's authority, and provided for the sharing between the parties of certain responsibilities.[82]

The protective doctrine of Aboriginal rights in the common law is distinct from the Aboriginal rights themselves. In *Côté*, the Court confirmed that although the doctrine of Aboriginal rights

> was a species of unwritten British law, it was not part of English common law in the narrow sense, and its application to a colony did not depend on whether or not English common law was introduced there.[83]

The Court acknowledged that the common law has protected the Aboriginal rights from the colonists and colonial law, but it emphasized that, in the present day, s. 35(1) of the *Constitution Act, 1982* constitutionalizes existing Aboriginal rights, not the imported common law doctrine protecting them.[84] The judiciary must understand this fundamental distinction[85] and accept the challenge of comprehending these *sui generis* inherent rights in terms of the Aboriginal jurisprudences in which they have their sources.[86]

Uniquely among those resident in Canada, therefore, Aboriginal peoples do not have to demonstrate their Aboriginal or treaty rights by reference to delegated powers or grants from the British sovereign or from Parliament; their constitutional rights are inherent in their own worldviews and legal arrangements. They are not fragmented lists of powers or permissions delegated from a sovereign; as explained above, they are, and have always been, comprehensive, holistic orders that developed independently of British legal traditions and that came to be extended consensually through treaties with other legal orders.[87]

These Aboriginal orders and treaties had the force of imperial law within the North American colonies. The remarkable thing is that, despite this, the British imperial order thereafter all but forgot about reconciling them until 1982.[88] The imperial statutes that established delegated self-rule and responsible government for the colonies never sought to reconcile these new powers with the pre-existing Aboriginal orders or with the empire's treaty obligations to Aboriginal peoples. The governmental structures these statutes created with care for the colonists embodied the key principles of provincial federalism[89] but were silent about the Aboriginal orders and treaty federalism.[90] They exemplified implicitly the principles of constitutionalism, the rule of law, and respect for minorities, but never applied those principles to Aboriginal peoples or their rights. They established for the immigrant population a democracy[91] that excluded the Aboriginal peoples.[92]

CONCLUSION

The constitutional reforms of 1982 provide a restorative vantage point from which to address Aboriginal peoples' sense of being surrounded by injustice on account of the indignities, humiliations, and dominations wrought by the colonial order. The constitutional affirmation of treaty and Aboriginal rights was designed to prevent the federal and provincial orders of government, as well as the judiciary, from flouting or overlooking Aboriginal rights or their underlying principles, with a view to securing equality and dignity in Canada for Aboriginal peoples and their rights. The ultimate purpose of these reforms was to create constitutional conditions—a legal and epistemic pluralism[93] protected by the constitutional order from pragmatic, majoritarian politics—within which Aboriginal peoples and Canadians could rediscover good relations and live together on the shared land more compatibly. These reforms were implemented not to make governmental action or judicial analysis easier, but rather to make them more just.

Because of these reforms, and because of the theories that underlie them, the judiciary now has the tools to protect the Aboriginal legal orders and to implement the Aboriginal jurisprudences within the Canadian constitutional structure. The Royal Commission on Aboriginal Peoples, after listening to Aboriginal peoples and leading academics, has done an inspiring job of elucidating some of the changes necessary to realize such pluralism.[94]

The reality, however, has sometimes failed to fulfil the promise of the reforms. In *Van der Peet*, for example, the majority decision focused its test for identifying Aboriginal rights on the facts about, and the status of, particular activities involving Aboriginal peoples in abstraction from the Aboriginal jurisprudences that have regulated them throughout time and from which they derive their constitutional significance. This approach disregards and eviscerates Aboriginal jurisprudences; in doing so, it violates the inherent spirit of the teachings, laws, and societies to which they belong.

In *Côté*, the Supreme Court held that each substantive Aboriginal right will normally include the incidental right to teach the relevant Aboriginal custom or tradition, in order to ensure the survival and continuity of that tradition or custom.[95] To date, however, the Court has not comprehended or internalized the significance of this conclusion. It has not allowed this incidental right to teach Aboriginal jurisprudences to inform its own approach to Aboriginal rights analysis.[96] Its attempts to identify and determine Aboriginal rights have ignored Aboriginal jurisprudences—their teachings, their performances, and their manifestations—in favour of an external Anglo-Canadian legal analysis focused on certain exercises and activities. In part, no doubt, this is because neither courts nor lawyers have properly introduced the Aboriginal teachings into litigation concerning Aboriginal rights. They have not yet acknowledged Aboriginal Elders and law-keepers as expert witnesses on Aboriginal law and jurisprudence and have not asked them properly to share their teachings with the courts.

Accurate identification and elaboration of the rights constituted within this *sui generis* system cannot take place without appropriate introduction to the media and orientation of Aboriginal jurisprudences. The Canadian judiciary has a constitutional responsibility to respect Aboriginal jurisprudences, not to show—or to tolerate—disrespect or indignities toward them.[97]

Aboriginal Elders and knowledge-keepers have corresponding constitutional responsibilities to teach Aboriginal jurisprudences, through dialogue with the legislatures, with the bureaucracy, with the judiciary, and with Canadians generally. They have to assist the courts and governments to displace the colonial order and the systemic discrimination that has suffused its institutions, laws, and policies and that so often is taken as natural, neutral, and justified. Each of these manifestations of egregious colonialism has serious negative consequences for Aboriginal peoples and their constitutional rights.

The Canadian judiciary must break free of the constructed Eurocentric image of Aboriginal societies to learn Aboriginal jurisprudences and how they inform Aboriginal rights. Aboriginal jurisprudences are integral to each aspect of authentic legal analysis of Aboriginal rights. To take full account of them, the judiciary needs the consensual authority of the Aboriginal peoples and the benefit of the teachings of their Elders and law-keepers. With such authority and such teachings, courts will be in a position properly to identify, define, interpret, and give meaningful context to Aboriginal rights, to reconcile such rights with the Canadian legal order in a fair and just way that shows them proper respect, and to tell when external limitations on such rights can legitimately be justified.

Both Canadians and Aboriginal peoples have the educational capacity to broaden and strengthen support for the constitutional order and treaty federalism. Instead of widening and deepening the divide in Canada between the order of prosperity and the order of survival, and instead of playing off the constitutional order against Aboriginal rights, Canadians need to work more effectively together for the benefits that such socially urgent—and constitutionally mandated—collaboration will bring to all. Otherwise, the constitutional practice will not become an avenue that opens to a postcolonial order, but will remain in large part a symbol of bad faith, sharp practice, and marginalization of Aboriginal teachings and jurisprudence. That result would reflect ongoing dishonour on the Crown and on Canada.

NOTES

[1] *R. v. Van der Peet*, [1996] 2 S.C.R. 507 at paras. 17–20 [*Van der Peet*], relying on Michael Asch & Patrick Macklem, "Aboriginal Rights and Canadian Sovereignty: An Essay on *R. v. Sparrow*" (1991)

29 Alta. L. Rev. 498 at 502 [Asch & Macklem, "Aboriginal Rights and Canadian Sovereignty"] and Brian Slattery, "Understanding Aboriginal Rights" (1987) 66 Can. Bar Rev. 727 at 776 [Slattery, "Understanding Aboriginal Rights"].

[2] My use of the concept of Aboriginal orders is derived from Algonquian languages. It is meant to be a neutral term with which to discuss the *sui generis* structure of the kinship relationships embedded in the ecological law of creation. That law is comprehended and developed by Aboriginal teachings, ceremonies, and fundamental values, which, in turn, are represented by activities and beliefs. These relationships have generated consensual alliances and confederations among the families, clans, or bands, in which no family occupies a permanently dominant position or is credited with an inherent right to govern. These teachings lay down fundamental jurisdiction, principles, and ceremonies for the conduct of affairs. The concept of Aboriginal legal orders is used to avoid being excessively general (confederations) or narrow (bands). The Supreme Court has held in *R. v. Pamajewon*, [1996] 2 S.C.R. 821 [*Pamajewon*], that the Aboriginal right to self-government, if it exists as a constitutional right, cannot be framed in excessively general terms; in *Mitchell v. M.N.R.*, [2001] 1 S.C.R. 911 [*Mitchell*], on the other hand, it held at paras. 20–21 that Aboriginal rights cannot be framed too narrowly.

[3] Section 35(1) is found in Part II of the *Constitution Act, 1982*, being Schedule B to the *Canada Act 1982* (U.K.), c. 11 [*Constitution Act, 1982*], entitled "Rights of the Aboriginal Peoples of Canada." It provides that "[t]he existing aboriginal and treaty rights of the aboriginal peoples of Canada are hereby recognized and affirmed." The proclamation of the *Constitution Act, 1982* removed the last vestige of British authority over the Canadian constitution.

[4] *Van der Peet*, *supra* note 1 at para. 30. See also *ibid.* at para. 20; *R. v. Sundown*, [1999] 1 S.C.R. 393 at para. 35.

[5] *Delgamuukw v. British Columbia*, [1997] 3 S.C.R. 1010 at para. 2 [*Delgamuukw*] (explaining the jurisprudential framework for s. 35(1)). The Court recognized the jurisprudential framework for analyzing Aboriginal rights embedded in s. 35(1) in *R. v. Sparrow*, [1990] 1 S.C.R. 1075 [*Sparrow*] (affirming an Aboriginal right to fish "for food and social and ceremonial purposes") and developed and elaborated it in a series of subsequent decisions: *Van der Peet*, *supra* note 1; *R. v. N.T.C. Smokehouse Ltd.*, [1996] 2 S.C.R. 672; *R. v. Nikal*, [1996] 1 S.C.R. 1013; *R. v. Gladstone*, [1996] 2 S.C.R. 723 [*Gladstone*]; *Pamajewon*, *supra* note 2; *R. v. Adams*, [1996] 3 S.C.R. 101 [*Adams*]; *R. v. Côté*, [1996] 3 S.C.R. 139 [*Côté*]; and *Mitchell*, *supra* note 2.

[6] To describe and evaluate the Aboriginal peoples' orders, the Court has used the concepts "social organization," "political structures," "societies," and "culture": D*elgamuukw*, *ibid.* at para. 42 (Aboriginal title arises out of the prior social organization and distinctive cultures of Aboriginal peoples on that land); *Van der Peet*, *ibid.* at para. 74 ("[Aboriginal rights] arise from the prior social organization and distinctive cultures of aboriginal peoples on [a] land"); *Côté*, *ibid.* at para. 41 ("distinctive culture" of the Algonquin people); *Mitchell*, *ibid.* at para. 9 ("organized, distinctive societies with their own social and political structures").

[7] Hans Kelsen, *Pure Theory of Law*, trans. by Max Knight (Berkeley: University of California Press, 1967). Such fundamental norm, called the "grundnorm" or basic norm, of any legal system generates many affirmations of the norm, some express and some implied.

[8] H.L.A. Hart, *The Concept of Law*, 2d ed. by Penelope A. Bulloch & Joseph Raz (Oxford: Clarendon Press, 1994). The rule of recognition expresses that there are conventional criteria, agreed upon by officials, for determining which rules are and which are not part of a given legal system.

[9] *Sui generis* is a concept developed by judicial interpretation; it is not in the text of s. 35, *supra* note 3. *Sui generis* is derived from the Latin language: *su* (of its own) connects with *generis*, genitive of *genus* (kind), meaning self-generating: being the only example of its kind. It is translated in English as constituting a class of its own: whatever is absolutely unique or distinctive about something. The expression was created by European scholastic philosophy to indicate an idea, an entity, or a reality that cannot be included in a wider concept, and that is structurally outside legally defined categories: a species that heads its own genus. In other words, a distinct legal knowledge. The legal concept of *sui generis* first appeared in *Guerin v. The Queen*, [1984] 2 S.C.R. 335 at 382, 387 [*Guerin*] (Indians' interest in the land is *sui generis*). *Sparrow*, *supra* note 5 at 1108, built on *Guerin*'s concept of *sui*

generis, adding (*ibid.* at 1112) that Aboriginal rights must be defined with reference to the Aboriginal perspective on their meaning and that courts must be careful to avoid applying traditional common law property concepts as they develop their understanding of these *sui generis* rights. In *Van der Peet*, *supra* note 1, the majority, in its analysis of the nature of Aboriginal rights, did not call such rights *sui generis*; it did, however, use the related concept of "distinct," stating (at para. 71) that a tradition or custom that is distinct is one that is unique—"different in kind or quality; unlike." It said that a culture with a distinct tradition must claim that in having such a tradition it is different from other cultures; a claim of distinctness is, by its very nature, a claim relative to other cultures or traditions. It does not explain how different comparative jurisprudences can be reconciled in a manner that does not undermine Aboriginal jurisprudences. Elsewhere, the Court has held *sui generis* rights to be distinct from those in other legal orders: see *e.g. R. v. Simon*, [1985] 2 S.C.R. 387 at 404 [*Simon*] (Indian treaties *sui generis* from international law); *R. v. Sioui*, [1990] 1 S.C.R. 1025 at 1056 [*Sioui*] (Aboriginal treaties *sui generis* from British colonial law); *Sparrow*, *supra* note 5 at 1108, 1111–12 (Aboriginal rights *sui generis* from British common law); *Delgamuukw*, *supra* note 5 at paras. 112–14 (Aboriginal title *sui generis* in being different from "normal" proprietary interests, in being irreducible to either common law or Aboriginal rules of property, and in arising from possession before the assertion of British sovereignty).

[10] *R. v. Badger*, [1996] 1 S.C.R. 771 at para. 76 [*Badger*]; *Mitchell*, *supra* note 2 at paras. 138–39.

[11] In *Delgamuukw*, *supra* note 5, the Court noted (at para. 140) that this has been a function of the types of s. 35 cases that have come before it: prosecutions for regulatory offences that necessarily proscribe discrete types of activity.

[12] The facts that make Aboriginal cultures distinctive operate in an analogous way to the facts that generate sovereignty in British law: see *Reference Re Secession of Quebec*, [1998] 2 S.C.R. 217 at para. 142 [*Quebec Secession Reference*] ("No one doubts that legal consequences may flow from political facts, and that 'sovereignty is a political fact for which no purely legal authority can be constituted . . .'," H.W.R. Wade, "The Basis of Legal Sovereignty" (1955) Cambridge L.J. 172 at 196 [Wade, "The Basis of Legal Sovereignty"]).

[13] Donna Greschner, "Aboriginal Women, The Constitution and Criminal Justice" (1992) 26 U.B.C. L. Rev. (sp. ed.) 338 at 342, cited in *Mitchell*, *supra* note 2 at para. 134, Binnie J., concurring.

[14] *Sparrow*, *supra* note 5 at 1110:
> The constitutional recognition afforded by [s. 35(1)] therefore gives a measure of control over government conduct and a strong check on legislative power. While it does not promise immunity from government regulation in a society that, in the twentieth century, is increasingly more complex, interdependent and sophisticated, and where exhaustible resources need protection and management, it does hold the Crown to a substantive promise. The government is required to bear the burden of justifying any legislation that has some negative effect on any aboriginal right protected under s. 35(1).

See also *Delgamuukw*, *supra* note 5 at para. 126; *Côté*, *supra* note 5 at para. 74 ("The text and purpose of s. 35(1) do not distinguish between federal and provincial laws which restrict aboriginal or treaty rights, and they should both be subject to the same standard of constitutional scrutiny").

[15] In *Delgamuukw*, *ibid.*, the Court concluded at paras. 180–81 that provincial laws of general application have not since Confederation had the constitutional competence to extinguish Aboriginal rights. Compare *Van der Peet*, *supra* note 1 at paras. 133, L'Heureux-Dubé J., dissenting, and 232, McLachlin J. (as she then was), dissenting.

[16] See *Sparrow*, *supra* note 5 at 1110, rejecting the Crown's argument that s. 35 was merely precatory, not entitled to constitutional protection:
> By giving aboriginal rights constitutional status and priority, Parliament and the provinces have sanctioned challenges to social and economic policy objectives embodied in legislation to the extent that aboriginal rights are affected. Implicit in this constitutional scheme is the obligation of the legislature to satisfy the test of justification.

Compare *ibid.* at 1085.

[17] In *Delgamuukw*, *supra* note 5, the Court stated at para. 186 that "[u]ltimately, it is through negotiated settlements, with good faith and give and take on all sides, reinforced by the judgments

of this Court, that we will achieve what I stated in *Van der Peet*, [*supra* note 1] at para. 31, to be a basic purpose of s.35(1)—'the reconciliation of the pre-existence of aboriginal societies with the sovereignty of the Crown'. Let us face it, we are all here to stay." See also *Van der Peet, ibid.* at para. 43 (Aboriginal rights are "the means by which that prior occupation is reconciled with the assertion of Crown sovereignty over Canadian territory"), 44, 57; *Gladstone, supra* note 5 at para. 72 ("the recognition of the prior occupation of North America by aboriginal peoples or . . . the reconciliation of aboriginal prior occupation with the assertion of the sovereignty of the Crown"). The reconciliation is the convergence of two fundamental facts derived from two distinct lands, two distinct systems of law and two distinct forms of society.

[18] *Sparrow, supra* note 5 at 1105 ("Section 35(1) . . ., at the least, provides a solid constitutional base upon which subsequent negotiations can take place"); *Delgamuukw, ibid.* at para. 186 ("Those negotiations should also include other aboriginal nations which have a stake in the territory claimed. Moreover, the Crown is under a moral, if not a legal, duty to enter into and conduct those negotiations in good faith"). Compare *Van der Peet, ibid.* at para. 230, McLachlin J. (as she then was), dissenting (s. 35(1) "seeks not only to reconcile these claims with European settlement and sovereignty but also to reconcile them in a way that provides the basis for a just and lasting settlement of aboriginal claims consistent with the high standard which the law imposes on the Crown in its dealings with aboriginal peoples").

[19] *Van der Peet, ibid.* at para. 23: "In *Sparrow* [*supra* note 5], this Court held at p. 1106 that s. 35(1) should be given a generous and liberal interpretation in favour of aboriginal peoples: 'When the purposes of the affirmation of aboriginal rights are considered, *it is clear that a generous, liberal interpretation of the words in the constitutional provision is demanded*" [emphasis added in *Van der Peet*].

[20] *Van der Peet, ibid.* at para. 25 ("The fiduciary relationship of the Crown and aboriginal peoples also means that where there is any doubt or ambiguity with regards to what falls within the scope and definition of s. 35(1), such doubt or ambiguity must be resolved in favour of aboriginal peoples. . . . This interpretive principle applies equally to s. 35(1) of the *Constitution Act, 1982* and should, again, inform the Court's purposive analysis of that provision").

[21] *Van der Peet, ibid.* at para. 25.

[22] *Sparrow, supra* note 5 at 1107–8, 1114.

[23] The Court's use of the term "distinctive" and "distinct" has generated much confusion. Initially, in *Calder v. British Columbia (A.G.)*, [1973] S.C.R. 313 [*Calder*], the Court did not qualify the term "society": see *e.g. ibid.* at 328, Judson J.: "the fact is that when the settlers came, the Indians were there, organized in societies and occupying the land as their forefathers had done for centuries." Later, in *Sparrow, ibid.* at 1099, the Court used "distinctive culture" to mean a characteristic culture to be observed on its own, not to mean a "distinct" culture, one different in kind from others and requiring comparison and evaluation from a separate vantage point. This approach attempts to use the phrase "distinctive" culture or societies to characterize the pre-contact Aboriginal jurisprudences and orders. Sometimes, however, the Court has used "distinctive" when it seemed instead to mean "distinct": unique, different in kind or quality, or unlike. "Distinct" is another way of characterizing these societies as *sui generis*: see *Van der Peet, supra* note 1 at para. 71. (On *sui generis*, see *supra* note 9.) Elsewhere, the majority in *Van der Peet, ibid.* held that the "integral to distinctive culture" test did not require rights-bearing Aboriginal cultures to be distinct: compare *ibid.*, paras. 55–59, 71–72. The dissenting judges in *Van der Peet* criticized the majority on this point: see *ibid.* at paras. 151–54, 162, L'Heureux-Dubé J., at paras. 254, 256–59, McLachlin J. (as she then was). See also Andrea Bowker's analysis of "distinctive" and "distinct" in "*Sparrow*'s Promise: Aboriginal Rights in the B.C. Court of Appeal" (1995) 53 U.T. Fac. L. Rev. 1 at 28–29 [Bowker, "Sparrow's Promise"].

[24] *Van der Peet, supra* note 1, identified the appropriate principles for defining, refining, and clarifying Aboriginal rights. See *ibid.* at paras. 30–31 ("what s. 35(1) does is provide the constitutional framework through which the fact that aboriginals lived on the land in distinctive societies, with their own practices, traditions and cultures, is acknowledged and reconciled with the sovereignty of the Crown. The substantive rights which fall within the provision must be defined in light of this purpose; the

aboriginal rights recognized and affirmed by s. 35(1) must be directed towards the reconciliation of the pre-existence of aboriginal societies with the sovereignty of the Crown"), 20 ("The Court must n[ot] lose sight of the generalized constitutional status of what s. 35(1) protects").

[25] In *Delgamuukw, supra* note 5, the Court held that the specific content of Aboriginal title, which has not been definitively addressed, either at common law or under s. 35(1), is a *sui generis* interest in land based on Aboriginal law and occupation: see paras. 111 ("Aboriginal title is a right in land and, as such, is more than the right to engage in specific activities which may be themselves aboriginal rights"), 133 ("Aboriginal title at common law is protected in its full form by s. 35(1)"). Compare *Adams, supra* note 5 at para. 30 (Aboriginal title simply one manifestation of the doctrine of Aboriginal rights). L'Heureux-Dubé J., in her concurring opinion in *Adams, supra* note 5 at para. 62, and her dissenting opinion in *Van der Peet, supra* note 1 at para. 119, affirmed that Aboriginal rights can be incidental to Aboriginal title but need not be: they are severable from and can exist independently of Aboriginal title.

[26] *Van der Peet, supra* note 1 at para. 28, had previously explained that "s. 35(1) did not create the legal doctrine of aboriginal rights; aboriginal rights existed and were recognized under the common law." Through the enactment of s. 35(1), "a pre-existing legal doctrine was elevated to constitutional status"; in other words, s. 35(1) had achieved "the constitutionalization of those rights" (*ibid.* at para. 29).

[27] *Delgamuukw, supra* note 5 at para. 136 ("I hasten to add that the constitutionalization of common law aboriginal rights by s. 35(1) does not mean that those rights exhaust the content of s. 35(1)").

[28] The Court has recognized that Aboriginal peoples are the constitutional bearers of ancient dignitary rights that are linked to Aboriginal jurisprudences, order, peace, security, and authority. Neither the federal nor provincial governments may disregard any longer the heritage or the rights of Aboriginal peoples. The dignity of Aboriginal peoples, in Cree called *kisteyittakusiwin* or *nikaneyittakusiw*, need not be justified in reference to Eurocentric legal categories; it is something inherent in personhood and human development.

[29] *Quebec Secession Reference, supra* note 12.

[30] *Ibid.* at paras. 32 ("In order to endure over time, a constitution must contain a comprehensive set of rules and principles which are capable of providing an exhaustive legal framework for our system of government. Such principles and rules emerge from an understanding of the constitutional text itself, the historical context, and previous judicial interpretations of constitutional meaning"), 53 ("the recognition of these constitutional principles . . . could not be taken as an invitation to dispense with the written text of the Constitution").

[31] *Ibid.* at para. 49 ("These [underlying] principles inform and sustain the constitutional text: they are the vital unstated assumptions upon which the text is based"); see generally *ibid.* at paras. 49–54. *Campbell v. British Columbia (A.G.)* (2000), 189 D.L.R. (4th) 333, 2000 BCSC 1123 [*Campbell*], noted (at para. 65) that the preamble to the *Constitution Act, 1867* (U.K.), 30 & 31 Vict., c. 3, reprinted in R.S.C. 1985, App. II, No. 5, "endowed Canada 'with a Constitution similar in Principle to that of the United Kingdom.' In considering this Preamble," the court added, "the Supreme Court of Canada has recognized that there are a number of constitutional principles and powers not set out in writing in the *Constitution Act, 1867* which nevertheless are fundamental to the Constitution." It held that "British imperial policy, reflected in the instructions given to colonial authorities in North America prior to Confederation, recognized a continued form, albeit diminished, of aboriginal self-government after the assertion of sovereignty by the Crown. This imperial policy, through the preamble to the *Constitution Act, 1867*, assists in filling out 'gaps in the express terms of the constitutional scheme'": *ibid.* at para. 68.

[32] *Quebec Secession Reference, ibid.* at para. 49 ("These defining [underlying] principles function in symbiosis. No single principle can be defined in isolation from the others, nor does any one principle trump or exclude the operation of any other").

[33] *Ibid.* at para. 72 ("The essence of constitutionalism in Canada is embodied in s. 52(1) of the *Constitution Act, 1982*, which provides that '[t]he Constitution of Canada is the supreme law of Canada, and any law that is inconsistent with the provisions of the Constitution is, to the extent of the inconsistency, of no force or effect.' Simply put, the constitutionalism principle requires that all

government action comply with the Constitution. The rule of law principle requires that all government action must comply with the law, including the Constitution").

[34] *Ibid.* The doctrine of parliamentary supremacy is an underlying political doctrine. Its legal force in Canada derives from the preamble to the *Constitution Act, 1867, supra* note 31, which states that the Constitution of Canada is "a Constitution similar in Principle to that of the United Kingdom": see *New Brunswick Broadcasting v. Nova Scotia (Speaker of the House of Assembly)*, [1993] 1 S.C.R. 319 at 375–78. In the national politics of the United Kingdom, parliamentary supremacy is the seventeenth- and eighteenth-century principle that the Parliament of the United Kingdom was supreme over all other governmental institutions, including the monarch and the courts. It prevented judicial review of representative legislation. Professor Hogg has stated that federalism is inconsistent with the idea that "omnicompetent" parliamentary sovereignty prevents judicial review of the wisdom or policy of legislation: see Peter W. Hogg, *Constitutional Law of Canada*, 3d ed. (Scarborough, Ont.: Carswell, 1992) at 301–7 [Hogg, *Constitutional Law*]; Jeffrey Denys Goldsworthy, *The Sovereignty of Parliament: History and Philosophy* (Oxford: Clarendon Press, 1999) at 2–3. L. Crispin Warmington, ed., *Stephen's Commentaries on the Laws of England*, 21st ed. (London: Butterworths, 1950) vol. 3 at 288, states, "no direct authority in the shape of decided cases can be adduced in support of the legislative omnipotence of Parliament." In *Constitutional Fundamentals* (London: Stevens, 1980) at 68, William Wade wrote that British lawyers have been brainwashed "in their professional infancy by the dogma of legislative sovereignty." Earlier, Wade had stated: "The rule of judicial obedience [to parliamentary sovereignty] is in one sense a rule of common law, but in another sense—which applies to no other rule of common law—it is the ultimate *political* fact upon which the whole system of legislation hangs": Wade, "The Basis of Legal Sovereignty, *supra* note 12 at 188 [emphasis in original]. In the past, this idea of parliamentary supremacy allowed Canadian courts to uphold federal legislation imposing unilateral restrictions on Aboriginal and treaty rights. The theory of parliamentary supremacy underwent some recent erosion in the United Kingdom itself when that country joined the European Union and submitted to the jurisdiction of the European Court on Human Rights.

[35] *R. v. Marshall*, [1999] 3 S.C.R. 456 at para. 4 [*Marshall*].

[36] *Ibid.* at para. 3.

[37] *Ibid.* at paras. 5–6. Although this "trade clause" is framed as a restraint on the ability of the Mi'kmaq to trade with non-government individuals, the Court found that it reflected a grant to them of the positive right to bring the products of their hunting, fishing, and gathering to a truckhouse to trade.

[38] *Ibid.* at para. 4. In modern terms, Binnie J. found, "necessaries" amounts to a "moderate livelihood" that "includes such basics as 'food, clothing and housing, supplemented by a few amenities', but not the accumulation of wealth" (*ibid.* at para. 59). Compare *R. v. Van der Peet*, [1993] 5 W.W.R. 459 (B.C.C.A.) at paras. 146 and 191 [*Van der Peet* (C.A.)] (aff'd by *Van der Peet, supra* note 1), where Lambert J.A., dissenting, suggests the notion of "moderate livelihood" in the context of a commercial Aboriginal right.

[39] *Marshall, ibid.* at paras. 7, 35.

[40] *Ibid.* at para. 37 [emphasis in original; underscoring in original deleted]; see also *ibid.* at para. 22 (British encouragement of the Mi'kmaq "hunting, fishing and gathering lifestyle"). The defence experts, Drs. John Reid and William Wicken, generally agreed with Dr. Patterson's evidence regarding the assumptions underlying and "implicit" in the treaty: *ibid.* at para. 39.

[41] As explained by Sujit Choudhry & Robert Howse, "Constitutional Theory and The *Quebec Secession Reference*" (2000) 13 Can. J.L. & Jur. 143 at 151–54.

[42] Jurisprudence was understood originally to be a monopoly of the college of the Pontiffs (*Pontifex*), which, comprising the only experts (*periti*) in the *jus* of traditional law (*mores maiorum*, a body of oral laws and customs transmitted "by father to son"), retained an exclusive power of judgment on facts. Pontiffs indirectly created a body of laws by their pronouncements (*sententiae*) on single concrete (*judicial*) cases. In an analogous way, the Aboriginal teachings, traditions, customs, oral history, practices, and perspectives establish *sui generis* Aboriginal law and orders available to be known, studied, and applied. Aboriginal knowledge is concerned with the study of Aboriginal teachings; its principles are best translated in English as "Aboriginal jurisprudences." It is based on ecological

understanding and linguistic conventions, unlike Eurocentric law, which is created by the artificial man-state and derived from theology or morals. The Cree say that jurisprudence sets relationships into order (*kwayaskotchikatew* or *nahawastâsuw*).

[43] *Delgamuukw, supra* note 5 at para. 82 ("although the doctrine of aboriginal rights is a common law doctrine, aboriginal rights are truly *sui generis*"); *Van der Peet, supra* note 1 at paras. 17, 20 (s. 35(1) recognizes and affirms rights that are Aboriginal, because they are Aboriginal).

[44] *Van der Peet, ibid.* See also *Campbell, supra* note 31 at para. 106.

[45] See the elegant works of John Borrows: *Recovering Canada. The Resurgence of Indigenous Law* (Toronto: University of Toronto Press, 2002); "Constitutional Law from a First Nation Perspective: Self-Government and the Royal Proclamation" (1994) 28 U.B.C. L. Rev. 1; "With or Without You: First Nations Law (in Canada)" (1996) 41 McGill L.J. 629 [Borrows, "With or Without You"]; "Frozen Rights in Canada: Constitutional Interpretation and the Trickster" (1997) 22 Am. Indian L. Rev. 37. See also J. Dumont, "Justice and Aboriginal Peoples" (1990) [unpublished paper, Manitoba: Public Inquiry Into the Administration of Justice and Aboriginal Peoples] (on Anishinabe Jurisprudence); Justice S. Clark, "Aboriginal Customary Law: Literature Review" (1990) [unpublished paper, Manitoba: Public Inquiry Into the Administration of Justice and Aboriginal Peoples].

[46] In Aboriginal knowledge, Aboriginal jurisprudence creates and structures the sovereignty and dignity of the Aboriginal peoples. Aboriginal societies are not formal associations of people with similar interests or concepts of Eurocentric self-rule or self-government. See generally, Borrows, "With or Without You," *ibid.*

[47] On performance legal cultures, see generally Bernard J. Hibbits, "'Coming to Our Senses': Communication and Legal Expression in Performance Cultures" (1992) 41 Emory L.J. 873. In synesthetic performance cultures, a legal act that modern lawyers would associate with one sense may be understood also to exist in another sensory dimension. On synesthesia generally, see Lawrence E. Marks, *The Unity of the Senses: Interrelations Among the Modalities* (New York: Academic Press, 1978). On the comparative prominence of synesthesia among "primitive and archaic" peoples, see Heinz Werner, *Comparative Psychology of Mental Development* (New York: International Universities Press, 1948) at 86–88.

[48] Canada, *Report of the Royal Commission on Aboriginal Peoples: Perspectives and Realities,* vol. 4, (Ottawa: Supply and Services Canada, 1996) at 454 [*Final Report of RCAP*]. See also Inuit Circumpolar Conference for Indian and Native Affairs, Canada, *The Participation of Indigenous Peoples and the Application of Their Environmental and Ecological Knowledge in the Arctic Environmental Protection Strategy,* vol. 1 (Ottawa: Inuit Circumpolar Conference, 1993) at 27–37.

[49] United Nations Economic and Social Council, Sub-Commission on Prevention of Discrimination and Protection of Minorities, Commission on Human Rights, *Preliminary Report of the Special Rapporteur, Protection of the Heritage of Indigenous Peoples,* UN ESC, UN Doc. E/CN.4/Sub.2/1994/31 (1994) at para. 8 [*Preliminary Report*]. For a more comprehensive analysis, see Marie Battiste & James Sa'ke'j Youngblood Henderson, *Protecting Indigenous Knowledge and Heritage* (Saskatoon, Sask.: Purich, 2000).

[50] *Preliminary Report, ibid.* These insights were codified in the *Principles and Guidelines for the Protection of the Heritage of Indigenous Peoples* (1995) that merged the concepts of Indigenous knowledge and heritage: see G.A. Res. 95-12808 (E), UN GAOR, 40th Sess., UN Doc. E/CN.4/Sub. 2/1995/3, (1995) at paras. 12–13. See also Siegfried Wiessner & Marie Battiste, "The 2000 Revision of the United Nations Draft Principles and Guidelines on the Protection of the Heritage of Indigenous People" (2000) 13 St. Thomas L. Rev. 383.

[51] *Delgamuukw, supra* note 5 at para. 126 (prior occupation is relevant "because aboriginal title originates in part from pre-existing systems of aboriginal law").

[52] Eurocentrism is the manifestation of ethnocentrism by Europeans. See generally, J.M. Blaut, *The Colonizer's Model of the World: Geographical Diffusionism and Eurocentric History* (New York: Guilford Press, 1993); Samir Amin, *Eurocentrism,* trans. by Russell Moore (New York: Monthly Review Press, 1989).

[53] Robert M. Cover, "Foreword: *Nomos* and Narrative" (1983) 97 Harvard L. Rev. 4 at 9. See also

Anthony T. Kronman, "Precedent and Tradition" (1990) 99 Yale L.J. 1029 at 1066 ("We must respect the past because the world of culture that we inherit from it makes us who we are. The past is not something that we, as already constituted human beings, choose for one reason or another to respect; rather, it is such respect that establishes our humanity in the first place").

[54] In the Westminster tradition that originated in England, unwritten constitutional conventions, precedents, royal prerogatives, and custom collectively constitute constitutional law.

[55] In the *Coronation Oath Act, 1688* (U.K.), 1 Will. & Mar., c. 6, the king and queen solemnly promise and swear to govern the people of the kingdom of England, and the dominions thereto belonging, according to the statutes in Parliament agreed on and the laws and customs of the peoples. This oath created a constitutional compact with the English people in the dominions. As Sir William Blackstone notes in his *Commentaries on the Law of England,* 14th ed. (Oxford: Clarendon Press, 1765–69) at bk. 1, c. 6, the *Coronation Oath* is a compact or contract for life between the sovereign and the peoples of the United Kingdom and the Commonwealth.

[56] Roberto Mangabeira Unger, *Law in Modern Society: Toward a Criticism of Social Theory* (New York: Free Press, 1976) at 242 (arguing that the search for the latent and living law—not the law of prescriptive rules or of bureaucratic polities, but the elementary code of human interaction—has been the staple of the lawyer's art where this art was practised with the most depth and skill).

[57] In *Guerin, supra* note 9 at 376, Dickson J. (as he then was) described Aboriginal title as a "legal right derived from the Indians' historic occupation and possession of their tribal lands." See also *Van der Peet, supra* note 1 at paras. 40, 50; *ibid.* at para. 230, McLachlin, J. (as she then was), dissenting ("a prior legal regime giving rise to aboriginal rights" was implicit in the *Sparrow* decision (*supra* note 5) on s. 35(1)); *Delgamuukw, supra* note 5 at paras. 126, 148 (Aboriginal title arises out of prior occupation of the land by Aboriginal peoples and out of the relationship between the common law and pre-existing systems of Aboriginal law); *Badger, supra* note 10 at para. 76 ("Aboriginal rights flow from the customs and traditions of the native peoples").

[58] *Delgamuukw, ibid.* at paras. 13, 95–98 (discussing spiritual song, dance, and performance, which tie them to their land and government).

[59] See *Delgamuukw, ibid.* at paras. 82, 114; *Van der Peet, supra* note 1 at paras. 17, 20; *Roberts v. Canada,* [1989] 1 S.C.R. 322 at 340 [*Roberts*] ("aboriginal title pre-dated colonization by the British and survived British claims of sovereignty"); *Badger, supra* note 10 at para. 76.

[60] *Van der Peet, ibid.* at para. 19 [emphasis in original] ("*Aboriginal* rights cannot . . . be defined on the basis of the philosophical precepts of the liberal enlightenment"). This prohibits European jurisprudences and laws from operating in the analysis or definition of Aboriginal rights and jurisprudences. On rights in Eurocentric jurisprudences and categories, see generally Matthew H. Kramer, ed., *Rights, Wrongs and Responsibilities* (New York: Palgrave, 2001); A. John Simmons, *Justification and Legitimacy: Essays on Rights and Obligations* (Cambridge, U.K.: Cambridge University Press, 2001); Judith Jarvis Thomson, *The Realm of Rights* (Cambridge, Mass.: Harvard University Press, 1990); Ronald Dworkin, *Taking Rights Seriously* (Cambridge, Mass.: Harvard University Press, 1978).

[61] *Delgamuukw, supra* note 5 at para. 130 ("the *sui generis* nature of aboriginal title precludes the application of 'traditional real property rules' to elucidate the content of that title"); *St. Mary's Indian Band v. Cranbrook (City),* [1997] 2 S.C.R. 657 at para. 14; *Mitchell v. Peguis Indian Band,* [1990] 2 S.C.R 85 at 108, Dickson C.J., concurring; *Canadian Pacific Ltd. v. Paul,* [1988] 2 S.C.R. 654 at 678; *Guerin, supra* note 9 at 382.

[62] See McLachlin, J.'s summary, in dissent, of British common law principles in *Van der Peet, supra* note 1 at paras 263–75, especially at para. 269 ("It may now be affirmed with confidence that the common law accepts all types of aboriginal interests, 'even though those interests are of a kind unknown to English law'").

[63] *Sparrow, supra* note 5 at 1112.

[64] *Delgamuukw, supra* note 5 at para. 148: "if, at the time of sovereignty, an aboriginal society had laws in relation to land, those laws would be relevant to establishing the occupation of lands which are the subject of a claim for aboriginal title. Relevant laws might include, but are not limited to, a

land tenure system or laws governing land use." See generally *ibid.* at paras. 147–48. Judicial reliance on the Aboriginal jurisprudences and perspectives is consistent with s. 27 of the *Canadian Charter of Rights and Freedoms*, Part I of the *Constitution Act, 1982, supra* note 3 [*Charter*], which provides: "This *Charter* shall be interpreted in a manner consistent with the preservation and enhancement of the multicultural heritage of Canadians."

[65] See *e.g. Van der Peet, supra* note 1 at paras. 38–40 ("'Traditional laws' and 'traditional customs' are those things passed down, and arising, from the pre-existing culture and customs of aboriginal peoples"), 68; *ibid.* at para. 262, McLachlin J. (as she then was), dissenting; *Delgamuukw, supra* note 5 at paras. 84–88, 114, 126, 145–48; *Mitchell, supra* note 2 at paras. 27–35, 37, 48. In *Campbell, supra* note 31 at paras. 83–88, the court held that Indigenous legal systems in North America continued after the arrival of Europeans and survived Canadian Confederation, and that courts in Canada have enforced laws made by Aboriginal societies. This, in the court's view, demonstrates that Aboriginal laws and such rules, whether they result from custom, tradition, agreement, or some other decision-making process, meet A.V. Dicey's classic definition of a law as "any rule which will be enforced by the courts": *Law of the Constitution*, 10th ed. (London: Macmillan, 1959) at 40.

[66] Chief Judge E.T. Durie of the Maori Land Court of New Zealand and Chairman of the Waitangi Tribunal, "Biculturalism and the Politics of Law" (Address to University of Waikato, 2 April 1993) quoted by Judge A.G. McHugh in "The New Zealand Experience in Determination of Native or Customary Title: Effect of Title Grants and Need for a New Title System" (Address to Supreme Court and Federal Court judges of Australia at their 1995 conference in Adelaide).

[67] See *Mitchell, supra* note 2 at para. 35.

[68] Ward Hunt Goodenough, *Cooperation in Change: An Anthropological Approach to Community Development* (New York: Russell Sage Foundation, 1963) at 7.

[69] A. Irving Hallowell, *Culture and Experience* (Philadelphia: University of Pennsylvania Press, 1955) and "Ojibwa Ontology, Behavior, and World View" in Stanley Diamond, ed., *Primitive Views of the World* (New York: Columbia University Press, 1969) at 49.

[70] *Van der Peet, supra* note 1 at para. 37, quoting with approval from *Worcester v. Georgia*, 31 U.S. (6 Pet.) 515 (1832) (U.S.S.C.) [*Worcester*] at 542, 559 (emphasis added in *Van der Peet* deleted). Compare *Sioui, supra* note 9 at 1053. Hall and Judson JJ. in *Calder, supra* note 23, each quoted with approval Marshall C.J.'s general description of Aboriginal societies in North America: see *ibid.* at 383 and 328, respectively.

[71] *Van der Peet, ibid.* at para. 106, L'Heureux-Dubé J. As the majority noted *ibid.* at para. 40, the meaning of the word "tradition" in English is "that which is 'handed down [from ancestors] to posterity'" (*The Concise Oxford Dictionary*, 9th ed., (1995)); the term "ancestral" in the French translation of s. 35(1), "which *Le Petit Robert* 1 (1990) dictionary defines as '*[q]ui a appartenu aux ancêtres, qu'on tient des ancêtres'*, suggests that the rights recognized and affirmed by s. 35(1) must be temporally rooted in the historical presence—the ancestry—of aboriginal peoples in North America": *ibid.* at para. 32 [emphasis in original].

[72] *Delgamuukw, supra* note 5 at paras. 144–48. See also *ibid.* at para. 114 (Aboriginal title recognized by the *Royal Proclamation of 1763*, reprinted in R.S.C. 1985, App. II, No. 1 [*Royal Proclamation, 1763*] but arising from the prior occupation of Canada by Aboriginal peoples). Compare *Mitchell, supra* note 2 at para. 67, Binnie J., concurring ("It has been almost 30 years since this Court emphatically rejected the argument that the mere assertion of sovereignty by the European powers in North America was necessarily incompatible with the survival and continuation of aboriginal rights: *Calder* . . ."); *Roberts, supra* note 59 at 340 ("aboriginal title pre-dated colonization by the British and survived British claims of sovereignty"); and *Worcester, supra* note 70 at 545 (imperial Crown grants "asserted a title against Europeans only, and were considered as blank paper so far as the rights of the natives were concerned"). In the unreported 1884 decision in the *Ontario Boundaries* case, cited and discussed in Kent McNeil, "Aboriginal Nations and Québec's Boundaries: Canada Couldn't Give What It Didn't Have" in Daniel Drache & Roberto Perin, eds., *Negotiating With a Sovereign Québec* (Toronto: J. Lorimer, 1992) 107 at 113, the Privy Council held that assertions of sovereignty would not be accepted by English courts where a pre-existing sovereign entity had claim to the territory

(based on actual mastery of the territory).

[73] The Court has emphasized the plasticity of sovereignty in foreign affairs rather than the absolute power within national or domestic boundaries. This tradition of the British imperial power was crystallized in the *Royal Proclamation, 1763, ibid.* See *e.g. Mitchell, ibid.* at paras. 9–10 (with the Crown assertion "that [out of] sovereignty over the land, and ownership of its underlying title, vested in the Crown . . . arose an obligation to treat aboriginal peoples fairly and honourably, and to protect them from exploitation, a duty characterized as 'fiduciary'"); *Delgamuukw, ibid.* at paras. 126, Lamer C.J., for the majority (the law of aboriginal title "seeks to afford legal protection to prior occupation in the present-day"), 200, La Forest J., concurring (*Royal Proclamation* bears witness to British policy of respecting Aboriginal peoples' right to occupy their ancestral lands).

[74] *Mitchell, ibid.* at para. 10 ("European settlement did not terminate the interests of aboriginal peoples arising from their historical occupation and use of the land. To the contrary, aboriginal interests and customary laws were presumed to survive the assertion of sovereignty, and were absorbed into the common law as rights, unless (1) they were incompatible with the Crown's assertion of sovereignty, (2) they were surrendered voluntarily via the treaty process, or (3) the government extinguished them. . . . Barring one of these exceptions, the practices, customs and traditions that defined the various aboriginal societies as distinctive cultures continued as part of the law of Canada"). These questionable exceptions arise in colonial law, not in imperial or Canadian constitutional law. The suggestion here that Aboriginal laws were "absorbed into the common law" is contrary to *Delgamuukw, ibid.* at paras. 82 ("although the doctrine of aboriginal rights is a common law doctrine, aboriginal rights are truly *sui generis*"), 133 (Aboriginal title at common law is protected in its full form by s. 35(1), but "s.35(1) did not create aboriginal rights; rather, it accorded constitutional status to [Aboriginal] rights which were 'existing' in 1982") and 136 ("the constitutionalization of common law aboriginal rights by s.35(1) does not mean that those rights exhaust the content of s.35(1)"), and to *Côté, supra* note 5 at para. 48 ("the doctrine [of Aboriginal rights] was a species of unwritten British law, it was not part of English common law in the narrow sense"). See also *The Queen v. Secretary of State for Foreign & Commonwealth Affairs*, [1981] 4 C.N.L.R. 86 (Eng. C.A.) [*Secretary of State*]; *Guerin, supra* note 9; and *Van der Peet, supra* note 1 at paras. 263–75, McLachlin, J. (as she then was), dissenting on other grounds. The Court has not accepted the necessity of the "sovereign incompatibility" test: see *Mitchell, ibid.* at paras. 9, 63–64. Extinguishment of *sui generis* rights protected by imperial law is both difficult and extraordinary: see *Delgamuukw, ibid.* at paras. 172–83; *Sparrow, supra* note 5 at 1097–99.

[75] Only in the specific situation of settlement by British subjects of uninhabited territory was English law deemed to be imported: see R.T.E. Latham, *The Law and the Commonwealth* (Westport, Conn.: Greenwood Press, 1970) at 516–17. If the territory was inhabited, English law did not automatically replace the Aboriginal legal system: *ibid.* The International Court of Justice in *Western Sahara (Advisory Opinion)*, [1975] I.C.J. Rep. 12 at 39 declared: "the State practice of the relevant period indicates that territories inhabited by tribes or peoples having a social and political organization were not regarded as terrae nullius. It shows that in the case of such territories the acquisition of sovereignty was not generally considered as effected unilaterally through 'occupation' of terra nullius by original title but through agreements concluded with local rulers." See also *ibid.* at 75, 85–87, 124, 171, 173.

[76] *Delgamuukw, supra* note 5 at para. 145. See also *Delgamuukw v. British Columbia*, [1993] 5 C.N.L.R. 1 (B.C.C.A.) at para. 46 [*Delgamuukw* (C.A.)], citing *Mabo v. Queensland* [*No. 2*], [1992] 5 C.N.L.R. 1 (H.C.A.) at 51 [*Mabo*]; *Côté, supra* note 5 at para. 49. According to *Secretary of State, supra* note 74 at 91–93, the *Royal Proclamation, 1763, supra* note 72, "was regarded as of high constitutional importance. . . . [It] was equivalent to an entrenched provision in the Constitution of the colonies in North America. It was binding on the Crown 'so long as the sun rises and the river flows'. . . . It was an unwritten provision . . . [that] was binding on the legislature of the Dominion and the Provinces just as if there had been included in the [1867] statute a sentence: 'The aboriginal peoples of Canada shall continue to have all their rights and freedoms as recognized by the royal proclamation of 1763.'"). In *Mabo, ibid* at 43, Brennan J. emphasized the importance of distinguishing between sovereignty and ownership as follows: "It is only the fallacy of equating sovereignty and beneficial ownership of land that gives rise to the notion that native title is extinguished by the acquisition of sovereignty." See

also Leroy Little Bear, "A Concept of Native Title" (1982) 5:2 Canadian Legal Aid Bulletin 99; James Youngblood Henderson, Marjorie L. Benson & Isobel Findlay, *Aboriginal Tenure in the Constitution of Canada* (Scarborough, Ont.: Carswell, 2000).

[77] The imperial instructions, letters patent, proclamations, imperial commissions, and courts all protected Aboriginal orders: see *Royal Proclamation, 1763, ibid.*; *Colonial Laws Validity Act,* 1863 (U.K.), 28 & 29 Vict., c. 63; *An Act to remove Doubts as to the Exercise of Power and Jurisdiction by Her Majesty within divers Countries and Places out of Her Majesty's Dominions, and render the same more effectual,* 1843 (U.K.), 6 & 7 Vict., c. 94, ss. 9, 12, 129; *Constitution Act, 1867, supra* note 31. See also *Campbell, supra* note 31 at paras. 68–70; *Mohegan Indians v. Connecticut*, Certified Copy Book of Proceedings Before Commission of Review 1743 (1769) at 191–92, discussed in Joseph Henry Smith, *Appeals to the Privy Council from the American Plantations* (New York: Octagon, 1965) at 422–42; Mark D. Walters "*Mohegan Indians v. Connecticut* (1705–1773) and the Legal Status of Aboriginal Customary Laws and Government in British North America" (1995) 33 Osgoode Hall L.J. 785; *Secretary of State, ibid.* at 91–93; *Van der Peet, supra* note 1 at para. 36; Mark D. Walters, "The 'Golden Thread' of Continuity: Aboriginal Customs at Common Law and Under the Constitution Act, 1982" (1999) 44 McGill L.J. 711; Slattery, "Understanding Aboriginal Rights," *supra* note 1 at 737–38; Brian Slattery, "Aboriginal Sovereignty and Imperial Claims" (1991) 29 Osgoode Hall L.J. 681; and Kent McNeil, *Common Law Aboriginal Title* (Oxford: Clarendon Press, 1989) at 110–16, 181–83.

[78] Hogg, *Constitutional Law, supra* note 34 at 27–44.

[79] See *supra* note 76 and the sources cited there.

[80] *Van der Peet, supra* note 1 at para. 263, McLachlin J. (as she then was), dissenting on other grounds.

[81] *Ibid.* at para. 275. Compare to McLachlin C.J.'s summary of the operation of British law in *Mitchell, supra* note 2 at paras. 9–10 ("English law, which ultimately came to govern aboriginal rights, accepted that the aboriginal peoples possessed pre-existing laws and interests, and recognized their continuance in the absence of extinguishment, by cession, conquest, or legislation").

[82] *Delgamuukw, supra* note 5 at para. 131 (Aboriginal title "should not be taken to detract from the possibility of surrender to the Crown in exchange for valuable consideration").

[83] *Côté, supra* note 5 at para. 49, quoting Slattery "Understanding Aboriginal Rights," *supra* note 1 at 737–38. This confirmation clarifies Lamer, C.J.'s earlier remarks in *Van der Peet, supra* note 1 at paras. 27–29 that Aboriginal rights existed and were recognized in 1973 in the *Calder* decision [*supra* note 23] as under the common law, and that the interests protected by s. 35(1) must be identified through an explanation of the basis for the legal doctrine of Aboriginal rights, not through an explanation of why that legal doctrine now has constitutional status. Compare *Van der Peet, ibid.* at para. 114, L'Heureux-Dubé J., dissenting on other grounds ("Aboriginal interests arising out of natives' original occupation and use of ancestral lands have been recognized in a body of common law rules referred to as the doctrine of aboriginal rights: . . . [t]hese principles define the terms upon which the Crown acquired sovereignty over native people and their territories"); *Mitchell, supra* note 2 at para. 114, Binnie J., concurring (common law concept of Aboriginal rights built around the doctrine of sovereign succession in British colonial law). As regards the sovereign succession in New France, see *Adams, supra* note 5 at paras. 31–33 and *Côté, ibid.* at paras 43–54 (constitutional protection of s. 35(1) extends to Aboriginal customs, practices, and traditions that may not have achieved legal recognition under the colonial regime of New France prior to the transition to British sovereignty in 1763).

[84] *Van der Peet, ibid.* at para. 17.

[85] The judicial confusion on this point results from a propensity to define Aboriginal rights with reference to the colonial law reception of British law and sovereign succession in the colonies instead of with reference to the *sui generis* Aboriginal jurisprudences and the protection they received in imperial law. In *Mitchell, supra* note 2 at para. 150, for example, Binnie, J., concurring, argues that the existing language of s. 35(1) cannot be construed as a wholesale repudiation of the common law. This argument assumes, mistakenly, that the common law, and not the Aboriginal jurisprudences, was the source of Aboriginal rights because of the common law's role in protecting Aboriginal rights.

Binnie J. suggests (*ibid.*) that the notion of incompatibility with the new sovereignty, one of the defining characteristics of sovereign succession in British colonial law, was therefore a limitation on the scope of Aboriginal rights. This is an old colonial legal immunity argument that excuses the Crown from having to account for its actions and precludes an adjudicator from reaching the merits of a claim. It forgets that *Sioui, supra* note 9, rejected (at 1056) the application of British colonial law to Aboriginal peoples' *sui generis* rights and that *Sparrow, supra* note 5, rejected (at 1097–99) the Crown's argument that extinguishment may take place where the sovereign authority is exercised in a manner "necessarily inconsistent" with the continued enjoyment of Aboriginal rights. The constitutional purpose of s. 35(1) is to reconcile the Aboriginal framework with the sovereignty of the Crown, not with extinguishments of these rights. Apart from the consensual treaties, no legitimate sovereign succession existed in respect of Aboriginal rights protected by imperial law and the common law. It could strongly be argued that the repatriation of the constitution in 1982 was the appropriate time of sovereign succession; it was then that Aboriginal peoples with Aboriginal rights under s. 35 became an essential part of the Canadian federated sovereignty. This innovative notion of shared sovereignty in the constitution of Canada generates a convergence rather than a juxtaposition of sovereignty over Aboriginal territories. The converged sovereignty was supposed to protect the Aboriginal rights under imperial and common law, a task the common law failed to accomplish when it accommodated extinguishment of Aboriginal rights by cession, conquest, or legislation. The historic failures of the common law and Canadian law have not been enshrined in the constitutional order: see *Sparrow, ibid.* at 1091 ("an existing aboriginal right cannot be read so as to incorporate the specific manner in which it was regulated before 1982"), 1099 ("an aboriginal right should not be defined by incorporating the ways in which it has been regulated in the past").

[86] See *e.g. Van der Peet, supra* note 1 at paras. 3 (s. 35, like other constitutional provisions, must be understood "in the light of the interests it was meant to protect"), 21 (such an approach is consistent with the fact that what s. 35 is recognizing and affirming are "rights" and helps situate Aboriginal peoples' rights in relation to Canadian society as a whole). The notion of inherent rights and powers is familiar to the common law courts. They themselves have always asserted inherent jurisdiction that can be precluded neither by Parliament (*Crevier v. Québec (A.G.)*, [1981] 2 S.C.R. 220) nor by the standards of the *Charter, supra* note 64 (*R.W.D.S.U. v. Dolphin Delivery Ltd.*, [1986] 2 S.C.R. 573). Although inherent rights may be unfamiliar to delegated constitutional governments, residual powers are not.

[87] Other jurisprudences, such as positivism, view laws holistically, as a system with a life of its own, but that system's orders are viewed as legislatively determined by an artificial state. In natural law, individuals have rights derived from juridical morality rather than the state, and view the order as a unified political system and an autonomous whole distinguishable from law's universal, hierarchical, and singular intellectual structure.

[88] See *Campbell, supra* note 31 at paras. 68, 78–81 (federal–provincial division of powers in 1867 was a division "internal" to the Crown, which did not extinguish Aboriginal rights, including rights of self-government akin to legislative powers to make laws). See generally Peter W. Hogg & Mary Ellen Turpel, "Implementing Aboriginal Self-Government: Constitutional and Jurisdictional Issues" (1995) 74 Can. Bar Rev. 187.

[89] *Quebec Secession Reference, supra* note 12 at paras. 35, 55–60.

[90] See generally James [Sákéj] Youngblood Henderson, "Empowering Treaty Federalism" (1995) 58 Sask. L. Rev. 241 [Henderson, "Empowering Treaty Federalism"].

[91] *Quebec Secession Reference, supra* note 12 at paras. 61–69.

[92] Henderson, "Empowering Treaty Federalism," *supra* note 90 at 319–25.

[93] On legal pluralism, see generally Roderick A. Macdonald, "Metaphors of Multiplicity: Civil Society, Regimes and Legal Pluralism" (1998) 15 Ariz. J. Int'l & Comp. L. 69, and H. W. Arthurs, *"Without the Law": Administrative Justice and Legal Pluralism in Nineteenth-Century England* (Toronto: University of Toronto Press, 1985). A growing body of scholarship speaks of legal pluralism, of the significant normative dimension of all social relations, of law deeply imbricated within social relations rather than imposed by the state or other external forces. See *e.g.* Marc Galanter, "Justice in Many Rooms:

Courts, Private Ordering, and Indigenous Law" (1981) 19 J. Legal Pluralism 1; Sally Engle Merry, "Legal Pluralism" (1988) 22 Law & Soc'y Rev. 869; and John Griffiths, "What is Legal Pluralism?" (1986) 24 J. Legal Pluralism 1. This view of modern law acknowledges the importance of the state and of professional actors, but does not privilege state or professional contributions to law over those of other participants in social institutions such as the family, the community, the marketplace, and the workplace, which generate ubiquitous normative regimes. Studies show that the state does not enjoy a monopoly over the production of law. It never did. To the contrary, all institutions are sites for the production of law: see *e.g.* Sally Falk Moore, "Law and Social Change: The Semi-Autonomous Social Field as an Appropriate Subject of Study" (1973) 7 Law & Soc'y Rev. 719; Stuart Henry, *Private Justice: Towards Integrated Theorising in the Sociology of Law* (Boston: Routledge & Kegan Paul, 1983); David Sugarman, ed., *Legality, Ideology and the State* (London: Academic Press, 1983); Barbara Yngvesson, "Making Law at the Doorway: The Clerk, the Court, and the Construction of Community in a New England Town" (1988) 22 Law & Soc'y Rev. 409; and Robert C. Ellickson, *Order Without Law: How Neighbors Settle Disputes* (Cambridge, Mass.: Harvard University Press, 1991). On epistemic pluralism see Frank I. Michelman, "Brennan and Democracy" (1998) 86 Cal. L. Rev. 399 at 420; Kathleen M. Sullivan, "Epistemic Democracy and Minority Rights" (1998) 86 Cal. L. Rev. 445.

[94] *Final Report of RCAP, supra* note 48.

[95] *Côté, supra* note 5 at paras. 27, 31, 56 ("to ensure the continuity of aboriginal practices, customs and traditions, a substantive aboriginal right will normally include the incidental right to teach such a practice, custom and tradition to a younger generation").

[96] The Court's decisions have created a viciously circular argument. It assumes that it is competent to define an activity as an Aboriginal right without any knowledge of or training in a foreign legal system. In its ignorance, the Court has denied some activities recognition as Aboriginal rights and has therefore also denied protection to the incidental rights to teach about them. The Court, in other words, is not exercising the power to recognize and affirm, but the jurispathic power to deny or change *sui generis* Aboriginal rights on the basis of common law characterizations. Using the common law to trump the *sui generis* rights is prohibited in the constitutional convergence. It generates in the definitional process a perception of bias against Aboriginal jurisprudences that is difficult, if not impossible, to overcome.

[97] "There is a tendency, operating at times unconsciously, to render [Indigenous] title conceptually in terms which are appropriate only to systems which have grown up under English law. But this tendency has to be held in check closely": *Amodu Tijani v. Southern Nigeria (Secretary)*, [1921] 2 A.C. 399 (P.C.) at 403. Compare *Van der Peet, supra* note 1 at paras. 264, 268–70, McLachlin J. (as she then was), dissenting on other grounds (the common law acknowledged Aboriginal categories unknown to Canadian law). See also *Delgamuukw* (C.A.), *supra* note 76 at paras. 53–59, 130–31, 199, Macfarlane J.A. (rediscovering the danger that old, inappropriate legal concepts could be unconsciously applied to *sui generis* Aboriginal rights in a way that would fail to uphold the purposes of s. 35(1)). In contemplating what might be occurring "unconsciously," it is important to consider the language judges use, or do not use, to describe the concepts and issues raised in a case: see Bowker, "Sparrow's Promise," *supra* note 23.

PART 2

Substantive Arguments

INDIGENOUS RIGHTS AND THE *LEX LOCI* IN BRITISH IMPERIAL LAW

Russel Lawrence Barsh

In *Mabo v. Queensland*, the High Court of Australia concluded that

> Native title has its origin in and is given its content by the traditional laws acknowledged by and the traditional customs observed by the Indigenous inhabitants of a territory. *The nature and incidents of native title must be ascertained as a matter of fact by reference to those laws and customs.*[1]

Four years later, in *Wik Peoples and Thayorre People v. Queensland*, the High Court held that whether a Crown grant had extinguished Native title

> in a particular case would depend, not on theoretical possibilities discovered by an examination of the nature of legal instruments, but by evidence concerning *the possible reconciliation or inconsistency of the two legal regimes* and the concurrent enjoyment of rights deriving from them, as a matter of fact.[2]

In brief, the High Court recognized the persistence of an Indigenous legal regime that continues to define and protect land rights in the absence of an unavoidable conflict with national laws. It remains to be seen how narrowly the High Court construes the notion of inconsistency.[3]

Similarly, the Supreme Court of Canada referred to Indigenous laws in *R. v. Van der Peet*[4] as a guide for identifying "aboriginal rights" under s. 35 of the *Constitution Act, 1982*.[5] Aboriginal rights are based on "the pre-existing societies of aboriginal peoples," and must be found by reference to the "aboriginal perspective," including the "practices, traditions and customs" of particular Aboriginal peoples.[6] *Van der Peet* anticipated the Supreme Court's conclusion in *Delgamuukw v. British Columbia*[7] that

> if, at the time of [British] sovereignty, an aboriginal society had laws in relation to land, those laws would be relevant to establishing the occupation of lands which are the subject of a claim for aboriginal title. Relevant laws might include, but are not limited to, a land tenure system or laws governing land use.[8]

To be sure, the Supreme Court has nowhere accepted the argument that Indigenous laws are sufficient in themselves to make a claim.[9]

Do these complementary Australian and Canadian decisions represent advances in the judicial protection of Indigenous peoples? If we look no further than the Australian and Canadian domestic case law of the past 150 years, the answer is affirmative. A wider examination of British Imperial and Commonwealth jurisprudence, however, directs us to precisely the opposite conclusion: Australia and Canada have long been at odds with the British constitutional tradition of respecting annexed nations' local laws. Legal pluralism not only has a rich history in British law, but was a core principle of the Imperial legal system from which Australia and Canada have only recently begun to emerge as distinct and independent states. Viewed against this background, the Australian High Court and Canadian Supreme Court have scarcely begun to restore the status of Indigenous laws as part of the common law to the extent that British courts would have required in 1763.

ANGLO-NORMAN FOUNDATIONS

This story begins when Britain was still a Roman province. The primary aim of Roman imperial policy was to patronize and Latinize outlying regions, rather than to replace Indigenous populations with Roman emigrants;[10] hence, local customary law was ordinarily respected unless it was incompatible with specific imperial decrees.[11] Indeed, local customs were so generally applied that in 319 A.D., the Emperor Constantine felt it necessary to clarify that "the authority of custom and long-continuing usage . . . is not to prevail to the extent of overcoming either reason or statute."[12] Because the Roman imperial administrative system was highly decentralized and largely relied upon local people to serve as censors (civil magistrates) and jurors, there was ample opportunity for local laws to persist in memory and practice.[13] After Rome withdrew its legions, central authority in England collapsed, and invaders such as the Saxons, Jutes, and Danes brought their laws with them to their scattered British settlements.

Legal pluralism continued after the Norman invasion. Royal judges had to deal with the laws of chartered towns, fairs, feoffs (or fiefdoms—estates granted to feudal vassals with some measure of local "baronial" jurisdiction), guilds, and various other geographical and social communities within England itself.[14] By the time James I assumed the thrones of England and Scotland in 1603, there were also several distinct countries to contend with: England, Wales, Scotland, and Ireland, as well as Berwick, Jersey, Guernsey, and the Isle of Man. In the seventeenth century, of course, plantations were established in the Caribbean and North America; in the eighteenth and nineteenth centuries, the realm included (to varying degrees) hundreds of African and south Asian kingdoms.

Although the earliest royal courts were preoccupied with centralization, central control of judicial administration and decision making was achieved gradually and with a minimum of interference in local substantive laws.[15] When travelling on circuit with the sovereign (i.e., on eyre), for example, royal judges inquired into the local customs applicable to realty and fealty and routinely applied them, so far as they were compatible with the sovereign's interests in retaining ultimate control and maximizing his income from local fines, forfeitures, and wardships.[16] In practice, the jurisprudence of medieval and renaissance England respected the continuity of local laws, and expectations were reasonably based upon local laws and customs.[17] As the Anglo-Norman kingdom grew and absorbed its neighbours, however, there was a tendency to enact more laws at London, and to attempt greater administrative centralization and standardization, resulting in more frequent and complex problems of conflicts of laws.

Indeed, the term "liberty" originally connoted a grant of royal protection for the continuity of local customs, laws, and law making rather than individuals' freedom from restraint or excessive laws (as John Stuart Mill used "liberty"). The early Anglo-Norman kings granted hundreds of liberties to abbeys, markets, towns, and individual subjects,[18] leading to several centuries of disputes over the extent to which the sovereign's writs run to persons residing within the liberty.[19] In one such case, arguably the first to discuss the principles of metropolitan law later synthesized by Lord Coke and Lord Mansfield, the judges of King's Bench concluded that a liberty must be proven by a written grant or by conquest.[20] "Conquest" assumed a different meaning in medieval English law than it does today, a point to which I will return. Referring to conquest was ordinarily a way of claiming a liberty by dint of long usage. If a liberty had been exercised since the Norman conquest, royal judges presumed it to have been conferred or confirmed by William the Conqueror, even in the absence of a recorded grant.[21]

The United Kingdom today[22] includes three countries that coalesced with England by significantly different means: Wales, by military defeat in 1282; Ireland, a colony or "settlement" backed by military expeditions, which began in the time of Henry IV; and Scotland, by treaty and inheritance in 1603, through the marriage of Henry VIII's sister Margaret to the Scottish king James IV). The Isle of Man and the Channel Islands are regarded as subject to the English sovereign but not as part of the United Kingdom; the Isle of Man was originally a possession of the Scottish realm, and the Channel Islands were already possessions of Dukes of Normandy before the Norman seizure of England in 1066. Questions have arisen since Tudor times as to the powers of the English sovereign and Parliament to legislate for different territories in the British Isles, and the extent to which Acts of Parliament are presumed to apply to different parts of the British Isles without express words to that effect.

As the Empire grew and the number and diversity of the sovereign's dominions[23] increased, English jurists gradually shifted from a simple classification scheme based on the circumstances of each dominion's original submission to the Crown to an even more complex but less determinate scheme based on the degree of integration of each territory into the Imperial metropolis. The more integrated territories such as Ireland were treated as presumptively subject to general parliamentary acts, while demographically, culturally, or politically less integrated territories such as India were presumed to be subject only to laws that referred to them or suited their particular circumstances. By the 1930s, this approach bifurcated because some territories, such as Canada, were gradually disengaging from the United Kingdom.[24] The United Kingdom proper was consolidating itself legally, and the overseas dominions were growing practically independent of the British Parliament, long before the official transfers of sovereignty that dissolved the Empire, piecemeal, in the wake of the Second World War.

THE TUDOR CONSTITUTION AND LORD COKE

The choice-of-laws regime applied to the consolidated British Isles evolved from three cases decided just as the first British settlements were established in North America. The best known today is *Calvin's Case*,[25] but two earlier decisions are equally relevant, if somewhat less eloquent.

The central issue in the *Countee de Derby's Case*[26] was whether a general Act of Parliament applied automatically to realty on the Isle of Man. Queen Elizabeth's judges of Common Pleas reasoned that because the Isle of Man was a "conquest," laws enacted by the English Parliament could not apply there in the absence of some express legislative reference to that effect. According to the judges, the legislation at issue

> does not apply to the said Isle nor its estates, nor any does any other Statute made in England without special and express provision to that effect; and it is the same in the case of Ireland, where the people are governed by the Laws and Acts of Parliament of their country, and not by any Law of this country excepting an Act of Parliament that provides expressly that it is a Law for Ireland and Wales.[27]

In *Le Case de Tanistry*,[28] conversely, the issue was whether English courts should apply Irish customary law to a dispute over the inheritance of land in Ireland. The judges of King's Bench outlined three tests for the application of local customs: the custom must be ancient, "certain," and have a "reasonable" purpose.[29] Although tanistry was ancient and certain, it appeared fundamentally unfair and injurious to persons who would qualify as heirs under English law, and therefore would not be respected by an English court. *Le Case de Tanistry* left open the possibility that other Irish customs of comparable antiquity and certainty had survived the introduction of the common law by the conqueror.[30]

What did Tudor judges mean by the term "conquest"? "Conquest" has its roots etymologically in the classical Latin terms *con quaestus* (or *con quaesitus*), literally "with an inquiry," such as a formal investigation or legal proceeding before a *quaestor* (Roman magistrate).[31] *Conquisitus* was used in medieval Latin to refer to "acquiring [something] other than by inheritance."[32] Roman jurists used the terms *victoria* or *deditio* to signify a military victory over other nations, not *con quaesita*.[33] It would have been proper for a medieval scholar to write *bello quaesita* ("acquired in war"), but *quaesita* or *conquisitus* would have simply implied a lawful acquisition without specifying its precise nature.

Significantly, "conquest" long retained its original Latin meaning in Scottish law. "A subject purchased with money acquired by industry and economy, is in the true sense conquest," Lord Kames explained in a classic treatise. "But land, or any other subject, purchased with borrowed money, is no conquest; except as far as the subject may be of greater value than the price paid for it."[34] In other words, property acquired by means of *personal effort*, rather than by inheritance, is a conquest. The acquisition may be through any lawful means, so long as there is genuine consideration. For a commoner, conquests may be by contract or purchase; for a sovereign, by treaty or cession. What is significant for our purposes here is the fact that hostilities are irrelevant. The contract or treaty is the instrument of conquest, not the sword.

Tudor judges accordingly used "conquest" to identify inhabited territories that had been added to the English realm by sovereign effort, whether peacefully by treaty or by military might, not to signify that these territories had been defeated by force of arms. Ireland and Scotland were both classified as conquered, for example, although Ireland was annexed by force and Scotland by treaty. "Conquest" was therefore used to signify the sovereign's personal role in the acquisition, whether as a warrior or as a diplomat. In *Calvin's Case*, however, Lord Coke used "conquest" as if it could refer only to a military victory, and thereby left a legacy of juridical confusion.

The actual facts in *Calvin's Case* deserve more than passing attention. Robert Calvin was born in Scotland three years after James I ascended the throne of the united kingdoms of England, France,[35] Ireland, and Scotland. Calvin inherited a freehold estate in England, from which he was dispossessed by Richard and Nicholas Smith. In response to Robert's writ to King's Bench, the Smiths argued that Robert could not properly proceed in an English court because he was not English but an alien—that is, a Scot born under and governed by Scottish laws. Thus two profound constitutional issues were presented: the definition of alien for the purpose of regulating access to English justice; and, even if the Scots were not aliens from the vantage point of English law, whose laws applied to land disputes between English and Scots.

It is not insignificant that Lord Coke began his opinion with a lengthy dissertation on the meaning of *ligeance* (i.e., allegiance). The key underlying principle in his analysis is the personal (*in personam*) nature of sovereignty and jurisdiction.

> [I]t appeareth that ligeance, and faith and truth which are her members and parts,

are qualities of the mind and soul of man, and cannot be circumscribed within the predicament [i.e., precondition] of *ubi* [location].[36]

Allegiance and subjection comprise a relationship.

> Ligeance is the mutual bond and obligation between the King and his subjects, whereby his subjects are called his liege subjects, because they are bound to obey and serve him; and he is called their liege lord, because he should maintain and defend them.[37]

Although Coke's approach anticipated the social contract theory of John Locke, Coke himself attributed sovereignty to the law of nature and believed that allegiance can arise from birth or by the operation of laws and treaties amongst rulers, as well as by the subject's personal consent.[38]

Lord Coke then applied the principle of the *Countee de Derby's Case* to Scotland. As a "conquest," Scotland became subject to the authority of the sovereign, and the Scots accordingly became English subjects rather than aliens.[39] Robert Calvin was therefore entitled, as a subject, to the protection of writs in English courts, although his own indigenous Scottish laws had remained in force and still largely governed his status.[40] Coke, unfortunately, argued that this result was dictated by the law of nature, however, rather than by equity or judicial precedents. The sovereign is free to do what he pleases with the laws of a "conquered" kingdom, Coke explained, "seeing that he hath *vitae et necis potestam*" (power of life and death) over the inhabitants.[41] By this dictum, Coke associated the authority of the sovereign with his generosity in sparing the lives of defeated people, rather than (as in the actual case of Scotland) the terms of the treaty of allegiance or cession.

Lord Coke's analysis left two important constitutional questions unresolved: does Parliament have competence to modify the laws of a conquered territory, or is this power reserved to the sovereign as a matter of royal prerogative? If there is a treaty of cession or association, must the sovereign or Parliament respect its terms? These points were not litigated until the establishment of the Caribbean sugar colonies, and in Lord Mansfield's sweeping judgment in *Campbell v. Hall*[42] on the eve of the American Revolution.

THE BRITISH PLANTATIONS IN AMERICA

Restoration and the Royal Prerogative

The narrow holding of *Calvin's Case* (i.e., that the sovereign's writ reaches every corner of the British dominions) was reaffirmed shortly after the restoration in *Dutton v. Howell*,[43] a complaint of false imprisonment against the British governor of Barbados. The plaintiff was English by birth, so the Privy Council could simply have focused their analysis on the plaintiff's personal allegiance to the king, which could not logically have been lost by virtue of his settling in a British overseas territory.[44] Instead, the Privy Council reopened the question of which laws applied to territories outside England. Did the common law apply to Barbados and thereby provide the plaintiff with a remedy?

According to the Privy Council, the fact that Barbados had been uninhabited prior to British settlement was dispositive of the legal issues.[45]

> The Truth is, certain subjects of *England*, by Consent of their Prince, go and possess an uninhabited desert Country; the Common Law must be supposed their Rule, as 'twas their Birthright, and as 'tis the best, and so to be presumed their Choice; and not only that, but even as Obligatory, 'tis so.[46]

English subjects were presumed to retain their allegiance and their system of laws, much in the spirit of Tudor conceptions of the personal nature of jurisdiction, and "if an Injury [be done to a subject], 'tis relievable somewhere in the King's Dominions."[47] Although this was a sufficient basis for deciding the case at bar, the Privy Council reiterated the "conquest" language of *Calvin's Case*. "The reason of a Conqueror's Power to prescribe Laws" for a conquered country, the Privy Council observed,

> is the Conqueror's Clemency, in saving the Lives of the conquered, whom, by the Strict Right of War, he might have destroyed; or [else it is] the presumed Chance of subjection, which the conquered Prince and People threw themselves upon, when they first engaged in the War.[48]

Like Lord Coke's remark in *Calvin's Case*, this was not only *dictum* but unsupported by any examples.

The nature and consequences of "conquest" were revisited in *Blankard v. Galdy*,[49] where the issue was whether an English statute punishing office-buying could be applied to a British colonial official in Jamaica. Lord (then Chief Justice) Holt's reprise of Lord Coke's formula is worthy of quotation at length:

> 1st, In case of an uninhabited country newly found out by *English* subjects, all laws in force in *England* are in force there; so it seems to be agreed.
>
> 2dly, Jamaica being conquered, and not pleaded to be parcel of the kingdom of *England*, but part of the possessions and revenue of the Crown of *England*, the laws of *England* did not take place there, until declared so by the conqueror or his successors. The *Isle of Man* and *Ireland* are part of the possessions of the Crown of *England*; yet retain their ancient laws[.][50]

The persistence of the *lex loci* (in this instance, Spanish laws) was reasonable and appropriate, Lord Holt opined, because it would take time to establish English institutions in the new territory; meanwhile, the Jamaican authorities would unavoidably continue to legislate and regulate local affairs on the island.[51] Lord Holt suggested that the same rule would apply to an "infidel country" as far as practicable: "their laws by conquest do not entirely cease, but only such as are against the law of God."[52] Unlike the Privy Council's *obiter* in *Dutton*, *Blankard* remained close to Tudor conceptions of "conquest" and legal pluralism. Unfortunately, the holding permitted a serious injustice to persist, and (as we shall see) was overturned by the same court nearly a century later.

British and French forces were manoeuvring for control of Acadia when the cases governing annexed territories were summarized in a 1722 Privy Council memorandum:

> 1st. That if there be a new and uninhabited country found out by *English* subjects, as the law is the birthright of every subject, so, wherever they go, they carry their laws with them, and therefore such new found country is to be governed by the laws of *England*; though after such country is inhabited by the *English*, acts of parliament, made in *England*, without naming the foreign plantations, will not bind them . . .
>
> 2dly. Where the King of *England* conquers a country, it is a different consideration: for there the conqueror, by saving the lives of the people conquered, gains a right and property in such people; in consequence of which he may impose upon them what law he pleases. But,
>
> 3dly. Until such laws [are] given by the conquering prince, the laws and customs of the conquered country shall hold place; unless where these are contrary to our religion, or enact anything that is *malum in se*, or are silent; for in all such cases the laws of the conquering country shall prevail.[53]

Presumably intended as a basis for drafting letters patent and royal instructions to colonial governors, the 1722 memorandum closely paraphrased *Dutton* and *Blankard,* with a focus on the exercise of the royal prerogative. The legal implications of peaceful cessions or treaties remained to be addressed, however.

The issue of "conquest" was again raised in another Jamaican office-buying case, *Rex v. Vaughan*,[54] which aroused the wrath of Lord Mansfield. "If these transactions are believed to be frequent, it is time to put a stop to them," Lord Mansfield raged, fittingly on the very eve of the American Revolution. "A terrible Consequence would result to the Public, if every Thing that such an Officer is concerned in Advising the disposal of, should be set up to *Sale*."[55] The king had never extended the requisite laws[56] to Jamaica, however, as Lord Holt had found in *Blankard*, so Lord Mansfield contrived to reclassify Jamaica as a settled colony, rather than a conquest. This device was also unsatisfactory, he concluded, because the plaintiff had invoked Tudor anti-bribery legislation that clearly had never been intended to apply to overseas territories.

"If *Jamaica* was considered as a *Conquest*, they would retain their old Laws, till the Conqueror had thought fit to alter them," Lord Mansfield reasoned carefully.

> If it is considered a *Colony*, (which it ought to be, the old Inhabitants having left

the Island), then these Statutes are positive Regulations of Police, not adapted to the Circumstances of a new Colony; and therefore no Part of that Law of *England* which every Colony, from Necessity, is supposed to carry with them at their first Plantation.

Moreover, since "[no] Act of Parliament made after a Colony is planted, is construed to extend to it, without express Words shewing the Intention of the Legislature to be that it should," it would be improper to apply more recent anti-bribery laws to Jamaican territory.[57] Lord Mansfield's solution to these logical obstacles was to find a duty of honourable conduct implied in the letters patent that Jamaican officials received from the king. They had not violated any English legislation applicable to Jamaica by buying their offices; rather, they had broken their personal commitments to the Crown.

Lord Mansfield and the Royal Proclamation
This, then, was the law of the British Empire at the time of the Mi'kmaq treaties at issue in *Simon*[58] and *Marshall*[59] and the Royal Proclamation of 7 October 1763.[60] Assuming that the execution and (by the subsequent Royal Proclamation) affirmation and implementation of these treaties eliminates any possibility of classifying Atlantic Canada as vacant in 1752–1763, it would appear to follow unavoidably that the Indigenous laws of the region were to remain in force except where modified expressly by the Crown—at least amongst the Mi'kmaq, if not within the limits of lawful British settlements such as the cities of Halifax or Annapolis Royal. Two important questions remain unanswered: the effect of the treaties themselves, and the division of powers between the sovereign and Parliament. *Campbell v. Hall*[61] squarely addressed both of these questions.

Campbell v. Hall is especially relevant to Canada. Great Britain had acquired the French Caribbean island of Grenada as well as New France (Acadia and Québec) by the 1763 Treaty of Paris. The Royal Proclamation of 1763, which the Supreme Court has characterized as the original guarantee of Aboriginal peoples' rights,[62] established a new framework for the administration of both territories. Like the Aboriginal nations of North America, the residents of Grenada argued that the Royal Proclamation entrenched rights they had secured in treaties previously made with the British sovereign.

In their wartime capitulation to British naval forces, the residents of Grenada were able to secure a promise that their private property would be respected and that export taxes would not be raised.[63] The royal governor of the island subsequently raised the export tax on Grenadan sugar without the consent of the local assembly, an act that Grenadans challenged at King's Bench as *ultra vires*—that is, unconstitutional.

Lord Mansfield began his analysis by reiterating the principle in *The Countee of Derby's Case*: "the laws of a conquered country continue in force, until they are altered by the conqueror."⁶⁴ He then distinguished the legislative power of Parliament from the exercise of royal prerogative (the sovereign acting alone on his or her own authority). In the exercise of his or her prerogative powers of war and peace, the sovereign may bring new territories into the Empire upon whatever terms he or she pleases. Once brought within the Empire, however, "conquered" territories become subject to the powers of Parliament, and Parliament alone. This formula has two important corollaries. The first is that the power of the sovereign to alter the laws of conquered territories is itself limited by constitutional restrictions on the sovereign's prerogative. Thus, the sovereign

> cannot make any new change contrary to fundamental principles: he cannot exempt an inhabitant from that particular dominion; as for instance, from the laws of trade, or from the power of parliament, or give him privileges exclusive of his other subjects.⁶⁵

A treaty of peace must therefore be constitutional in the sense of being compatible with the supremacy of Parliament and the rule of law.

A second corollary is that the treaty of peace itself is a constitutional instrument.

> [T]he articles of capitulation upon which the country is surrendered, and the articles of peace by which it is ceded, are sacred and inviolable according to their true intent and meaning.⁶⁶

Parliament cannot alter the conditions offered and agreed to by the sovereign. In the case of Grenada, the conditions included a ceiling on sugar taxes. Furthermore, the Royal Proclamation subsequently authorized the Grenadans to convene a local assembly, which implicitly terminated the remaining prerogative authority of the sovereign. Hence, the governor lacked any authority to meddle in sugar taxes or any other internal affairs of the Grenadans once their rights were entrenched by treaty and the Royal Proclamation.

The events that shaped the legal foundations of British Canada parallel the events that Lord Mansfield found dispositive in *Campbell v. Hall*. France ceded its interests in Acadia and Québec to Great Britain, and France's Indigenous allies subsequently entered into separate treaties of peace and allegiance with the British king, who responded with a Royal Proclamation expressly guaranteeing the property and security of his new subjects. No provision was made by treaty or in the Royal Proclamation for a form of local First Nations self-government, but in the absence of an express directive in the treaty or Royal Proclamation changing the "political form of government" of First Nations, the laws and political institutions of First Nations must be presumed to have remained the same.⁶⁷

It may be objected that the First Nations of eastern Canada never capitulated to British forces, nor ceded their territories to the sovereign. Lord Mansfield implied that conquest results from an exercise of military might; following the reasoning of the Privy Council in *Dutton v. Howell*, it is this fact that justifies the sovereign's exercise of prerogative power to change the laws of the conquered country when fixing the terms of peace. But while *Campbell v. Hall* involved a military victory and capitulation, Lord Mansfield also stated as a general rule:

> If a king (says the book) comes to a kingdom by conquest, he may change and alter the laws of that kingdom; *but if he comes to it by title and descent,* he cannot change the law of himself without the consent of parliament.[68]

It is therefore possible to imagine cases in which the sovereign did not have the opportunity to put the inhabitants to the sword as a matter of fact, yet negotiated the terms upon which they chose freely to associate themselves with Great Britain. Surely, countries that freely associated themselves with the Crown and Empire should not have fewer rights or be more vulnerable to parliamentary control than countries that were defeated in war.

It is important to clarify the distinction between conquered and settled additions to the realm, as Lord Mansfield understood it:

Conquered	*already populated*	local laws persist until expressly modified, unless they are immoral or unjust
Settled	*vacant when found*[69]	English laws fill the vacuum

It is also appropriate to reflect briefly on the law of treaties in Lord Mansfield's time. Non-Christian societies—even the piratical Barbary Powers—were regarded as independent states capable of making binding treaties.[70] No less an authority than Hugo Grotius, in his influential 1646 treatise *De Jure Belli et Pacis*, observed that the capacity to enter into binding treaties was "so common to all men that it does not admit to any distinction of religion."[71] Early European jurists also agreed that a state does not lose its international personality merely by placing itself by treaty under the protection of a stronger power.[72] All European empires routinely employed treaties with non-Christian powers in Asia, the Americas, and Africa to secure trade concessions, acquire strategic ports, and, through a combination of protectorates and outright cessions, to widen their spheres of influence and enlarge their metropolitan territories.[73] It was therefore no leap to conceive of protected nations as possessing internal laws of their own, which continued to apply to disputes arising within their borders.

THE GLOBAL BRITISH EMPIRE

Legal Pluralism in British India

British sovereignty over much of the Indian subcontinent was established within a few decades after the Royal Proclamation of 1763 and offers us the opportunity to see how Crown lawyers understood Lord Mansfield's constitutional rule in *Campbell v. Hall* whilst it was still fresh in their minds.

The accession of British sovereignty in India was gradual and piecemeal.[74] Most of the Empire's claims on the subcontinent were founded upon treaties with Native rulers, and treaties often included specific delegations of jurisdiction to the East India Company or to the sovereign.[75] The complex mosaic of treaty relationships resulted in a mosaic of regional jurisdictional accommodations and court systems.[76] Local customary laws were routinely respected, as were the religious laws of Hindus and Muslims.[77] British judges conceived of this as a policy dictated by "justice, equity, and good conscience," however, rather than a duty imposed on Imperial courts by constitutional law.[78] Similarly, acts of Parliament were not applied in India except as required by their express terms, and judges explained that general British laws were not suited to India's circumstances,[79] not that constitutional principles placed a burden on Parliament to express its intention to change the local laws of an acquired territory. These fictions preserved the appearance of Imperial supremacy, and provided a justification for the rare circumstances in which British judges felt compelled to disregard local customs, whilst in practice following Lord Mansfield's formula for resolving conflicts of laws.

This did not mean that customary laws survived undiminished. Litigants engaged in forum-shopping and chose British courts and British laws when it was expedient to do so.[80] Forum-shopping was undoubtedly encouraged by the demographic complexity and urbanization of India, which made it likely that parties would come from different castes, ethnic groups, and religions.[81] The popularity of British tribunals led to the rapid erosion of traditional legal expertise among Native-born advocates and magistrates.[82] Clumsy efforts at codification and the restraints of precedent also took a toll.

As Duncan Derrett has observed, the early British governors of India came from a Britain that was still a patchwork of local, canon, and royal jurisdictions, so they had no intellectual difficulty grasping the idea of treating India's numerous tribes, castes, and confessions as distinct communities with separate laws.[83] Significantly, however, British administrators and judges placed on the litigants a strict burden of proof of applicable customary laws.[84] A rebuttable presumption in favour of applying British laws to fill a local normative vacuum reverses the perspective of *Campbell v. Hall*, at least in principle. The significant extent to which the courts of British India nevertheless applied Indigenous law in practice may reflect power dynamics and the extent to which Hindu and Muslim legal traditions were already extensively documented and therefore indisputably manifest.

Legal Pluralism in British Africa

British Africa may be a better comparison with Canada. The Empire neither sought nor exercised much effective control over Africans or Canada's First Nations until the middle to late nineteenth century. Africans and Canada's First Nations did not seek, and were never afforded, the same level of social and economic integration with Britons as the peoples of the Indian subcontinent. Whereas India was consolidated administratively before 1900, British Africa still consisted of numerous treaty-based protectorates until the Second World War, and Canada was still negotiating the status of its northern territories during the Cold War.[85] It is useful for our purposes here that the applicability and nature of African tribal law was frequently the subject of appeals to the Privy Council, leaving a rich judicial record at the highest level of the Imperial legal system.

> [I]n spite of the circumstances under which English law was received in any part of West Africa, whether by settlement conquest or cession, the change of sovereignty did not result in the disappearance of customary laws.[86]

Customary laws throughout Africa were generally respected,[87] at least where they could be "reconciled with the institutions or the legal ideals of civilized society,"[88] which generally was to say British conceptions of natural justice.[89] Customary laws could be extinguished by incompatible legislation, but only where this result was the "manifest intention" of the legislature.[90] In *Malomo v. Olushola*,[91] for example, the West African Court of Appeal refrained from invalidating customary oral gifts of land in Nigeria, although they violated the British Statute of Frauds. These principles, together with the demographic complexion of most of British Africa, resulted in the great majority of disputes continuing to be governed by customary laws.[92]

On the whole, as the Privy Council explained in *Oke Lanipekun Laoye v. Amao Oyetunde*, it had always been the policy of the British Empire to respect Native customs "in so far as possible and in so far as they have not been varied or suspended by statutes or ordinances," provided they are not "barbarous."[93] This policy had often been affirmed in the express terms of the constitutional instruments under which overseas territories had been acquired and settled, such as letters patent and royal charters.[94] Furthermore, the Privy Council conceded that "it is the assent of the native community that gives a custom its validity," rather than its recognition by the Crown or by the courts.[95] Customary laws continue to change, just like the common law.[96] "The chief characteristic of native law is its flexibility."[97] The *lex loci* was not sought in books or immemorial tradition but in contemporary practices that remained sufficiently widespread to form the basis of local people's personal expectations.[98] "A customary law that once prevailed may now exist in a modified form owing to modern political, social and economic developments," the East African Court of Appeal decided in *The Kabaka's Government v. Kitonto*.[99]

> The new or modified custom may be deemed to have acquired the force of law if it is shown that the members of the community recognize it as an obligatory rule which

regulates the conduct of persons within that community.[100]

A dramatic illustration of these principles is *Santeng* per *Ohemeng v. Darkwa*,[101] in which the plaintiff successfully argued that his expulsion from a sacred society had been accomplished in violation of customary procedures. Both the substantive right upon which the claim was founded (belonging to a tribal sacred society) and the standard of fair process for a taking of the right were derived from the *lex loci*.[102] Of course, it could be said that the local procedural standard was upheld only because it was consistent with British notions of fairness.[103] However, there were cases in which customary principles were enforced that simply could not be reconciled with British social norms prevailing at the time, such as those involving the inheritance rights of the offspring of polygamous marriages.[104] The Privy Council went a step beyond *Darkwa* in a subsequent Ghanaian appeal and upheld the authority of Native courts to refer disputes to traditional elders councils.[105] There was no statutory basis for the referral; it was upheld as an application of customary law.[106] Likewise, in *Macauley v. P.C. Bongay (No. 3)*,[107] the West African Court of Appeal upheld a chief's physical expulsion of a British squatter as an exercise of the authority conferred on chiefs by customary law.

British judges often confronted complex conflicts of tribal laws. The basic rule in British West Africa was to look to the legal regime expressly or impliedly chosen by the parties.[108] The form of the transaction could be dispositive: if the parties were Natives but they used an English deed to transfer interests in land, for example, it would be presumed that they intended to be bound by English law.[109] On the other hand, a customary interest in land remained subject to the Native legal regime that had created it,[110] and a customary holder could convey only the interests that he himself possessed under customary laws.[111] If the parties came from two different Indigenous societies, British courts adopted Native choice-of-law rules. In *Mphumeya v. R.*,[112] the defendant, an Ngoni woman, was charged with stealing money from her Mchewa husband. It was held on appeal that the wife of a Mchewa man is subject to Mchewa law under both Mchewa and Ngoni law, and that Mchewa law does not shield wives from criminal liability for acts within the household.[113]

The existence of Native land rights under Native laws was recognized in a variety of circumstances. The Privy Council concluded, for example, that an 1861 treaty ceding the port of Lagos to the Crown for protection from slavers had not disturbed the Native inhabitants' property rights, ruling: "A mere change of Sovereignty is not to be presumed as meant to disturb the right of private owners."[114] The Crown bore the burden of proving that it had obtained title by treaty, and the 1861 treaty's silence was fatal to the Crown's claims.[115] The Privy Council also relied on customary Nigerian land-tenure law when determining to whom compensation should be paid for a compulsory acquisition by the Crown.[116] The dispute was between the actual occupant of the land and the chief of the district. Although the chief possessed a kind of "usufruct" throughout his domain, the Privy Council held that compensation was due mainly to those who actually occupied the land in accordance with customary laws. A third party (a local headman) had meanwhile obtained a Crown patent for the same tract and argued that he was the true owner, rather than the occupants. However, the Nigerian judges held that, under local customs, the headman merely became a trustee for the lawful occupants; the Privy Council adopted this conclusion.[117]

Native customary law was not always dispositive of disputes in which the Crown itself had an interest. At issue in *Cook v. Sprigg*[118] was a trade concession granted to an English merchant by the paramount chief of Pondoland, prior to the latter's cession of Pondoland to the Crown. British authorities in the Cape Colony subsequently chose to disregard the grant, and the Privy Council ultimately concluded that this was an act of state beyond the control of municipal courts.[119] Nonetheless, the Privy Council also noted that the treaty of cession contained no reference to the protection of pre-existing interests, that the trade concession had merely been at the chief's pleasure under Pondo law, and that it probably was void under Pondo law because the headmen of the affected district had never ratified it. Likewise, in a case challenging the validity of the Crown railway grants to Cecil Rhodes, the Privy Council conceded that although property rights "hardly less precise than our own" existed in many African legal systems, and as such were entitled to protection, it could not discover any evidence that the Native rulers of Zimbabwe had ever respected individual land rights. In the absence of a pre-existing system of land rights, the Empire was free to dispose of the territory as it pleased following its annexation.[120]

The Privy Council not only held that customary law governs tenure relationships within Indigenous communities, then, but also that courts may resort to customary law in determining the effect of treaties and Crown grants on Native title. It is fair to say that the Australian High Court in *Wik* and the Supreme Court of Canada in *Delgamuukw* added nothing to what the Privy Council had ruled in African appeals sixty years earlier.

THE PROBLEM WITH CANADA

Canadian courts did not consider the application of Indigenous laws until *Van der Peet* and *Delgamuukw*. Why? Canada inherited the same Imperial legal jurisprudence as the British territories in Africa and south Asia; thus, *Campbell v. Hall* should have applied to Canada from the beginning. When the Supreme Court of Canada heard its first Indian treaty hunting appeals in the 1960s, British courts were still routinely applying customary laws in appeals from African territories. Canadian jurists could not have been completely unaware of this apparent inconsistency; why did they never address it?

To attempt an answer, we must return to the time of *St. Catherine's Milling and Lumber Co. v. The Queen*,[121] decided twenty years after Confederation, when the Canadian state was still in its infancy. Indigenous laws were not directly at issue, because the land in dispute had already been surrendered to the Crown by treaty for disposal. Nor were any Indigenous people parties to the proceedings. The courts were asked to decide a narrow constitutional issue: whether the surrendered land was still sufficiently "Indian" to fall within the relevant federal head of powers: s. 91(24) of the *British North America Act, 1867*.[122] Lord Watson advised the queen that her Privy Council had not settled any other constitutional questions, such as

> the right to determine to what extent, and at what periods, the disputed territory, over which the Indians still exercise their avocations of hunting and fishing, is to be taken up for settlement and other purposes.[123]

Hence, Lord Watson's often-cited characterization of Aboriginal peoples' interests ("the tenure of the Indian was a personal and usufructuary right, dependent upon the good will of the Sovereign") was intended to apply to disputes between branches of the Canadian government over ceded and surrendered lands, rather than disputes with Indigenous peoples themselves;[124] besides, its negative implications for Indigenous peoples' land rights were contradicted by subsequent decisions of the Privy Council.[125] Canada nevertheless continued to develop its approach to First Nations as if *St. Catherine's* had wholly settled the issues of land rights and customary land tenure laws. Aboriginal peoples' ability to challenge this approach was limited by their lack of electoral franchise, by administrative interference from Ottawa, by provincial recalcitrance, and by legislation making it an offence to raise funds for the purpose of pursuing Indian land claims.[126]

The United States established tribal court systems in the 1880s.[127] Canada did not emulate this policy;[128] instead, reserves were included in the new Confederation's wider project of achieving unity and "peace, order, and good government" through a system of uniform criminal laws and a national police force. In the United States, hundreds of Native courts provided the opportunity (at least) for Indigenous customary laws and ordinances to be applied and developed.[129] American Indian tribal courts have won exclusive original jurisdiction over most disputes involving Indians, Indian lands, and Indian self-government,[130] including disputes over property interests created by tribal customary laws.[131] Such diversity of law is reminiscent of British Africa, but stands in sharp contrast to the situation in Canada.

Canada's continued eschewal of Indigenous law today may reflect the shadow of Québec nationalism and unity fears. The existence of a separate and distinct legal system in Québec has scarcely been a major point of the unity debate, but separate legal systems for hundreds of First Nations may be perceived as more threatening.[132] Québec was less of an issue in the 1880s, when Canada's territorial integrity was more threatened by the expansion of American settlement into the northern prairies, based on American treaties with prairie nations such as the Dakota and Blackfoot, who spanned the Forty-ninth Parallel and lived directly in the path of the planned Canadian national railroad.[133] Canadian efforts to seal off the border included the hastily negotiated Treaties Nos. 1 through 7 (1871–1878),[134] close on the heels of omnibus American treaties with the Sioux and Blackfoot confederacies in 1868. Canada was in direct competition with the United States for prairie nations' respect and loyalty, at a time when Ottawa was relatively weak and poor. The United States could offer more cash and trade to western First Nations, so Ottawa offered them physical safety and the rule of law.

Once the international border was effectively closed, Canadian implementation of the Crown's responsibilities to First Nations may have been influenced by developments in Imperial policy and international law following the *Berlin General Act, 1885*, in which the Empire and other great powers eliminated the customary requirement of Indigenous consent for the annexation of overseas territories.[135] Over the next five years, Whitehall moved quickly to consolidate and harmonize the Empire's metropolitan jurisdiction. The *British Settlements Act, 1887* recognized the sovereign's prerogative to appoint courts for British settlements, defined as "any British possession which has not been acquired by cession or conquest";[136] the *Foreign Jurisdiction Act, 1890* extended the uniform jurisdiction of British courts to all overseas subjects, as if "by the cession or conquest of territory," regardless of the actual means by which particular territories had been acquired (i.e., whether "by treaty, capitulation, grant, usage, sufferance [or] other lawful means").[137] The Privy Council subsequently construed the *Foreign Jurisdiction Act, 1890* as a non-justiciable act of state converting all protectorates into "conquests" (in the current sense of that term)—that is, abolishing any restrictions on parliamentary powers that may have been contained in specific treaties between the Empire and Native rulers.[138]

The act of state doctrine is problematic in British constitutional law, if it results in shielding Crown officers from accountability to the law for their treatment of subjects.[139] Indeed, in *Vayjesingji Joravarsingji v. Secretary of State for India*, Lord Dunedin was careful to explain that "when a territory is acquired by a sovereign state *for the first time, that* is an act of state."[140] Once a new regime has been established, in which Native rights or title have been recognized by treaty, legislation, or otherwise, the Crown's new subjects are entitled, like all other subjects, to judicial protection from ministers of government.[141] The defence of act of state has generally been upheld only in cases involving the liberties or property rights of plaintiffs who are not subjects of the Crown.[142] Even the exercise of the royal prerogative in foreign affairs is no longer shielded from judicial review in cases where the "legitimate expectations" of subjects are threatened.[143] The constitutionality of the *Foreign Jurisdiction Act, 1890* is therefore contextual rather than absolute.

In any event, the main result of the *Foreign Jurisdiction Act, 1890* was to collapse much of the jurisdictional complexity of the Native states of India and tribal protectorates in Africa, without any generalized effect on the continuing recognition and application of Indigenous laws in those territories. To be sure, Parliament and the councils of individual colonies enacted statutes and orders altering the jurisdiction of Native courts and applying some substantive British laws to disputes within Native communities.[144] Under *Campbell v. Hall*, Parliament could have done this all along, provided that it did so expressly and in conformity with any applicable treaty of cession. The novelty, then, was disregarding the specific legal facts of each overseas territory's history, and applying the same principles of statutory construction to all overseas territories. Because constitutional law required that Parliament express itself clearly, and presumed against any changes in subjects' status or rights, the impact of harmonized Imperial jurisdiction on Indigenous legal systems could only be gradual.

There was a countercurrent to harmonization, however, for while the Empire was busy consolidating the Imperial legal system in territories inhabited chiefly by Indigenous peoples, Parliament was simultaneously delegating more local self-governing authority to British settlers in Canada, Australia, New Zealand, and South Africa, which were drifting towards independent statehood. Strictly speaking, these dominions were not "settled," in the legal sense used by Lord Mansfield in *Campbell v. Hall*, because they had Indigenous populations with which (in all but Australia) the Crown had made alliances by treaty. All four dominions had become predominantly European demographically as a matter of fact, and their respective immigrant populations were actively seeking to convert this evolving fact into a legal conclusion. The *Colonial Laws Validity Act, 1865*[145] confirmed that laws enacted by colonial assemblies were effective without prior Imperial ministerial approval, albeit still subject to general Imperial legislation. In the *Statute of Westminster, 1931*,[146] the Empire reversed the presumption in *Campbell v. Hall* that general Imperial acts apply to British settlers overseas. These two Imperial statutes gave the legislative assemblies of settlers in Canada, Australia, New Zealand, and South Africa greater independence in regulating their own domestic affairs, but did not expressly subordinate the Indigenous peoples of those territories to their legislative supremacy, nor in any way extinguish Indigenous laws. In subsequent administrative actions and judicial decisions, however, settlers assumed that Indigenous peoples had only such rights as settlers themselves chose to recognize legislatively.[147] I suggest that this was incompatible with the basic constitutional principles elucidated in *Campbell v. Hall*.[148]

On the eve of the Second World War, a prominent Canadian sociologist explained that respect for Aboriginal customary laws should be temporary, at most, because the goal of Indigenous administration was complete assimilation.[149] Although the United States had begun a national program to "organize" Indian tribes for self-government during the Depression, many congressmen likewise regarded this as a transitional measure rather than a further entrenchment of inherent rights, and by 1946 there was widespread talk on Capitol Hill of "terminating" Indian tribes.[150] Canada legislatively subjected Indians to those "laws of general application from time to time in force in any province" in 1951;[151] two years later, Congress delegated to state governments civil and criminal jurisdiction over many Indian reservations.[152] Was Ottawa constitutionally competent to sweep away Indigenous legal systems by means of this broad delegation of legislative powers to the provinces?[153]

The constitutional status of Indigenous laws was addressed only indirectly when the Supreme Court first had occasion to consider treaty rights in the 1960s. *Sikyea v. The Queen*[154] and *R. v. George*[155] involved conflicts between hunting rights secured by treaty and regulations issued under the *Migratory Birds Convention Act, 1917*. The legal issue was whether the legislation necessarily governed the exercise of the treaty rights. The trial court in *Sikyea* held that treaty rights had not been affected because the legislation did not expressly extinguish them.[156] The Court of Appeal reversed, however, and the Supreme Court summarily upheld the reversal without further discussion. In *George*, the defendant had been hunting inside an Indian reserve, raising a question of the effect of s. 87 (now s. 88) of the *Indian Act, 1951*. Cartwright J. argued that, for "the honour of the Sovereign," the treaty right must be upheld,[157] but the majority agreed with Martland J. that the opposite result was required by the plain meaning of the statutory text:

> Subject to the terms of any treaty and any other Act of Parliament of Canada, all laws of general application from time to time *in force in any province* are applicable to and in respect of Indians in the province . . . [emphasis added].

Since the *Migratory Birds Convention Act* was unquestionably a law of general application in force in the provinces, Parliament had apparently intended to subject treaty rights to federal regulation.[158]

The majority decision in *George* was incompatible with the "well-known general principle that statutes that encroach upon the rights of the subject, whether as regards person or property, are subject to 'strict' construction," which is to say that any doubts must be resolved "in favour of an interpretation that leaves private rights undisturbed."[159] Ironically, the Privy Council had reminded Canada of this principle barely a year after the enactment of s. 87 of the *Indian Act, 1951*.[160] Nevertheless, even after *Van der Peet*, the Supreme Court has not fully corrected the constitutional error in *George* nor fully revived the recognition of Indigenous law in the spirit of *Campbell v. Hall.*

Indeed, Lord Denning's judgment in *Indian Association of Alberta*[161] identified the relevant principles of Imperial constitutional law more clearly than any subsequent decision of the Supreme Court of Canada. Lord Denning made a point of discussing the existence of Aboriginal laws (albeit in somewhat dated and offensive language):

> They had their chiefs and headmen to regulate their simple society and to enforce their customs. I say "to enforce their customs" because in early societies custom is the basis of law. Once a custom is established it gives rise to rights and obligations which the chiefs and headmen will enforce. These customary laws are not written down. They are handed down by tradition from one generation to another. Yet beyond doubt they are well established and have the force of law within the community.[162]

Significantly, the foregoing paragraph appeared under the subheading "Aboriginal rights and freedoms," which suggests—correctly, in the light of *Calvin's Case* and *Campbell v. Hall*—that Aboriginal rights are protected by respecting Aboriginal laws. "[I]t was of first importance to pay great respect to their laws and customs," Lord Denning explained in his overview of British policy, "and never to interfere with them except when necessary in the interests of peace and good order."[163] He characterized the Royal Proclamation of 7 October 1763 as an "entrenched provision" of the constitutions of the British colonies in North America, which is to say that it was equivalent to an irrevocable royal charter, and concluded that it was necessarily also entrenched by implication in the *Constitution Act, 1867.*[164] As a result, all the Aboriginal rights and freedoms contemplated by the Royal Proclamation have been entrenched in the constitution of Canada since 1763, and they would have remained entrenched after the *Constitution Act, 1982* even if that legislation had made no reference to them.

CONCLUSION

The status of customary laws in English courts was always an issue. Even within England itself, there were many linguistic and ethnic groups and historical jurisdictions; royal judges were continually confronted with problems of ascertaining local customary laws and reconciling them with national legislation. As the realm expanded through war, treaties, feudal feoffs, and aristocratic marital liaisons, the problem of choosing between parliamentary acts and local customs increased as well. Far from being unusual, respect for legal pluralism was more a fact of life and law in Tudor times than it is today. As the multiethnic, legally diverse British state expanded into a world empire, its highest courts maintained a tradition of pluralism. On the whole, the local laws of Indigenous and tribal peoples and religious communities were respected and applied as Imperial common law.

Legal pluralism can be two-edged, as many contemporary writers have argued.[165] A pluralistic legal system is by definition unequal; different individuals and communities within the same state are subject to different laws. Respect for local laws may perpetuate inequalities within, and between, neighbouring groups. As the Supreme Court of Canada wisely observed in the *Reference re Secession of Québec*,[166] however, achieving equality among groups in fact may require some inequality in law, particularly where some groups are vulnerable minorities subject to persistent discrimination. Achieving real equality can be advanced through legal pluralism if there is strict respect for the rule of law: all action taken by government must be clearly and explicitly authorized by democratically enacted laws, consistent with the constitution and with generally accepted principles of justice, such as the principle that courts will construe legislation strictly against any interference with a citizen's rights.[167]

There is an important but (in Canada) neglected relationship of respect for the *lex loci* and for the larger goal of ensuring respect for the rule of law. Rule of law reflects a belief in the value of stability and continuity of rules—that is, of ensuring that citizens are capable of knowing the laws, and making plans based on the assumption that laws will not change dramatically or unpredictably. Respect for decided cases (*stare decisis*), generality (rules apply to broad categories of persons rather than individuals), prospectivity (rules apply to future conduct), and universality (equal treatment under law) are logical corollaries of the rule of law. The fundamental spirit of the rule of law is therefore "to promote and protect legitimate expectations" arising from our past transactions and from the normative framework in which those transactions occurred.[168]

In the British constitutional tradition, legislation is the instrument of change, and, "[a]s a body of evolving principle, the common law provides stability and continuity."[169] Hence, to maintain the rule of law, judges must construe legislation against any dramatic or implied change in the common law. "To alter any clearly established principle of law, a distinct and positive legislative enactment is necessary and statutes are not presumed to alter the common law further or otherwise than the Act expressly declares."[170] Likewise, courts must not alter the plain meaning of legislation by inferring the real intention of the legislature.[171] "Parliament, under our constitution, is sovereign only in respect of what it expresses by the words used in the legislation it has passed."[172] The fact that Canada has adopted a written charter of rights does not render these British constitutional principles obsolete or irrelevant. On the contrary, I suggest that strict observance of such traditional constitutional principles is more important than ever, if First Nations are to survive.

It is difficult to avoid the conclusion that Canada, Australia, and New Zealand fell by the wayside of Imperial constitutional development simply because British settlers and their descendants, rather than colonial officers directly accountable to London, controlled all the domestic courts and assemblies. In other words, the difference between British Africa, where tribal law was routinely enforced, and Canada, where First Nations law was utterly disregarded, is solely a result of the growing *de facto* majority power of immigrants, and has nothing whatsoever to do with constitutional law.

Viewed through the lens of British Imperial legal history, *Delgamuukw* is not an innovative breakthrough, but a return to fundamental constitutional principles that were improperly disregarded by Canadian courts for more than a century. It remains to be seen whether the non-Aboriginal citizens of Canada and their elected government, who profited for generations from the courts' failure to abide by British law, are now prepared to abide by the constitutional framework upon which Canada was originally founded.

NOTES

[1] [1992], 175 C.L.R. 1 at 58 [*Mabo*]; 107 A.L.R. 1 at 42, Brennan J. for the majority [emphasis added]. The term "customary law" is fraught with misleading implications, for example that it is "traditional," ancient, superstitious, unconscious, or unchanging. See James S. Read, "Customary Law under Colonial Rule" in Henry Francis Morris & James S. Read, eds., *Indirect Rule and the Search for Justice: Essays in East African Legal History* (Oxford: Clarendon Press, 1972) 167 at 169–74. I prefer to use the terms *lex loci* or "Indigenous laws," where my meaning will not be misconstrued.

[2] (1996), 187 C.L.R. 1; 141 A.L.R. 129 at 273–74, Kirby J. [*Wik*] [emphasis added]; see also *ibid.* at 185, Toohey J.

[3] Two questions may arise: whether sovereign intentions to override Indigenous laws are clearly expressed, and whether the conflict or inconsistency has a substantial adverse impact on the interests of other citizens. Compare the American rule, first articulated in *Worcester v. Georgia*, 31 U.S. (6 Pet.) 515 (1832), that the rights of an Indian tribe, whether granted by legislation or reserved by a treaty, can be defeated only by explicit legislative extinguishment. U.S. law does not recognize the persistence of Indigenous law as such; however, Indian tribes enjoy a sphere of local legislative and judicial authority within which they can articulate and apply traditional or customary laws. See Russel L. Barsh, "Putting the Tribe into Tribal Courts: Possible? Desirable?" (1999) 8 Kan. J.L. & Pub. Pol'y 74 [Barsh, "Putting the Tribe into Tribal Courts"].

[4] [1996] 2 S.C.R. 507 at 544–46, Lamer C.J. [*Van der Peet*], quoting *Mabo*, *supra* note 1, and equating the term "traditional laws," as used in *Mabo*, with the phrase "pre-existing societies" used in his own analysis. In turn, *Van der Peet* was cited with approval by Toohey J. in *Wik*, *supra* note 2 at 185.

[5] Schedule B to the *Canada Act 1982* (U.K.), 1982, c. 11.

[6] *Van der Peet*, *supra* note 4 at 553–56, Lamer C.J. The Court imposed two significant limitations on the use of Native customs and practices to define the scope of Aboriginal rights: they must deal with matters "integral to the distinctive cultures of Aboriginal peoples," and they must be reconciled generally with "the Canadian legal and constitutional structure." The second limitation is arguably consistent with the Privy Council decisions discussed *infra* in notes 88 and 125; the first is not, and constitutes a peculiarly Canadian concession to non-Indigenous interests. For discussion, see Russel L. Barsh & James Y. Henderson, "The Supreme Court's *Van der Peet* Trilogy: Naïve Imperialism and Ropes of Sand" (1997) 42 McGill L.J. 3.

[7] [1997] 3 S.C.R. 1010 at 1100, Lamer C.J. [*Delgamuukw*]; see also *ibid.* at 1099–1100: "the source of aboriginal title appears to be grounded both in the common law and in the aboriginal perspective

on land; the latter includes, but is not limited to, their systems of law."

[8] *Ibid.* at 1100. In *M.N.R. v. Mitchell*, [2001] 1 S.C.R. 911 at 952–53, McLachlin C.J. maintained in *dictum* that a broad doctrine of "sovereign incompatibility" is not applicable to Aboriginal rights in Canada; rather, conflicts between Aboriginal rights and the claims of others should be governed only by the tests of extinguishment, infringement, and justification outlined in *Van der Peet, supra* note 4. In a separate concurring opinion, Binnie J. argued (*ibid.* at 986–87) that Aboriginal rights "cannot [be] wholly cut loose from either their legal or historical origins"; accordingly, extinguishment of at least some of them may be implicit in the historical assertion of Crown sovereignty over Canada. This argument echoes the "plenary power" doctrine in American Indian law, first articulated in *Lone Wolf v. Hitchcock*, 187 U.S. 553 (1903) at 565–67, and recently rephrased by the United States Supreme Court as the doctrine of "implicit divestiture," *e.g.*, in *U.S. v. Wheeler*, 435 U.S. 313 (1978).

[9] The Supreme Court has not yet pursued the implications of these decisions for the role of customary law in construing *treaty* rights under s. 35, for example in its decisions in *R. v. Marshall*, [1999] 3 S.C.R. 456 [*Marshall*], [1999] 3 S.C.R. 533. The World Court has ruled that Portuguese treaties with the Native rulers of India must be interpreted as they were understood by the Indigenous grantors, in the light of the conceptual categories used by Indigenous legal systems: *Right of Passage over Indian Territory (Merits)*, 1960 I.C.J. Rep. 6 at 37.

[10] *E.g.* Stephen L. Dyson, *The Creation of the Roman Frontier* (Princeton: Princeton University Press, 1985) at 271–78. On colonies of Romans, chiefly of demobilized legionnaires, see Edward Togo Salmon, *Roman Colonization under the Republic* (Ithaca: Cornell University Press, 1970). The Latin term *colonus* literally meant "farmer"; hence, *colonia* was a farm or plantation (with the implication of being made on virgin soil).

[11] A. Arthur Schiller, "Custom in Classical Roman Law" in Alison Dundes Renteln & Alan Dundes, eds., *Folk Law: Essays in the Theory and Practice of* Lex Non Scripta (New York & London: Garland Publishing, 1994) 39; A. Arthur Schiller, *Roman Law: Mechanisms of Development* (The Hague: Mouton, 1978) at 538–39 [Schiller, *Roman Law*]. Classical Roman lawyers conceived of *ius non scripta* ("unwritten law") as the historical foundation of their legal system, and frequently used terms such as *mos provinciae* ("provincial mores"), *consuetudo regionis* ("custom of the region"), and *consuetudo loci* ("local custom") to refer to the unwritten laws of non-Roman peoples: Schiller, *Roman Law*, *ibid.* at 262–64.

[12] Schiller, *Roman Law*, *ibid.* at 263. Long-continuing usage appears as *diuturna usus*. On the general jurisprudence of Roman "trusteeship" (*fides*) of allied nations (*amici*), protectorates (*clientelae*), and Latinized provinces (*socii*), see E. Badian, *Foreign Clientelae (264–70 B.C.)* (Oxford: Clarendon Press, 1958). On the earliest Roman treaties of protection and their shifting interpretation, see Percy Cooper Sands, *The Client Princes of the Roman Empire under the Republic* (New York: Arno Press, 1975) at 10–48.

[13] J.F. Drinkwater, *Roman Gaul: The Three Provinces, 58 BC–AD 260* (London & Canberra: Croon Helm, 1983) at 93–114; Tenney Frank, *Roman Imperialism* (New York: MacMillan, 1914) at 104.

[14] See John Hudson, *The Formation of the English Common Law: Law and Society in England from the Norman Conquest to Magna Carta* (London & New York: Longmans, 1996) at 24–51, for an overview.

[15] *Ibid.* at 16–20; S.F.C. Milsom, *Historical Foundations of the Common Law* (London: Butterworths, 1969) at 1–25; R.F. Hunnisett, *The Medieval Coroner* (Cambridge, U.K.: Cambridge University Press, 1961). A similar approach was adopted by the Norman lords of medieval Sicily, as described by Harold J. Berman in *Law and Revolution: The Formation of the Western Legal Tradition* (Cambridge, Mass.: Harvard University Press, 1983) at 419–57.

[16] See *e.g.* Martin Weinbaum, ed., *The London Eyre of 1276* (Leicester: The London Record Society, 1976) at 5, 21, 76, 134, 324, 488, 514, 517, 523 (customary laws of London applied by royal judges). Paul R. Hyams, *King, Lords and Peasants in Medieval England: The Common Law of Villeinage in the Twelfth and Thirteenth Centuries* (Oxford: Clarendon Press, 1980) at 69–72, discusses the routine use of customary laws in local (as opposed to aristocratic) inheritance disputes.

[17] Henry de Bracton, *On the Laws and Customs of England*, trans. by Samuel E. Thorne (Cambridge, Mass.: Harvard University Press, 1968), refers to local customs ninety-one times (ascertained from

the electronic version of this translation available from the Harvard Law School Library <http://hls5.law.harvard.edu.bracton/Common/>. See also Ranulf de Glanville, *The Treatise on the Laws and Customs of the Realm of England Commonly Called Glanville*, ed. by G.D.G. Hall (Oxford: Clarendon Press, 1993) at 75–79, 113, 147.

[18] Privileges and exemptions granted by William I were usually styled *libertas* in the original instruments, compiled by David Bates, ed., *Regesta Regum Anglo-Normannorum: The Acta of William I (1066–1087)* (Oxford: Clarendon Press, 1998). In a grant to the Abbey of Abingdon in 1127, Henry I used the words *perpetuo tenendum et habendum . . . in legitima et liberrima potestate sua et justicia* ("to have and to hold forever . . . in their free power and justice"), and his grant to Kenilworth Priory in 1132 spoke of *libertatibus et consuetudinibus et quietationibus terris et ecclesiae pertinentibus* ("the liberties, customs and immunities of the lands and churches concerned"). Henry II made his grant of a town to William Fitz Robert in 1179 *cum omnibus libertatibus et liberis consuetudinus suis* ("with all of its liberties and free customs"). See also R.C. Van Caenegem, ed., *English Lawsuits from William I to Richard I* (London: Selden Society, 1990) at 1:211, 1:234, 2:562. Van Caenegem compiled more than fifty early cases involving "liberties," some of them based on grants made by pre-Conquest English rulers, as in the celebrated case of the monks of St. Albans and the Bishop of Lincoln (1159–1163): *ibid.* at 2:368–78. Liberties could also be claimed by the presumption of an ancient grant as implied from long usage—that is, by prescription: see *infra* note 21.

[19] E.g. *Michael Dunwich's Case*, Coram Rege Roll No. 137 (Trin. 1293); *Bishop of Worcester's Case*, Coram Rege Roll No. 139 (Hil. 1294); *Adam Henwick's Case*, Coram Rege Roll No. 142 (Mich. 1294); *Devon Stannaries Case*, Coram Rege Roll No. 187 (Hil. 1307) [*Devon Stannaries*]; G.O. Sayles, ed., *Select Cases in the Court of King's Bench under Edward I* (London: The Selden Society, 1936–1939) 2: 143; 3:1, 37, 158 [Sayles, *Select Cases*]. The City of London enjoyed a "liberty" of enforcing its own laws: Weinbaum, *supra* note 16 at 279–80. A liberty was understood to be a grant of a part of the sovereignty of the Crown. Hence, in *John Lovel v. John de Boys* (1279), the justices of the Common Bench ruled that a liberty cannot be devised inconsistent with the original grant, for the subject "cannot give that which belongs to the king": Paul A. Brand, ed., *The Earliest English Law Reports* (London: Selden Society, 1996) 1:106.

[20] *The Bishop of Hereford's Case*, Coram Rege Roll No. 136 (Pach. 1293); Sayles, *Select Cases, ibid.*, 2:142.

[21] An exclusive proprietary right to fish at a particular place could also be claimed by grant or prescription: *Le Case del Royall Piscarie de la Banne* (1610), Davis 55, 80 E.R. 540; *Lord Fitzwalter's Case* (1674), 1 Mod. 105, 86 E.R. 766; *Carter v. Murcot* (1768), 4 Burr. 2162 at 2164, 98 E.R. 127, Lord Mansfield. This exclusive right to fish (and thus, implicitly, to regulate the fishery) was originally called *libera piscaria* ("liberty of fishing") as in *Lord Fitzwalter's Case, ibid*. Some later cases confusingly translate *libera piscaria* as a "free [*i.e.*, public] fishery" and refer to proprietary fisheries as a "several fishery": *Smith v. Kemp* (1692), 2 Salk. 637, 91 E.R. 537, Lord Holt C.J.; *Seymour v. Lord Courtenay* (1771), 5 Burr. 2814 at 2817, 98 E.R. 478, Lord Mansfield.

[22] For a more detailed review of the United Kingdom's territorial development, see E.C.S. Wade, *Constitutional and Administrative Law*, 11th ed. by A.W. Bradley & K.D. Ewing (London & New York: Longmans, 1993) at 38–47.

[23] I use "dominion" to refer to a territory captured, held, or possessed by the sovereign, without necessarily being integrated into the core "realm" governed by the Parliament at London. This is different from the use of "Dominion" in the *Statute of Westminster, 1931* (U.K.), 22 & 23 Geo. V, c. 4, s. 2 as a term of art to refer to relatively self-governing territories such as Canada.

[24] Hence, as a matter of constitutional convention as well as Realpolitik, the authority of the British Parliament to legislate for these departing territories was diminished: *British Coal Corp. v. R..*, [1935] A.C. 500 at 520 (Canada); also *Ndlwana v. Hofmeyr*, [1937] A.C. 229 at 237 (South Africa).

[25] (1608), 7 Co. Rep. 1a, 77 E.R. 377 (K.B.) [*Calvin's Case* cited to Co. Rep.].

[26] (1598), 2 And. 115, 123 E.R. 575 (C.P.).

[27] *Ibid.*, 2 And. 115 at 116 [author's translation from the original, which follows]:

ne lier le dit Isle ne l'enheritans de ceo ne ascun auter Statute fait en Angliterr sans especiall

& expresse Ordinance pur ceo; & est en mesme case come Ireland, ou le people est rule per les Leys & Acts de Parlement de leur terre, & nemy per ascun Ley de ceo terre sinon que sont per Act de Parlement que ordean Ley expressment pur eux de Ireland, & Wales.

[28] (1606), Davis 28, 80 E.R. 516 (K.B.), discussed and followed as recently as *Mercer v. Denne*, [1904] 2 Ch. 534 at 550, a dispute over customary fishing rights.

[29] In the original: "Le commencement del custome . . . doet estre sur reasonable ground & cause. . . . Custome doet estre certaine. . . . Custome doet aver continuance sans interruption de temps dont memory ne Court": *ibid.*, Davis 28 at 33. The judges added that custom cannot override royal prerogatives: "Custome que se exalt sur le prerogative del Roy, ceo est void auxy envers le Roy": *ibid.*

[30] What local practices were "reasonable," and therefore compatible with the English legal regime, was rarely adjudicated over the next three centuries. An exception was *Chamberline v. Harvey* (1696), 5 Mod. 186 at 190, 87 E.R. 598, which held that the slavery law of Barbados "is only *lex loci*, and adapted to that particular place (as the law of *Stannaries* in *Cornwall*), and extends only to that country"; hence, a slave taken from Barbados to England could not be deprived of his liberty whilst on English soil. The parenthetical reference is to the case of the *Devon Stannaries*, supra note 19. However, in *Re Rucker ex parte Rucker* (1834), 3 Deacon & Chitty's Reports (Bankruptcy) 704, it was held that Antiguan law defines slaves as realty, so the disposition of a slave in Antigua must be decided under Antiguan laws.

[31] Ordinarily, the Roman *quaestor* was responsible for treasury accounts and trusts: Schiller, *Roman Law*, supra note 11 at 186–87. Medieval English legal texts written in Latin accordingly used *quaestor* to mean "chancellor" or a judge in chancery.

[32] Jan Frederik Niermeyer, *Mediae Latinitatis Lexicon Minus* (Leiden, The Netherlands: E.J. Brill, 1976) at 251, 877–78. The same Latin roots give us the French words *question* and *acquerir* (to acquire or purchase) and the English *quest, inquest, question, query,* and *acquire*.

[33] Roman jurists distinguished between a *provincia togatae* ("province with togas"), a Romanized territory associated with Rome, and a *colonia* settled by Roman citizens: Salmon, *Roman Colonization under the Republic*, supra note 10 at 147–49. Provinces and colonies were likewise distinguished from *amici* or friendly powers aligned with Rome by treaty, most of which eventually submitted to Roman "protection": Badian, *supra* note 12 at 25–32.

[34] Henry Home Lord Kames, *Elucidations Respecting the Common and Statute Law of Scotland* (London: T. Cadell, 1777) at 40–41. This is comparable to the meaning of *conquets* in pre-Napoleonic French law: "les immeubles acquis par le mari & la femme pendant leur communauté" ("realty acquired by a man and wife during their marriage"): Claude-Joseph de Ferriere, *Dictionnaire de Droit et de Pratique, nouvelle edition* (Toulouse: J. Dupleix, 1779) 1:342.

[35] *Calvin's Case, supra* note 25, was decided at a time when the English monarch still asserted claims by inheritance to the French Crown and periodically occupied coastal French realms such as Normandy and Bordeaux.

[36] *Calvin's Case, ibid.* at 7a.

[37] *Calvin's Case, ibid.* at 5a. Coke used the example of subjects' duty to follow the sovereign into war, and the corresponding royal obligation to pay and protect loyal soldiers: *ibid.* at 8a. It followed that royal writs must run wherever the sovereign's subjects are found and require protection: *ibid.* at 9b. Lord Mansfield revisited this issue in *Mostyn v. Fabrigas* (1774), 1 Cowp. 161, 98 E.R. 1021 (K.B.) [*Mostyn* cited to Cowp.], a claim of false imprisonment against the British military governor of the island of Minorca.

> [I]t is impossible that there ever could exist a doubt, but that a subject born in *Minorca* has as good a right to appeal to the King's courts of justice, as one who is born within the sound of Bow bell. . . . Therefore to lay down in an *English* court of justice such a monstrous proposition, as that a governor acting by letters patent under the great seal, is accountable only to God, and his own conscience; that he is absolutely despotic, and can spoil, plunder, and injure his Majesty's subjects, both in their liberty and property, with impunity, is a doctrine that cannot

be maintained [emphasis in original].

Mostyn, ibid., at 171, 175. Interestingly, Lord Mansfield used the Inuit of Labrador as a hypothetical case of a territory under the King's authority where there were no local courts of justice capable of protecting the inhabitants from abuse, so that redress must necessarily be provided by the courts in England: *Ibid.* at 181.

[38] *Calvin's Case, ibid.*, at 12b–14b, 17b–18a. Nonetheless, Coke argued that the subject owes allegiance to the Crown in its capacity as "an hieroglyphic of the laws," rather than owing allegiance to the sovereign's body; hence, it follows that a ruler who disregards the laws can command no one's allegiance: *ibid.* at 11b–12a.

[39] *Ibid.* at 25a. It should be noted that Coke believed that pagans were *perpetui inimici*, incapable of becoming friends or subjects, and incapable of bringing any actions in law: *ibid* at 17a–17b. He cited no case law or practice to support this view, and it was laid firmly to rest in *Omichund v. Barker* (1744), 1 Atk. 21, 26 E.R. 15 (Ch.). Coke also maintained that "conquered" pagan kingdoms lose all of their laws automatically, and must be governed by the sovereign according to "natural equity" because pagan laws are repugnant to Christianity and to the law of nature: *Calvin's Case, ibid.* at 17a. He cited no case law or examples of this assertion, either; it was not followed by the evolving British Empire in law or practice.

[40] The reasoning in *Calvin's Case, ibid.* was applied to Wales in *Witrong v. Blany* (1674), 3 Keble 401 at 402, 84 E.R. 789 (K.B.). For historical background on Welsh law see Huw Pryce, *Native Law and the Church in Medieval Wales* (Oxford: Clarendon Press, 1993). For applications of *Calvin's Case* to Ireland, see *e.g. Craw v. Ramsay* (1669), 2 Vent. 1 at 4, 86 E.R. 273 (C.P.), and *Cartwright v. Pettus* (1676), 2 Chan. Cas. 214 at 222, 22 E.R. 916 (Irish law applies to the partition of lands in Ireland).

[41] *Calvin's Case, ibid.* at 17b.

[42] (1774), 1 Cowp. 204, 98 E.R. 848 (K.B.) [cited to Cowp.].

[43] (1693), Show. P.C. 24, 1 E.R. 17 [*Dutton* cited to Show. P.C.].

[44] Although a resident of Barbados, the injured party in *Dutton, ibid.* was English by birth, and was presumed to be English by allegiance. Hence, this was the reverse of the situation in *Calvin's Case, supra* note 25, where the injured party was Scottish by birth but claimed allegiance to the English sovereign by virtue of Scotland's union with England.

[45] *Dutton, ibid.* at 31.

[46] *Ibid.* at 32.

[47] *Ibid.* at 30.

[48] *Ibid.* at 31. The Privy Council's reading of the *iure belli* is suspect in that it does not acknowledge the possibility that a just war can ever be waged against England. In any event, the Privy Council observed (*ibid.*) that "Conquest *est res odiosa*, and never to be presumed; besides, 'tis the People, not the Soil, that can be said to be conquered." By definition, a vacant land cannot be conquered; contrariwise, vacancy must clearly be demonstrated *as a matter of fact*, out of considerations of justice to the inhabitants.

[49] (1693), 2 Salk. 411, 91 E.R. 356 (K.B.) [*Blankard* cited to Salk.]. *Collett v. Lord Keith* (1802), 2 East 260, 102 E.R. 368 (K.B.) involved the alleged abuse of power by British officials in the Cape Colony; the plaintiff argued that Dutch law applied to the substantive question but the court disposed of the case on defects of pleading.

[50] *Blankard, ibid.* at 411 [emphasis in original].

[51] *Ibid.* at 412.

[52] *Ibid.* This statement does not appear in the report of *Blankard* in 4 Mod. 222, 87 E.R. 359.

[53] *Memorandum of Decision on Appeal to the King in Council of Foreign Plantations* (1722), 2 P. Wms. 75, 24 E.R. 646 [emphasis in original].

[54] (1769), 4 Burr. 2494, 98 E.R. 308 (K.B.) [*Vaughan* cited to Burr.].

[55] *Ibid.* at 2499. Persistent abuse of office by British colonial officials was one of the grievances set out in the American Declaration of Independence six years later.

[56] Statute of 5 & 6 Edw. VI, c. 16.

[57] *Vaughan, supra* note 54 at 2500 [emphasis in original].

INDIGENOUS RIGHTS & BRITISH IMPERIAL LAW   117

[58] *Simon v. The Queen*, [1985] 2 S.C.R. 387 [*Simon*].
[59] *Marshall, supra* note 9.
[60] Privy Council Register, Geo. III, vol 3. at 102; R.S.C. 1985, App. II, No. 1.
[61] *Campbell v. Hall, supra* note 42.
[62] *Guerin v. The Queen*, [1984] 2 S.C.R. 335. The relevance of *Campbell v. Hall, ibid.* to the analysis of First Nations' rights under the Royal Proclamation of 1763 was not lost on Justice Hall in *Calder v. Attorney-General of British Columbia*, [1973] S.C.R. 313 at 394–96, or Lord Denning M.R. in *R. v. Secretary of State for Foreign and Commonwealth Affairs ex parte Indian Association of Alberta*, [1982] 2 W.L.R. 641 (C.A.) at 647 [*Indian Association of Alberta*].
[63] *Campbell v. Hall, ibid.* at 205–6. "Capitulation" did not imply an unconditional surrender, but precisely the opposite: *capitulae* ("chapters") were the enumerated terms and conditions of a treaty: Charles Henry Alexandrowicz, *An Introduction to the History of the Law of Nations in the East Indies* (Oxford: Clarendon Press, 1967) at 99 [Alexandrowicz, *History of the Law of Nations*]. Compare the Anglo-Huron battlefield treaty at issue in *R. v. Sioui*, [1990] 1 S.C.R. 1025.
[64] *Campbell v. Hall, ibid.* at 209.
> It is left by the constitution to the king's authority to grant or refuse a capitulation: if he refuses, and puts the inhabitants to the sword or exterminates them, all the lands belong to him. If he receives the inhabitants under his protection and grants them their property, he has a power to fix such terms and conditions as he thinks proper. He is intrusted with making the treaty of peace: he may yield up the conquest, or retain it upon what terms he pleases. These powers no man ever disputed, neither has it hitherto been controverted that the king might change part or the whole of the law or political form of government of a conquered dominion:

ibid. at 209–10. Lord Mansfield did not state that a "conquest" is necessarily preceded by an unconditional surrender or military defeat; it can be purely diplomatic.
[65] *Ibid.* at 209.
[66] *Ibid.* at 208. In *Rex v. Cowle* (1759), 2 Burr. 834 at 850–55, 97 E.R. 987 (K.B.), likewise, Lord Mansfield held that the king's writs run to] Berwick because it was conquered and subsequently granted a charter that subjects its inhabitants to English laws. As acts of royal prerogative, charters were deemed irrevocable and inviolable, like treaties. Joseph Chitty, Jr., *A Treatise on the Law of the Prerogatives of the Crown: and the Relative Duties and Rights of the Subject* (London: Butterworth, 1820) at 29, 32, 119, 125.
[67] In *(A.G.) v. Stewart* (1817), 2 Mer. 143, 35 E.R. 895 (Ch.) [*Stewart* cited to Mer.], there was a question of whether the English Mortmain Act (9 Geo. II, c. 1) applied to realty in Grenada. Sir William Grant M.R. observed in *dictum* that English rather than French law was "the received and acknowledged law of the island," despite the implication of *Campbell v. Hall* that French law should persist in this "conquered" territory: *Stewart, ibid.* at 158. He did not pursue this anomaly further, however, holding simply that the Mortmain Act was meant to prevent an evil peculiar to England, and therefore could not be considered general legislation applicable throughout the British dominions.
[68] *Campbell v. Hall, supra* note 42 at 211 [emphasis added], citing *Calvin's Case, supra* note 25, and no doubt thinking of Scotland.
[69] The reasoning and result in *Dutton, supra* note 43, following the dictum in *Calvin's Case, ibid.* The fact of "settlement" implied the vacancy (*terra nullius*) of the land in question at the time of British entry; there could be no "conquest" because there was no one to "conquer," by the sword or by treaty. However, British courts never considered a fact situation in which a treaty of cession *partitioned* the territory between the original inhabitants and British settlers, creating two geographically distinct jurisdictions. Such was the usual result of North American Indian treaties, affirmed explicitly by the Royal Proclamation of 1763, and it would naturally follow from the British Imperial legal framework of the time that Indian law would apply within lands reserved by the treaties, and English law would apply within the ceded settlements. As shown below (see *infra* notes 74–120 and accompanying text), the nineteenth century British decisions in Africa and India arrived at a similar result by a different path: they treated jurisdiction as *personal,* rather than territorial. Hence, Natives were governed by Native laws, Englishmen by English laws, unless substantial justice required some other result.

[70] Jörg Manfred Mössner, "The Barbary Powers in International Law" in Charles Henry Alexandrowicz, ed., *Grotian Society Papers* (The Hague: Martinus Nijhoff, 1972) 197; *The Helena* (1801), 4 C.Rob. 4, 165 E.R. 515.

[71] "Nam id ius ita omnibus hominibus commune est, ut religionis discrimen non admittat": Hugo Grotius, *De Jure Belli et Pacis Libri Tres, in quibus Jus Naturae et Gentium, item Juris Publici praecipua explicantur* (Washington, D.C.: Carnegie Institution, 1913) lib. II, c. XV, s. 8 at 266. See also Emerich de Vattel, *Le Droit des Gens, ou, Principes de la Loi Naturelle appliqués à la Conduite et aux Affaires des Nations et des Souverains* (Washington, D.C.: Carnegie Institution, 1913) lib. I, c. XII, s. 162 at 1: 363 with respect to capacity to enter into treaties,

> la différence de Religion y est absolument étrangère. Les Peuples traitent ensemble en qualité d'hommes, & non en qualité de Chrétiens, ou de Musulmans. Leur salut commun éxige qu'ils puissant traiter entr'eux, & traiter avec sûreté.

[72] Grotius, *ibid.,* lib. II, c. XV, s. 7 at 265–66. In *Le Droit des Gens, ibid.,* lib. II, c. XII, s. 155 at 1: 389, Vattel says of a protected state: "il peut faire de Traités & contracter des Alliances, á moins qu'il n'ait expressément renoncé á ce droit sans le Traité de Protection." See also Henry Wheaton, *Elements of International Law: With a Sketch of the History of the Science* (Philadelphia: Carey, Lea & Blanchard, 1836) at 51–52, and *Worcester v. Georgia, supra* note 3 at 554. Today, this principle is reflected in the rule that treaties must be construed against any relinquishment of sovereignty.

[73] Alexandrowicz, *History of the Law of Nations, supra* note 63; Charles Henry Alexandrowicz, *The European-African Confrontation: A Study in Treaty-Making* (Leiden: A.W. Sijthoff, 1973) [Alexandrowicz, *European-African Confrontation*]; M.F. Lindley, *The Acquisition and Government of Backward Territory in International Law; Being a Treatise on the Law and Practice Relating to Colonial Expansion* (London: Longmans, Green, 1926).

[74] As Lord Brougham observed in *Mayor of Lyon v. East India Company* (1836), 1 Moo. P.C. 175 at 274–75, 12 E.R. 782 [*Mayor of Lyon*]. See also *Elphinstone v. Bedreechund* (1830), 1 Kn. 316 at 336–38, 12 E.R. 340 (P.C.), and *Ex-Rajah of Coorg v. East India Company* (1860), 29 Beav. 300 at 307–8, 59 E.R. 642 (P.C.), in which the Privy Council reasoned that no rights vested in Native rulers until the final cessation of hostilities and definitive treaty of peace with the Crown.

[75] William Lee-Warner, *The Native States of India* (New York: AMS Press, 1971). Similarities between British treaty-making in India, British and American treaties with Native Americans, and the Romans' use of treaties in their piecemeal acquisition of Celtiberia (Spain) are noted by Frank, *supra* note 13 at 232: in particular, the tactical uses of dishonesty by Imperial agents. In India as well as the Far East, the sovereign often acted in right of the protected state, and to the extent delegated by treaty, rather than in his capacity as the ruler of Great Britain. See *e.g. Imperial Japanese Government v. D.O. Co.*, [1875] A.C. 644; *Secretary of State for Foreign Affairs v. Charlesworth, Pilling & Co.*, [1901] A.C. 373.

[76] See Harihar Prasad Dubey, *A Short History of the Judicial Systems of India and Some Foreign Countries* (Bombay: N.M. Tripathi, 1968) for a survey of British India's crazy quilt of specialized and local courts.

[77] M.B. Hooker, *Legal Pluralism: An Introduction to Colonial and Neo-colonial Laws* (Oxford: Clarendon Press, 1975) at 60–70, 95–99; M.P. Jain, "Custom as a Source of Law in India" in Renteln and Dundes, *supra* note 11 at 49; Lloyd I. Rudolph & Susanne Hoeber Rudolph, *The Modernity of Tradition: Political Development in India* (Chicago: University of Chicago Press, 1967) at 253–93; J. Duncan M. Derrett, *Religion, Law and the State in India* (New York: Free Press, 1968) at 274–320.

[78] Hooker, *ibid.* at 66; J.D.M. Derrett, "Justice, Equity and Good Conscience" in J.N.D. Anderson, ed., *Changing Law in Developing Countries* (London: Allen and Unwin, 1963) 144. In the minds of British judges of the nineteenth century, classifying choice-of-law rules as matters of equity rather than law implied a modest degree of additional flexibility in their application.

[79] As was the holding, for example, in *Mayor of Lyon, supra* note 74.

[80] Mark Galanter, "The Displacement of Traditional Law in Modern India" (1968) 24 Journal of Social Issues 65; Derrett, *supra* note 77 at 279–80, 286–88. In British Burma, customary laws were respected in principle but sidelined to a greater extent in practice because the Burmese embraced British law in their struggle against Native despots. See Maung Maung, *Law and Custom in Burma*

and the Burmese Family (The Hague: Martinus Nijhoff, 1963) at 20–36; Maung Maung, *Burma in the Family of Nations* (Amsterdam: Djambatan, 1957) at 75–79; J.S. Furnivall, *Colonial Policy and Practice: A Comparative Study of Burma and Netherlands India* (New York: New York University Press, 1956) at 131–36.

[81] Indian courts did not produce a jurisprudence of choice-of-laws in multiethnic disputes, however. Because some disputes undoubtedly crossed caste or ethnic lines, it is reasonable to suppose that the litigants in such disputes—no doubt to the profound relief of the judges—contented themselves with the application of imported principles of English common law.

[82] Derrett, *supra* note 77 at 277.

[83] *Ibid.* at 281. Castes were generally treated as autonomous communities in the same way as tribes: *ibid.* at 291. The American historian James Bryce, in *The Ancient Roman Empire and the British Empire in India; The Diffusion of Roman and English Law Throughout the World; Two Historical Studies* (New York: Oxford University Press, 1914) at 47–49, 108–9, noted that respect for local law was a hallmark of both empires. It was the "line of least resistance" for bureaucracies, he noted; "[t]hey accepted and carried on what they found."

[84] Derrett, *supra* note 77 at 285. This was not the approach taken in Africa, where Native judges presided over most courts, and where it was apparently assumed that the trier of fact possessed first-hand knowledge of customary laws. See Read, *supra* note 1 at 188–90.

[85] The last of the "numbered" treaties ceding Native territories in Canada to the Crown were executed in the 1920s, followed by the northern land-claims settlements made after 1975 that are "deemed" to be treaties by s. 35 of the *Constitution Act, 1982*. On the relationship between Canadian sovereignty in the Arctic and the settlement of northern land claims, see Russel L. Barsh, "Demilitarizing the Arctic as an Exercise of Indigenous Self-Determination" (1986) 55 Nordic J. Int'l L. 208.

[86] William Cornelius Ekow Daniels, *The Common Law in West Africa* (London: Butterworths, 1964) at 349.

[87] Hooker, *supra* note 77 at 113, 129. In the absence of applicable legislation, Nigerian courts ordinarily applied "the native law and custom (or customary law) prevailing in the jurisdiction or binding between the parties, so far as it is not repugnant to natural justice, equity or good conscience" or with applicable legislation: E.A. Keay & S.S. Richardson, *The Native and Customary Courts of Nigeria* (London: Sweet and Maxwell, 1966) at 227. Also see Read, *supra* note 1 at 167–68, 174.

[88] *In re Southern Rhodesia*, [1919] A.C. 211 at 233. In this oft-quoted but generally misinterpreted case, the Indigenous people in question reputedly had been the subjects of a despotic ruler who did not respect any form of land tenure; hence, there was (ostensibly) no Native law to apply. Apart from any question of the accuracy of the law lords' ethnography, it is clear that the case did not establish a general principle that Indigenous laws are presumed to be irreconcilable with the common law. See the text *infra* to note 120; *Amodu Tijani v. Southern Nigeria (Secretary of State)*, [1921] 2 A.C. 399 [*Amodu Tijani*]; *Eshugbayi Eleko v. Government of Nigeria*, [1931] A.C. 662 [*Eshugbayi Eleko*] at 672.

[89] Hooker, *supra* note 77 at 130–37. This exception was rarely invoked, however, except in cases where British courts refused to enforce slavery, debt-bondage, or the forced removal of children from their birth mothers: Read, *supra* note 1 at 176–80; Keay & Richardson, *supra* note 87 at 233–38; Harold Child, *The History and Extent of Recognition of Tribal Law in Rhodesia* (Salisbury, Rhodesia: Rhodesia Government, Ministry of Internal Affairs, 1965) at 15–16 [Child, *Recognition of Tribunal Law in Rhodesia*]. British colonial courts upheld the discretionary customary authority of chiefs to expel troublemakers (*Macauley v. P.C. Bongay (No. 3)* (1932), 36 A.L.R. (S.L.) 319 (W.A.C.A.)), as well as polygamous succession and the levirate: Keay & Richardson, *ibid*. In *Gwao bin Kilimo v. Kisunda bin Ifuti* (1938), 1 T.L.R.(R.) 403 at 405, the High Court of Tanganyika ruled that the customary liability of parents for the actions of their adult children was repugnant to natural justice. However, the offender was a civil servant who had been "removed from the sphere of tribal influence and sanctions" for some time (*i.e.*, he no longer was bound by customary law). Parental liability was upheld in Rhodesia, moreover (Child, *ibid.*), and not struck down anywhere else in British Africa. Repugnancy remains an issue in British conflicts-of-laws cases, *e.g.*, *Sowa v. Sowa*, [1960] 3 All E.R. 196 (Ghanaian woman's right to support under a polygamous tribal custom marriage not enforceable

in England); but compare *Ohochuku v. Ohochuku*, [1960] 1 All E.R. 253 (an English court will not grant a divorce from a polygamous tribal custom marriage celebrated in Nigeria).

[90] Keay & Richardson, *ibid.* at 240–41 and cases cited therein.

[91] (1955), 14 W.A.C.A. 12.

[92] Eugene Cotran, "The Place and Future of Customary Law in East Africa" in *East African Law Today* (London: British Institute of International and Comparative Law, 1966) 72 at 74. Lord Denning, author of the *Indian Association of Alberta* judgment, *supra* note 62, participated in the London conference that produced this volume, and wrote the introductory chapter.

[93] [1944] A.C. 170 at 172–73, upholding the applicability of Native customary law to the selection of chiefs despite the fact that a 1933 ordinance required chiefs to maintain "order and good government." British imposition of this duty on chiefs did not expressly address their selection and therefore offered "no ground for overruling the traditional law and custom in the matter": *ibid.* at 174. The determination of compliance with applicable Native customs was subsequently entrusted by ordinance to the discretion of the governor after "due inquiry." The Privy Council construed this procedural standard in *Memudu Lagunju v. Olubadan-in-Council*, [1952] A.C. 397, concluding that it barred a judicial remedy.

[94] Thus, for example, the 1889 Charter of Rhodesia provided that "[i]n the administration of justice to the said peoples or inhabitants careful regard shall always be had to the customs and laws of the class or tribe or nation to which the parties respectively belong." Quoted and discussed in Child, *Recognition of Tribal Law in Rhodesia*, *supra* note 89 at 9. See Read, *supra* note 1 at 167, n. 2, for some of the relevant East African orders in council.

[95] *Eshugbayi Eleko*, *supra* note 88 at 673.

[96] "I wish we had never used the phrase [native law and custom]," one British administrator in Tanganyika complained. "It means no more than 'the common law of Tanganyika.' The common law of England is English native law and custom": Read, *supra* note 1 at 172.

[97] *Brima Balogun v. Oshodi* (1929), 10 N.L.R. 36 at 53, Webber J., reversed on other grounds *sub nom. Oshodi v. Balogun* (1936), 4 W.A.C.A. 1; accord, *Golightly v. Ashrifi* (1955), 14 W.A.C.A. 676 at 684.

[98] Cotran, *supra* note 92 at 73–74. Needless to say, African magistrates gradually absorbed much of the British jurisprudence to which they were continually exposed, and British codification schemes made African tribal law considerably less flexible and less meaningful to Africans: *ibid.* at 78; Keay & Richardson, *supra* note 87 at 229; Read, *supra* note 1 at 180, 193–99; Sally Falk-Moore, "Treating Law as Knowledge: Telling Colonial Officers What to Say to Africans About Running 'Their Own' Native Courts" (1992) 26 Law & Soc. Inquiry 11; Antony N. Allott, "The Future of African Law" in Hilda Kuper & Leo Kuper, eds., *African Law: Adaptation and Development* (Berkeley: University of California Press, 1965) 216.

[99] [1965] E.A. 278 at 284, Crabbe J.A.

[100] *Ibid.*, reversing a ruling of the Uganda High Court that Native courts could enforce only customary laws in existence in 1940, *i.e.*, on the date of the Uganda ordinance creating the Native court system. See Read, *supra* note 1 at 207–9, for more Ugandan cases on the evolving nature of customary law, and Keay & Richardson, *supra* note 87 at 228–29, for a brief summary of Nigerian law on this point. Needless to say, many of the changes in customary laws reflected Anglicization. See *e.g. Lewis v. Bankole* (1908), 1 N.L.R. 81 (adaptations to English forms of individual land tenure); *Golightly v. Ashrifi*, *supra* note 97 (adaptations to English ideals of democratic selection in the case of chiefs).

[101] (1940), 6 W.A.C.A. 52.

[102] There were also cases in which Indigenous law was successfully advanced as a defence against criminal responsibility, *e.g.*, on grounds of provocation or self-defence, as in *R. v. Nunguyashi* (1941), 8 E.A.C.A. 55, or in *R. v. Karonga and 52 Others* (1913), 5 E. Afr. L.R. 50. In the latter case, community leaders' belief that they had acted properly in burning an alleged witch to death was the basis for a significant reduction in the charges upon which they were convicted.

[103] Compare *Caldwell v. Vanvlissengen* (1851), 9 Hare. 415, 68 E.R. 571, which contends that the courts never apply foreign laws, but rather adopt reasonable principles of decision discovered in foreign

laws and thus make them British laws.

[104] *Bangbose v. Daniel*, [1955] A.C. 107 at 117, and the Chinese polygamy cases cited therein, at 118. See, too, the principle upheld in *Pappoe v. Kweku*, (1924) F.C. 158 (Full Court of Nigeria) at 161 [*Pappoe*], that the head of a lineage is not accountable for losses of the personal property of the lineage. Hooker, *supra* note 77 at 132 criticizes *Pappoe* as either politically motivated or a misinterpretation of local laws.

[105] *Opanin Asong Kwasi v. Joseph Richard Obuadabong Larbi*, [1952] A.C. 165. Referrals to peacemakers (mediation) have become routine in many American Indian tribal court systems; see *e.g. Navajo Nation v. Ethelyn Begay* (23 September 1997), No. CP-CR-2759-96 Navajo Nation Court of Appeal, dismissing the charges against a defendant who had complied with referral to a peacemaker. Many tribal court decisions are available on-line from the American Indian Lawyer Training Program (AILTP) at <http://www.tribal-institute.org/lists/decision.htm>.

[106] The Privy Council agreed with the Supreme Court of the Gold Coast that the ordinances creating the territory's judicial system "did not sweep away the judicial powers of the Native kings and chiefs"; thus, "native customary law governs not only the substantive law administered by the Native tribunals, but also their practice and procedure" except in so far as they have been expressly modified by legislation: *ibid.* at 172. The question of whether a party can withdraw from the elders' proceedings before a decision is made was also resolved by reference to customary law: *ibid.* at 179.

[107] *Supra* note 89. See to similar effect *Quechan Tribe v. Rowe*, 531 F.2d 408 (9th Cir., 1976) (Indian tribes have inherent power to expel undesirables).

[108] *Enimil v. Tuakyi* (1950), 13 W.A.C.A. 8 at 9. If one of the parties was English, it was often presumed that they had chosen English law unless there were substantial reasons of justice to hold otherwise: see e.g. *Koney v. Union Trading Co. Ltd.* (1934), 2 W.A.C.A. 188 at 191. See also *Osagwu v. Dominic Soldier*, [1959] N.R.N.L.R. 39, in which the Northern Rhodesian High Court expressly ruled that the local law applicable is the law of the parties, not of the forum (discussed in Keay and Richardson, *supra* note 87 at 259–60).

[109] *Kwesi-Johnson v. Effie* (1953), 14 W.A.C.A. 254; *Vanderpuye v. Plange* (1942), 8 W.A.C.A. 170; *U.A.C. v. Kwadjo Apaw* (1936), 3 W.A.C.A. 114. English law was also presumed to apply to marriages celebrated in Christian churches: *Smith v. Smith* (1924), 5 N.L.R. 105 at 107; *Ajayi v. White* (1945), 18 N.L.R. 41 at 44. These presumptions were subject to rebuttal, however. In *Nelson v. Nelson* (1951), 13 W.A.C.A. 248, the defendant was a family trustee under customary law who used funds under his care to purchase and later re-sell land for his own profit. To avoid substantial injustice, the court disregarded the English-style conveyances and decided the case entirely under customary law. See also *Shaheen v. Duralia* (1920), 36 A.L.R. (S.L.) 3.

[110] Keay & Richardson, *supra* note 87 at 250, 256, 260, 271.

[111] See *e.g. Enimil v. Tuakyi*, *supra* note 108, in which a customary interest, seized and sold in execution of a judgment and later mortgaged by the purchaser and re-sold by the mortgagee, was held still to be subject to customary laws after twenty years. Compare *Alade v. Aborisade*, [1962] W.N.L.R. 74 at 83–84. See also *Munyae and Muthwa v. Kilili and Maithya* (Uganda 1962), 10 Court of Review Law Reports 5, holding that while a tenancy conferred no vested rights under Kamba law, a tenant who had been in peaceable possession for thirty-five years acquired ownership as a matter of natural justice. See Read, *supra* note 1 at 178.

[112] (1956), 1 A.L.R. Mal. 344 (Malawi Criminal Appeals).

[113] Compare *Means v. District Court* of the *Chinle Judicial District*, (11 May 1999), Navajo, No. SC-CV-61-98, in which the Navajo Supreme Court held that the defendant, a Lakota Sioux, had subjected himself to Navajo law by marrying and cohabiting with a Navajo woman. Available on-line from AILTP, *supra* note 105.

[114] *Amodu Tijani*, *supra* note 88, extended to other Nigerian Native lands by *Sunmonu v. Disu Raphael*, [1927] A.C. 881 at 884.

[115] Compare *West Rand Central Mining Co. v. The King*, [1905] 2 K.B. 391 at 406 [*West Rand Mining*], in which the petitioner sought compensation from the Crown for gold seized by the South African Republic during the Boer War, on the theory that the Crown succeeded by conquest to the

liabilities of the republic. "The considerations which applied to peaceable cession raise such different questions from those which apply to conquest that it would answer no useful purpose to discuss them in detail." *West Rand Mining, ibid.* is the first Imperial decision after *Campbell v. Hall, supra* note 42, to distinguish between the consequences of peaceful annexation and the seizure of property during the course of a war.

[116] *Sakariyawo Oshodi v. Moriamo Dakolo,* [1930] A.C. 667 [*Sakariyawo Oshodi*]; distinguished, *Nalukuya v. Director of Lands,* [1957] A.C. 325 at 333, in the case of Fiji, which had a different history and system of social organization.

[117] *Sakariyawo Oshodi, ibid.* at 670.

[118] [1899] A.C. 572 at 575–77.

[119] *Ibid.* at 579. Compare *Johnson v. M'Intosh,* 21 U.S. (8 Wheat.) 543 (1823), which involved a land grant made to an individual settler prior to the treaty of cession to the United States. The United States Supreme Court held that a treaty of cession extinguishes the pre-existing Indigenous legal regime in the absence of express terms to the contrary. However, in *Worcester v. Georgia, supra* note 3, the Supreme Court later ruled that treaties with Indian tribes must be construed against any implied loss of Indigenous sovereignty. See similarly *Duff Development Co. v. Kelantan Government,* [1924] A.C. 797 (treaty of protection did not extinguish Native ruler's sovereignty); *The King v. Earl of Crewe, ex parte Sekgome,* [1910] 2 K.B. 576 at 619, Kennedy L.J.: "What the idea of a Protectorate excludes, and the idea of annexation on the other hand would include, is that absolute ownership which was signified by 'dominium' in Roman law."

[120] *In re Southern Rhodesia, supra* note 88. To the extent that they protect royal prerogative, these cases are consistent with the criteria for the application of customary laws enunciated by the judges in the *Case of Tanistry, supra* note 28.

[121] (1888), 14 A.C. 46 (P.C.) [*St. Catherine's*], aff'g (1887), 13 S.C.R. 577.

[122] (U.K.), 30 & 31 Vict., c. 3, now styled the *Constitution Act, 1867.* The province of Ontario argued that the land at issue fell within s. 109 of the same Act, which reserved Crown lands in each of the provinces to the provincial governments, subject to "any Interest other than that of the Province in the same." *St. Catherine's, ibid.,* held that Ottawa lacked any constitutional authority to dispose of the surrendered land by lease; Ottawa then tried to recoup the expenses of acquiring the surrender in *Dominion of Canada v. Province of Ontario,* [1910] A.C. 637, which also did not address the nature of Indian nations' unsurrendered rights.

[123] *St. Catherine's, ibid.* at 60.

[124] "There was a great deal of learned discussion at the Bar with respect to the precise quality of the Indian right, but their Lordships do not consider it necessary to express any opinion on the point": *ibid.* at 54–55. It is probably fair to say that Lord Watson's "personal and usufructuary" remark was an ill-chosen legal fiction for settling a difficult point of Canadian federalism, rather than a deliberative ruling on the treatment of Indigenous peoples.

[125] *Amodu Tijani, supra* note 88; see also *In re Southern Rhodesia, supra* note 88 at 234, Lord Sumner:

> [T]here are indigenous peoples whose legal conceptions, though differently developed, are hardly less precise than our own. When once they have been studied and understood, they are no less enforceable than rights arising under English law.

Although the Privy Council could not discern a Native land tenure system to enforce in the Rhodesian case, they found enforceable Native law in Nigeria. The existence of Native land rights under Indigenous tenures is therefore not settled universally as a matter of law, but is a question of fact in the specific case—that is, what the Supreme Court of Canada was unable to recognize until nearly a century later, in *Delgumuukw, supra* note 7.

[126] Paul Tennant, *Aboriginal Peoples and Politics: The Indian Land Question in British Columbia, 1849–1989* (Vancouver: University of British Columbia Press, 1990) especially at 96–113; E. Brian Titley, *A Narrow Vision: Duncan Campbell Scott and the Administration of Indian Affairs in Canada* (Vancouver: University of British Columbia Press, 1986) at 135–61. The offence was created by a 1927 amendment to the *Indian Act*: S.C. 1927, c. 32, s. 6; R.S.C. 1927, s. 141; repealed S.C. 1951, c.

29, s. 123; see Tennant, *ibid.* at 111–12. Ottawa was willing to litigate Native title claims during this period only on the condition that First Nations agree in advance to the extinguishment of their rights (with money compensation) if they were successful: Titley, *ibid.* at 143. Extinguishment continued to be demanded even after the recognition of "aboriginal and treaty rights" in the *Constitution Act, 1982*: see Canada, *Living Treaties: Lasting Agreements; Report of the Task Force to Review Comprehensive Claims Policy* (Ottawa: Department of Indian Affairs and Northern Development, 1985) at 10–13.

[127] On the original policy behind the American tribal court system, see Russel L. Barsh & James Y. Henderson, "Tribal Courts, the Model Code, and the Police Idea in American Indian Policy" (1976) 40 Law & Contemp. Probs. 25. Supreme Court decisions have eroded the personal and subject-matter jurisdiction of tribal governments and their courts over the past fifteen years; see *e.g. Brendale v. Confederated Tribes of the Yakima Nation*, 492 U.S. 408 (1989); *Duro v. Reina*, 495 U.S. 676 (1990); *South Dakota v. Bourland*, 508 U.S. 679 (1993).

[128] Surprisingly little has been written critically on the history of thinking behind Canada's Indian policies, in view of the fact that the courts played virtually no role in shaping Native rights until the 1980s. The best overview of changing administrative ideas on local self-government continues to be Wayne Daugherty & Dennis Madill, *Indian Government under Indian Act Legislation 1868–1951* (Ottawa: Department of Indian and Northern Affairs, 1980).

[129] Although customary laws are rarely mentioned in federal or tribal courts (see Barsh, "Putting the Tribe in Tribal Courts," *supra* note 3), they have occasionally been challenged as violations of civil rights: see *In re Sah Quah*, 31 F. 327 (D. Alaska, 1886) (slavery); *Santa Clara Pueblo v. Martinez*, 436 U.S. 49 (1978) (gender discrimination in tribal membership rules). Read, *supra* note 1, observes (at 181–82) that there was far more litigation involving customary laws in British West Africa than in East Africa, and attributes this to the fact that the West African Native court system was older and attended by a larger and more active, longer-established Indigenous bar.

[130] See *e.g. Williams v. Lee*, 358 U.S. 217 (1959) at 222; *McClanahan v. Arizona Tax Commission*, 411 U.S. 164 (1971); *National Farmers Union Insurance Co. v. Crow Tribe*, 471 U.S. 845 (1985).

[131] *Chilkat Indian Village v. Johnson*, 870 F.2d 1469 (9th Cir., 1989) (the authority to dispose of Tlingit clan-house carvings is a matter of Tlingit customary law that must be decided by a Tlingit court).

[132] On the contemporary relationship between Québecois nationalism and First Nations' self-determination, see Russel L. Barsh, "Aboriginal Peoples and Quebec: Competing for Legitimacy as Emerging Nations" (1997) 21 American Indian Culture & Research Journal 1, and Russel L. Barsh, "The Aboriginal Issue in Canadian Foreign Policy" (1995) 12 Int'l J. Can. Stud. 107.

[133] This is the thread that runs through George F.G. Stanley's classic study, *The Birth of Western Canada: A History of the Riel Rebellions* (Toronto: University of Toronto Press, 1961). See also Howard Palmer & Tamara Palmer, *Alberta: A New History* (Edmonton: Hurtig, 1990) at 29–70 for an overview of the interactions of railroad, settlement, and Indian policies in relation to fears of the United States. For background on earlier Canadian fears of American motives, see Peter B. Waite, *The Life and Times of Confederation 1864–1867: Politics, Newspapers, and the Union of British North America* (Toronto: University of Toronto Press, 1962) at 28–34.

[134] Alexander Morris, *The Treaties of Canada with the Indians of Manitoba and the North-West Territories; Including the Negotiations on Which They Were Based, and other Information Relating Thereto* (Toronto: Belfords Clark, 1880). Morris, lieutenant-governor of Manitoba and Canada's first treaty commissioner, felt that securing the complete allegiance of prairie nations was "one of the gravest of the questions" facing Canada after Confederation: *Ibid.* at 2.

[135] Alexandrowicz, *European-African Confrontation*, *supra* note 73 at 46–47. The American delegation at the Berlin conference strenuously objected to this conclusion, arguing that "recognition of the right of native races . . . to dispose freely of themselves and of their hereditary soil" was recognized in international law: *ibid.* at 47. It is noteworthy that the final act of the conference imposed upon the British Empire and other contracting parties the duty to adopt measures for "the protection of the indigenous populations and the improvement of the moral and material conditions of existence." See c. I, s. 6 and c. VI of the *General Act of the Conference . . . respecting the Congo, signed at Berlin, 26 February 1885* in Clive Parry, ed., 165 Consolidated Treaty Series 485 (Dobbs Ferry, NY: Oceana,

1978). Also see Stig Förster, Wolfgang J. Mommsen & Ronald Robinson, eds., *Bismarck, Europe, and Africa: The Berlin Africa Conference 1884-1885 and the Onset of Partition* (Oxford: Oxford University Press, 1988).

[136] (U.K.) 50 & 51 Vict., c. 54, s. 6.

[137] (U.K.) 53 & 54 Vict., c. 37, ss. 1, 2. By s. 6 of this act, "persons enjoying Her Majesty's protection . . . shall include all subjects of the various princes and states in India." See also the *Pacific Islanders Protection Act, 1872*, 35 & 36 Vict., c. 19, s. 1, authorizing the British courts to punish "outrages" against Indigenous people inhabiting any part of the Pacific "not being in Her Majesty's dominions, nor within the jurisdiction of any civilized power."

[138] *India (Secretary of State) v. Sardar Rustam Khan*, [1941] A.C. 356; *Sobhuza II v. Miller*, [1926] A.C. 518 at 524; *R. v. Earl of Crewe, ex parte Sekgome*, supra note 119. It is difficult to escape the conclusion that Indigenous peoples lost more ground in Canada than elsewhere in the British Empire during this period because of their numerical minority, which meant that they represented less of a threat to British settlers, and less of a potential grassroots force in colonial politics, compared to India or British Africa.

[139] As forcefully affirmed by *Entick v. Carrington* (1765), 19 State Trials 1030 at 1066–67.

[140] (1924), L.R. 51 I.A. 357 at 360 [emphasis added].

[141] Thus, in *Ex parte Mwenya*, [1960] 1 Q.B. 241, the Court of Appeal held that writs of habeas corpus run wherever the Crown exercises dominion, regardless of the precise nature or source of that dominion. This follows the reasoning in *Mostyn*, supra note 37.

[142] See *e.g. Nissan v. Attorney General*, [1970] A.C. 179; *Walker v. Baird*, [1892] A.C. 491.

[143] *Schmidt v. Home Secretary*, [1969] 2 Ch. 149, Lord Denning; followed in *Laker Airways v. Board of Trade*, [1977] 2 All E.R. 182 at 193, Lord Denning M.R.; *R. v. Secretary of State for Foreign & Commonwealth Affairs, ex parte Everett*, [1989] All E.R. 655 at 660, Taylor L.J.; and in Canada, *Operation Dismantle v. The Queen*, [1985] 1 S.C.R. 441 at 464–74, Wilson J., concurring. "It is the duty of the courts to be alert now as they always have been to prevent abuses of the prerogative": *Chandler v. Department of Public Prosecutions*, [1964] A.C. 763 at 811, Lord Devlin. But see *Council of Civil Service Unions v. Minister for Civil Service*, [1985] 1 A.C. 374 (H.L.) at 418, Lord Roskill, shielding at least some exercises of prerogative from review.

[144] Keay & Richardson, supra note 87, and Derrett, supra note 77, offer the most detailed accounts of legislative reforms of Native court systems after 1890.

[145] (U.K.) 28 & 29 Vict., c. 63.

[146] (U.K.) 22 Geo. V, c. 4, especially ss. 2–4.

[147] For recent critical studies see *e.g.* Tennant, supra note 126, on British Columbia, and William C. Wicken, *Mi'kmaq Treaties on Trial: History, Land, and Donald Marshall Junior* (Toronto: University of Toronto Press, 2002) on Nova Scotia. On both coasts of Canada, settlers used their colonial assembles to legislate away the lands and resources of Aboriginal peoples, often in disregard of instructions received from the sovereign and Imperial ministers.

[148] *Supra* note 42. The Australian High Court in *Mabo*, supra note 1, appears to agree.

[149] C.W.M. Hart, "The Problem of Laws" in C.T. Loram & T.F. McIlraith, eds., *The North American Indian Today* (Toronto: University of Toronto Press, 1943) 251.

[150] See our critical assessment of this project in Russel L. Barsh & James Y. Henderson, *The Road: Indian Tribes and Political Liberty* (Berkeley: University of California Press, 1980) at 96–132.

[151] *Indian Act, 1951*, c. 29, s. 87 as continued by R.S.C. 1952, c. 149. This provision is now s. 88 of the *Indian Act*, R.S.C. 1985, c. I-5.

[152] Act of 15 August 1953, Pub. L. No. 83-280, c. 505, 67 Stat. 588. The jurisdictional consequences of the act for the sixteen states that exercise "mandatory" or "optional" powers in accordance with its terms have been construed most thoroughly in: *Kennerly v. District Court*, 400 U.S. 423 (1971); *Bryan v. Itasca County*, 426 U.S. 373 (1976); and *Washington v. Confederated Bands of Yakima Indian Nation*, 439 U.S. 463 (1979). It is significant that Public Law 83-280, like s. 87 of the *Indian Act, 1951*, contains an express savings clause for treaty rights.

[153] S. 87 (now s. 88) of the *Indian Act, 1951* subjected "Indians" to provincial laws "of general applica-

tion" (laws that do not single out Aboriginal people for separate treatment) that are consistent with relevant federal laws and treaties. This formula describes a large or small legislative space, depending upon who bears the burden of proof with regard to generality and consistency. After *Simon, supra* note 58, and *R. v. Sparrow*, [1990] 1 S.C.R. 1075, the Supreme Court seemed inclined to place the burden of proof on the Crown, taking account of the constitutional entrenchment of "aboriginal and treaty rights" by s. 35 of the *Constitution Act, 1982*. Before 1982, the constitutionality of s. 87 (now s. 88) of the *Indian Act* could be attacked only as an unacceptable delegation to the provinces of exclusively federal legislative power. Under s. 35, there is also a question of whether provincial laws are broadly incompatible with the retained "aboriginal and treaty rights" of the Aboriginal peoples concerned—in particular, if Aboriginal peoples bear a heavy financial burden of challenging provincial laws one by one.

[154] [1964] S.C.R. 642 [*Sikyea*].

[155] [1966] S.C.R. 267 [*George*].

[156] [1964] 2 C.C.C. 325. Compare *Simon, supra* note 58 at 413, which suggested that legislation may regulate the exercise of a treaty right without extinguishing the right.

[157] *George, supra* note 155 at 279.

[158] *Ibid.* at 280–81.

[159] *Canada (A.G.) v. Hallett & Carey*, [1952] A.C. 427 at 450–51, Lord Radcliffe. Of course, recent Supreme Court decisions grounded on s. 35 of the *Constitution Act, 1982* go much farther to protect treaty rights than earlier general constitutional principles of statutory construction.

[160] *Ibid.*

[161] *Supra* note 62. The Indian Association of Alberta argued that the British Parliament could not use the *Constitution Act, 1982* to cut off the Empire's treaty obligations to First Nations without First Nations' consent; see also *Manuel v. Attorney General*, [1983] Ch. 77. Three of the provinces made an equally unsuccessful parallel argument against the validity of the *Constitution Act, 1982*, based on claims of retained sovereignty in *Re Amendment of the Constitution of Canada*, [1981] S.C.R. 753 at 801–6.

[162] *Indian Association of Alberta, ibid.* at 645, Lord Denning M.R.

[163] *Ibid.*

[164] *Ibid.* at 647–48, citing *Campbell v. Hall, supra* note 42.

[165] See *e.g.* Jörg Fisch, "Law as a Means and as an End: Some Remarks on the Function of European and Non-European Law in the Process of European Expansion" in W.J. Mommsen & J.A. de Moor, eds., *European Expansion and Law: The Encounter of European and Indigenous Law in 19th- and 20th-Century Africa and Asia* (Oxford & New York: Berg, 1992) 15 at 27–32; Hooker, *supra* note 77 at 2.

[166] [1998] 2 S.C.R. 217 at 261–62.

[167] It is significant that the International Labour Organization's (ILO) influential *Convention on Indigenous and Tribal Peoples, 1989* (No. 169) supports the application of Indigenous laws to the extent that such laws are consistent with human rights and fundamental freedoms. Such limitations on sovereignty have been objectionable to some, but not most, contemporary international Indigenous leaders. See Russel L. Barsh, "Indigenous Peoples and the Idea of Individual Human Rights" (1995) 10 Native Studies Review 35. The text of the 1989 ILO convention, its current status with respect to ratifications, and authoritative interpretations of its provisions by ILO bodies are available on-line from ILOLEX <http://www.ilo.org/ilolex/english/index.htm>.

[168] As very persuasively argued by T.R.S. Allan, *Law, Liberty, and Justice: Legal Foundations of British Constitutionalism* (Oxford: Clarendon Press, 1993) at 25. Naturally, non-Aboriginal Canadians may feel that *their* legitimate expectations of continuity are violated by the resurrection of Indigenous rights and legal regimes. But this is an inherent problem of justice in an unequal society: the strong will always prefer to maintain the status quo, whilst the weak seek to change it. At least we may argue in the Indigenous case that the goal of reform is to restore in some practical contemporary format the status quo ante, restoring the legitimate expectations of the weak at the expense of the most recent gains of the strong. In any event, as a practical matter, Canada's Aboriginal peoples must convince other Canadians that they too will benefit in the long run.

[169] *Ibid.* at 79. This approach is consistent with parliamentary sovereignty because the meaning of a statute "will inevitably be dependent, to some degree, on the expectations of those subject to its requirements," and a statute "can only be understood in its context, which extends to the expectations of the interpreter": *ibid.* at 79, 92.

[170] *Wills v. Bowley*, [1983] 1 A.C. 57 (H.L.) at 78, Lord Lowry. Also see *R. v. Hallstrom, ex parte W. (No. 2)*, [1986] 2 All E.R. 306 at 314, McCullough J., referring to the "canon of construction that Parliament is presumed not to enact legislation which interferes with the liberty of the subjects without making it clear that this was its intention."

[171] We often say that we are looking for the intention of Parliament, but that is not quite accurate. We are seeking the meaning of the words which Parliament used. We are seeking not what Parliament meant but the true meaning of what they said: *Black-Clawson International v. Papierwerke Waldhof-Aschaffenberg*, [1975] A.C. 591 at 613, Lord Reid. This is necessarily exactly the opposite of the approach taken in treaty interpretation, where the aim is not to protect the subject from an abuse of state power, but to ensure that the parties' own expectations are realized.

[172] *Ibid.* at 638, Lord Diplock.

CONTINUITY OF ABORIGINAL RIGHTS

Kent McNeil

Note: Professor McNeil submitted this paper for inclusion in this book well before the Nova Scotia Court of Appeal released its decision in R. v. Marshall, *[2004] 2 C.N.L.R. 211. Cromwell J.A.'s decision for the court in that case includes extensive discussion of the continuity issue (at paras. 157–181); his conclusions on some points are substantially the same as those that Professor McNeil had already reached independently. The congruence between the two presentations is, therefore, coincidental. The version of Professor McNeil's paper published below takes account of, and incorporates reference to, the* Marshall *decision. On 29 April 2004, the Supreme Court of Canada granted leave to appeal the* Marshall *decision. At this writing, the appeal is awaiting oral argument before the Court.*—Ed.

In 1982, the existing Aboriginal and treaty rights of the Aboriginal peoples of Canada were recognized and affirmed, without definition, by s. 35(1) of the *Constitution Act, 1982*.[1] Attempts during four constitutional conferences in the 1980s to define those rights were largely unsuccessful.[2] As a result, the onerous task of definition has been left to the courts. Since 1990, the Supreme Court of Canada has responded to this challenge in a series of decisions that have attempted to give some content to Aboriginal rights.[3] In two decisions in particular, *R. v. Van der Peet*[4] and *Delgamuukw v. British Columbia*,[5] the Court provided crucial guidelines for the identification and proof of Aboriginal rights, including Aboriginal title to land.

The *Van der Peet* and *Delgamuukw* decisions have already generated extensive discussion and commentary.[6] In this paper, I do not intend to provide any broad analysis of these cases, nor to revisit issues that have already been discussed in detail elsewhere. My goal is much more modest. I will focus on a specific aspect of these decisions that has not, as far as I know, received much attention: their discussion of the continuity of an Aboriginal right from the time it would have been acknowledged by the common law to the time a court is called upon to recognize its current existence as a constitutionally protected right.[7] The fundamental issue to be addressed is this: is proof of continuity a requirement for establishing existing Aboriginal rights in all cases, or is it only required when Aboriginal claimants rely on practices, customs, and traditions subsequent to European contact, or on occupation of land subsequent to European sovereignty, to establish their rights? I will start by examining how this matter was dealt with in *Van der Peet* and subsequent Supreme Court decisions involving Aboriginal rights other than title to land, and then consider the relevance of continuity to proof of Aboriginal title by examining the *Delgamuukw* decision.

CONTINUITY AND ABORIGINAL RIGHTS

The *Van der Peet* case involved a charge laid under the federal *Fisheries Act*[8] against Dorothy Van der Peet, a member of the Sto:lo Nation in British Columbia, for illegal sale of ten salmon. She claimed that she had an Aboriginal right, protected by s. 35(1) of the *Constitution Act, 1982*, to sell the salmon. Chief Justice Lamer, for a majority of the Supreme Court, held that she had failed to establish an Aboriginal right to exchange fish for money or other goods. In so holding, Lamer C.J. created what is known as the "integral to the distinctive culture" test for Aboriginal rights. According to this test, for an Aboriginal right to be established, it is necessary to prove that it was "an element of a practice, custom or tradition integral to the distinctive culture of the aboriginal group" prior to contact with Europeans.[9] Dorothy Van der Peet was convicted because she could not meet this test in respect of the Aboriginal right she had claimed.

Although the "integral to the distinctive culture" test has several elements, my present concern is exclusively with its continuity aspect. Chief Justice Lamer began his discussion of continuity by acknowledging how difficult it might be for Aboriginal peoples to prove what their practices, customs, and traditions had been prior to European contact.

> It would be entirely contrary to the spirit and intent of s. 35(1) to define aboriginal rights in such a fashion so as to preclude in practice any successful claim for the existence of such a right. The evidence relied upon by the applicant and the courts may relate to aboriginal practices, customs and traditions post-contact; it simply needs to be directed at demonstrating which aspects of the aboriginal community and society have their origins pre-contact. It is those practices, customs and traditions that can be rooted in the pre-contact societies of the aboriginal community in question that will constitute aboriginal rights.[10]

From this passage, Lamer C.J. appears to have regarded continuity as the means for linking post-contact practices, customs, and traditions with pre-contact Aboriginal societies, so that very real difficulties of proof would be lessened. In other words, the requirement of continuity would appear to apply only where post-contact practices, customs, and traditions were relied upon, not where an Aboriginal people was able to provide sufficient independent proof of pre-contact practices, customs, and traditions.

In the next paragraph of his judgment, Lamer C.J. elaborated on the relevance of continuity to proof of Aboriginal title. This key paragraph needs to be quoted in full:

I would note in relation to this point the position adopted by Brennan J. in *Mabo*, *supra*, where he holds, at p. 60, that in order for an aboriginal group to succeed in its claim for aboriginal title it must demonstrate that the connection with the land in its customs and laws has continued to the present day:

> ... when the tide of history has washed away any real acknowledgement of traditional law and any real observance of traditional customs, the foundation of native title has disappeared. A native title which has ceased with the abandoning of laws and customs based on tradition cannot be revived for contemporary recognition.

The relevance of this observation for identifying the rights in s. 35(1) lies not in its assertion of the effect of the disappearance of a practice, custom or tradition on an aboriginal claim (I take no position on that matter), but rather in its suggestion of the importance of considering the continuity in the practices, customs and traditions of aboriginal communities in assessing claims to aboriginal rights. It is precisely those present practices, customs and traditions which can be identified as having continuity with the practices, customs and traditions that existed prior to contact that will be the basis for the identification and definition of aboriginal rights under s. 35(1). Where an aboriginal community can demonstrate that a particular practice, custom or tradition is integral to its distinctive culture today, and that this practice, custom or tradition has continuity with the practices, customs and traditions of pre-contact times, that community will have demonstrated that the practice, custom or tradition is an aboriginal right for the purposes of s. 35(1).[11]

Although the last two sentences in this passage, if taken out of context, might be regarded as imposing a general requirement of continuity, Lamer C.J.'s comments on continuity as a whole reveal that this cannot have been what he meant. In the first place, his refusal to take a position on the assertion by Brennan J. (as he then was) in *Mabo* that Native title can be lost by discontinuance of the traditional connection with the land shows that Lamer C.J. did not intend to make continuity of practices, customs, and traditions from the time of contact with Europeans a requirement for Aboriginal rights to exist today.[12] Moreover, we have seen that Lamer C.J.'s express reason for mentioning continuity in the first place was to avoid imposing impractical burdens of proof on Aboriginal claimants.[13] As his obvious intention was to lessen the burden of proof for Aboriginal peoples, he cannot have meant to increase that burden at the same time by imposing an additional requirement of continuity that would have to be met even if pre-contact practices, customs, and traditions establishing an Aboriginal right could be proven independently.[14]

In cases where an Aboriginal right is established by proof of a pre-contact practice, custom, or tradition, it will, of course, still have to be shown that the present-day activity alleged to be an exercise of that right does in fact fall within the right's scope.[15] In other words, there has to be a sufficient connection between the present-day activity and the right in the sense that the activity is encompassed by the definition of the right, but there is no need to show continuity between the two over time from contact to the present. Moreover, failure to demonstrate that the present-day activity is sufficiently connected with the right would not invalidate the right itself; it would simply mean that that particular activity does not qualify as an exercise of the right.

This understanding of continuity is confirmed by the Supreme Court's decision in *R. v. Gladstone*,[16] delivered the same day as *Van der Peet*. In *Gladstone*, the defendants were able to prove that, as members of the Heiltsuk Nation in British Columbia, they had an Aboriginal right to harvest and sell herring spawn on kelp in commercial quantities. The evidence that led a majority of the Court to accept that the Heiltsuk had traded herring spawn on a commercial scale prior to contact with Europeans consisted of an entry in Alexander Mackenzie's journal in 1793, an entry by Dr. William Tolmie (a fur trader) in his journal in 1834, and testimony by Dr. Barbara Lane (an expert witness). In his majority judgment, Lamer C.J. said that "[t]he evidence presented in this case . . . is precisely the type of evidence which satisfies this [continuity] requirement," as described in *Van der Peet*.[17] He elaborated as follows:

> The evidence of Dr. Lane, and the diary of Dr. Tolmie, point to trade of herring spawn on kelp in "tons." While this evidence relates to trade post-contact, the diary of Alexander Mackenzie provides the link with pre-contact times; in essence, the sum of the evidence supports the claim of the appellants that commercial trade in herring spawn on kelp was an integral part of the distinctive culture of the Heiltsuk prior to contact.[18]

Lamer C.J.'s decision in *Gladstone* therefore affirms that the purpose of the continuity doctrine in this context is to permit evidence of post-contact practices, customs, and traditions to be used to prove pre-contact practices, customs, and traditions.

However, in *R. v. Adams*,[19] Lamer C.J. appears to have placed a different interpretation on this aspect of his judgments in *Van der Peet* and *Gladstone*. After concluding that the evidence showed that the Mohawks had fished for food in Lake St. Francis in what is now Quebec at the time of contact with the French in 1603 and that this was a significant part of their life from that time, he concluded that this was "sufficient to satisfy the *Van der Peet* test."[20] He nonetheless went on to say this:

> As part of the second stage of the *Van der Peet* analysis, *there must be "continuity"* between aboriginal practices, customs and traditions that existed prior to contact and a particular practice, custom or tradition that is integral to aboriginal communities today: *Van der Peet, supra*, at para. 63; *Gladstone, supra* at para. 28. This part of the *Van der Peet* test has been met as well. The evidence of numerous witnesses at trial proves the existence of continuity. . . . This was the way of their ancestors, and these practices continued into the present.[21]

The words I have emphasized in this passage might suggest that Lamer C.J. viewed his own judgments in *Van der Peet* and *Gladstone* as imposing a requirement of proof of continuity up to the present, even where the requisite pre-contact practices, customs, or traditions have been proven. However, this interpretation should be rejected, as it is inconsistent with what the chief justice actually said in *Van der Peet*, and with the way he applied the concept of continuity in *Gladstone*.[22] What he must have meant in *Adams* is that the present-day fishing activities of the Mohawks are sufficiently connected with their pre-contact fishing practices, customs, and traditions to come within the scope of the Aboriginal right to fish for food that had already been proven by the evidence.[23]

Moreover, we have seen that Lamer C.J., in *Van der Peet*, expressly avoided taking a position on Brennan J.'s views in *Mabo* on the effect of loss of traditional laws and customs on Aboriginal rights. In the passage Lamer C.J. quoted from *Mabo*, Brennan J. was referring not to establishment of Native title, but to subsequent loss of it through the disappearance of the traditional laws and customs that supported it. In this respect, there is a significant divergence between Australian and Canadian law. In Australia, Native title rights, which include hunting and fishing rights as well as title to land, are based not just on the existence but also on the actual content of traditional laws and customs in relation to the subject matter of the right.[24] Australian courts have therefore taken the position that the disappearance of the supporting laws and customs results in loss of the right.[25] In Canada, Aboriginal rights can arise from the existence of practices that were integral to distinctive Aboriginal cultures at the time of contact with Europeans, regardless of whether those practices were governed by Aboriginal laws or customs.[26] In other words, while Aboriginal laws and customs would be sources of Aboriginal rights, in Canada they are not the only sources.[27]

However, though proof of continuity does not seem to be a requirement for establishing Aboriginal rights in Canada where the requisite pre-contact practices, customs, or traditions have been established in another way, the question remains whether an Aboriginal right that was supported by a practice, custom, or tradition at the time of European contact could be lost in Canada if the practice, custom, or tradition ceased to be engaged in or followed. Although Lamer C.J. expressly avoided this question in *Van der Peet*, he did say this:

> I would note that the concept of continuity does not require aboriginal groups to provide evidence of an unbroken chain of continuity between their current practices, customs and traditions and those which existed prior to contact. It may be that for a period of time an aboriginal group, for some reason, ceased to engage in a practice, custom or tradition which existed prior to contact, but then resumed the practice, custom or tradition at a later date. Such an interruption will not preclude the establishment of an aboriginal right. Trial judges should adopt the same flexibility regarding the establishment of continuity that, as is discussed, *infra*,

they are to adopt with regards to the evidence presented to establish the prior-to-contact practices, customs and traditions of the aboriginal group making claim to an aboriginal right.[28]

Although these remarks were made in the context of proof of continuity where post-contact practices, customs, and traditions are relied upon, they nonetheless reveal that suspension of practices, customs, and traditions will not necessarily cause loss of the Aboriginal rights derived from them. This was confirmed by McLachlin J. (dissenting on other grounds) in *Van der Peet*, when she said:

> The continuity requirement does not require the aboriginal people to provide a year-by-year chronicle of how the event has been exercised since time immemorial. Indeed, it is not unusual for the exercise of a right to lapse for a period of time. Failure to exercise it does not demonstrate abandonment of the underlying right.[29]

But this might still leave open the possibility of an Aboriginal right being lost if there was an actual disappearance of the practice, custom, or tradition, rather than just suspension of the exercise of it.

Before discussing further whether the disappearance of practices, customs, and traditions can cause loss of Aboriginal rights, I should point out two things. First, I am troubled by the very concept of disappearance in this context. Customs and traditions seldom disappear; instead, they undergo modification as societies and cultures change to take account of new circumstances.[30] As for practices, they may cease, but what is to prevent them from being resumed at some time in the future? If that happens, it would seem to be more appropriate to regard them as having been suspended in the interim. So the distinction between disappearance and suspension may in fact be a false one.

Second, I think it is essential, at the risk of repetition, to clarify the onus of proof in this context. If Aboriginal people rely on a post-contact practice, custom, or tradition, it appears from Lamer C.J.'s judgment in *Van der Peet* that the onus will be on them to prove continuity to the satisfaction of the court.[31] However, if they are able to establish the existence of the right by direct proof of a pre-contact practice, custom, or tradition, then if that right could be lost by the disappearance of the practice, custom, or tradition (which I doubt, for reasons given below), the onus should be on the Crown to prove loss of the right in this way. Otherwise, Aboriginal people would end up having to prove that no loss of the right had occurred, which would involve proving continuity up to the present in addition to proving the pre-contact practice, custom, or tradition. As discussed above, this does not appear to be what Chief Justice Lamer had in mind when he discussed the matter of continuity.[32]

However, I think there are good reasons why Aboriginal rights, once established by proof of pre-contact practices, customs, and traditions, should not be lost, even if the practices, customs, and traditions upon which they were originally based have not been followed for a long time. First of all, Aboriginal rights that are based on pre-contact practices, customs, and traditions would have become enforceable at common law when that law was received into the part of Canada where the right arose.[33] Lamer C.J. affirmed this in *Van der Peet* when he said that s. 35 of the *Constitution Act, 1982* conferred constitutional protection on "aboriginal rights [that] existed and were recognized under the common law."[34] In the case of an Aboriginal practice that was not rooted in Aboriginal law or custom,[35] this means that juridical force would have been given to the practice by the common law, so that a legally enforceable right would have been created when the common law was received.[36] From then on, the practice could be engaged in as of right. As a general rule, legal rights, whether derived from custom or the common law, are not lost as a result of non-user. In *Re Yateley Common*, Foster J. said in regard to a customary right to a common:

> A right of common is a legal right, and it is exceedingly difficult to prove that a person having such a legal right has abandoned it. Non-user, if the owner of the right has no reason to exercise it, requires something more than an immense length of time of non-user. It is essential that it is proved to the court's satisfaction that the owner of the legal right has abandoned the right—in the sense that he not only has not used it but intends never to use it again. The onus lies fairly and squarely on those who assert that the right has been abandoned.[37]

So non-user of an Aboriginal right, for no matter how long, should not by itself cause the right to disappear, any more than non-user causes other legal rights to disappear.[38]

Conferral of common law recognition on Aboriginal rights therefore should be sufficient to prevent those rights from being lost without some positive act of extinguishment, even if the practices, customs, and traditions on which those rights were originally based have not recently been followed or observed. Once the *Van der Peet* test has been met by proof that those practices, customs, and traditions were integral to the Aboriginal people's distinctive culture at the time of European contact, the resultant rights would be enforceable as common law rights[39] and so would no longer need to be supported by continuance of those practices, customs, and traditions.[40] However, even if Aboriginal rights were based solely on Aboriginal custom or law (rather than on common law recognition of Aboriginal practices, customs, and traditions), those rights should not be lost as a result of not being exercised, even for long periods of time. In this respect, they deserve to be treated in the same way as customary rights in England,[41] which, as we have seen, are not lost by non-user, even if not exercised for long periods of time.[42] This is further illustrated by Lord Denman C.J.'s observation in *Scales v. Key* in 1840 that the jury's finding in that case "that the custom had existed till 1689, was the same in effect as if they had found that it had existed till last week, unless something appeared to shew that it had been legally abolished."[43] In the more recent case of *Wyld v. Silver*, Lord Denning M.R. affirmed this approach by rejecting the notion that a right to hold a fair could be lost by non-user:

> I know of no way in which the inhabitants of a parish can lose a right of this kind once they have acquired it except by Act of Parliament. Mere disuse will not do. And I do not see how they can waive it or abandon it. No one or more of the inhabitants can waive or abandon it on behalf of the others. Nor can all the present inhabitants waive or abandon it on behalf of future generations.[44]

So extinguishment of a customary right in England will occur only if the custom is expressly abolished by or is clearly inconsistent with a statute,[45] in much the same way as Aboriginal rights could only be legislatively extinguished in Canada (prior to receiving constitutional protection in 1982)[46] by or pursuant to a clear and plain enactment.[47]

The proposition that Aboriginal rights recognized by the common law cannot be lost by non-user is supported by Supreme Court jurisprudence. In *Sioui*,[48] the Court considered whether rights that had been affirmed by a treaty between the Hurons of Lorette and the British Crown in 1760 were protected in 1982 against provincial legislation by s. 88 of the *Indian Act*.[49] Among other things, the Crown contended that "non-user of the treaty over a long period of time may extinguish its effect."[50] Delivering the unanimous judgment of the Court, Lamer J. (as he then was) pointed out that the Crown had cited no authority for this contention. He then said that he did "not think that this argument carries much weight: a solemn agreement cannot lose its validity merely because it has not been invoked."[51] Although this rejection of extinguishment by non-user relates only to treaty rights, there seems to be no reason in principle why Aboriginal rights should be treated differently,[52] especially given that treaties often affirmed pre-existing Aboriginal rights.[53]

In summary, the concept of continuity, as formulated by Chief Justice Lamer in *Van der Peet* and applied by him in *Gladstone*, serves the purpose of lessening the burden of proof of Aboriginal rights by allowing Aboriginal claimants to use post-contact practices, customs, and traditions to prove the pre-contact practices, customs, and traditions necessary to establish Aboriginal rights.[54] Proof of this kind of continuity back in time is therefore required only when post-contact practices, customs, and traditions are relied upon. When, on the other hand, the *Van der Peet* "integral to the distinctive culture" test can be met by direct proof of pre-contact practices, customs, and traditions, the Aboriginal right will be established without any need to show continuity in the sense Lamer C.J. envisaged. In the latter situation, however, it will still be necessary to determine whether the present-day activity that is alleged to be an exercise of that right actually comes within its scope. If it does, the next issue is whether the right had been extinguished at any time prior to receiving constitutional recognition in 1982. Voluntary surrender of the right by treaty aside,[55] it seems that the only way extinguishment could have occurred would have been by or pursuant to clear and plain legislation, enacted by a constitutionally competent legislative body.[56]

As we have seen, these principles are supported both by the *Sioui* decision in relation to treaty rights, and by common law doctrine in relation to the continuation of legal rights generally, including legal rights arising in England from custom. Once proven, customary rights continue, even if not exercised for long periods of time, in the absence of unambiguous legislative extinguishment. As with Aboriginal rights in Canada, the concept of continuity is used to facilitate proof of a custom back to the time when it must have been in existence to qualify for legal recognition; it is not necessary to prove that the exercise of a custom, once shown to have existed at that time, has continued. Moreover, the onus of proving that a custom or an Aboriginal right has been extinguished is on the party so alleging, and is not easily met.[57]

CONTINUITY AND ABORIGINAL TITLE TO LAND

The *Delgamuukw* case arose from claims by the Wet'suwet'en and Gitxsan (spelled "Gitksan" in the judgments) nations to Aboriginal title and self-government over their traditional territories in British Columbia. The Supreme Court did not decide the merits of the claims, in part because the trial judge had not accorded adequate respect and weight to the Wet'suwet'en and Gitxsan oral histories.[58] However, in the principal judgment in the case, Chief Justice Lamer did define Aboriginal title in reasonably clear terms and provide significant direction on how it can be proven.[59]

> In order to make out a claim for aboriginal title, the aboriginal group asserting title must satisfy the following criteria: (i) the land must have been occupied prior to sovereignty, (ii) if present occupation is relied on as proof of occupation pre-sovereignty, there must be a continuity between present and pre-sovereignty occupation, and (iii) at sovereignty, that occupation must have been exclusive.[60]

The second requirement, relating directly to the matter of continuity, need be met only "if present occupation is relied on." In other words, in situations where Aboriginal claimants are able to meet the other two requirements by direct proof of exclusive occupation at the time the Crown asserted sovereignty, there should be no need to prove continuity.

This interpretation is confirmed by Lamer C.J.'s elaboration on the second requirement. Referring to his judgment in *Van der Peet*, he said that he had acknowledged in that case that

> . . . it would be "next to impossible" (at para. 62) for an aboriginal group to pro-

vide conclusive evidence of its pre-contact practices, customs and traditions. What would suffice instead was evidence of post-contact practices, which was "directed at demonstrating which aspects of the aboriginal community and society have their origins pre-contact" (at para. 62). The same concern, and the same solution, arises with respect to the proof of occupation in claims for aboriginal title, although there is a difference in the time for determination of title. Conclusive evidence of pre-sovereignty occupation may be difficult to come by. Instead, an aboriginal community may provide evidence of present occupation as proof of pre-sovereignty occupation in support of a claim to aboriginal title. What is required, in addition, is a *continuity* between present and pre-sovereignty occupation, because the relevant time for the determination of aboriginal title is at the time before sovereignty.[61]

This passage is entirely consistent with our earlier analysis of the *Van der Peet* decision and with the reason why Lamer C.J. introduced the concept of continuity in Aboriginal rights cases.[62] His evident intention was to make proof of Aboriginal rights, including title, easier by permitting evidence of post-contact practices, customs, and traditions or post-sovereignty occupation to be introduced and relied upon. He did not intend to make proof of Aboriginal rights and title more difficult by imposing a requirement of continuity in all cases, even when sufficient direct evidence of the pre-contact practices, customs, and traditions or pre-sovereignty occupation is available.

Lamer C.J. went on to say that "there is no need to establish 'an unbroken chain of continuity' (*Van der Peet*, at para. 65) between present and prior occupation," especially because

> [t]o impose the requirement of continuity too strictly would risk "undermining the very purpose of s. 35(1) [of the *Constitution Act, 1982*] by perpetuating the historical injustice suffered by aboriginal peoples at the hands of colonizers who failed to respect" aboriginal rights to land (*Côté, supra,* at para. 53).[63]

He also made it clear that "the fact that the nature of occupation has changed would not ordinarily preclude a claim for aboriginal title, as long as a substantial connection between the people and the land is maintained."[64] Taken out of context, statements such as these might be interpreted to mean that there is a general requirement of continuity for proof of Aboriginal rights and title. However, given that these passages all appear in his judgment under the heading "[i]f present occupation is relied on as proof of occupation pre-sovereignty, there must be a continuity between present and pre-sovereignty occupation,"[65] it is apparent that he was limiting the application of the concept of continuity to that situation.[66]

If Aboriginal title is proven by sufficient evidence of exclusive occupation of the claimed lands at the time of Crown assertion of sovereignty,[67] Aboriginal title will have vested at common law in the Aboriginal occupants as a community at that historical moment.[68] Once vested, Aboriginal title continues until surrendered to the Crown or extinguished by clear and plain legislative enactment.[69] Moreover, the burden of proving extinguishment of Aboriginal rights, including title, is on the Crown or other party so alleging.[70] Given these well-established principles, it is understandable that Lamer C.J. limited the requirement of proving continuity to situations where present (or at least post-sovereignty) occupation is relied upon to prove occupation at the time of Crown assertion of sovereignty.[71] If Aboriginal people had to prove post-sovereignty continuity even in cases where occupation at the time of sovereignty had been established, they would be required in effect to prove that their title had not been extinguished or otherwise lost. In addition to conflicting with Supreme Court decisions involving Aboriginal rights, such a requirement would be inconsistent with common law principles regarding property rights.

Once property and other legal rights, including rights arising from custom, are vested, they are presumed by the common law to continue until proven to have been extinguished, transferred, or otherwise relinquished.[72] The application of this fundamental principle to personal property is revealed by the rule that a chattel, even if lost, is presumed not to have been abandoned in the absence of evidence that the owner intended to give up his or her rights to it.[73] Regarding land, although title can be statutorily extinguished by adverse possession for the limitation period in some jurisdictions, the onus of proving adverse possession for the requisite time is clearly on the person attempting to establish title in this way.[74] Discontinuance of possession by the paper-titleholder, for no matter how long, will not start the time period running unless someone else has actually acquired adverse possession of the land.[75]

So even if Aboriginal title could be lost by failure to maintain a substantial connection with the land, common law principles would require that the Crown bear the onus of proving that that had happened. But is it even possible for Aboriginal title to be lost in this way? In *Delgamuukw*, Chief Justice Lamer said that Aboriginal title "is a *right to the land* itself."[76] Relying on *Canadian Pacific Ltd. v. Paul*,[77] he rejected the notion that "aboriginal title is a non-proprietary interest which amounts to no more than a licence to use and occupy the land and cannot compete on an equal footing with other proprietary interests."[78] Clearly, Aboriginal title is a real property interest, though it is unlike any other interest known to the common law because it is *sui generis* in several respects.[79] Statutory limitation periods aside, since at least *Magna Carta* of 1215 the common law has not permitted interests in land to be lost by the wrongful taking of land, whether by private individuals or by the Crown.[80] This common law protection for property rights is so fundamental that it must extend to Aboriginal title.[81] Dispossession of Aboriginal peoples should not, therefore, amount to the kind of discontinuance of connection with the land that might result in loss of title.[82]

But could Aboriginal title be lost by discontinuance of the connection with the land in circumstances amounting to abandonment? This is doubtful. At common law, lawful title to land, once acquired, probably cannot be given up or lost by abandonment.[83] It might be argued, however, that even if this is so, Aboriginal title is *sui generis* and therefore is not subject to a restriction arising mainly out of seisin and feudal conceptions of real property in England.[84] Be that as it may, there are other reasons why Aboriginal title probably cannot be lost by abandonment.[85] First, it is held communally, and it appears that communal rights cannot be waived or abandoned, particularly where the interests of future generations would be jeopardized.[86] And even if the Royal Proclamation of 1763 authorized surrender of Aboriginal title to the Crown,[87] this had to be done at a public assembly, held for that purpose, of the Indian tribe or nation whose lands were involved. No informal surrender of Aboriginal title by abandonment was contemplated or sanctioned.[88] There are thus good reasons for concluding that Aboriginal title cannot be lost by abandonment. But even if it could be, the onus of proving an intention to abandon would be on the party so alleging, and would not be easy to meet.[89]

CONCLUSIONS

Our examination of Chief Justice Lamer's decisions in *Van der Peet*, *Gladstone*, and *Delgamuukw* has revealed a consistent approach to the matter of continuity in regard to both Aboriginal title to land and other Aboriginal rights.[90] In these contexts, continuity involves a substantial maintenance of an Aboriginal people's pre-Crown sovereignty occupation of the land in the case of title, or of their pre-European contact practices, customs, and traditions in the case of other Aboriginal rights. However, continuity of this sort has to be shown only when Aboriginal peoples rely on post-sovereignty occupation or post-contact practices, customs, and traditions as evidence of their pre-sovereignty occupation or pre-contact practices, customs, and traditions. If they are able to produce adequate direct evidence of their pre-sovereignty occupation or pre-contact practices, customs, and traditions, then proof of continuity from that time is unnecessary. In other words, continuity applies backward in time to sovereignty or contact, not forward in time from those moments in history.

Although Lamer C.J. indicated in the cases we have discussed that, where post-sovereignty occupation or post-contact practices, customs, and traditions are relied upon, continuity must relate back to the time of Crown sovereignty or European contact, he also said that it is unnecessary to show "an unbroken chain of continuity."[91] In addition to allowing for gaps, this must mean that it is unnecessary to show continuity all the way back to the time of sovereignty or contact, for if that could be shown then the occupation requisite for title at the time of sovereignty, or the practices, customs, and traditions requisite for other

Aboriginal rights at the time of contact, could be proven directly in most cases without any need to rely on post-sovereignty occupation or post-contact practices, customs, and traditions. As Lamer C.J.'s express intention in allowing post-sovereignty occupation and post-contact practices, customs, and traditions to be relied upon was to make proof of Aboriginal title and other Aboriginal rights easier,[92] proof as far back as sovereignty or contact should not be necessary. All that should be required is sufficient evidence of post-sovereignty occupation or post-contact practices, customs, and traditions to raise a presumption that the land was occupied at the time of Crown assertion of sovereignty, or that the practices, customs, and traditions were in existence at the time of European contact.[93]

So if proof of continuity back to Crown sovereignty or European contact is unnecessary, how far back does the evidence have to reach? The case law on Aboriginal rights and title so far has not answered this question. There are, however, well-established rules regarding proof of custom in England, and in this respect English custom is closely analogous to the practices, customs, and traditions necessary to establish Aboriginal title.[94] Like Aboriginal practices, customs, and traditions, English custom must be proven from a particular historical moment: namely, 1189, when Richard I became king.[95] As that is almost always impossible, judges have sensibly decided that evidence that the custom was in existence as far back as living witnesses can remember will raise a presumption that the custom existed in 1189.[96] The burden of rebutting the presumption then shifts to the party opposing the custom; it can be met by showing, for example, that the custom did not exist or could not have existed in 1189.[97] This practical approach to proof of custom is supported by a legal maxim, by which courts are expected "to give effect to everything which appears to have been established for a considerable course of time, and to presume that what has been done was done of right, and not in wrong."[98] As Bramwell L.J. said in *Mayor of Penryn v. Best*, "every supposition, not wholly irrational, should be made in favour of long-continued enjoyment."[99]

The main rationale for holding that proof of a custom as far back as the memory of living witnesses goes is *prima facie* sufficient is to avoid placing an impossible burden of proof on those who seek to establish customs. As we have seen, Lamer C.J. used the same rationale in *Van der Peet* when he said that Aboriginal peoples can rely on post-European contact practices, customs, and traditions to establish their Aboriginal rights.[100] There is thus good reason to apply the same standard of proof in both these situations, so that proof that the relevant practice, custom, or tradition has been in place for as long as any witnesses can remember will raise a presumption that it was in existence at the time of contact.[101] As with custom in England, it would then be open to the Crown or other party contesting the Aboriginal right to prove that the practice, custom, or tradition has a more recent origin.[102]

The presumption utilized by the courts in relation to proof of custom does not apply to proof of title to land. Real property interests have always been of such vital importance in the common law that the courts have developed a different set of rules where title to land is concerned. As I have already discussed the application of these rules to Aboriginal title in detail elsewhere,[103] I will provide only a brief summary here. First of all, anyone who is in occupation of land is presumed to have a valid title.[104] If occupation can be proven,[105] there is no need to show that it has been continuous for as far back as living witnesses can remember, or indeed for any period of time at all. The burden of rebutting the presumption of title arising from occupation is therefore on anyone who challenges the validity of the occupier's title. But the law goes even further in protecting the occupier, for those challenging the occupier's right to the land will succeed only if they can show that they either have a better title than the occupier or are claiming the land on behalf of someone who has a better title.[106] It is not sufficient for challengers to prove that a third party has a better title, as that will not give them any right to acquire the lands themselves. These rules have been affirmed and applied in so many cases that their validity is beyond dispute. There is no doubt that they are fundamental to the common law of real property.[107]

As discussed elsewhere, there is no reason in principle why these rules in relation to proof of title to land generally should not apply to Aboriginal title.[108] Proof that an Aboriginal community had exclusive occupation of land at any time after Crown assertion of sovereignty should give rise to a presumption of Aboriginal title.[109] In other words, despite what Lamer C.J. said in *Delgamuukw* about proof of continuity being required if present occupation is relied upon,[110] there should be no need to show continuity of occupation for a presumption of Aboriginal title to arise, any more than there is a need to show continuity of occupation for any other occupier to have a presumptive title. If the Aboriginal community proves the requisite occupation,[111] the burden should then be on the Crown, if it disputes their title, to rebut the presumption of title by showing either that the land was unoccupied and therefore became Crown land unburdened by Aboriginal title at the time of assertion of sovereignty, or that the Aboriginal title was validly surrendered to the Crown or extinguished by legislation at some time after sovereignty had been asserted. Failing that, the presumptive Aboriginal title should prevail.

Canadian courts often treat Aboriginal claims as if the issues raised are ones of first impression. In one sense, this is appropriate, because these claims are unique to the circumstances of the Aboriginal peoples and their historical relationships with the Crown, and do involve complex cross-cultural issues, including the interplay of very different legal systems.[112] However, in contexts where there are relevant principles and rules in the common law that could be adapted and applied to

Aboriginal claims without discounting Aboriginal difference and distorting their rights,[113] judges should at least take those principles and rules into consideration. In particular, if the common law would provide advantages to Aboriginal peoples in proving or defending their rights, judges should have very good reasons for not extending the benefit of the common law to them.[114] Regarding proof of Aboriginal rights, including Aboriginal title to land, the common law does contain principles and rules that would help alleviate the heavy burden that Aboriginal peoples face in establishing their rights. As judges develop the concept of continuity that the Supreme Court has sketched out in this context, they should be informed by these principles and rules and apply them in ways that do not cause Aboriginal peoples to be disadvantaged.

NOTES

[*] I owe a debt of gratitude to Liza Bowman for her excellent research assistance for this paper, and to Brent Arnold for his help and suggestions. James Guest, Douglas Harris, Brian Slattery, and Kerry Wilkins also provided very helpful comments, for which I am most grateful. The financial support of the Social Sciences and Humanities Research Council of Canada is also gratefully acknowledged.

[1] Schedule B to the *Canada Act 1982* (U.K.), 1982, c.11.

[2] See Kent McNeil, "The Decolonization of Canada: Moving Toward Recognition of Aboriginal Governments" (1994) 7 Western Legal History 113 at 122–26, reprinted in Kent McNeil, *Emerging Justice? Essays on Indigenous Rights in Canada and Australia* (Saskatoon: University of Saskatchewan Native Law Centre, 2001) 161 at 168–71 [McNeil, *Emerging Justice?*].

[3] Treaty rights, on the other hand, depend on the terms, both written and unwritten, of the particular treaty in question. So although the Supreme Court has developed principles for treaty interpretation, it has not defined and could not define treaty rights in any general way. Some of the leading cases on treaty rights are *Simon v. The Queen*, [1985] 2 S.C.R. 387 [*Simon*]; *R. v. Sioui*, [1990] 1 S.C.R. 1025 [*Sioui*]; *R. v. Badger*, [1996] 1 S.C.R. 771 [*Badger*]; *R. v. Sundown*, [1999] 1 S.C.R. 393; *R. v. Marshall*, [1999] 3 S.C.R. 456 [*Marshall I*]; *R. v. Marshall*, [1999] 3 S.C.R. 533 [*Marshall II*]. For recent critical analysis of the Court's principles of treaty interpretation, see Gordon Christie, "Justifying Principles of Treaty Interpretation" (2000) 26 Queen's L.J. 143. Treaty rights will not be discussed in this paper.

[4] [1996] 2 S.C.R. 507 [*Van der Peet*].

[5] [1997] 3 S.C.R. 1010 [*Delgamuukw*].

[6] For a sampling of the academic commentary, see John Borrows, "Frozen Rights in Canada: Constitutional Interpretation and the Trickster" (1997) 22 Am. Indian L. Rev. 37 [Borrows, "Frozen Rights"]; John Borrows, "Sovereignty's Alchemy: An Analysis of *Delgamuukw* v. *British Columbia*" (1999) 37 Osgoode Hall L.J. 537; Russel Lawrence Barsh & James Youngblood Henderson, "The Supreme Court's *Van der Peet* Trilogy: Naive Imperialism and Ropes of Sand" (1997) 42 McGill L.J. 993; Catherine Bell, "New Directions in the Law of Aboriginal Rights" (1998) 77 Can. Bar Rev. 36; Nigel Bankes, "*Delgamuukw*, Division of Powers and Provincial Land and Resource Laws: Some Implications for Provincial Resource Rights" (1998) 32 U.B.C. L. Rev. 317; Kerry Wilkins, "Of Provinces and Section 35 Rights" (1999) 22 Dal. L.J. 185; Owen Lippert, ed., *Beyond the Nass Valley: National Implications of the Supreme Court's Delgamuukw Decision* (Vancouver: Fraser Institute, 2000); Brian Slattery, "Making Sense of Aboriginal and Treaty Rights" (2000) 79 Can. Bar Rev. 196; Gordon Christie, "*Delgamuukw* and the Protection of Aboriginal Land Interests" (2000–2001) 32 Ottawa L. Rev. 85; Kent McNeil, "Aboriginal Title and Section 88 of the *Indian Act*" (2000) 34 U.B.C. L. Rev. 159; McNeil, *Emerging Justice?*, *supra* note 2; and papers posted online: Delgamuukw/Gisday'wa National Process <http://www.delgamuukw.org>.

[7] The concept of continuity is also used to determine whether the present Aboriginal claimants are sufficiently connected with the Aboriginal people who had the right at the time it was recognized by the common law: see *e.g. R. v. Powley*, [2003] 2 S.C.R. 207, 2003 SCC 43 at paras. 12, 23, and 27 [*Powley*] (involving Métis hunting rights). I am grateful to Kerry Wilkins for reminding me of this. While obviously an important issue, it will not be addressed in this paper.

[8] R.S.C. 1970, c. F-14, now R.S.C. 1985, c. F-14.

[9] *Van der Peet, supra* note 4 at paras. 46, 60.

[10] *Ibid.* at para. 62.

[11] *Ibid.* at para. 63. Lamer C.J.'s reference to *Mabo* in this passage is to *Mabo v. Queensland [No. 2]* (1992), 175 C.L.R. 1 [*Mabo*].

[12] See *R. v. Marshall*, [2004] 1 C.N.L.R. 211 (N.S.C.A.) at paras. 157–81, Cromwell J.A. [*Marshall*], leave to appeal to the S.C.C. granted 29 April 2004, [2004] 2 C.N.L.R. iv. In Australia, the consequences of Brennan J.'s approach were starkly revealed in *Yorta Yorta Aboriginal Community v. Victoria* (2002), 194 A.L.R. 538 [*Yorta Yorta*], where the High Court held that an Aboriginal community lost its Native title because, as a result of the impact of European settlement, it had not maintained its traditional laws and customs in relation to the land.

[13] See text accompanying note 10, *supra*, and *Marshall, ibid.* at paras. 160, 170, 173, 177. It is also consistent with the way Lamer C.J. actually applied the continuity concept in *Van der Peet, supra* note 4 at para. 89, where he held that the evidence of trade of salmon with the Hudson's Bay Company did not prove the existence of a pre-contact practice, custom, or tradition of trading salmon because "[t]he trade of salmon between the Sto:lo and the Hudson's Bay Company does not have the necessary continuity with Sto:lo culture pre-contact to support a claim to an Aboriginal right to trade salmon."

[14] However, as Kerry Wilkins has pointed out to me, it needs to be acknowledged that, in many cases, direct evidence of pre-contact practices, customs, and traditions will be inadequate. So, as a practical matter, Aboriginal claimants will often have to rely on post-contact evidence.

[15] See *Powley, supra* note 7 at para. 45, where the Supreme Court found that the requisite continuity existed because the hunting right claimed by Steve Powley and Roddy Powley fell "squarely within the bounds of the historical practice grounding the right." See also *Marshall, supra* note 12 at paras. 176–77.

[16] [1996] 2 S.C.R. 723 [*Gladstone*]. See also *Marshall, supra* note 12 at para. 173.

[17] *Gladstone, ibid.* at para. 28.

[18] *Ibid.*

[19] [1996] 3 S.C.R. 101 [*Adams*].

[20] *Ibid.* at paras. 45–46.

[21] *Ibid.* at para. 47. See also *R. v. Côté*, [1996] 3 S.C.R. 139 [*Côté*], handed down the same day as *Adams, ibid.*, where Lamer C.J. relied (at para. 69) on the same paragraphs from the *Van der Peet, supra* note 4, and *Gladstone, supra* note 16, decisions to conclude that, once it has been shown that the Aboriginal right in question is supported by practices, customs, or traditions that existed prior to contact, "there must also be 'continuity'" between those practices, customs, or traditions and "a particular practice, custom or tradition that is integral to Aboriginal communities today." As in *Adams*, the defendants in *Côté* were able to show this kind of continuity.

[22] See paras. 62 and 63 of his judgment in *Van der Peet, ibid.*, quoted in text accompanying notes 10 and 11. In para. 28 of *Gladstone, ibid.*, he simply explained how the continuity doctrine, as described in *Van der Peet*, applied to the facts in *Gladstone*: see text accompanying notes 16–18. Although Lamer C.J. relied on para. 63 from *Van der Peet* and para. 28 from *Gladstone* as authority for his statement in *Adams* that there must be continuity between pre-contact and present-day practices, customs, and traditions, I do not think those paragraphs support making continuity a general requirement. On the contrary, we have seen that he used the concept of continuity in those earlier cases to make proof of Aboriginal rights easier, not harder. Moreover, in his post-*Adams* judgment in *Delgamuukw, supra* note 5 at para. 83, Lamer C.J. referred to his discussion of continuity in *Van der Peet* and repeated that the reason why Aboriginal peoples can rely on post-contact practices, customs, and traditions is that, "given that many aboriginal societies did not

keep written records at the time of contact or sovereignty, it would be exceedingly difficult for them to produce (*Van der Peet* at para. 62) 'conclusive evidence from pre-contact times about the practices, customs and traditions of their community.'" See also *Marshall, supra* note 12 at paras. 174–77.

[23] See also the dissenting judgment of McLachlin J. (as she then was) in *Van der Peet, ibid.* at para. 249, where she said in reference to the "continuity requirement" that "[a]ll that is required is that the people establish a link between the modern practice and the historic aboriginal right." This must be what she had in mind, as well, in her recent judgment in *Mitchell v. M.N.R.*, [2001] 1 S.C.R. 911 at para. 12 [*Mitchell*], when she said that "an aboriginal claimant must prove a modern practice, tradition or custom that has a reasonable degree of continuity with the practices, traditions or customs that existed prior to contact" (see also para. 26). In *Mitchell*, she also affirmed that the "flexible application of the rules of evidence [mandated by the *Van der Peet* decision] permits, for example, the admissibility of evidence of post-contact activities to prove continuity with pre-contact practices, customs and traditions" (para. 29). As it would make no sense to say that the common law "permits" the admissibility of evidence of post-contact activities to prove continuity, or to describe that as a "flexible application of the rules of evidence" if proof of such continuity were required, McLachlin C.J. must have used the term "continuity" in two senses: first, to mean that when a post-contact practice, custom, or tradition is relied upon, it must be traced to a pre-contact practice, custom or tradition; and second, to mean that there has to be a link between a current activity and an Aboriginal right established by proof of a pre-contact practice, custom, or tradition, in the sense that the activity comes within the scope of the right. McLachlin C.J. was nonetheless able to avoid actually applying these concepts of continuity in *Mitchell* because she found (at para. 51) that the respondent had failed to prove that the Mohawks of Akwesasne had "an ancestral practice of transporting goods across the St. Lawrence River for the purposes of trade" (the basis for the claimed Aboriginal right, as she characterized it) at the time of contact with Europeans. She had already determined at para. 41 that "[o]nly if this ancestral practice is established does it become necessary to determine whether it is an integral feature of Mohawk culture with continuity [in the second sense described above, I think] to the present day."

[24] See *e.g. Mabo, supra* note 11; *Commonwealth v. Yarmirr* (2001), 184 A.L.R. 113 (H.C.A.); *Western Australia v. Ward* (2002), 191 A.L.R. 1 (H.C.A.). For critical discussion, see Kent McNeil, "The Relevance of Traditional Laws and Customs to the Existence and Content of Native Title at Common Law" in *Emerging Justice?, supra* note 2 at 416.

[25] See *Yorta Yorta, supra* note 12. See also *Marshall, supra* note 12 at paras. 157–81.

[26] In *Gladstone, supra* note 16, all the evidence of pre-contact trade in herring spawn relied upon by the Court related to Heiltsuk practices, not to Heiltsuk laws or customs. However, this is not to suggest that the Heiltsuk lacked laws or customs in this regard; it just means that proof of their existence is not a requirement for Aboriginal rights in Canada. For an illuminating discussion of the Heiltsuk herring spawn fishery and the *Gladstone* decision, see Douglas C. Harris, "Territoriality, Aboriginal Rights, and the Heiltsuk Spawn-on-Kelp Fishery" (2000) 34 U.B.C. L. Rev. 195.

[27] See also *Adams, supra* note 19; *Côté, supra* note 21; *Delgamuukw, supra* note 5; *Mitchell, supra* note 23.

[28] *Van der Peet, supra* note 4 at para. 65.

[29] *Ibid.* at para. 249.

[30] See Black C.J.'s dissenting opinion in the full Federal Court of Australia in *Yorta Yorta Aboriginal Community v. Victoria* (2001), 180 A.L.R. 655, and Gaudron and Kirby JJ.'s dissenting opinion in the same case in the High Court, *supra* note 12 at paras. 112–19.

[31] See the last sentence in the passage from his judgment accompanying note 11, *supra*.

[32] See text accompanying notes 10–18. See also *Marshall, supra* note 12 at paras. 157–81. Moreover, the Supreme Court has affirmed on several occasions that the burden of proving extinguishment of an Aboriginal right is on the Crown or other party so alleging: see *e.g. R. v. Sparrow*, [1990] 1 S.C.R. 1075 at 1099 [*Sparrow*]; *Badger, supra* note 3 at para. 41, Cory J.; *Gladstone, supra* note 16 at paras. 31–38, Lamer C.J., para. 106, La Forest J., dissenting on other grounds; *Côté, supra* note 21 at para. 72, Lamer C.J., para. 97, La Forest J.

[33] This date will vary, depending in part on whether the area in question was previously part of French

Canada or was acquired directly by the British Crown.

34 *Van der Peet, supra* note 4 at para. 28.

35 Aboriginal rights rooted in Aboriginal law or custom would have existed as rights in Aboriginal legal systems before the common law was received.

36 This conclusion is based on a positivist view of law. I acknowledge the possibility that there could also be a natural right to engage in the practice, especially if the livelihood of the Aboriginal people in question depended on it. For an argument in favour of Aboriginal rights that relies in part on the right of a people to the necessities of life, see Brian Slattery, "Aboriginal Sovereignty and Imperial Claims" (1991) 29 Osgoode Hall L.J. 681.

37 [1977] 1 All E.R. 505 (Ch.) at 510.

38 See the quotation from McLachlin J.'s judgment in *Van der Peet* accompanying note 29. See also *Ward v. Ward* (1852), 7 Ex. 838, at 839; *Gotobed v. Pridmore* (1970), 115 Sol. Jo. 78 (C.A.) [*Gotobed*]. In *Tehidy Minerals Ltd. v. Norman*, [1971] 2 Q.B. 528 (C.A.) at 553 [*Tehidy*], Buckley L.J. said: "Abandonment of an easement or of a profit à prendre can only, we think, be treated as having taken place where the person entitled to it has demonstrated a fixed intention never at any time thereafter to assert the right himself or to attempt to transmit it to anyone else." Nor can rights in relation to natural resources be lost by non-user. For example, mere failure to exercise a riparian right to use water, for however long, does not result in loss of the right at common law: see *Sampson v. Hoddinott* (1857), 1 C.B. (N.S.) 590 (C.P.) at 611, aff'd 3 C.B. (N.S.) 596 (Ex. Ch.).

39 See *Roberts v. Canada*, [1989] 1 S.C.R. 322 at 340, where Wilson J., in a unanimous judgment, decided that the law of Aboriginal title is "federal common law." This characterization was applied by the Lamer C.J. in *Côté, supra* note 21 at para. 49, to an Aboriginal right to fish.

40 It is arguable that if the practices, customs, and traditions ceased between the time of contact with Europeans (the relevant time for them to be integral to the distinctive culture of the Aboriginal people in question, according to the *Van der Peet* test), and the reception of the common law (the time when the practices, customs, and traditions would be recognized by the common law as giving rise to Aboriginal rights), there would be nothing for the common law to recognize. However, this may also be indicative of the problematic nature of the time frame utilized in *Van der Peet*: see Borrows, "Frozen Rights," *supra* note 6; Barsh & Henderson, *supra* note 6.

41 Custom is defined in Sir Alexander Turner Kingcome & D.R. Christie, eds., *Halsbury's Laws of England*, 4th ed., vol. 12(1) (London: Butterworths, 1998) at para. 601, as "a particular rule which has obtained either actually or presumptively from time immemorial in a particular locality and obtained the force of law in that locality, although contrary to, or not consistent with, the general common law of the realm."

42 *Ibid.* at para. 624.

43 (1840), 11 Ad. & E. 819 (Q.B.) at 825–26. See also *Heath v. Deane*, [1905] 2 Ch. 86 at 93–94 [*Heath*]; *New Windsor Corporation v. Mellor*, [1975] 3 All E.R. 44 (C.A.) at 50–51, Lord Denning M.R., at 53, Browne L.J.

44 [1963] 1 Ch. 243 (C.A.) at 255–56 [*Wyld*].

45 *Halsbury's Laws of England, supra* note 41, vol. 12(1) at para. 646. In *Re Tucktoo and Kitchooalik* (1972), 27 D.L.R. (3d) 225 (N.W.T.T.C.), aff'd *Re Kitchooalik and Tucktoo* (1972), 28 D.L.R. (3d) 483 (N.W.T.C.A.) [*Kitchooalik*], Morrow J. held that the rule that customs can be abolished only by statute applies to Inuit customs relating to adoption, and that the legislation would have to be either repugnant to those customs, or directly or by implication intended to abolish them.

46 In *Van der Peet, supra* note 4 at para. 28, Lamer C.J. said that "[s]ubsequent to s. 35(1) [of the *Constitution Act, 1982*] aboriginal rights cannot be extinguished and can only be regulated or infringed consistent with the justificatory test laid out by this Court in *Sparrow*." This was affirmed by McLachlin C.J. in *Mitchell, supra* note 23 at para. 11.

47 See *Sparrow, supra* note 32 at 1099; *Gladstone, supra* note 16 at paras. 31–38; *Delgamuukw, supra* note 5 at para. 180. Note, however, that voluntary surrender of Aboriginal rights by treaty is possible in Canada. For detailed discussion, see Kent McNeil, "Extinguishment of Aboriginal Title in Canada: Treaties, Legislation, and Judicial Discretion" (2001–2002) 33 Ottawa L. Rev. 301.

⁴⁸ *Supra* note 3.
⁴⁹ R.S.C. 1970, c. I-6, now R.S.C. 1985, c. I-5.
⁵⁰ *Sioui, supra* note 3 at 1066.
⁵¹ *Ibid.* Note that Lamer J. said specifically that the proposition that "a treaty could be extinguished merely because it had not been relied upon in litigation . . . is untenable": *ibid.*
⁵² In the context of s. 35(1) of the *Constitution Act, 1982*, the Supreme Court has held that justification of infringement of treaty rights should be treated in the same manner as justification of infringement of Aboriginal rights: see *Badger, supra* note 3 at paras. 74–79, Cory J.; *Marshall I, supra* note 3 at para. 64, Binnie J.; *Marshall II, supra* note 3 at para. 32. For a contrary view, see Leonard I. Rotman, "Defining Parameters: Aboriginal Rights, Treaty Rights, and the *Sparrow* Justificatory Test" (1997) 36 Alberta L. Rev. 149.
⁵³ In *Sioui*, the clause of the treaty being relied upon probably did just that. It provided that the Hurons were "allowed the free Exercise of their Religion, their Customs, and Liberty of trading with the English" (*Sioui, supra* note 3 at 1031), and the accused were exercising their religion and customs when charged under provincial legislation. See also *Simon, supra* note 3 at 409, where Dickson C.J. held that, even though the Micmac Treaty of 1752 "did not *create* new hunting or fishing rights but merely *recognized* pre-existing rights" [emphasis in original], it was still a treaty for the purposes of s. 88 of the *Indian Act, supra* note 49.
⁵⁴ The issue of whether continuity must be shown as far back as European contact will be discussed below in the Conclusions to this paper.
⁵⁵ Although the issue cannot be discussed here, surrender of Aboriginal rights may be problematic because, as Lamer C.J. made clear in *Delgamuukw, supra* note 5 at paras. 115, 125–32, they are communal rights that are intended to benefit future as well as present generations. As Lord Denning observed in the quotation from *Wyld* accompanying note 44, one generation should not be able to waive or abandon communal rights on behalf of future generations. See also Leroy Little Bear, "Aboriginal Rights and the Canadian 'Grundnorm'" in J. Rick Ponting, ed., *Arduous Journey: Canadian Indians and Decolonization* (Toronto: McClelland and Stewart, 1986) 243; McNeil, *supra* note 47 at 304–8. However, the Royal Proclamation of 1763, reprinted in R.S.C. 1985, App. II, No. 1, may have provided authority for the surrender of Aboriginal land rights. Moreover, the surrenderability of Aboriginal title to the Crown was affirmed by Lamer C.J. in *Delgamuukw* at para. 131 (without reference to the Royal Proclamation), despite the inherent limit that prevents uses of the land by the Aboriginal titleholders "which are inconsistent with continued use by future generations of aboriginals" (para. 154). For critical commentary on the inherent limit, see Kent McNeil, "The Post-*Delgamuukw* Nature and Content of Aboriginal Title" in McNeil, *Emerging Justice?, supra* note 2, 102 at 116–22 [McNeil, "Post-*Delgamuukw*"].
⁵⁶ See McNeil, *supra* note 47. In *Delgamuukw, ibid.* at paras. 172–83, Lamer C.J. held that provincial legislatures have had no jurisdiction since Confederation to extinguish Aboriginal rights because those rights are within the core of federal jurisdiction over "Indians, and Lands reserved for the Indians" (*Constitution Act, 1867* (U.K.) 30 & 31 Vict., c. 3, s. 91(24)), and so are protected against extinguishment by provincial laws by the doctrine of interjurisdictional immunity.
⁵⁷ See *supra* note 32, and notes 43–46 and accompanying text. This protection is part of the respect that the common law accords to vested rights generally, as there is a strong presumption against legislative interference with them: see *e.g. Spooner Oils Ltd. v. Turner Valley Gas Conservation Board*, [1933] S.C.R. 629 at 638, Duff C.J.; *Attorney-General for Canada v. Hallet and Carey Ltd.*, [1952] A.C. 427 (P.C.), esp. at 450, Lord Radcliffe; *Colet v. The Queen*, [1981] 1 S.C.R. 2 at 10; Ruth Sullivan, *Sullivan and Driedger on the Construction of Statutes*, 4th ed. (Markham, Ont.: Butterworths, 2002) at 412–16.
⁵⁸ *Delgamuukw, supra* note 5, especially at paras. 78–108, Lamer C.J. The case was therefore sent back to trial, though a re-trial has not taken place. On use of oral histories in court, see Lori Ann Roness & Kent McNeil, "Legalizing Oral History: Proving Aboriginal Claims in Canadian Courts" (2000) 39:3 Journal of the West 66; John Borrows, "Listening for a Change: The Courts and Oral Tradition" (2001) 39 Osgoode Hall L.J. 1.

59 For discussion of Lamer C.J.'s definition of Aboriginal title, see McNeil, "Post-*Delgamuukw*," *supra* note 55.
60 *Delgamuukw, supra* note 5 at para. 143.
61 *Ibid.* at para. 152 [emphasis in original]. See also paras. 83, 101. Note that La Forest J., concurring in the result, took a more flexible approach to continuity where present occupation is relied upon. In his view, "continuity may still exist where the present occupation of one area is connected to the pre-sovereignty occupation of another area": *ibid.* at para. 197 (see also para. 198).
62 See text accompanying notes 10–13. See also *Marshall, supra* note 12 at paras. 178–81.
63 *Delgamuukw, supra* note 5 at para. 153. Regarding *Côté*, see *supra* note 21.
64 *Delgamuukw, ibid.* at para. 154.
65 *Ibid.* before para. 152 [underlining removed].
66 See also *ibid.* at para. 151, where Lamer C.J. said that "in the case of title, it would seem clear that any land that was occupied pre-sovereignty, and which the parties have maintained a substantial connection with since then, is sufficiently important to be of central significance to the culture of the claimants" (see also *ibid.* per La Forest J. at para. 199). Once again, the chief justice's obvious intention was to make proof of Aboriginal title easier by not requiring the claimants actually to prove that their connection with the land was of central significance to their distinctive culture, as per the *Van der Peet* test. Surely he could not have meant that they must show that they have maintained a substantial connection with the land since sovereignty in all cases, given that he went on to explain, in the paragraphs immediately following, that continuity must be shown "[i]f present occupation is relied on as proof of occupation pre-sovereignty": *ibid.*, heading before para. 152 [underlining removed]. This was confirmed by Daigle J.A. in *R. v. Bernard* (2003), 230 D.L.R. (4th) 57 (N.B.C.A.) at para. 58 [*Bernard*], who said that Lamer C.J.'s requirement in *Delgamuukw* for continuity as an element for proof of Aboriginal title "only applies in cases where present occupation is relied on as proof of pre-sovereignty occupation" (see also paras. 131–32). Leave to appeal *Bernard* was granted by the Supreme Court of Canada on 29 April 2004, [2004] 2 C.N.L.R. iv.
67 Difficult questions arise as to when this might have occurred in various parts of Canada: see *e.g.* Kent McNeil, "Aboriginal Nations and Quebec's Boundaries: Canada Couldn't Give What It Didn't Have" in McNeil, *Emerging Justice?, supra* note 2, 1. In its recent decision in *Bernard, ibid.*, the New Brunswick Court of Appeal accepted the trial judge's ruling that British sovereignty over the Northwest Miramichi River area in what is now northern New Brunswick had been acquired in 1759, as that was when the British "took possession of the land" or acquired "de facto control over the area": para. 61, Daigle J.A.; see also paras. 443, 446, Robertson J.A. See also *Marshall, supra* note 12 at para. 73, where Cromwell J.A. stated that there was no dispute on appeal over the trial judge's findings that British sovereignty had been acquired over mainland Nova Scotia in 1713 and over Cape Breton in 1763.
68 In *Delgamuukw, supra* note 5 at para. 145, Lamer C.J. said that "aboriginal title crystallized at the time sovereignty was asserted."
69 In *Delgamuukw*, Lamer C.J. affirmed that Aboriginal title, like other Aboriginal rights, could be extinguished prior to the enactment of s. 35 of the *Constitution Act, 1982,* only by clear and plain legislation enacted by a constitutionally competent legislative body: *ibid.* at para. 180. Regarding surrender of Aboriginal title, see *supra* note 55, and *infra* notes 86–87 and accompanying text.
70 See *supra* note 32.
71 However, an argument will be made in the Conclusions to this paper that the requirement that Aboriginal peoples actually prove continuity of their occupation even in this context offends common law principles in relation to title to land.
72 See authorities cited *supra* in notes 37–38, 42–45. See also *Moffat v. Kazana*, [1969] 2 Q.B. 152 at 156, where Wrangham J. said that the owners of the money in question in the case "remain the true owners of the money unless they . . . had divested . . . themselves of the ownership by one of the recognised methods, abandonment, gift or sale."
73 See *Williams v. Phillips* (1957), 41 Cr. App. R. 5 (U.K. Div. Ct.); *Simpson v. Gowers* (1981), 32 O.R. (2d) 385 (C.A.). For discussion, see A.H. Hudson, "Is Divesting Abandonment Possible at Common Law?" (1984) 100 Law Q. Rev. 110. The rule that there must be an intention to abandon applies to

real property as well in the context of easements and profits à prendre: see *Swan v. Sinclair*, [1924] 1 Ch. 254 (C.A.), aff'd [1925] A.C. 227 (H.L.); *Gotobed*, supra note 38; *Tehidy*, supra note 38.

[74] See *Keefer v. Arillotta* (1976), 13 O.R. (2d) 680 (C.A.); *Masidon Investments Ltd. v. Ham* (1984), 45 O.R. (2d) 563 (C.A.) [*Masidon Investments*]; *J.A. Pye (Oxford) Ltd. v. Graham*, [2003] 1 A.C. 419 (H.L.) at 427, Lord Browne-Wilkinson.

[75] *Wallis's Cayton Bay Holiday Camp Ltd. v. Shell-Mex*, [1974] 3 All E.R. 575 (C.A.), applied in *Masidon Investments, ibid*. See also Eileen E. Gillese, *Property Law: Cases, Text and Materials*, 2nd ed. (Toronto: Emond Montgomery, 1990) at 12:8.

[76] *Delgamuukw*, supra note 5 at para. 140 [emphasis in original].

[77] [1988] 2 S.C.R. 654 at 677.

[78] *Delgamuukw*, supra note 5 at para. 113.

[79] *Ibid*. at paras. 112–15. For discussion, see McNeil, "*Post-Delgamuukw*," supra note 55.

[80] For detailed discussion, see Kent McNeil, *Common Law Aboriginal Title* (Oxford: Clarendon Press, 1989) at 18–63, 93–95 [McNeil, *Common Law Aboriginal Title*].

[81] See Kent McNeil, "Aboriginal Title as a Constitutionally Protected Property Right" and "Racial Discrimination and Unilateral Extinguishment of Native Title" in McNeil, *Emerging Justice?*, supra note 2, 292 and 357, respectively.

[82] Lamer C.J. suggested this himself in *Delgamuukw*, supra note 5 at para. 153, when he gave the following reason why "an unbroken chain of continuity" need not be established: "The occupation and use of lands may have been disrupted for a time, perhaps as a result of the unwillingness of European colonizers to recognize aboriginal title." See also the quotation accompanying note 63, *supra*.

[83] See *Jones v. McLean*, [1931] 2 D.L.R. 244 (Man. C.A.) at 247, Prendergast C.J.M., at 252, Fullerton J.A. See also McNeil, *Common Law Aboriginal Title*, supra note 80 at 63–73.

[84] The common law abhorred an abeyance of seisin, in part because that would mean no one was responsible for the feudal services and incidents of tenure. This is probably what led Maitland to remark that "[i]t seems very doubtful whether a man could (or can) get rid of a seisin once acquired, except by delivering seisin to some one else": Frederick Pollock & Frederic William Maitland, *The History of English Law Before the Time of Edward I*, 2d ed. (Cambridge: Cambridge University Press, 1898, reissued 1968), vol. 2 at 55 n. 2.

[85] It should be noted that American law apparently does allow Indian title to be lost by abandonment: see *e.g. United States v. Arredondo*, 6 Pet. 691 (1832) at 747–48; *Williams v. Chicago*, 242 U.S. 434 (1917); *United States v. Santa Fe Pacific Railroad*, 314 U.S. 339 (1941) at 354–58; *Turtle Mountain Band of Chippewa Indians v. United States*, 490 F.2d 935 (1974) at 947–48. However, Indian title in the United States is a non-proprietary right of occupancy: *Tee-Hit-Ton Indians v. United States*, 348 U.S. 272 (1955). As Aboriginal title in Canada is an interest in land that is proprietary (see text accompanying notes 76–79), this aspect of American law is inapplicable here. See discussion in McNeil, *Common Law Aboriginal Title*, supra note 80 at 258–67. Compare *Ontario (A.G.) v. Bear Island Foundation*, [1985] 1 C.N.L.R. 1 (Ont. S.C.) at 77, where Steele J. found, *inter alia*, that the Aboriginal title of the Temagami Indians had been extinguished because they "abandoned their traditional use and occupation" of their lands. Although his decision was affirmed on appeal, [1989] 2 C.N.L.R. 73 (Ont. C.A.), [1991] 2 S.C.R. 570, the Supreme Court did not mention abandonment, holding only that the Temagami Indians' land rights had been validly surrendered by adhesion to a treaty. Moreover, at 575, the Supreme Court said it did "not necessarily follow" from their acceptance of Steele J.'s factual findings that they agreed "with all the legal findings based on those facts. In particular, we find that on the facts found by the trial judge the Indians exercised sufficient occupation of the lands in question throughout the relevant period to establish an aboriginal right." The Court said that Steele J. had been misled in this regard by certain considerations, including his finding that the Temagami Indians had failed to prove "that, as an organized society, they continued to exclusively occupy and make aboriginal use of the Land Claim Area from 1763 or the time of coming of settlement to the date the action was commenced": *ibid*. at 574–75, quoting [1985] 1 C.N.L.R. 1 at 21. For further discussion, see Kent McNeil, "The High Cost of Accepting Benefits from the Crown: A Comment on the Temagami Indian Land Case" in McNeil, *Emerging Justice?*,

supra note 2, 25 [McNeil, "High Cost"].

[86] See the quotation from *Wyld* accompanying note 44.

[87] See *supra* note 55.

[88] On the Royal Proclamation's requirements for the surrender of Aboriginal title, see Brian Slattery, *The Land Rights of Indigenous Canadian Peoples* (Saskatoon: University of Saskatchewan Native Law Centre, 1979), especially at 312–13; McNeil, "High Cost," *supra* note 85 at 41–48. See also *Chippewas of Sarnia Band v. Canada (A.G.)* (1999), 40 R.P.R. (3d) 49 (Ont. Sup. Ct.), aff'd [2001] 1 C.N.L.R. 56 (Ont. C.A.), leave to appeal refused [2001] 3 S.C.R. vi, S.C.C.A. No. 63. However, in *Chippewas of Sarnia* the Court of Appeal, in *obiter* at paras. 206–19, affirmed its controversial ruling in *Ontario (A.G.) v. Bear Island Foundation*, *supra* note 85, that the surrender provisions of the Royal Proclamation had been repealed by the *Quebec Act* (U.K.), 14 Geo. 3, c. 83. For critical commentary, see McNeil, *ibid.* at 42–44.

[89] See quotation from *Re Yateley Common* accompanying note 37. See also *Gotobed v. Pridmore*, *supra* note 38. Note that in *Marshall*, *supra* note 12 at para. 241, Cromwell J.A. dismissed the Crown's argument that loss of connection with the land amounted to abandonment. In doing so, he relied on his conclusion that proof of continuity is not required where exclusive occupation at the time of Crown sovereignty has been established by direct evidence. He also found on the facts that abandonment had not occurred.

[90] Although *Adams*, *supra* note 19, and *Côté*, *supra* note 21, discussed *supra* in notes 19–23 and accompanying text, might indicate some confusion regarding this matter, I think this is due to inappropriate use of the term "continuity" in the context of the requirement that the present-day activity must come within the scope of the Aboriginal right that has been shown to exist. See also discussion at note 23, *supra*, of McLachlin C.J.'s decision in *Mitchell*, *supra* note 23.

[91] *Van der Peet*, *supra* note 4 at para. 65, repeated, in the context of Aboriginal title, in *Delgamuukw*, *supra* note 5 at para. 153.

[92] See text accompanying notes 10 and 61.

[93] An approach like this was taken by Merkel J. in the Federal Court of Australia in his recent decision in *Rubibi Community v. Western Australia* (2001), 112 F.C.R. 409 at para. 79.

[94] Although the matter cannot be pursued in this paper, an examination of how customary law is proven in former British colonies elsewhere might provide useful parallels as well. For an introduction to this complex matter, see A.N. Allott, "The Judicial Ascertainment of Customary Law in British Africa" (1957) 20 Mod. L. Rev. 244.

[95] See *Halsbury's Laws of England*, *supra* note 41, vol. 12(1) at paras. 607–8, 620–22.

[96] See *Jenkins v. Harvey* (1835), 1 C.M. & R. 877 (Ex.) at 894; *Bastard v. Smith* (1837), 2 M. & Rob. 129 (Q.B.) at 136 [*Bastard*]; *Hammerton v. Honey* (1876), 24 W.R. 603 (H.C.) at 604 [*Hammerton*]; *Angus v. Dalton* (1877), 3 Q.B.D. 85 at 104; *Mercer v. Denne*, [1904] 2 Ch. 534, aff'd [1905] 2 Ch. 538 (C.A.).

[97] See *Bastard*, *ibid.* at 136; *Hammerton*, *ibid.* at 604.

[98] *Gibson v. Doeg* (1857), 2 H. & N. 615 (Ex.) at 623, Pollock C.B., applied by Joyce J. to a customary right to quarry stone on the waste of a manor in *Heath*, *supra* note 43 at 93.

[99] (1878), 3 Ex. D. 292 (C.A.) at 299, applied in *Heath*, *ibid.* at 93. See also *Cocksedge v. Fanshaw* (1779), 1 Doug. K.B. 119 at 132; *Roe d. Johnson v. Ireland* (1809), 11 East 280 (K.B.) at 284; *Brocklebank v. Thompson*, [1903] 2 Ch. 344 at 350; *Egerton v. Harding*, [1975] Q.B. 62 (C.A.). In *Attorney General v. Lord Hotham* (1823), Turn. & R. 209 (Ch.) at 218, Plumer M.R. said: "Very high judges have said they would presume any thing in favour of a long enjoyment and uninterrupted possession."

[100] See text accompanying note 10.

[101] The rule that a custom is presumed to be valid if shown to be in existence for as far back as living memory goes was applied in Canada in the context of an Inuit custom of adoption by the Northwest Territories Court of Appeal in *Kitchooalik*, *supra* note 45 at 488, relying on *Bastard v. Smith*, *supra* note 96.

[102] Compare L'Heureux-Dubé J.'s dissenting judgments in *Van der Peet*, *supra* note 4 at paras. 164–79, and *R. v. N.T.C. Smokehouse Ltd.*, [1996] 2 S.C.R. 672 at paras. 45, 62, 73, where she rejected Lamer

C.J.'s pre-contact time frame for proof of Aboriginal rights, advocating instead an approach that would recognize rights based on practices, customs, and traditions that have been integral to distinctive Aboriginal cultures "*for a substantial continuous period of time*": *Van der Peet* at para. 175 [emphasis in original]. She said that the actual length of this period "will depend on the circumstances and on the nature of the aboriginal right claimed," but suggested that it should be in the range of twenty to fifty years: *ibid.* at para. 177, relying on Brian Slattery, "Understanding Aboriginal Rights" (1987) 66 Can. Bar Rev. 727 at 758. See also her concurring judgments in *Gladstone, supra* note 16 at paras. 133–35, 143–45, and *Adams, supra* note 19 at para. 66. Her twenty- to fifty-year period is similar to the period that will usually suffice to raise a presumption of a valid custom at common law: see *Halsbury's Laws of England, supra* note 41, vol. 12(1) at para. 622. However, unlike in the case of English custom, L'Heureux-Dubé J. does not appear to have envisaged that proof of an Aboriginal right could be rebutted by evidence of non-existence of the practice, custom, or tradition before the twenty- to fifty-year period.

[103] See Kent McNeil, "The Onus of Proof of Aboriginal Title" (1999) 37 Osgoode Hall L.J. 775, reprinted in McNeil, *Emerging Justice?, supra* note 2, 136 [McNeil, "Onus of Proof"].

[104] See *Whale v. Hitchcock* (1876), 34 L.T. 136 (Div. C.A.); *Emmerson v. Maddison*, [1906] A.C. 569 (P.C.) at 575; *Wheeler v. Baldwin* (1934), 52 C.L.R. 609 (H.C.A.), esp. at 621–22; *Allen v. Roughley* (1955), 94 C.L.R. 98 (H.C.A.) at 136–41. This presumption is usually expressed as a presumption of title from *possession*, but since possession (a matter of law) is presumed from occupation (a matter of fact), it is not necessary in this context to distinguish between them. On the difference between occupation and possession, see McNeil, *Common Law Aboriginal Title, supra* note 80 at 6–8.

[105] On proof of occupation, see McNeil, *ibid.* at 197–204.

[106] See *Roe d. Haldane and Urry v. Harvey* (1769), 4 Burr. 2484 (K.B.) at 287–88; *Goodtitle d. Parker v. Baldwin* (1809), 11 East 488 (K.B.) at 495; *Asher v. Whitlock* (1865), L.R. 1 Q.B. 1; *Danford v. McAnulty* (1883), 8 App. Cas. 456 (H.L.) at 460–61, 462, 464–65; *Perry v. Clissold*, [1907] A.C. 73 (P.C.) at 79–80; *City of Vancouver v. Vancouver Lumber Company*, [1911] A.C. 711 (P.C.) at 720; *McAllister v. Defoe* (1915), 8 O.W.N. 175 (Ont. K.B.), aff'd (1915), 8 O.W.N. 405 (Ont. C.A.); *Swaile v. Zurdayk*, [1924] 2 W.W.R. 555 (Sask. C.A.); *Pinder Lumber and Milling Co. v. Munroe*, [1928] S.C.R. 177; *Oxford Meat Co. Pty. v. McDonald*, [1963] S.R.(N.S.W.) 423 (N.S.W.S.C.) at 425–27.

[107] For confirmation of these rules in leading texts, see Edward Coke, *The First Part of the Institutes of the Laws of England; or a Commentary upon Littleton*, 19th ed. by Charles Butler (London: J. and W.T. Clarke et al., 1832) at 239a, n. 1; William Blackstone, *Commentaries on the Laws of England*, 16th ed. (London: T. Cadell and J. Butterworth and Son, 1825) vol. 2 at 196, vol. 3 at 177, 180; Frederick Pollock & Robert Samuel Wright, *An Essay on Possession in the Common Law* (Oxford: Clarendon Press, 1888) at 22–25, 91–100; John M. Lightwood, *A Treatise on Possession of Land* (London: Stevens and Sons, 1894) at 125, 146–47, 294–95; Robert Megarry & William Wade, *The Law of Real Property*, 6th ed. by Charles Harpum (London: Sweet & Maxwell, 2000) at 87–94; E.H. Burn, *Cheshire and Burn's Modern Law of Real Property*, 15th ed. (London: Butterworths, 1994) at 26–29; *Halsbury's Laws of England, supra* note 41, vol. 39(2) at para. 267. For discussion and further references, see McNeil, *Common Law Aboriginal Title, supra* note 80 at 42–43, 46–49, 56–58.

[108] See McNeil, "Onus of Proof," *supra* note 103.

[109] If exclusive occupation at the time of Crown assertion of sovereignty is proven, then of course an actual Aboriginal title will have been established, not just a presumptive title.

[110] See text accompanying note 60.

[111] Past as well as present occupation should give rise to this presumption of Aboriginal title: see McNeil, "Onus of Proof," *supra* note 103 at 794–96 (*Emerging Justice?* at 152–54).

[112] See generally John Borrows, *Recovering Canada: The Resurgence of Indigenous Law* (Toronto: University of Toronto Press, 2002).

[113] For an insightful discussion of ways in which courts have used Aboriginal difference (and sameness) to the disadvantage of Aboriginal peoples, see Patrick Macklem, "First Nations Self-Government and the Borders of the Canadian Legal Imagination" (1991) 36 McGill L.J. 382.

[114] See articles cited in note 81, *supra*. Admittedly, the Supreme Court has said on occasion that common

law property principles do not necessarily apply to Aboriginal rights and title, given the latter's *sui generis* nature: see *e.g. Guerin v. The Queen*, [1984] 2 S.C.R. 335 at 381–82, Dickson J.; *Sparrow, supra* note 32 at 1112; *St. Mary's Indian Band v. Cranbrook (City)*, [1997] 2 S.C.R. 657 at paras. 14–16. However, the reasons the Court has generally given for this are to avoid distortion of Aboriginal rights and title by inappropriately trying to fit them into common law categories, to respect the intentions of Aboriginal peoples and the Crown when they negotiate agreements, and to prevent injustice. These goals are not inconsistent with applying common law principles that would assist Aboriginal peoples in the often difficult task of proving or defending their rights.

MÉTIS ABORIGINAL TITLE IN CANADA

Achieving Equality in Aboriginal Rights Doctrine

Larry N. Chartrand

> *Yes, she was written, this song of praise—*
> *Come sing the glory*
> *Of the Bois-Brulés.*
> Pierre Falcon, "Song of the Battle of Seven Oaks," 1816

Delgamuukw v. British Columbia[1] is generally acknowledged to be one of the most important cases in Canadian Aboriginal law. Because of it, the Aboriginal title claims of the Métis peoples in Canada have a far better chance of acceptance than previously. This improvement stems largely from the test Lamer C.J. adopted for determining the appropriate cutoff date for proving Aboriginal title.[2] In *Delgamuukw*, Chief Justice Lamer held that Aboriginal title depends on possession of land at the time the Crown asserted sovereignty over the area. This determination places Métis peoples in a more favourable position than if they had to prove, for example, that they had occupied territory since "time immemorial."

Contrast this with what is required under *Van der Peet*[3] for asserting other Aboriginal rights. Strict application of *Van der Peet* would have left the Métis at a distinct disadvantage because the legal test required proof that the relevant activity, custom, or tradition had existed prior to European contact. The Métis, obviously, could not meet this test; they are, by definition, a people of mixed European and Indian ancestry. The Supreme Court of Canada addressed this predicament in the recent *Powley* decision,[4] modifying the *Van der Peet* test so that Métis communities need prove only that they engaged in an activity, custom, or tradition integral to their distinctive culture prior to the effective establishment of European political and legal control in the area.[5]

The dilemma that the Métis faced because of *Van der Peet* in claiming other Aboriginal rights is not as obvious in the context of Aboriginal title claims because of the different relevant time frame for proving Aboriginal title. Requiring proof of title as of the date the Crown asserted sovereignty in a given area may or may not be prejudicial to the Métis, depending on how one defines "assertion of sovereignty."

The Supreme Court of Canada has now prescribed what the Métis[6] must do to claim Aboriginal rights successfully. The Court has yet to deal with how the Métis may succeed in claiming Aboriginal title. Will the Court feel compelled to modify the test for asserting Aboriginal title, as it has done for other Aboriginal rights when the claimant group is Métis? The answer to this question will depend on how the Court defines the term "assertion of sovereignty." One option is to define the assertion of sovereignty as the moment when the Crown, through some documentary instrument (proclamation, treaty, statute), declares that it has sovereignty over an area. Another is to define the assertion of sovereignty as the moment when the Crown has followed up its mere assertion of sovereignty by instrument with actual physical and meaningful control over the territory by occupation. The thesis presented here is that the latter approach is the appropriate one.

When entertaining Métis claims to Aboriginal title, we must consider initially the appropriate analytical approach to apply to such claims. Must a Métis community prove Aboriginal title based on its Indian ancestors' occupation and use of land (what I call the "trace theory"), or must it prove Aboriginal title based on its own existence as an autonomous and distinct people?

This paper argues that the trace theory is problematic on a number of theoretical and practical grounds. The preferred approach, I argue, is for a Métis community to assert Aboriginal title based on its own existence as a separate, autonomous Aboriginal people. Such a conclusion is consistent with *Powley*, where the Supreme Court of Canada expressly rejected the trace theory in respect of Métis Aboriginal rights claims.

Given the serious, and arguably insurmountable, problems with the trace theory, scholars and courts concerned with Métis claims of Aboriginal right have sought alternative means for the Métis to avoid the consequences of the "European contact" cutoff date.[7] The obvious alternative is resort to a test that would explicitly incorporate a relaxed, more flexible cutoff date specifically for Métis, not for First Nations, claims. This is exactly what the Supreme Court of Canada did in *Powley*. In doing so, I believe the Court created problems where none really existed.

I do not advocate the adoption of either the trace theory or the alternative cutoff date approach. Instead, I argue for resolving the Métis Aboriginal rights and title dilemma by defining with greater precision the concepts of "contact" for the purpose of proving Aboriginal rights and "assertion of sovereignty" for the purpose of proving Aboriginal title. This means applying pre-existing legal principles, reflected in early English case law, regarding the acquisition of territory with a greater understanding of the historical context of Aboriginal–European contact. By doing so, I will argue, it is unnecessary to carve out an exception to the existing Aboriginal rights doctrine to meet the unique circumstances of the Métis. Indeed, the interpretation I offer would result in greater harmonization of Aboriginal law principles generally without a need to create a separate and more relaxed test for the Métis: a test that First Nations would no doubt regard as unfair.

I will first consider which approach the courts ought to apply in respect of Métis claims; I then offer a position on how the principle of "assertion of sovereignty" ought to be defined. But before addressing these substantive issues, I would like to discuss very briefly the dilemma I face as an Aboriginal legal academic writing on issues of Aboriginal law.

Although this paper is about applying the doctrine of Aboriginal rights and title as it is currently understood, I do so with the greatest of hesitation, because of a growing critical perspective of the jurisprudence surrounding this field of law and the fact that, by uncritically applying Aboriginal rights doctrine, I am indirectly supporting an inequitable legal regime. This paper does not address at length the inequality of peoples or how this inequality continues to be manifest in Canadian Aboriginal rights jurisprudence. Neither does it attempt to expose how Aboriginal law doctrine continues to be grounded in a colonial ideology that, notwithstanding certain "favourable decisions," continues to deny Aboriginal peoples true equality among the peoples of the world. Others have written extensively on these issues; I will not repeat these important works here.[8] I will assume, for the purposes of this paper, that the current state of the law regarding Aboriginal rights and title in Canada is legitimate, even though I know it not to be.

THE LEGAL CONTEXT OF MÉTIS RIGHTS

Section 35(2) of the *Constitution Act, 1982* includes the Métis among the three major classifications of Aboriginal peoples in Canada. By reason of this inclusion, the Métis are capable of possessing Aboriginal and treaty rights. Relying on this recognition, Métis groups have brought forth a number of Aboriginal and treaty rights claims. Most claims to date have involved Métis as defendants to charges against them for provincial hunting or fishing offences. Few cases involve positive claims based on treaty rights or Aboriginal title. One such case is the *Dumont*[9] decision. This case from Manitoba can be accurately characterized as a treaty rights case brought by Métis who are descendants of those entitled to land pursuant to s. 31 of the *Manitoba Act*.[10] Thus far, there is only one Métis case involving a positive claim to Aboriginal title. The *Morin* case claims title over much of the land in northwestern Saskatchewan.[11]

The Supreme Court of Canada has stated that Aboriginal title claims fall within the general framework of Aboriginal rights analysis. In other words, Aboriginal title is a subset of Aboriginal rights generally. The Court, however, made it clear that Aboriginal title is a distinct species of Aboriginal right because it involves a substantive claim to land, as opposed to a right to practise certain activities on land; this difference, the Court has said, is sufficient to warrant imposing a different cutoff time for anchoring title claims than for Aboriginal rights claims.[12]

Notwithstanding this distinction, Aboriginal rights are quite appropriately seen as falling along a continuum, depending on the degree to which the right being asserted is connected to a particular geographical location. In other words, Aboriginal rights can be seen as a function of the degree to which land is seen as a necessary part of being able to exercise the right. The Court explained in the following terms the relationship between Aboriginal rights and land:

> [A]boriginal rights . . . fall along a spectrum with respect to their degree of connection with the land. At the one end, there are those aboriginal rights which are practices, customs and traditions that are integral to the distinctive aboriginal culture of the group claiming the right. However, the "occupation and use of the land" where the activity is taking place is not "sufficient to support a claim of title to the land." Nevertheless, those activities receive constitutional protection. In the middle, there are those activities which, out of necessity, take place on land and indeed, might be intimately related to a particular piece of land. . . . At the other end of the spectrum, there is aboriginal title itself. . . . [A]boriginal title confers more than the right to engage in site-specific activities. . . . What aboriginal title confers is the right to the land itself.[13]

In *Van der Peet*,[14] the Court held that the test for proving Aboriginal rights requires proof that the right claimed formed an integral part of the distinctive culture of the Aboriginal people in question. The test as stated requires that the right not have emerged as a result of European influence. Consequently, the claimants must prove that the right was in existence prior to contact with Europeans.[15]

The Supreme Court in *Van der Peet* was aware of the problem such a legal test for proving Aboriginal rights would pose for the Métis. In response, Chief Justice Lamer presented two potential options for addressing the unique circumstances of the Métis.[16]

One option was to treat Métis claims differently from Indian or Inuit claims. He left open the possibility of developing a test for Aboriginal rights specific to the Métis: a separate body of Aboriginal rights law developed to meet the unique Métis circumstances. This option would entail that Métis rights are dependent on Métis society itself, distinct from any prior reference to either their European or their Indian antecedents. The rights of the Métis flow from their own source as a separate "organized society." Thus, Métis Aboriginal rights would turn on whether the Métis, as a distinct and independent people, satisfied the necessary criteria (whatever those criteria are) for proving Aboriginal rights or title.

The other option presented was to "trace" Métis rights through the Métis's Indian ancestors. For example, the Métis could claim rights that existed prior to European contact that were exercised by their Cree, Ojibway, or other First Nation ancestors, depending on the circumstances.

Seven years later, when the first Métis rights case reached the Supreme Court of Canada, the Court expressly rejected the trace theory. It held that

> [such a] theory [trace] in effect would deny to Métis their full status as distinctive rights-bearing peoples whose own integral practices are entitled to constitutional protection under s. 35(1). . . . [A]s long as the practice grounding the right is distinctive and integral to the pre-control Métis community, it will satisfy this prong of the test.[17]

Although the Court in *Van der Peet* was dealing with Aboriginal rights, as opposed to claims of Aboriginal title, these same options—the "trace theory" and the "alternative time frame" approach—also have relevance to potential Métis Aboriginal title claims. Either may be argued in a Métis Aboriginal title claim to avoid the potential for unfairness from the superficial assumption that sovereignty can be "asserted" by mere declaration. However, as I shall argue subsequently, this perceived unfairness becomes more illusory than real if courts recognize that "assertion of sovereignty," properly understood, requires effective occupation of the territory in addition to a mere declaration. Before turning to this issue, however, I will examine the "trace theory" option.

THE TRACE THEORY OF PROVING MÉTIS RIGHTS AND TITLE

There is a tendency in judicial and scholarly thought to suppose that the Aboriginal rights of the Métis are somehow connected to the fact that Métis have Indian ancestry: that without this ancestry, they would have no basis for claiming Aboriginal rights. Indeed, Indian ancestry is often mistakenly looked upon as the very source of Métis Aboriginal rights.

As mentioned at the outset, the trace theory was attractive because it provided a way for Métis claims to Aboriginal lands and rights to avoid the seemingly insurmountable obstacle posed by the doctrine of Aboriginal rights, as understood by the courts. Prior to *Powley*, strict application of the Aboriginal rights test would have meant that no Métis group could ever claim an Aboriginal right. The inclusion of the Métis in s. 35(2) of the *Constitution Act, 1982* would have been a hollow victory and a cruel hoax. The trace theory permitted Métis groups to avoid this predicament by tracing their Aboriginal rights from their First Nations ancestors. It also meant there would be no need to argue for the development of a separate body of Aboriginal law unique to the Métis. Under the trace theory, it would be possible to authenticate Métis Aboriginal rights within the existing unmodified *Van der Peet* test. For example, there would be no need to create for the rights claims of Métis a "time consideration" different from that already used for proving Aboriginal rights (prior to contact) or Aboriginal title (at the time sovereignty is asserted).

Dale Gibson, writing for the Royal Commission on Aboriginal Peoples, supported the trace theory because he assumed the prevalence of European authority prior to the emergence of Métis "socio-cultural entities."[18] He explained in these words the distinction between the trace theory and the independent nation theory and his preference for the former:

> The first [theory] traces Métis rights to the ancient rights of the peoples from whom Métis peoples derive their Aboriginal ancestry. From that point of view, these rights are older than Métis peoples themselves. The other view is that Métis Aboriginal rights were not derived from those of the ancestral Aboriginal nations but sprang into existence when the Métis themselves were born as a distinct people....
>
> Which view is more valid probably depends upon context. For cultural and political purposes, such as the design of arrangements appropriate to the present and future needs and aspirations of Métis people, the second approach seems better suited. New peoples emerged from Aboriginal-European contact and the development of distinctive communities and folk-ways. That fact cannot be ignored by Canadians today or by those who are concerned about the shape of Métis life of tomorrow. For legal purposes, however, the first approach seems more likely to apply. The very notion of Aboriginal rights, in a legal sense, has to do with entitlements carried over from a pre-existing legal order into a newly established legal system. By the time the Métis communities came into being as cohesive socio-cultural entities, a European-derived legal and governmental system (albeit rudimentary in some regions) had been in place for some time. It seems unlikely that any Canadian courts would recognize, in addition to the Aboriginal rights possessed by First Nations citizens, an entirely distinct second order of Aboriginal rights held by new social entities that did not exist when the European-based order first asserted jurisdiction.[19]

Gibson's assumption is that "cohesive" Métis collectivities did not exist when the "European-based order first asserted jurisdiction." However, he does not support this assumption with any analysis or authorities. In addition, he seems to take no account of the varying geographical and temporal patterns of European contact and penetration into the west. We know from *Powley* that an independent, self-identifying Métis community existed in the Sault Ste. Marie area before effective Crown control. The Court held that the date when effective control in the area transferred from the Métis and Ojibway peoples to the English was the period just before 1850.

As for the western Métis, a significant body of historical research supports the birth of a separate Métis identity and consciousness in the northwest as early as the 1770s.[20] The events of 1812–1816 (and in particular the Battle of Seven Oaks) are not the genesis of Métis nationalism, as many have assumed,[21] but rather overt manifestations of an already pre-existing distinct Métis identity. John Foster argues, for example, that it is more appropriate to look to the processes and social relationships that gave rise to a unique and separate identity for the plains Métis:

> Thus, the critical feature in explaining Métis ethnogenesis is not mixed ancestry;

rather, it is the historical circumstances and processes which saw some children enculturated differently than those children associated with Indian bands or with the very few Euro-Canadian communities that could be said to exist in the pre-settlement west.[22]

According to Foster, it was the practice of "wintering" by the Montreal-based fur traders in the last quarter of the eighteenth century that gave rise to the "Plains Métis." Fur-traders would marry Indian women to secure trade alliances and would "winter" by or near their wives' Indian communities. The common experiences of the "freeman," in living "apart from the Indian band and the trading post laid the basis for his children to be enculturated in circumstances distinct from that of the band or the post."[23]

> It is to wintering in the fur trade, not in the 1870s, however, but in the 1770s, that scholars must look to identify the circumstances and the processes which gave rise to the Métis on the Western Plains.[24]

> With the marriage of his children to the children of other freeman families and with their pursuit of his ways, the process of Métis enthnogenesis on the Western Plains, as early as the first quarter of the nineteenth century, was complete.[25]

Unlike First Nations, Métis groups claiming Aboriginal rights must show that their distinct Métis collective identity first arose before the cutoff date prescribed for determining the nature and content of such rights. The earlier a distinct Métis community can be said to have formed, the better are its chances of proving its existence prior to the relevant cutoff date. The above discussion shows that there is considerable support for the existence of distinct Métis communities before the 1800s. Regardless, Gibson's assumption must now be seriously questioned in light of more recent literature dealing with the origins of Métis ethnogenesis, and now *Powley*. Reliance on the trace theory becomes unnecessary and less attractive if Métis communities can demonstrate the existence of a separate and distinct identity prior to any authoritative European presence in Red River or other parts of the Northwest.

Regardless, there are other problems with applying the trace theory to Métis rights and title claims.

PROBLEMS WITH THE TRACE THEORY

There are two ways of conceiving how a Métis person could exercise rights by tracing them through to First Nation antecedents. First, individual Métis could argue that they are entitled to exercise Aboriginal rights because they are direct descendants of individuals from, for example, a Cree band. Although they may identify with a Métis group for social and political reasons, they are claiming legal rights not based on any collective entitlement of the Métis group *per se*, but because of their own individual Cree ancestry. *R. v. Chevrier*[26] illustrates this form of tracing. There, Justice Wright recognized that the accused was unregistered and therefore not an Indian under the *Indian Act*, "but he traces his descent from a member of a tribe that was a signatory to this treaty."[27] As a result, the accused was immune from any provincial legislation that infringed his treaty right, because provinces do not have the power to take away rights originally granted to Indians.[28] Thus, a "Métis" person was able to exercise Cree treaty rights by tracing his ancestry to those who belonged to the tribe when it signed treaty.[29]

It is arguable that such cases are not even properly considered Métis rights cases *per se*: that they are the by-products of an increasingly exclusionary *Indian Act* system of determining status.[30] This type of individual tracing, however, should not be confused with the application of the trace theory to Métis groups as groups. Different considerations apply in that context.[31]

The second form of tracing involves the idea that a Métis individual could exercise rights by belonging to a Métis group that has, as a group, inherited a First Nation's group rights.[32] The source of a Métis group's collective rights would not, however, be based on the group's own independent ability to assert collective rights, but on those rights it has "inherited" from the First Nation society as a result of forming a new separate group that traces its roots, in part, to the First Nation society.[33] To date, case law has not carefully distinguished between these two approaches to tracing.

Even if the courts were correct in applying this second, collective society form of tracing where appropriate, there would be serious problems with this approach to proving Aboriginal rights for Métis. The first concerns the theoretical inconsistency between asserting rights from one's ancestral community and at the same time asserting one's own autonomy and independence as a distinct people. The second is that the trace theory, despite perhaps eluding the prejudicial cutoff dates faced by the Métis, may still confront the requirement that Aboriginal rights not arise as a result of European influence. There are difficulties for the Métis with this related dilemma.[34] Is it possible to dissect Métis rights so that only that part which is Indian in origin gains constitutional protection whereas the European part does not? I will now briefly discuss these two interrelated problems with the trace theory.

Preserving a Distinct Métis Identity

The first, again, is that the more the rights of the Métis are dependent on their Aboriginal ancestry, the more difficult it is for the Métis to justify their distinctness. By tracing the legal entitlements of the Métis to Indian communities, is one not at the same time denying the autonomy and independence of the Métis as a distinct and separate people? There is a fundamental contradiction between

Métis claims of distinctiveness and the assertion of rights based on the practices, traditions, and customs of another group. To claim rights as Indian rights that happen also to belong to the Métis is to deny the very existence of a separate Métis people. Justice Lambert of the British Columbia Court of Appeal, in commenting on the source of Métis rights, agrees that Métis rights must arise from the Métis themselves, as Métis, and not through their Indian ancestors.

> Métis' aboriginal rights must rest on Métis customs, traditions and practices which formed an integral part of their distinctive culture. They cannot rest on Indian aboriginal rights because if they did they would be Indian aboriginal rights held by Métis and not Métis aboriginal rights. That would surely introduce too much complexity into the already difficult questions of biology and genealogy governing questions of entitlement to aboriginal rights.[35]

As I have written elsewhere, if we push the "Indian card" too far, we may risk losing our own separate and unique identity.[36] Such an approach also has the effect of denying an important and integral part of our identity and existence as a people: our European ancestry. To accept only one part of our ancestry to the exclusion of the other is to deny our mixed-blood heritage: to look at our history and worldview from a skewed and incomplete perspective. If the law is going to be true to our mixed heritage, it must accept our European heritage. Any other approach would, quite simply, deny our very identity. However, recognizing our European heritage does not necessarily mean both parts of our heritage are on equal footing. It may be that one part of our heritage is more dominant than the other part. It is quite true, as others have noted, that Métis tend to emphasis the Indian traditions and cultures over the European.[37]

In *Powley*, the Crown argued that the Métis must be able to prove their rights by tracing them back to their Indian ancestors' communities. The respondent Powleys argued that their rights are not derivative of

> the practices of their pre-contact Indian ancestors, and that it is the practices of the Métis people themselves that were integral to the Métis way of life before the time of effective European control that provides the source for Métis rights.[38]

The Supreme Court agreed with the respondents that Métis rights find their source in their own identity as Métis communities. The Court does not require Métis communities to trace their rights through to their Indian ancestors to prove their rights. They can stand alone based on their own communities' practices, customs, and activities:

> [T]he recognition of Métis rights in s. 35 is not reducible to the Métis' Indian ancestry.... By analogy [to the *Van der Peet* test], the test for Métis practices should focus on identifying those practices, customs and traditions that are integral to the Métis community's distinctive existence and relationship to the land.... The focus should be on the period after a particular Métis community arose and before

it came under the effective control of European laws and customs.... We reject the appellant's argument that Métis rights must find their origin in the pre-contact practices of the Métis' aboriginal ancestors. This theory in effect would deny the Métis their full status as distinctive rights-bearing peoples whose own integral practices are entitled to constitutional protection under s. 35(1).[39]

The Court made it clear, however, that this approach does not preclude the Métis community from inheriting practices, customs, and traditions from their Indian ancestors' communities. It just means that the sole relevant issue is whether the custom or practice is and was integral to the distinctive culture of the "Métis" community. This is what the Métis community claiming the right must prove, regardless of whether the practice was integral to the original Indian community. Thus, the source of the Métis right is in the Métis community even when it is based on a practice originally inherited from their Ojibway ancestors. Such recognition does not involve tracing the right to the Ojibway community. This is an important distinction.

The Question of "European Influence"
The Court in *Powley* did not mention the specification, in *Van der Peet*, that community practices cannot be Aboriginal rights if they arise solely as a result of European influence. Does this omission mean that, for the Métis, practices that arose solely as a result of European influence can be recognized as Métis Aboriginal rights? Justice Sharpe, writing for the Ontario Court of Appeal, had this to say:

> Of course, one cannot ignore that s. 35 protects "aboriginal" rights and that [it] is the aboriginality of the Métis that is constitutionally protected.... [O]ne would expect the nature of Métis rights to correspond in broad outline with those of Canada's aboriginal peoples.[40]

This suggests that Aboriginal rights must "look Aboriginal" to be recognized. There is not enough in the judgment to explain how this notion would work if applied to practices fundamental to Métis culture. It does give rise, however, to serious concerns. Different people, depending on their perception of what "being Indian" looks like, could reach different conclusions as to whether a Métis activity is "Indian enough" to warrant protection as an Aboriginal right.[41] Moreover, many Métis activities and customs very dear to their culture—Métis fiddling and Métis land-use customs, for instance—have European origins. Yet these inherited European customs are integral to distinctive Métis culture. On a strict application of the Court of Appeal's stated view, these customs might not be recognized as sufficiently Aboriginal because they don't correspond in broad outline with those of Indians generally. Legal tests that result in such absurd results should be avoided. In the result, Justice Sharpe, having rejected resort to a direct tracing requirement, seems to require a characteristically vague form of "general indirect tracing" that is likely to lead to greater uncertainty. The Supreme Court of Canada did not expressly adopt or reject this proposition.

The fact that the Court said that the *Van der Peet* test must apply by analogy and not directly, and that the test must be modified to take into account the unique circumstances of the Métis, suggests that it did not want to deny the recognition of Métis rights even where they arise as a result of European influence. Indeed, the Court's decision to base the test on the period between European contact and European control must recognize implicitly that European influence is inevitable. Moreover, all one really need do to sidestep this threat to Métis rights is to characterize all Métis practices, customs, and traditions as inherently blended, such that no one practice can be characterized as solely the result of European influence. It is natural to suppose that Métis European and Ojibway heritage would each influence the evolution of any given practice or tradition. Such practices could no longer properly be regarded as either European or Ojibway; they are instead new and distinctly Métis practices. To what extent this is true of actual Métis practices or traditions remains to be seen pursuant to case-by-case analysis.

The Mechanics of Tracing

Another, more practical problem with the direct or indirect trace theory is that it recognizes only one part of Métis heritage. If the Métis were claiming rights from their Indian ancestors, to which of their several Indian ancestors would they trace their rights? Métis are a mixture of French or English and any number of First Nations backgrounds. Sorting through such backgrounds would render the tracing exercise essentially arbitrary. But assume that one could determine that a particular Métis community's predominant Indian ancestral heritage is Cree, and that it is possible under Cree tradition for Cree sub-groups to be composed of mixed Cree and European heritage. How then does the Métis group possess Cree Aboriginal rights? Must not the new Métis group be considered, for this purpose, a sub-group of the Cree? If so, difficult questions arise as to the nature of Cree law and the political autonomy of new Cree "bands." What customs, laws, and practices does Cree law require of new sub-groups (bands) to ensure continuity with the original Cree group? If these laws and customs were not followed, at what point would the new Métis group no longer be regarded as a Cree sub-group? And once it ceased to be Cree, how logical would it be to trace its rights from its Cree predecessors?

An example might illustrate the problem. Imagine that a Métis community with predominantly Cree ancestry occupies land in central Saskatchewan and wishes to assert a claim for Aboriginal title. Based on the trace theory, it would argue that it has a right to occupy the land because it can trace its Aboriginal title through to the Cree. To do so, it is arguable, the Métis community would have to characterize its right to occupy the land as that of a new "band" according to Cree custom. The nature and scope of the Métis title to land would then be dependent on the nature and scope of the title that was recognized to belong to their Cree ancestors. But what if Métis use of land is different from Cree use of land?

Consider the fact that Métis land use was a mixture of uses similar to those of their Indian ancestors, hunting and fishing, but also involved the division of lands, held individually, on a more permanent basis, similar to the French seigniorial system of land tenure.[42] Can newly emerged individual "Cree bands" develop their own unique and distinct forms of land tenure and still remain Cree? To what extent is Cree land law "universal" throughout the Cree nation? This unique Métis use of land may be inconsistent with and unknown to the Cree's understanding of their relation to land. The idea of individual ownership of land is often regarded as foreign to them.[43] How is it possible, then, to trace Métis rights to land if the land use patterns of the Métis are qualitatively different and distinct from those of the Cree?

Because of all these practical and theoretical inconsistencies within the trace theory, courts should be encouraged to reject its use for Métis title claims (as *Powley* has already done for Métis Aboriginal rights) and to examine such claims on the basis that the Métis are separate and autonomous Aboriginal collectivities. The source of Métis title must be derived from their own sense of collective identity as independent Aboriginal societies.

AN ALTERNATIVE THEORY FOR PROVING MÉTIS ABORIGINAL TITLE

The preferred approach to proving Métis Aboriginal title is one that is based on their independent status as an Aboriginal society. As explained previously, it is impossible and a contradiction to assert Métis group rights as an independent autonomous community by relying on the customs, traditions, and activities of an entirely different and distinct community. There may still be a strong moral connection to the mother society; certain customs and traditions may be carried over and continued. But from the day of severance, those customs and traditions are distinctly Métis, even though they may be the mirror image of their Indian predecessors' customs and traditions. Their Indian predecessors' customs and traditions may be relevant in proving the existence of the Métis community's customs and traditions, but they are not their source.[44]

In *Delgamuukw*, the Supreme Court held that the cutoff date in the case of a claim of Aboriginal title is the point at which the Crown asserted sovereignty.[45] Much of the remainder of this article will explore what is meant by the "assertion of Crown sovereignty" and the implications of this inquiry for the Métis. I intend to argue that the most logical and historically accurate definition to be given to that phrase is one that requires "effective occupation" by the Crown for its assertion of sovereignty to have any binding legal effect on the occupants of the territory in question. First, however, I shall briefly explore the trend towards harmonizing the definition of "European contact" with the definition of "assertion of sovereignty."

There is judicial support for the proposition that even the cutoff time of "European contact" for proving Aboriginal rights (other than Aboriginal title) is to be interpreted with reference to the moment when the Crown can be said to have effectively occupied the territory in question.[46] Acceptance of this conclusion would, of course, mean the virtual melding of the *Van der Peet* and *Delgamuukw* time frames into one general test for the assertion of all Aboriginal rights or title: for all Aboriginal peoples perhaps, not just in respect of the Métis.

In a recent law journal article, Mr. Justice Lambert of the British Columbia Court of Appeal predicted something quite similar. Lambert mused that the "assertion of sovereignty" test may likely "emerge" in the future as the appropriate test in all Aboriginal claims, regardless of whether they assert rights to hunt or claims of title to specific tracts of territory. Speaking on the impact of *Delgamuukw*, he predicted that

> [b]ecause the Court relied on the *Doctrine of Continuity* in *Delgamuukw* and set the time of establishing title as the date of sovereignty, which, for consistency, they must also do in self-government cases relying on aboriginal title, I would expect that the date of sovereignty will emerge as a consistent cut-off date throughout.[47]

As regards what this may mean for Métis, he added the following:

> And it would leave the Métis with a comprehensible basis for the assessment of Métis aboriginal rights. Surely Métis aboriginal rights cannot be entirely different in origin from Indian or Inuit aboriginal rights, and surely Métis aboriginal rights cannot be limited to the aboriginal rights of the First Nations people who joined in propagating the new and culturally vibrant Métis community.[48]

At the time Justice Lambert wrote, there were strong indications that any future court faced with the task of adjudicating Métis claims of Aboriginal right would likely choose the assertion of sovereignty as the appropriate alternative cutoff date. To some extent, this prediction came to fruition in the *Powley* litigation.[49]

At trial, Judge Vaillancourt of the Provincial Court saw no need to create a new test to resolve the Métis dilemma. He found support in *R. v. Adams*[50] for the view that "contact" has not been defined as one specific moment in time, but rather as a period of time, the beginning of which may be the first recorded meeting by a European and an Aboriginal group in a certain area, and the end the point at which the Europeans had firmly established "effective control" of the territory.[51] The period between initial contact and control could, therefore, in some cases, be quite lengthy.

In *Powley*, Judge Vaillancourt held that initial European contact in the Sault Ste. Marie area occurred when Jesuit missions were established in 1615. However, effective control did not pass to the European settlers until sometime between 1815 and 1850.[52] Justice O'Neill, of the Ontario Superior Court, upheld this decision on appeal, having found no legal error in Judge Vaillancourt's analysis on this point.[53] Before the Ontario Court of Appeal, the parties seem to have argued positions different from that held by Vaillancourt J. The appellant attorney general argued that there should be an alternative test for the Métis, based on a cutoff point defined as "effective Crown sovereignty."[54] The respondent Powleys argued that the test should be based on a period defined as "effective control."[55] It is unclear from the appeal court judgment whether the respondents were proposing a new alternative to the *Van der Peet* test for Métis or supporting Judge Vaillancourt's interpretation of *Adams*.

The Supreme Court resolved this uncertainty, expressly modifying certain elements of the "pre-contact test to reflect the distinctive history and post-contact ethnogenesis of the Métis, and the resulting differences between Indian claims and Métis claims."[56] That this modification is specific only to the Métis is clear from the Court's declaration that it is modifying the "pre-contact focus of the *Van der Peet* test when the claimants are Métis to account for the important differences between Indian and Métis claims."[57]

Both parties in the Court of Appeal had agreed that the cutoff date for the Sault Ste. Marie Métis is 1850. For the appellant, that was the date of effective Crown sovereignty; for the respondent, it was the date of effective control. It seems implicit from their agreement that both concepts are essentially the same. Certainly, that is my contention in this article. My argument is that the Crown's position is no different from that of the respondent. As I argue below, "effective Crown sovereignty" requires more than a mere assertion of sovereignty (by proclamation, letters patent, charter, or treaty with another European nation); rather, it requires demonstration of actual on-the-ground acquisition of sovereignty, with Crown officials physically present in the area and capable of enforcing its will. On this view, the cutoff dates for Métis Aboriginal rights and for Aboriginal title (generally) would be the same. Use of an "effective control" criterion in respect of Aboriginal title claims would also obviate any need to create a different test for Métis than for First Nations. One single, coherent legal test, applied to Métis and First Nations alike, would ensure harmony of relations and equality of doctrinal application.

Had Judge Vaillancourt's view prevailed, the definition of "European contact" could also have merged with the definition of "assertion of sovereignty," creating a single test for all Aboriginal right and title claims. There would have been no need to create a special test for Métis; the same test, of "effective occupation," could have served the needs of both Métis and First Nations communities, for both Aboriginal title and other Aboriginal rights claims. Unfortunately, the *Powley* decision now leaves open only the possibility of harmonizing Aboriginal title claims between Indian and Métis claimants. Perhaps the Supreme Court of Canada will in the future recognize that it wasn't actually modifying the *Van der Peet* test specifically for the Métis: that effective control had always been a part of the definition of "contact," and that *Van der Peet*, therefore, never posed a problem for Métis claimants.

The following section demonstrates that "effective control" is already a part of the meaning of "assertion of sovereignty" for purposes of Aboriginal title doctrine.

THE ASSERTION OF SOVEREIGNTY BY THE CROWN

An inquiry into when the Crown asserted sovereignty raises certain questions. What must the Crown prove to show that it succeeded in asserting sovereignty over a given territory? Must there be evidence of physical presence and administrative authority in the territory, or are assertions of sovereignty in the form of colonial instruments (paper claims), such as the 1670 Hudson's Bay Company (HBC) royal charter, sufficient?[58]

In the past, courts have rarely engaged in precise analysis of when Crown sovereignty took effect; sovereignty claims have been assumed, without much controversy, to be valid.[59] However, recent analyses by a number of legal scholars have presented credible and convincing arguments that sovereignty may not have been achieved over much of the territory in the Northwest until sometime after the introduction of the North-West Mounted Police in the late 1800s.[60]

In *Delgamuukw*, the Court did not need to consider what constitutes sufficient proof of a valid "assertion of sovereignty." The plaintiffs had conceded, for purposes of the case, that the Crown asserted its sovereignty in 1846, the year of the Oregon Boundary Treaty,[61] and the Court provided no guidance to lower courts facing this issue in future cases. Consequently, the issue of when sovereignty was asserted in British Columbia is not, as a matter of general law, conclusively settled.

One reason why dates of sovereignty have not been a contentious issue in Aboriginal rights cases is that First Nations rarely have difficulty in proving they occupied territory prior to a European Crown's assertion of sovereignty, regardless of the criteria used to establish sovereignty. There is usually ample anthropological and historical evidence available to prove occupation by First Nations well before the date of sovereignty. Thus, most Aboriginal cases are less concerned with the time sovereignty is asserted than with establishing continuing unextinguished

Aboriginal title to such lands.[62] For this reason, concurrence on this issue by all parties concerned has not been difficult to obtain. This has left the issue uncertain and without much detailed analysis.

In cases involving Métis, on the other hand, the dating of sovereignty is of considerably more importance because the occupation of territory by the Métis, as an independent people, may have begun very close to the time the Crown-asserted sovereignty.[63] A court's conclusion that a Métis people did not exist before the Crown's assertion of sovereignty would no doubt defeat any Aboriginal title claims by such a Métis people.

The limited case law dealing with assertions of Crown sovereignty in the context of Métis rights has yet to yield a consistent approach. In *R. v. McPherson*, for example, Judge Gregoire of the Manitoba Provincial Court did not even apply a cutoff date approach, opting instead to accept a test, formulated by Professor Slattery,[64] based on possession of land for a substantial period of time.[65] This approach is similar to the one adopted by Justice L'Heureux-Dubé in dissent in *Van der Peet*.[66] In *R. v. Morin and Daigneault*, Judge Meagher of the Saskatchewan Provincial Court held that the date sovereignty was asserted was 1870, the date when Rupert's Land and the Northwest Territories were admitted into Confederation.[67] In *R. v. Blais*, Judge Swail of the Manitoba Provincial Court held that 1818—the year that Britain and the United States settled their mutual boundary in the Convention of Commerce—was the date sovereignty was asserted.[68] There is, therefore, a general lack of consensus about the approach to be used to ascertain, let alone the date that ought to represent, the assertion of sovereignty by the British in the Northwest.

Academics have also offered different tests for determining the relevant date. Catherine Bell argues that the relevant date for Aboriginal rights claims ought to be the height of colonization.[69] Brian Slattery has argued more recently that the cutoff time should be the "transition date."[70] He argues for a relevant time that is common to both Aboriginal right and Aboriginal title claims, and argues that this time should be the moment when the Crown assumed a fiduciary relationship with the Aboriginal people, recognizing certain obligations that it owes the Aboriginal group.[71]

It is hard to determine the real differences among these various approaches. It may be more of a question of semantics than of actual substantive difference.[72] All seem to agree that effective control over the Aboriginal peoples is the relevant time. Whether the relevant moment is identified as the original date, the transition date, the peak of colonization, or effective Crown sovereignty is not important. What is important is that mere assertion of sovereignty is insufficient for purposes of determining the relevant date for proving the existence of Aboriginal rights and title. The relevant time is that of the actual acquisition of sovereignty.

In light of this discussion, I will now examine in greater detail what the courts have said about the assertion of sovereignty. What, from the judicial perspective, is required for successful assertion of Crown sovereignty over a given territory? Is the mere raw unilateral assertion of sovereignty sufficient? Or must the Crown also demonstrate an authoritative presence in the territory in question?

In answering this question, some judicial opinions appear to make distinctions based on the nature of the legal authority being relied on as evidence of the Crown's intention to acquire territory. For example, the case law appears to treat the various royal charters granted to third parties such as the HBC differently from other sources of Crown territorial intention, such as treaties with other European authorities and the United States. Thus, a useful way to proceed is to examine the effects on territorial acquisition of, first, various royal charters and second, the treaties that did not involve Aboriginal parties.

Royal Charters

The following analysis will first examine the principles of international law regarding territorial acquisition, then examine and contrast English and French colonial law. As will become evident, the principal difference is that, under international law, acquisition of territory by occupation is justified only if the territory is at the time *terra nullius*. Under English colonial law, however, the acquisition of territory by occupation could be effective even if the territory was under prior occupation, but only in respect of the lands of Indigenous non-Christian peoples.[73]

According to international law, acquisition of new territory required more than mere declarations of sovereignty by discovery or symbolic acts (such as planting a flag on a hillside).[74] Such pretensions may have amounted to an inchoate title, but in order to assert sovereignty successfully over a given territory, effective possession was also required to perfect the claim. In international law, effective possession could be acquired through occupation, cession, conquest, or prescription.

> Discovery, while not becoming in and of itself an accepted method of acquiring sovereignty over territory at international law, was treated as giving the discoverer's State an inchoate right against all other States of acquiring the sovereignty to the territory by taking actual possession of the territory within a reasonable time after discovery. The method of that possession . . . was by Occupation, if the land was previously *terra nullius* or by Cession, Conquest or Prescription, if it was not *terra nullius*.[75]

What amounts to effective occupation has evolved over the years. Lindley, writing on this question, described the criteria needed to establish effective occupation:

> There is now a general agreement that the essential point to look to is not whether there is present sufficient force to repel foreign intrusion, or whether the land is in fact being effectively exploited, but whether there has been established over it a

sufficient governmental control to afford security to life and property there. "The taking of possession," says Bluntschi, "consists in fact of organizing politically the recently discovered country, joined with the intention of their exercising power in the future."[76]

Lauterpacht further elaborated on the criteria needed. He said that effective possession requires both "possession and administration." Possession involves physical occupation of territory, while administration requires the establishment of "some responsible authority which exercises governing functions" in the territory.[77]

Under British colonial law, however, the methods of acquiring sovereignty did not always coincide with international law. Although acquisition of territory by conquest, cession, and settlement (occupation of vacant lands, in international law) does generally coincide with international law, there is an important difference between prescription in international law and annexation in British colonial law.

Under international law, the principle of prescription allows for the acquisition of sovereignty where lands are occupied by another society. But for acquisition by prescription to succeed, "[t]here must be, positively, an *actual assertion of sovereignty* supported by its exercise for a *long period*, and there must be, negatively, an *acquiescence* in the claim by the other party."[78] As Youssef states, the

> international law concept of Prescription loses importance in municipal law in that domestic courts are bound to give immediate effect to the will of their Sovereign without a prescriptive period or consideration of the former Sovereign's acquiescence or lack thereof.[79]

Slattery explains the relationship between international law and domestic English colonial law as follows:

> Once the Crown has asserted sovereignty over an area, or performed acts which presuppose its dominion, that territory is British for municipal purposes. The question of whether international legal criteria had been satisfied would not normally arise at the domestic level, and in any case would not entitle a municipal court to decline to give effect to an authoritative Crown claim. Where the Crown's territorial pretensions conflict with international norms, the former will prevail over the latter in the Sovereign's own courts. However, in the case of doubt, it appears that a court may refer to such norms for assistance in ascertaining the Crown's intent, on the principle that the Sovereign is presumed not to act in violation of international rules to which it subscribes.[80]

Although a municipal court cannot question an unambiguous formal assertion of sovereignty by the Crown, it does not necessarily follow that unilateral assertions of sovereignty in the form of orders or legislation are sufficient to establish sovereignty conclusively. A domestic court may conclude, as a matter of common law, that the Crown has acquired sovereignty over the territory only where it has also shown effective possession over the territory subject to the unilateral "documentary" assertion of sovereignty. In this regard, the court is not questioning the claim itself, but ascertaining when the claim begins to take legal effect. That does not take place until satisfaction of the effective occupation requirement.[81]

It is arguable that the requirement of effective occupation for territorial acquisition was recognized as part of the domestic law of England in the Privy Council decision of 1884 in the *Ontario Boundaries* case.[82] In speaking of the legal effect of the HBC charter of 1670, the Privy Council there affirmed the need for the Crown to perfect its documentary claim with actual occupation.

> I do not think one would be disposed to dispute the proposition that, so far as the Crown of England could give it, it [the Royal Charter of 1670] gave to the Hudson's Bay Company a right, if they were able to make themselves masters of the country, to the territory up to the sources of the rivers; but they did not make themselves masters of the whole of that country, for some other nation had come in the meantime.[83]

The "some other nation" mentioned by the Privy Council is the French, who began establishing fur trading posts in the interior of present-day Manitoba and Saskatchewan by the mid 1700s, before the English penetrated the interior.[84]

Implicit in the above dictum is the principle that the HBC needed to establish effective occupation in order to perfect the assertion in the charter of sovereignty over the Hudson Bay watershed.[85] That such occupation was needed is consistent with the wording of the charter itself, which states that lands within the boundaries of the charter are lands to be acquired "that are not already actually possessed by or granted to any of our Subjectes [sic] or possessed by the Subjectes [sic] of an other Christian Prince or State."[86] Thus, the charter's legal effect was to give a mandate to the company, within the boundaries prescribed, to obtain sovereignty, as agents, for the English Crown by subsequent occupation of territory within the limits of the charter, but in all cases to avoid conflict with other European powers, namely the French.

More important from an Aboriginal perspective is the extension of the above principle to non-European entities. According to the Privy Council, the presence of non-European nations also precluded the perfection of sovereignty unless the HBC actually acquired the effective occupation of the territory that was under the prior occupation of such Indigenous nations. In the 1899 decision of *Staples v. R.*,[87] the Privy Council held that the British Crown could not acquire sovereignty over a territory occupied by a non-European nation simply by issuing a royal charter. In order for the British Crown effectively to acquire sovereignty over a territory, there must be actual possession and control of the territory by the subjects authorized by the Crown under its various royal charters. Relying on the above Privy Council decisions, Kent McNeil concludes that

> [t]he cases just discussed [*Ontario Boundaries* and *Staples*] undermine further the assumption that the British Crown acquired sovereignty over the whole of the Hudson watershed by discovery and the issuance of the Royal Charter of 1670. So the better view is that the charter did not effectively grant the whole of the watershed to the Hudson's Bay Company, but merely authorized the Company to acquire sovereignty for the Crown and lands for itself by going out and taking control of the territory. To the extent that the territory was occupied and controlled by aboriginal nations, the Company would have had to assert and enforce jurisdiction over those nations and their lands before it could be in control… Beyond the limits of the posts, the Company's jurisdiction may have extended over its own employees, who included a few aboriginal persons, but virtually no attempt was made to govern the aboriginal nations generally or to control the territories occupied by them.[88]

This view is also consistent with the American understanding of the effect of European charters. Chief Justice Marshall held in *Worcester v. Georgia*[89] that such charters amounted to a grant to the beneficiaries of a right as against other Europeans to acquire lands within the boundaries of the charter that it was capable of acquiring by treaty, conquest, or cession. It was not automatic. The legal effect of colonial charters is clear from the following passage in the judgment:

> These motives for planting the new colony are incompatible with the lofty ideas of granting the soil and all its inhabitants from sea to sea. They demonstrate the truth, that these grants asserted a title against Europeans only, and were considered as blank paper so far as the rights of the natives were concerned.[90]

Although Marshall C.J. was speaking of early English charters that pertained to the east coast of present-day United States, such a view is consistent, as well, with the wording of the HBC charter. Michel Youssef, who studied the various charters issued by the English during the early colonial period, confirms that such an interpretation of the HBC charter is consistent with the general English approach to such matters.

> It was implied in these documents [charters] that the lands in question were not yet part of British dominions. Their discovery and acquisition was the expressed goal since the documents generally empowered the Patent-holders or Charter-holders to *acquire* unspecified lands not actually possessed by any allied Christian princes. Therefore, these were grants which operated *in futuro* [sic]. . . . Thus, these documents contain the clear indication that the Crown neither assumed that British sovereignty already extended to these vaguely defined territories nor purported to extend its sovereignty thereover by the simple expedient of issuing a Charter. Sovereignty had to be gained for the Crown by the Charter-holders who thereupon automatically have a vested colonial title by Crown grant. And where the lands were occupied by indigenous populations, sovereignty had to be gained by conquest.[91]

Indeed, as Youssef concludes, such charters, far from denying or ignoring the sovereignty of Aboriginal nations, are strong evidence of a competing First Nations sovereignty. Thus, even though the wording of the charter can be read to support an unencumbered claim of sovereignty over Rupert's Land, the courts have held that the claims contained in such charters are not complete until such time as the territory is actually possessed by English authority.[92] At most, such a document represents its beneficiaries' pretensions to acquire sovereignty as agents of the Crown.

In light of the above analysis, courts must now re-examine previous assumptions regarding the source and existence of Crown sovereignty. Indeed as Kent McNeil states, decisions such as *Re Labrador Boundary*,[93] *Re Eskimos*,[94] *Baker Lake*,[95] and *La Société de Developpement de la Baie James*,[96] which assumed that sovereignty was acquired over the Hudson Bay watershed territory by discovery and pursuant to a literal reading of the HBC charter, were made *per incuriam*[97] of the *Ontario Boundaries* and the *Staples* decisions.[98]

In integrating these important, but previously overlooked, Privy Council decisions, one can conclude that the HBC charter of 1670 authorized only an inchoate right to acquire sovereignty over lands within the boundaries prescribed. Where the lands were vacant, mere occupation would be sufficient to perfect the claim to sovereignty. Where the lands were occupied by Aboriginal nations, negotiations about such matters were expected to take place. Failing such negotiations, the English (or charter holders) were legally capable of acquiring sovereignty by establishing an authoritative presence (effective occupation) irrespective of the wishes and views of the Indigenous inhabitants.[99]

As Kent McNeil states,

> In order to determine what areas the Company acquired sovereignty over on behalf of the Crown, the historical record therefore has to be examined to see what areas the Company actually controlled.[100]

The question, in relation to the Métis, is whether the Métis occupied the territory as a distinct collectivity prior to the company asserting its own authority over the territory. Any such assessment requires a case-by-case, location-by-location analysis that is beyond the scope of this article. What is certain, however, from this perspective is that assertions of Crown sovereignty based on dates in official documents will have to be evaluated within this rich doctrinal framework.

It might be asserted that France or England effectively asserted sovereignty when their fur-trading posts appeared in the interior of the Northwest: that the presence of fur-trading posts in the surrounding territory constituted sufficient control to perfect a formal assertion of sovereignty. This appears to have been the view of Justice Monk of the Quebec Superior Court in the 1867 case of *Connolly v. Woolrich*.[101] He held that "discovery, [and] hunting and trading explorations"[102] were sufficient to establish occupation, and hence sovereignty, over the Athabaska region. With due respect to Justice Monk, however, such activities are hardly sufficient to constitute "effective control" of the region. Erection of an occasional trading post to encourage trade is arguably not sufficient for authoritative control over the territory.[103] It certainly falls short of the accepted international definitions of effective control.[104]

Many Métis communities developed near HBC trading posts. They were, however, free to develop as separate political communities, despite the HBC's mandate under its royal charter to exercise authority over such areas. Indeed, the HBC deliberately chose not to exercise authority over Aboriginal inhabitants, even within the immediate vicinity of its trading posts. It opted instead to share the area under mutual co-existence; neither group would interfere in the other's internal affairs. This non-interference policy is evident in the testimony given in 1857 before the Select Committee of the British House of Commons by the HBC Governor Sir George Simpson. When questioned on the exercise of the company's authority, Governor Simpson stated:

> [Mr. Grogan] What privileges or rights do the native Indians possess strictly applicable to themselves? — [Simpson] They are perfectly at liberty to do what they please; we never restrain Indians.
>
> [Grogan] Is there any difference between their position and that of the half-breeds? — [Simpson] None at all. They hunt and fish, and live as they please. . . . we exercise no control over them.[105]

Of the Métis community of Norway House, which had an HBC post, it has been said that it was allowed to develop on its own and that "[s]uch autonomous development had not been effectively interfered with by the HBC before 1870, and Canada did nothing to disturb the pattern. . . ."[106] As the quotation from Governor Simpson implies, Métis communities were not only independent and autonomous over land and territorial usage, they were also autonomous in respect of community governance. They developed their own unique customs and laws to govern the affairs of their community. Only if individual Indian or Métis were employed by the HBC did the company assert authority.[107]

This policy of non-intrusion would have been the norm even where Métis communities existed in proximity to European fur-trading posts. It would not have changed until there was a clear indication that the European authorities wished to exert authority over the Métis or Indian communities and had actually acquired such control. Notwithstanding subsequent legislation such as the *Canada Jurisdiction Act, 1803*, it is arguable that there was no such clear indication until well into the late 1800s, with the introduction of the North-West Mounted Police.

The various royal charters issued to companies such as the HBC can no longer be seen, therefore, as having established sovereignty automatically over the territory outlined in the charter. It is, however, still arguable that a European power could obtain sovereignty, even without effective occupation, pursuant to cessions in treaties with other European powers. In other words, it is argued that

England could acquire sovereignty over certain territory simply by being the beneficiary of an appropriate treaty with another European monarch, or with the United States. Such arguments, for example, have figured in deliberations in Métis hunting rights cases aimed at establishing for that purpose the date of Crown sovereignty.[108]

The Effect on Non-Europeans of Treaties Among Colonial Powers
The conclusion I reach above seems compelling as to the legal effects of the various royal charters, but does it apply, as well, to assertions of sovereignty not based on such grants? In other words, would England also have to acquire actual occupation of lands it had obtained by treaty from another European power?

If its decisions in *Calder*[109] and *Delgamuukw*[110] are any indication, the Supreme Court of Canada seems so far to assume that a treaty between the English Crown and another competing state, such as the United States, has the effect of establishing sovereignty over the relevant territory, regardless of the Aboriginal inhabitants in the territory.

In *Calder*, Justice Judson considered when British Columbia came under British sovereignty. He first discussed the 1818 Convention of Commerce between His Majesty and the United States of America, which settled the boundary between the United States and British territory along the 49th parallel east of the Rocky Mountains. At that time, the land west of the Rocky Mountains was in dispute between the United States and Britain. This dispute was not settled until 1846. Justice Judson stated that the area in question (territory claimed by the Nisga'a) came under British sovereignty in 1846 as a result of the Oregon Treaty. "This treaty extended the boundary along the 49th parallel. . . . There was no mention of Indian rights in any of these Conventions or the treaty."[111] His assumption is that Indian peoples did not have sufficient international legal standing to warrant recognition in the Oregon boundary treaty.

There are many problems with this assumption, as with all similar denials of First Nations' international legal personality. First, it is inherently racist and could be viewed as a colourable attempt to reintroduce through the back door the discredited "discovery" doctrine. Second, it does not necessarily follow from a treaty's omission to mention the competing rights of sovereign First Nations that the treaty beneficiaries automatically acquire full sovereignty or that the present occupiers lose legal status or rights. It is more appropriate, and more consistent with *Staples*[112] and with *Worcester*,[113] to argue that such an agreement between the United States and Britain settled, between themselves, only which one of them was to have the exclusive right of acquiring sovereignty over the territory in question. If unoccupied territory were exchanged, then sovereignty would have been perfected at the time of the treaty. If occupied territory were transferred, then sovereignty would have been perfected later: at the time of effective occupation.

Furthermore, it must be remembered that the Nisga'a did not dispute the assertion of sovereignty in *Calder*. They admitted the sovereignty of the Crown and argued instead for recognition of a common law right to Aboriginal title. Neither did the parties to the more recent *Delgamuukw* case dispute the Crown's acquisition of sovereignty in 1846. Chief Justice Lamer noted this when he referred to the lower court's view on the matter:

> McEachern C.J. found . . . , and the parties did not dispute on appeal, that British sovereignty over British Columbia was conclusively established by the Oregon Boundary Treaty of 1846.[114]

Although Lamer C.J. was correct in noting that the parties did not dispute the finding below on sovereignty, he does seem to overstate the decisiveness of McEachern C.J.'s ruling on the issue. In fact, Chief Justice McEachern was far from decisive:

> Because of the view I have of this case, I do not think it is necessary to make a specific finding about a date of British sovereignty over the northern part of the province. No specific argument was made by counsel on this question. For practical purposes, especially in the territory, it could well have been as early as the 1820s, but legally it may not have been until the creation of the colony in 1858. 1846 was the date chosen by Judson J. in *Calder*. In my view the actual date of British sovereignty, whether it be the earliest date of 1803 or the latest date of 1858, or somewhere in between, makes no difference.[115]

In the British Columbia Court of Appeal, both the majority judgment of Macfarlane J.A. and the minority judgment of Lambert J.A. adopted, without any legal analysis, the 1846 Oregon Treaty as the date sovereignty was asserted. However, it is important to note that Justice Macfarlane specifically limited his holding to the facts of the case before him, stating that "[f]or the purposes of this litigation sovereignty was asserted in 1846. . . ."[116]

Although Lambert J.A. did not provide any better analysis of the issue in respect of the facts of *Delgamuukw*, he did, unlike Macfarlane J.A., prescribe the criteria the Crown ought to have to meet to render a claim to sovereignty effective. He stated:

> Sovereignty, of course, does not occur when the first sea captain steps ashore with a flag and claims the land for the British Crown. Cook did that in 1778. Sovereignty involves both a measure of settled occupation and a measure of administrative control.[117]

However, he went on to acknowledge that "all counsel seemed content to treat 1846 as the date of British sovereignty."[118] He concluded by stating that none of the issues in *Delgamuukw* was affected by adopting the 1846 date. The main issues in *Delgamuukw* turned on the significance of sovereignty once it is asserted, not on when or how it is asserted. Nonetheless, Lambert J.A. has stated in clear language the criteria needed to perfect sovereignty over a territory. By his choice of criteria, he has, in essence, adopted the requirement of "effective occupation" as a common law criterion for establishing Crown sovereignty in North America. It is critical to note that Lambert J.A. did not distinguish between claims to sovereignty acquired by occupation and those acquired by treaty with another European power. The same criteria, it appears, would apply in either context. Thus, even if England had negotiated a treaty with the United States that had had the effect of withdrawing American claims over the disputed territory, England would nonetheless have had to perfect, by effective occupation, its now exclusive inchoate claim to sovereignty over the territory subject to the treaty. Of course, the treaty would have transferred to England those territories that were already under American sovereignty. It is a matter for historical inquiry how much territory the United States effectively occupied north of the 49th parallel east of the Rockies in 1818 and west of the Rockies in 1846.

Harry Slade and Robert Freedman, in a paper prepared for a conference dealing with *Delgamuukw*, came to similar conclusions about the gradual nature of territorial acquisitions:

> In our view sovereignty is not established when the first flag is planted on a piece of land; it is an ongoing process. It is important to make a distinction between the initial assertion of sovereignty and its perfection over time. This point was made by Deane and Gaudron JJ. in *Mabo v. State of Queensland* (1992), 107 A.L.R. 1 (H.C.A.) at p. 68:
>
>> In particular, contemporary international law would seem to have required a degree of actual occupation of a "discovered" territory over which sovereignty was claimed by settlement and it is scarcely arguable that the establishment by Phillip in 1788 of the Penal camp at Sydney cove constituted occupation of the vast areas of the hinterland of eastern Australia designated by his Commissions.
>
> If this view of sovereignty is tenable in Canada, then it is necessary to focus on the particular territory over which sovereignty is asserted.[119]

There are clues in *Delgamuukw* suggesting that effective control must be present for the Crown to assert sovereignty successfully. Brian Slattery is of the view that the decision can be read to support the proposition that more than the mere assertion of sovereignty is required. He explains:

> The Court states that the claimant group must show that it occupied the lands in question at the time at which the Crown "asserted sovereignty" over the lands. (par. 144) Elsewhere, however, it speaks of the time that sovereignty was "conclusively established". (par. 145) I suggest that the latter formulation is the more accurate one. In some instances, under Anglo-Canadian law, an unequivocal Crown claim to a certain territory is sufficient to establish Crown title to that territory for purposes

of domestic law. However, given the extensive claims to North American territories launched by various European powers in the early stages of colonization and the vagaries of colonial ambitions and rivalries over the years, it is preferable to specify the date when Crown sovereignty was actually established as the "cut-off date" for proving aboriginal title.[120]

Although there is little in *Delgamuukw* on point, what does exist suggests support for the requirement that the new European claimant perfect its inchoate sovereign claim by effective occupation, even where the territory had been subject to trade between European powers.

It is arguable that the same would be true in respect of the earlier treaties entered into by France and England, such as the Treaty of Utrecht, 1713 and the Treaty of Paris, 1763. Again, a historical factual analysis would have to ascertain the extent to which France had effective occupation of territory at the time of the treaty. As mentioned by Chief Justice Lamer in *Côté*, the French pattern of colonization likely precluded any such perfected claims to sovereignty by the French Crown in the Northwest.[121] For the French, the assertion of sovereignty was a gradual process never fully realized before their defeat in 1759 except upon a relatively small area around the St. Lawrence River. In the words of historian Olive Dickason, "assumption of sovereignty was one thing, realizing it with settlement would prove to be something else again."[122] The Indian tribes were too powerful and adept at diplomacy to allow the French to assert control beyond the immediate surroundings of the colony of New France.[123]

In short, the legal effect of treaties among European powers on the pre-existing rights of the Indigenous occupants is simply the confirmation and transfer of the "right to acquire" sovereignty within the boundaries stated in the treaty. In other words, these treaties amounted to nothing more than a transfer of the inchoate right to acquire sovereignty to the exclusion of the other party(ies) as agreed to in the treaty. Any other conclusion would entail the illogical proposition that peaceful relations between European powers were more prejudicial to the interests of the Indian tribes than a state of continuing warfare. Olive Dickason explains:

> The peace that was signed between Great Britain and the US in Paris in 1783 completely ignored the Amerindians. No provisions were made for their lands in the transfer of territory to the Americans; in particular, the cession of the Ohio Valley aroused a violent reaction on the part of British allies [e.g. Iroquois and Fox Nations]. Once more, Indians had to face the unpleasant fact that siding with the losing side in a European-style war meant loss of lands, even if they themselves had not been defeated. As the Iroquois bitterly observed, they had not been defeated in war, but they certainly were by the peace.[124]

In summary, the courts' treatment under colonial law of claims to sovereignty based on royal charters replicates the requirement in international law that the Crown perfect its claim to sovereignty by demonstrating "effective control" over the territory claimed in such a charter.

The same is not so clearly true, however, in respect of claims to sovereignty based on treaty arrangements between European colonizing powers or their North American descendants. There, the case law seems not to have embraced so clearly the same "effective control" requirement. This uncertainty appears to result largely from the fact that the courts have not turned their mind directly to the issue. They have tended to assume that such treaties result in the blanket confirmation of sovereignty over the territory. However, it is arguable that there is no logical justification for maintaining the distinction. On the contrary, there is every reason to extend the principle of effective occupation to claims based on treaty as well as to those based on royal charter.

Insistence in both spheres upon perfection by "effective control" would also be more consistent with contemporary principles of international human rights. In and of itself, this requirement would still fall well short of both the spirit and the intent of such principles[125] because it fails to accord any international legal personality to Aboriginal peoples. In this respect, adoption of this approach would not eliminate the discrimination inherent in domestic Aboriginal rights law; it would not achieve equality as between peoples. It would, however, confine the beast of discrimination within narrower, ascertainable limits, without disturbing either the foundations in domestic colonial law of contemporary Aboriginal rights jurisprudence or the authority of such leading decisions as *Delgamuukw*, *Sparrow*, or *Van der Peet*, which perpetuate the colonial myth.

It would do so by ascribing at least some limited legal significance to Indigenous peoples' actual presence in the relevant territory; the very fact of their presence would impose on the Crown an additional burden in the course of legitimate territorial acquisition. Instead of giving routine effect to blanket assertions of sovereignty over vast amounts of territory—assertions altogether unknown to the very Aboriginal communities affected by them—the "effective control" requirement would proceed case by case to inquire contextually whether, when, and how the relevant European authorities made plain to those already there their intention and capacity to control the territory they claimed to rule.

Some might argue that the "act of state" doctrine would not allow a court to question the Crown's unilateral assertions. This may be the case in other contexts, but the Supreme Court held in *Calder* that this doctrine does not apply to Aboriginal title claims. John Borrows explains:

> Canadian courts are not prevented from reviewing Sovereign acquisitions of new territory in cases dealing with Aboriginal title. The "Act of State" doctrine, which deals with this issue, was examined by the Supreme Court of Canada in the *Calder* case and was found not to apply. Justice Hall gave two reasons why it was inappropriate to extend the Act of State doctrine to cases dealing with Aboriginal title. First, "it has never been invoked in claims dependent on aboriginal title" and,

therefore, a finding that the Act of State doctrine applied to cases dealing with Aboriginal title would be unprecedented and unsupported by the jurisprudence. Second, the Act of State doctrine only deals with situations where a "Sovereign, in dealings with another Sovereign (by treaty of cession or conquest) acquires land." British Columbia did not acquire Gitksan and Wet'suwet'en land by a treaty or conquest. Therefore, this doctrine would have no application in examining assertions of Crown sovereignty because the courts would not be reviewing or enforcing a treaty between two sovereign states, nor would they be reviewing a grant of title from a previously conquered sovereign. As such, the courts would be permitted to review the effects of the Crown assertion of sovereignty over non-treaty Aboriginal peoples in British Columbia.[126]

In sum, an effective and valid confirmation of Crown sovereignty requires an assertion of sovereignty by royal prerogative manifest in a valid legal instrument, followed by (or endorsing) actual control by government officials of the relevant territory. The term "assertion of sovereignty" in *Delgamuukw* requires both these conditions to be present. Acceptance of this principle would obviate the need to distinguish Métis claims from First Nation claims, avoiding any unfairness as between the two kinds of claims. Both groups of Aboriginal peoples would benefit from the view that sovereignty crystallizes in a given territory only when there is both assertion and control by a European government. The Métis would benefit because effective English or Canadian control over an area may not have occurred until sometime after this mixed-ancestry community had formed as a distinct political society.

CONCLUSION

As mentioned at the outset, *Delgamuukw* has opened wider than before the door to successful Métis claims of Aboriginal title. Prior to *Delgamuukw*, it was not entirely clear how far back in time an Aboriginal group claiming title to land would have to show they occupied the land. Early on, it was thought that the group had to show occupation since "time immemorial."[127] The Court in *Delgamuukw* held, however, that the proper time frame was the date when the Crown asserted sovereignty. For Métis societies, born as distinct societies relatively recently (mid-1700s to 1800s, depending on the geographical and temporal pattern of fur-trade expansion), this second view is clearly the more congenial.

However, there are cases where strict application of a formalistic understanding of "assertion of sovereignty" could disadvantage Métis claims significantly. (Suppose, for example, that the HBC charter of 1670 turned out to be the moment of sovereignty in the Northwest.) Despite this concern, I have argued that it would be inappropriate for the courts to apply a trace theory to Métis title claims because of the practical and theoretical problems with its application. Neither, I have argued, is it appropriate to adopt, just for the Métis, an alternative time frame distinct from the "assertion of sovereignty" time frame, understood formalistically. That would create inequality between Métis and First Nations. It is already problematic that the Supreme Court of Canada, in *Powley*, has done just that with regard to the time frame for proving other Aboriginal rights. This mistake should not be repeated. The preferred approach is to define "assertion of sovereignty" with reference to a well-informed understanding of Aboriginal–European relations, as reflected in established international and colonial principles of territorial acquisition. These principles require that effective control of territory accompany any assertion of sovereignty before sovereignty can be validly acquired over an area.

The recent *Powley* case demonstrates that the Supreme Court of Canada is willing to create a new category of Aboriginal rights analysis specific to the Métis. The problem is that, in doing so, it has made the test for proving First Nations' Aboriginal rights more onerous than that for proving Métis Aboriginal rights. First Nations may argue that this development is unjustified and unfair. What is perhaps most unfortunate is that the Court need not have created a separate test for the Métis; it could have construed "European contact" as a period up to and including the time when the Crown exerted effective control in a given area. As long as a Métis group existed prior to this culminating moment, it would then have been capable of proving it had Aboriginal rights at the time of European contact. If this view took hold not as an exceptional scheme for Métis communities, but as a welcome adaptation of the generic European contact rule prescribed in *Van der Peet*, it would ensure harmony and consistency between Aboriginal rights and Aboriginal title claims. Such developments in the legal doctrine of Aboriginal rights and title would reflect more accurately the reality of European-Canadian relations generally and be a step toward greater harmony in our law and our society.

NOTES

[1] *Delgamuukw v. British Columbia*, [1997] 3 S.C.R. 1010, [1998] 1 C.N.L.R. 14 [*Delgamuukw*].
[2] Chief Justice Lamer wrote the majority judgment. Justice La Forest wrote a separate judgment concurring in the result. All references will be to the majority opinion unless otherwise specified.
[3] *R. v. Van der Peet*, [1996] 2 S.C.R. 507, 4 C.N.L.R. 177 [*Van der Peet*].
[4] This dilemma and how to overcome it is one of the major issues in *R. v. Powley*, [2003] 2 S.C.R. 207, [2003] 4 C.N.L.R. 321, 2003 SCC 43 [*Powley*], aff'g (2001), 53 O.R. (3d) 35 (C.A.) [*Powley* (C.A.)], aff'g (2000), 47 O.R. (3d) 30 (S.C.J.) [*Powley* (S.C.J.)], aff'g [1999] 1 C.N.L.R. 153 (Ont. Ct. J. (Prov. Div.)) [*Powley* (Prov. Ct.)]. The implications of *Powley* in overcoming the obvious barrier that a strict reading of *Van der Peet, ibid.* creates are discussed in more detail below.
[5] *Powley, ibid.* at para. 37.
[6] One of the most controversial issues in Canadian law concerns the criteria for determining who is Métis. The Supreme Court of Canada provided some guidance in *Powley, ibid.* Prior to *Powley*, there seemed to be agreement that a definition of Métis included, at a minimum, self-identity and community acceptance. The dispute concerned whether there was a need for a third criterion, requiring

demonstration of some objective indication of an individual's historical connection to a Métis family/ community. Both lower courts in *Powley* required, as a third criterion, some evidence of ancestral connection; they differed on whether there had to be direct evidence of genealogical descent (genetic connection) or whether ancestral family connection (which need not be genetic) is sufficient. The Court of Appeal deferred the issue, noting that the Powleys satisfy the more onerous test of genetic connection. It preferred to await a future case in which a litigant claimed to belong to a Métis community despite not having evidence of genealogical connection. The Supreme Court of Canada held in *Powley* that the indicia of Métis status under s. 35(1) of the *Constitution Act, 1982*, being Schedule B to the *Canada Act 1982* (U.K.), 1982, c. 4, are self-identification, ancestral connection, and community acceptance. It agreed, however, with Justice O'Neill (in *Powley* (S.C.J.), *supra* note 4) that there is should be no requirement for a minimum blood quantum, but rather some proof that the claimant's ancestors belonged to the historic Métis community by birth, adoption, or other means. The Court, therefore, went beyond the Court of Appeal, rejecting explicitly a genetic connection requirement, but did agree with the Court of Appeal that it should refrain from further elaboration without more extensive argument.

Because this paper does not directly address identity issues, I will not examine the matter further, except to say that a definition restricted to satisfying the criteria of individual self-identity and community acceptance (without a need to show ancestral family or genetic connection) would be more in line with principles of self-determination of peoples and with the international law concerning citizenship. This is not to say that ancestral connection requirements are not appropriate, but that the decision to apply them should rest with the Aboriginal people, not with the courts. See Larry Chartrand, *Métis Identity and Citizenship* (2001) 12 Windsor Rev. Legal Soc. Issues 5. See also Canada, *Report of the Royal Commission on Aboriginal Peoples*, vol. 4 (Ottawa: Supply and Services Canada, 1996), c. 5 "Métis Perspectives" [*Report of the Royal Commission*] and the research papers cited therein.

[7] These problems are discussed in more detail below. See *infra* notes 25–43 and accompanying text.

[8] See for example: Isabelle Schulte-Tenckhoff, "Reassessing the Paradigm of Domestication: The Problematic of Indigenous Treaties" (1998) 2 Rev. Const. Stud. 239; David Schneiderman, "Theorists of Difference and the Interpretation of Aboriginal and Treaty Rights" (1996) 14 International Journal of Canadian Studies 35; Patrick Macklem, "Distributing Sovereignty: Indian Nations and Equality of Peoples" (1993) 45 Stan. L. Rev. 1311; Paul Joffe, "Assessing the *Delgamuukw* Principles: National Implications and Potential Effects in Quebec" (2000) 45 McGill L.J. 155; John Borrows, "Sovereignty's Alchemy: An Analysis of *Delgamuukw v. British Columbia*" (1999) 37 Osgoode Hall L.J. 537; James Youngblood Henderson et al., *Aboriginal Tenure in the Constitution of Canada* (Scarborough, Ont.: Carswell, 2000); Patricia Monture-Angus, *Journeying Forward* (Halifax: Fernwood, 1999); Michel Youssef, *The Survival of Native Territorial Sovereignty in Canadian Land Claims Law* (LL.M. Thesis, Université d'Ottawa, 1994) [unpublished].

[9] *Dumont v. Canada (A.G.)*, [1990] 1 S.C.R. 25, [1990] 2 C.N.L.R. 19 [*Dumont*], rev'g [1988] 5 W.W.R. 193 (Man. C.A.) [*Dumont* (C.A.)] on the issue of standing.

[10] *Manitoba Act, 1870* (U.K.), 33 Vict. c. 3, reprinted in R.S.C. 1985, App. II, No. 8. See the minority judgment of O'Sullivan J.A. in *Dumont* (C.A.), *ibid.* at 198:

> The *Manitoba* Act sanctioned by Imperial legislation, is not only a statute; it embodies a treaty which was entered into between the delegates of the Red River settlement and the Imperial authority.

[11] *Morin v. The Queen* (Q.B. No. 619). This case has not gone to trial. Only pleadings are available at this time. The statement of claim was filed on 1 March 1 1994 in the Court of Queen's Bench in Saskatoon, Sask.

[12] In *Delgamuukw*, *supra* note 1, Chief Justice Lamer justified the distinction as follows (at paras. 144–45):

> In order to establish a claim to aboriginal title, the aboriginal group asserting the claim must establish that it occupied the lands in question at the time at which the Crown asserted sovereignty over the land subject to the title. The relevant time period for the establishment of title is, therefore, different than for the establishment of aboriginal rights to engage in specific activities. In *Van der Peet*, I held, at para. 60 that "[t]he time period that a court should

consider in identifying whether the right claimed meets the standard of being integral to the aboriginal community claiming the right is the period prior to contact...." This arises from the fact that in defining the central and distinctive attributes of pre-existing aboriginal societies it is necessary to look to a time prior to the arrival of Europeans. Practices, customs or traditions that arose solely as a response to European influences do not meet the standard for recognition as aboriginal rights.

On the other hand, in the context of aboriginal title, sovereignty is the appropriate time period to consider for several reasons. First, from a theoretical standpoint, aboriginal title arises out of prior occupation of the land by aboriginal peoples and out of the relationship between the common law and pre-existing systems of aboriginal law. Aboriginal title is a burden on the Crown's underlying title. However, the Crown did not gain this title until it asserted sovereignty over the land in question. Because it does not make sense to speak of a burden on the underlying title before that title existed, aboriginal title crystallized at the time sovereignty was asserted.

[13] *Ibid.* at para. 138.
[14] *Supra* note 3.
[15] *Ibid.* at paras. 60–61. The holding that Aboriginal rights are only those activities and customs that were of central significance to Aboriginal societies prior to contact with Europeans has been the subject of extensive academic and judicial criticism. Such a requirement is seen as "freezing" Aboriginal societies into a "museum"-like state of existence precluding the natural processes of evolution and adaptation necessary for societies to respond to outside influences. See for example John Borrows, "The Trickster: Integral to a Distinctive Culture" (1997) 8 Const. Forum Const. 27; Russel Barsh & James Youngblood Henderson, "The Supreme Court's *Van der Peet* Trilogy: Native Imperialism and Ropes of Sand" (1997) 42 McGill L.J. 993; Sebastien Grammond, "La Protection Constitutionnelle des Droits Ancestraux des Peuples Autochtones et L'arret Sparrow" (1991) 36 McGill L.J. 1382; Kent McNeil, "How Can Infringements of the Constitutional Rights of Aboriginal Peoples Be Justified?" (1997) 8 Const. Forum Const. 33. The minority judgments of L'Heureux-Dubé and McLachlin JJ. in *Van der Peet, ibid.* were also very critical of Chief Justice Lamer on this point. See *ibid.* at paras. 164–70, 244–50, respectively.
[16] *Van der Peet, ibid.* at paras. 66–67.
[17] *Powley, supra* note 4 at para. 38.
[18] Dale Gibson, "General Sources of Métis Rights" in *Report of the Royal Commission, supra* note 6, 271 at 281.
[19] *Ibid* at 280–81.
[20] John Foster, *Wintering, The Outsider Adult Male and the Ethnogenesis of the Western Plains Métis* (University of Alberta, 1993) [unpublished]. See also L. Heinemann, *An Investigation into the Origins and Development of the Métis Nation, the Rights of the Métis as an Aboriginal People, and their Relationship and Dealings with the Government of Canada* (Association of Métis and Non-Status Indians, 1984) [unpublished]; Jacqueline Peterson, "Many Roads to Red River: Métis Genesis in the Great Lakes Region, 1680–1815," in Jacqueline Peterson & Jennifer S.H. Brown, eds., *The New Peoples: Being and Becoming Métis in North America* (Winnipeg: University of Manitoba Press, 1985) 37 at 64. Peterson explains that the events of 1815–1816 resulted in a reformulation of symbols of identity that became more overt and expressive of an already pre-existing sense of distinct Métis identity. Historian Olive Dickason preferred to characterize the same events as a "catalyst which transformed mild awareness into conviction": see Olive Patricia Dickason, "'One Nation' in the Northeast to 'New Nation' in the Northwest: A Look at the Emergence of the Métis" in Peterson & Brown, *ibid.,* 19 at 31. See also Heather Devine, "Proto-Métis Community Formation and the Rise of the Métis People" (Paper presented to the Métis People in the 21st Century Conference, Indigenous Bar Association, June 2003) [unpublished].
[21] See for example Catherine Bell, "Who Are the Métis People in Section 35(2)?" (1991) 29 Alta. L. Rev. 351 at 359; *R. v. McPherson,* [1992] 4 C.N.L.R. 144 (Man. Prov. Ct.) at 149 [*McPherson*], rev'd on the issue of remedy (1994), 90 Man. R. (2d) 290 (Q.B.).
[22] Foster, *supra* note 20 at 4.

[23] *Ibid.* at 19.
[24] *Ibid.* at 7.
[25] *Ibid.* at 21.
[26] *R. v. Chevrier*, [1989] 1 C.N.L.R. 128 (Ont. Dist. Ct.).
[27] *Ibid.* at 130.
[28] *R. v. Ferguson*, [1993] 2 C.N.L.R. 148 (Alta. Prov. Ct. (Crim. Div.)) [*Ferguson*], aff'd [1994] 1 C.N.L.R. 117 (Alta. Q.B.) also illustrates that some mixed-blood individuals who are culturally and linguistically Cree may be socially and politically labelled Métis. At issue in this case was the meaning of the term "Indian" in para. 12 of the 1929 Alberta Natural Resources Transfer Agreement (NRTA), which took effect pursuant to s. 1 of the *Constitution Act, 1930* (U.K.), 20–21 Geo. V., c. 45. The court, in that context, interpreted "Indian" by reference to the *Indian Act*, R.S.C. 1927, c. 98, which had defined "Indian" in relation to lifestyle. Thus, Goodson J. held that Ferguson was an Indian for the purposes of the NRTA even though he was not registered under the more stringent rules in the present-day *Indian Act*. There are conflicting authorities in the prairies as to how to interpret this provision, which also appears, in identical language, in the NRTAs concluded with Saskatchewan and Manitoba. In *R. v. Grumbo*, [1998] 3 C.N.L.R. 172 [*Grumbo*], the Saskatchewan Court of Appeal held it to be inappropriate to interpret the term "Indians" in the NRTA without first determining whether the Métis at the time had Aboriginal rights that the NRTA would have protected. This view, in other words, required proof that Métis had Aboriginal rights to hunt. For further analysis of the implications of this decision, see Larry Chartrand, "Are We Indians or Are We Métis? A Commentary on *R. v. Grumbo*" (1999–2000) 31 Ottawa. L. Rev. 269 [Chartrand, "Are We Indians?"]. In *R. v. Blais*, [2003] 2 S.C.R. 236, [2003] 4 C.N.L.R. 219, 2003 SCC 44 [*Blais*], aff'g (2001), 156 Man. R. (2d) 53, [2001] 3 C.N.L.R. 187 (Man. C.A.) [*Blais* (C.A.)], aff'g [1998] 4 C.N.L.R. 103 (Man. Q.B.), aff'g [1997] 3 C.N.L.R. (Man. Prov. Ct.) [*Blais* (Prov. Ct.)], however, the Supreme Court of Canada held that the Manitoba NRTA was drafted with the intention that the Métis not be included within the term "Indians" as it was understood at the time. *Blais*, in effect, has now superseded *Grumbo*. It no longer matters for this purpose whether a Métis claimant can prove Aboriginal rights; the NRTA will never apply to a Métis who identifies as a Métis from a Métis community. As the Court made clear in *Blais, ibid.* at paras. 6, 42, that does not preclude a Métis from relying on Aboriginal rights pursuant to *Powley, supra* note 4. It just means that such a person cannot claim to be an Indian under the NRTA. However, if one meets the *Ferguson* criteria, then one may still be an Indian for NRTA purposes. *Blais* did not directly address the *Ferguson* scenario. Confusion will no doubt emerge when an individual's identity is not solidly in one camp or the other. For those who "live the Indian lifestyle," any association with a Métis identity could very well be seen as a negative factor threatening their ability to avail themselves of the NRTA's protection of hunting and fishing.
[29] Some defendants may have openly asserted Métis heritage and identity prior to being charged with a hunting offence. No doubt evidence of such identity is downplayed, as a matter of litigation strategy, to ensure success in arguing defences based on assertions of Indian lifestyle and acceptance. This is evident in Alberta when the courts use the "*Ferguson* test" in applying the NRTA defence to non-status Indians charged with hunting violations. In *R. v. Desjarlais*, [1996] 3 C.N.L.R. 113 (Alta. Q.B.), aff'g in part [1996] 1 C.N.L.R. 148 (Alta. Prov. Ct.), Clark J. applied the criteria established by Goodson J. in *Ferguson, ibid.* as to when an individual is "Indian enough" to be considered to be living an Indian lifestyle.
[30] See John Giokas & Paul Chartrand, "Who Are the Métis in Section 35? A Review of the Law and Policy Relating to Métis and 'Mixed-Blood' People in Canada" in Paul Chartrand, ed., *Who Are Canada's Aboriginal Peoples?* (Saskatoon: Purich, 2002) 83. These authors identify the processes that have led some individuals—referred to by the authors (at 106) as the "boundary Indians"—to self-identify as Métis on the basis of mixed heritage and to the removal, through compulsory enfranchisement, of their legal identity as Indians under the *Indian Act*. These individuals may have no cultural or genealogical connection to historically distinct Métis communities.
[31] *Ibid.* at 111.
[32] Mark Stevenson argues that Métis rights can validly arise either by inheritance or as part of the

unique and distinct Métis culture: "Section 35 and Métis Aboriginal Rights: Promises Must Be Kept" in Ardith Walken & Halie Bruce, eds., *Box of Treasures or Empty Box? Twenty Years of Section 35* (Penticton: Theytus, 2003) 63 at 71.

[33] The idea of autonomous political groups inheriting rights and privileges from their predecessor groups is not uncommon. On one level, Canada can be understood to have done so. When Canada became a nation independent from England, it was not reborn with an empty slate. It inherited rights and obligations from England.

[34] For a critique of the court's use of a cultural relativism model of analysis, see Macklem, *supra* note 8 at 1343–44. See also Marlee Kline, "The Colour of Law: Ideological Representations of First Nations in Legal Discourse" (1994) 2 Social and Legal Studies 45 at 119; Henderson et al., *supra* note 8 at 323. Henderson notes, *ibid.,* that the court's search for difference

> continues to value the "pure" over the composite, mixed, or mosaic. Such distinctions have historically not only created the racial masks, identities, and politics of Indians, Métis, and Inuit, but have also attempted to perpetuate the idea of "pure" or integral Aboriginal law and rights before European colonization. The result is to reject the Aboriginal compromises with the colonizers and their resulting inter- and intraculturality, cross-culturality, or syncretic visions as ineligible for constitutional protection.

The negative implications of this judicial approach for those that are by definition a mixed-heritage people are obvious. With respect to the Métis, see further Bell, *supra* note 21 at 366.

[35] *Delgamuukw v. British Columbia* (1993), 104 D.L.R. (4th) 470 (B.C.C.A.) at 654, Lambert J.A. dissenting [*Delgamuukw* (C.A.)]. *Delgamuukw, supra* note 1, reversed in part the majority judgment in *Delgamuukw* (C.A.), but without reference to this issue.

[36] Chartrand, "Are We Indians?" *supra* note 28 at 276.

[37] For example, Métis governance and social order processes have been noted to resemble those of the plains Ojibway. Like the plains Ojibway, the Métis had a main chief and several secondary chiefs. See Lawrence J. Barkwell, "Early Law and Social Control Among the Metis" in Samuel Corrigan & Lawrence Barkwell, eds., *The Struggle for Recognition: Canadian Justice and the Métis Nation* (Winnipeg: Pemmican, 1991) 7 at 30–32. Justice Sharpe, in *Powley* (C.A.), *supra* note 4, also acknowledged (at para. 119) that the Métis are closely related to the Ojibway and that this close relationship makes it appropriate to place some weight on pre-contact Ojibway hunting practice when considering how important hunting is to their Métis descendants.

[38] *Powley* (C.A.), *ibid.* at para. 99.

[39] *Powley, supra* note 4 at paras. 36–38.

[40] *Powley* (C.A.), *supra* note 4 at paras. 103–4.

[41] The Court, in presenting this view, is relying on a test, based on cultural relativism, that is inherently arbitrary. For further discussion of this concern see Larry Chartrand, *The Political Dimension of Aboriginal Rights* (LL.M. Thesis, Queen's University, 2001) at 55–67 [unpublished].

[42] The individual plots of land were held along rivers with narrow river fronts but extending back a considerable distance. According to Thomas Flanagan, *Métis Lands in Manitoba* (Calgary: University of Calgary Press, 1991) at 16, the "average river lot was about six chains wide" and two miles deep. Although similar to the French seigniorial system, these land use patterns, according to Robert Coutts, are actually adopted from the "infield and outfield system found in Scotland and brought to Red River by Selkirk settlers." See Robert Coutts, "The Role of Agriculture in an English Speaking Halfbreed Economy: The Case of St. Andrews, Red River" (1988) 4 Native Studies Review 67 at 73.

[43] For an excellent summary of how First Nations related to the land see *Report of the Royal Commission, supra* note 6, vol. 2 at 457–59.

[44] *Powley* (C.A.), *supra* note 4 at para. 120.

[45] *Delgamuukw, supra* note 1 at para. 145.

[46] *Powley* (Prov. Ct.), *supra* note 4 at para. 85.

[47] Hon. Mr. Justice Douglas Lambert, "*Van der Peet* and *Delgamuukw*: Ten Unresolved Issues" (1998) 32 U.B.C. L. Rev. 249 at 269 [emphasis in original]. It could be some time yet before the Supreme Court is prepared to revisit the test. In the recent *M.N.R. v. Mitchell,* [2001] 1 S.C.R. 911, the Court

reaffirmed the pre-contact *Van der Peet* test without even addressing the critical literature.

[48] Lambert, *ibid.*

[49] *Supra* note 4.

[50] *R. v. Adams*, [1996] 3 S.C.R. 101, 4 C.N.L.R. 1 [*Adams*].

[51] In *Adams, ibid.*, the Supreme Court of Canada had to decide when European contact occurred in the St. Lawrence River valley in order to determine the cutoff date for a claim of Aboriginal right to fish in Lake St. Francis brought by a Mohawk member of the St. Regis (Akwesasne) reserve in Quebec. The Court stated (at para. 46) that

> [t]he arrival of Samuel de Champlain in 1603, and the consequent establishment of effective control by the French over what would become New France, is the time which can most accurately be identified as "contact" for the purposes of the *Van der Peet* test.

[52] *Powley* (Prov. Ct.), *supra* note 4 at para. 90.

[53] *Powley* (S.C.J.), *supra* note 4 at para. 26.

[54] *Powley* (C.A.), supra note 4 at para. 95.

[55] *Ibid.* at para. 96.

[56] *Powley, supra* note 4 at para. 14.

[57] *Ibid.* at para. 18.

[58] In its statement of defence in the *Morin* claim to Aboriginal title in northwest Saskatchewan (see *supra* note 11 and accompanying text), the federal Crown argues that any of the 1670 HBC charter, the 1713 Treaty of Utrecht, or the 1763 Treaty of Paris is sufficient to prove the assertion of sovereignty to the territory claimed.

[59] For example, in *R. v. Sparrow*, [1990] 1 S.C.R. 1075 at 1103, 3 C.N.L.R. 160 at 177, the Supreme Court of Canada made the following remark:

> It is worth recalling that while British policy towards the native population was based on respect for their rights to occupy their traditional lands, a proposition to which the Royal Proclamation of 1763 bears witness, there was from the outset never any doubt that sovereignty and legislative power, and indeed the underlying title, to such lands vested in the Crown.

This statement was made without any detailed discussion as to why. The Court felt that the United States Supreme Court decision in *Johnson v. M'Intosh*, 21 U.S. (8 Wheat.) 543 (1823) was sufficient to justify its conclusion.

[60] See for example Kent McNeil, "Aboriginal Nations and Quebec's Boundaries: Canada Couldn't Give What It Didn't Have" in Daniel Drache & Roberto Perin, eds., *Negotiating With a Sovereign Québec* (Toronto: Lorimer, 1992) 107 [McNeil, "Aboriginal Nations"] and Youssef, *supra* note 8. The arguments in support of this point are set out in the text below.

[61] *Delgamuukw, supra* note 1 at para. 145.

[62] This may not be the case if the First Nation is asserting sovereignty itself or is concerned about territory it has occupied only recently.

[63] One need only examine the decision of Mahoney J. in *Baker Lake v. Canada*, [1980] 1 F.C. 518 [*Baker Lake*] to appreciate the negative implications for the Métis of a finding that 2 May 1670 was the date the English asserted sovereignty over Rupert's Land.

[64] Brian Slattery, "Understanding Aboriginal Rights" (1987) 66 Can. Bar Rev. 727 at 756.

[65] Ultimately, Gregoire J. did not apply this test; instead, he opted to "trace" the rights of the Métis, having concluded that the Big Eddy community would not be able to satisfy the "substantial period of time" test: *McPherson, supra* note 21 at 153.

[66] *Van der Peet, supra* note 3 at para. 175.

[67] *R. v. Morin and Daigneault*, [1996] 3 C.N.L.R. 157 (Sask. Prov.. Ct.) at 165. The judge's reasoning consisted of the following brief paragraph:

> There is no agreement on the date of the declaration of British sovereignty. As Crown Counsel stated, no evidence or law has been placed before the Court as to the date of assertion of British sovereignty. After examining the issue I am persuaded to agree with the Crown that sovereignty was asserted with the Imperial Order of 1870 when Rupert's Land and Northwest Territories were admitted into confederation.

This admission by the Crown was arguably quite generous in light of the Crown's assertions in its statement of defence in *Morin v. The Queen, supra* note 11.

[68] See Blais (Prov. Ct.), *supra* note 28 at paras. 127–29, citing *Calder v. British Columbia (A.G.)*, [1973] S.C.R. 313 [*Calder*].

[69] Catherine Bell, "Métis Constitutional Rights in Section 35(1)" (1997) 36 Alta. L. Rev. 180. Bell states in her paper at 189–90 that

> [i]t is only through the historical process of colonization which occurred before, during and after assertions of sovereignty that Aboriginal societies became fundamentally altered.... It refers to the actual dispossession of land, the imposition of one legal system over another, the amalgamation of autonomous political entities and gradual assimilation of the colonized.... British colonial law governing this process, and the actual relations between the colonizer and the colonized are the legal basis of Aboriginal rights recognized in s.35(1). Understood in this context, s.35(1) does not address injustices arising from a theoretical shift in legal and political regimes that occurs as a result of the assertion of sovereignty but actual injustices suffered by "peoples" as a corollary of British sovereignty through the historical process of colonization.

[70] Brian Slattery, "Making Sense of Aboriginal and Treaty Rights" (2000) 79 Can. Bar Rev. 196 at 218.

[71] *Ibid.* Paul Chartrand & John Giokas, "Defining 'The Métis People': The Hard Case of Canadian Aboriginal Law" in Chartrand, *supra* note 30, 268 at 286–87 have applied Slattery's "transition date" approach to the Métis of Red River and have concluded that the assumption of Canadian constitutional responsibility over the Métis there took place after the Crown agreed to the terms of the *Manitoba Act, 1870*, which protects Métis interests as a condition of the Métis agreement to allow Canada to acquire the territory.

[72] Bell, *supra* note 69 at 190 applies her "peak of colonization" approach to the Red River Métis and also chooses 1870 as the relevant time for determining Aboriginal rights claims of this group.

[73] See Robert A. Williams, *The American Indian in Western Legal Thought* (Oxford: Oxford University Press, 1990) at 317; David Elliot, "Aboriginal Title" in Brad Morse, *Aboriginal Peoples and the Law: Indian, Métis and Inuit Rights in Canada*, rev. 1st ed. (Ottawa: Carleton University Press, 1985) 48 at 59.

[74] Friedrich August Freiherr Von der Heydte, "Discovery, Symbolic Annexation and Virtual Effectiveness in International Law" (1935) 29 A.J.I.L. 448, referred to in Paul Joffe & Mary Ellen Turpel, *Extinguishment of the Rights of Aboriginal Peoples: Problems and Alternatives*, vol. 1 (Report of the Royal Commission on Aboriginal Peoples, June 1995) at 153 [unpublished]. But see L.C. Green, "Claims to Territory in Colonial America" in L.C. Green & Olive P. Dickason, *The Law of Nations and the New World* (Edmonton: University of Alberta Press, 1989) 1 at 15, where he argues that a symbolic act such as the "installation of markers, whether or not accompanied by other acts betokening possession, was regarded as a sufficient method of acquiring sovereignty during the early period of exploration." Other scholars, however, argue that symbolic discovery of territory was never sufficient to establish sovereignty (perhaps inchoate), because the European powers themselves refused from the outset to acknowledge such acts as sufficient to establish sovereignty. See Youssef, *supra* note 8 at 22–25; Brian Slattery, "Aboriginal Sovereignty and Imperial Claims" (1991) 29 Osgoode Hall L.J. 681 at 688–89.

[75] Youssef, *ibid.* at 18.

[76] M.F. Lindley, *The Acquisition and Government of Backward Territory in International Law* (New York: Negro Universities Press, 1969) at 141.

[77] L. Oppenheim, *International Law: A Treatise*, 8th ed. by H. Lauterpacht, vol. 1 (London: Longmans, Green, 1955) at 558.

[78] D.P. O'Connell, *International Law*, vol. 1 (London: Stevens and Sons, 1965) at 488 [emphasis in original].

[79] Youssef, *supra* note 8 at 35.

[80] Brian Slattery, *The Land Rights of Indigenous Canadian Peoples, as affected by the Crown's Acquisition of Their Territories* (Saskatoon: University of Saskatchewan Native Law Centre, 1979) at 63.

[81] This result is no different in kind from what occurs in the area of contract law. Contracts are routinely written up expressing intentions and obligations, but such contracts are not complete or valid until consideration has passed between the parties.

[82] *Re: Ontario Boundaries*, 11 August 1884, Privy Council, [unreported] [*Ontario Boundaries*]. This case is printed in *The Proceedings before the Judicial Committee of Her Majesty's Imperial Privy Council on the Special Case Respecting the Westerly Boundary of Ontario* (Toronto: Warwick and Sons, 1889) at 416–18. It is discussed in McNeil, "Aboriginal Nations," *supra* note 60 at 113.

[83] *Ontario Boundaries*, *ibid.*, quoted in McNeil, *ibid.* at 113.

[84] Arthur Ray, *Indians in the Fur Trade: Their Role as Hunters, Trappers, and Middlemen in the Lands Southwest of Hudson Bay, 1660–1870* (Toronto: University of Toronto Press, 1974) at 56.

[85] The text of the HBC charter of 1670 states that the company is to hold the lands (Rupert's Land, defined as the Hudson Bay watershed) as the "true and absolute Lordes and Proprietors of the same territory . . . TO BEE HOLDEN of us our heires and successors as of our Mannor of East Greenwich . . . in free and common Soccage" at 139. The charter is reproduced in E.E. Rich, ed., *Minutes of the Hudson's Bay Company, 1671–1674* (Toronto: Champlain Society, 1942) at 131–48.

[86] Rich, *ibid.* at 139.

[87] *Staples v. R.*, 27 January 1899, Privy Council [unreported] [*Staples*]. The case appears in Stephen Scott, *The Prerogative of the Crown in External Affairs and Constituent Authority in a Commonwealth Monarchy* (D. Phil. Thesis, Oxford University, 1968) [unpublished] at App. I. It is discussed in McNeil, "Aboriginal Nations," *supra* note 60 at 116.

[88] McNeil, "Aboriginal Nations," *ibid.* at 116–17.

[89] *Worcester v. Georgia*, 31 U.S. (6 Pet.) 515 (1832) [*Worcester*].

[90] *Ibid.* at 545.

[91] Youssef, *supra* note 8 at 87–88.

[92] For support for the contrary view that the HBC acquired complete "freehold" title to their charter territory, and thus complete sovereignty over it, see the references to Herman Merivale, the Permanent Under-Secretary of State for the Colonies, in *Delgamuukw v. British Columbia*, [1991] 3 W.W.R. 97 (B.C.S.C.) [*Delgamuukw* (S.C.)], aff'd. by *Delgamuukw* (C.A.), *supra* note 35, rev'd in part, without reference to the point, by *Delgamuukw*, *supra* note 1. Mr. Merivale, however, developed his views in 1858, prior to the Privy Council decisions in *Staples*, *supra* note 87 and *Ontario Boundaries*, *supra* note 82. These references cannot, therefore, be said to reflect the law on the matter accurately.

[93] [1927] 2 D.L.R. 401 (P.C.).

[94] [1939] S.C.R. 104.

[95] *Supra* note 63.

[96] [1975] Que. C.A. 166.

[97] *Per incuriam* is Latin meaning that a subsequent court has made a decision without knowledge of an earlier binding legal precedent.

[98] McNeil, "Aboriginal Nations," *supra* note 60 at 116.

[99] Under contemporary theories of international human rights, of course, colonization can never justify the acquisition of territory without the consent of the people colonized. The latter method of acquiring territory is, therefore, problematic from this standpoint. It ignores the right of all peoples to equality in their occupation of territory and their status as peoples. To the extent that it continues to be part of our domestic Aboriginal rights doctrine, this principle is in violation of fundamental human rights as reflected in numerous international documents.

[100] McNeil, "Aboriginal Nations," *supra* note 60 at 117.

[101] *Connolly v. Woolrich* (1867), 17 R.J.R.Q. 75 (Que. Sup. Ct.) at 83, 95.

[102] *Ibid.* at 83.

[103] This view is consistent with that of "some legal historians [who] have suggested that the French Crown never assumed full title and ownership to the lands occupied by aboriginal peoples in light of the nature and pattern of French settlement": *R. v. Côté*, [1996] 3 S.C.R. 139, 4 C.N.L.R. 26 at para. 46 [*Côté*]. Chief Justice Lamer did not decide the issue in *Côté*; he did, however, criticize the Quebec attorney general's submission that the French had not recognized any Indian rights in New France,

pointing out that the French regarded the Aboriginal peoples as allies, not as subjects, of France.

[104] See Lindley, *supra* note 76 at 157–59.

[105] U.K., *Report from the Select Committee on the Hudson's Bay Company* (London: House of Commons, 1857) Minutes of Evidence, at 91–92, cited in McNeil, "Aboriginal Nations," *supra* note 60 at 117–18.

[106] D.N. Sprague, "Administrative History of Métis Claims" at 30, CD-ROM: *For Seven Generations: An Information Legacy of the Royal Commission on Aboriginal Peoples* (Ottawa: Libraxus, 1997).

[107] For an excellent account of the extent to which the Crown asserted jurisdiction during the early historical period, see Hamar Foster, "Forgotten Arguments: Aboriginal Title and Sovereignty in *Canada Jurisdiction Act* Cases" (1992) 21 Man. L.J. 343. The HBC charter contained language that restricted to its "Colonyes Fortes and Plantacons Factors Masters Mariners and other Officers employed or to bee employed in any of the Territories and Landes aforesaid" the HBC's ability to make and apply its laws: see text at <http://www.solon.org/Constitutions/Canada/English/PreConfederation/hbc_charter_1670.html>. Professor Foster also considers the impact of the early legislation (the *Canada Jurisdiction Act, 1803* (U.K.), 43 Geo. 3, c. 138 and the *Regulation of the Fur Trade Act, 1821* (U.K.) 1 & 2 Geo. IV, c. 66) and concludes that it was never meant to apply to Aboriginal peoples not employed by European authorities. In his summary of the case law interpreting these early statutes, Foster concludes (Foster, *ibid.* at 387) that

> while most of the judges appear to have been of the view that the Indian Territories were part of His Majesty's dominions—a proposition that was by no means clear—they did not rule that the *Canada Jurisdiction Act* subjected Indians to colonial criminal law. On the contrary, Chief Justice Reid told the jury in the *Cadien* case that the statute did not apply to Indians unless they placed themselves in the employ of the fur company.

Although there was agreement that the relevant jurisdiction legislation did not have broad territorial scope, there was uncertainty whether the lands in the northwest were under Crown sovereignty. The majority of lower court decisions from the time seemed to assume that they were. However, these earlier colonial decisions, like the other, later cases Kent McNeil has cited (see *supra* notes 93–98 and accompanying text) must now be reinterpreted in light of *Ontario Boundaries*, *supra* note 82 and *Staples*, *supra* note 87. As Foster explains (*ibid.* at 382), there was a significant minority view that the "Indian Territories were not within Her Majesty's dominions. . . ." The Privy Council decisions must now be taken to have transformed the minority view into the majority view and to have effectively overruled those lower court colonial decisions to the contrary.

[108] See *Blais* (Prov. Ct.), *supra* note 28 at paras. 127–30. At the Manitoba Court of Appeal, the intervenor Métis National Council argued that the trial judge had erred in holding that the correct cutoff date was 1818, the year that Canada and the United States settled the boundary west of Lake of the Woods to the Rocky Mountains. It argued instead that the correct date was the date of "effective control" in Red River and that effective control was not in place until 1870, the year the people of Red River, upon receiving assurance that a new province would be created, agreed to submit to Canadian jurisdiction in the region. The Manitoba Court of Appeal did not disturb the lower court's conclusion on this point (see *Blais* (C.A.), *supra* note 28 at para. 51), but noted that this issue was not determinative, because the appellant had failed to prove the existence of an Aboriginal right. The Supreme Court of Canada (*Blais*, *supra* note 28) did not address this issue; it dealt exclusively with the NRTA claim.

[109] *Supra* note 68.

[110] *Supra* note 1.

[111] *Calder*, *supra* note 68 at 325–26.

[112] *Supra* note 87.

[113] *Supra* note 89.

[114] *Delgamuukw*, *supra* note 1 at para. 145.

[115] *Delgamuukw* (S.C.), *supra* note 92 at 235.

[116] *Delgamuukw* (C.A.), *supra* note 35 at 493.

[117] *Ibid.* at 655.

[118] *Ibid.*

[119] Harry Slade & Robert Freeman, "Aboriginal Rights: Pleading the Case" (Paper presented to the Pacific Business and Law Institute Conference on the Supreme Court of Canada Decision in *Delgamuukw*, February 1998) 8.1 at 8.16–8.17 [unpublished].

[120] Brian Slattery, "The Definition and Proof of Aboriginal Title" (Paper presented to the Pacific Business and Law Institute Conference on the Supreme Court of Canada Decision in *Delgamuukw*, February 1998) 3.1 at 3.14 [unpublished].

[121] *Côté, supra* note 103 at paras. 46–48.

[122] Olive Dickason, *Canada's First Nations*, 2nd ed. (Toronto: Oxford University Press, 1997) at 150.

[123] *Ibid.* at 99–166.

[124] *Ibid.* at 159.

[125] A growing body of international human rights law incorporates many fundamental principles relating to the recognition of Aboriginal peoples' right to self-determination and control of traditional territories. See for example James Anaya & Robert Williams, "The Protection of Indigenous Peoples' Rights over Lands and Natural Resources Under the Inter-American Human Rights System" (2001) 14 Harv. Hum. Rts. J. 33.

[126] Borrows, *supra* note 8 at 576–77. Borrows goes on to argue (*ibid.* at 577–85) that courts are not only capable of inquiring into the nature and validity of Crown assertions of sovereignty, they have an obligation to do so to ensure that the rule of law is upheld.

[127] See for example *Baker Lake, supra* note 63 at 562.

PART 3

Practical Consequences & Choices

FEAR, HOPE, AND MISUNDERSTANDING

Unintended Consequences and the Marshall Decision

Christopher P. Manfredi

As James Kelly has argued, the dramatic rise in Aboriginal rights cases decided by the Supreme Court is an important exception to a general decline in the judicialization of public policy during the *Charter of Rights and Freedoms* era.[1] In 1996 alone, the Court decided eight cases involving Aboriginal or treaty rights under section 35 of the *Constitution Act, 1982*.[2] Four of these decisions (*Badger, Nikal, Adams,* and *Côté*) resulted in the exemption of members of the relevant Aboriginal communities from hunting and fishing regulations in Alberta, British Columbia, and Québec.[3] In 1997, of course, the Court decided perhaps its most important Aboriginal rights case, *Delgamuukw v. British Columbia*.[4] At issue in *Delgamuukw* was a claim by the hereditary chiefs of the Gitksan and Wet'suwet'en peoples to Aboriginal title over approximately 58,000 square kilometres in British Columbia. The claim was unsuccessful at both the provincial trial and appellate court levels. The chiefs won a partial victory in the Supreme Court, which accepted the use of oral history to establish the existence of Aboriginal title, provided a definition of Aboriginal title, and held that Aboriginal title could be extinguished only by the federal government. At the same time, however, the Court recognized inherent limits to Aboriginal title, as well as federal and provincial authority to infringe Aboriginal rights under certain circumstances. In fact, the judgment did not so much resolve the "Aboriginal rights question" as establish a framework for working through that question, thus ensuring continuing judicial engagement in this politically contentious issue. Despite these limitations, *Delgamuukw* represents a landmark development in section 35 jurisprudence.[5]

Almost two years after *Delgamuukw*, Aboriginal rights would lead the Court even more deeply into the "political thicket" of Aboriginal rights when it delivered its initial judgment in *R. v. Marshall*.[6] On September 17, 1999 the Court announced that a 1760 treaty between the Crown and the Mi'kmaq people exempted Donald Marshall, Jr. from complying with federal regulations governing eel fishing.[7] The judgment encouraged Aboriginal groups to claim an extended right to catch lobster out of season, as well as to claim rights to exploit other resources, such as oil and lumber.[8] It also sparked a violent and ethnically charged confrontation between non-Aboriginal and Aboriginal fishers and between

Aboriginal fishers and federal enforcement officials. In November of 1999, the Court sought to moderate the situation by "clarifying" the scope of its earlier judgment, emphasizing that it applied exclusively to eels.[9] Indeed, the unexpected reaction to the original judgment is undoubtedly behind cautionary comments by Chief Justice Beverley McLachlin about the role of courts in constitutional litigation. In particular, one can hear echoes of *Marshall* in her warnings that "courts should take great care to express any change to the law in clear, precise language," and that "courts must be alive to the economic and social consequences of new pronouncements of law."[10]

Marshall is not, of course, the first judgment in the *Charter* era where unintended consequences made later judicial clarification necessary. In fact, the "*Marshall* incident" bears a striking resemblance to the Court's assessment of unreasonable trial delays in *Askov v. The Queen*.[11] In *Askov*, the Court issued a new set of guidelines for determining violations of the constitutional right to be tried within a reasonable time, confident that those guidelines would only "infrequently" result in stays of proceedings.[12] Instead, the judgment resulted in dismissals, stays, or withdrawals of almost 52,000 criminal charges involving more than 27,000 cases in Ontario alone between October 1990 and November 1991.[13] Expressing "shock" at this outcome, Justice Peter Cory conceded that the Court had been unaware of *Askov*'s potential impact.[14] The Court therefore felt compelled in a subsequent judgment—*R. v. Morin*—both to clarify and to modify the *Askov* ruling.[15]

Why did the Court find itself in the same predicament in *Marshall* as it had in *Askov*? I argue in this essay that the answer to this question is found in certain "attributes of adjudication" which constrain the Court's institutional policy-making capacity.[16] These attributes flow from the traditional structure of adjudication, which gives judicial policy making "its own habits of analysis" and "repertoire of solutions."[17] The result is a process that is passive, incremental, focused on rights and remedies, concerned with historical rather than social facts, and poorly suited to measuring the behavioural impact of decisions. There is, in other words, a tension between the type of analysis required to solve complex and multi-faceted social problems and the techniques used by the judicial process to gather, process, and evaluate information.

JUDICIAL POLICY MAKING AND UNREASONABLE TRIAL DELAYS

In a series of cases decided during the 1980s, the Supreme Court consistently recognized that trial delays caused by limited institutional resources could be excused under certain circumstances.[18] However, obviously concerned by government failure to provide new resources for the judicial system, the Court decided to lay down more stringent guidelines in *Askov*. The general principle articulated by Justice Cory for a majority of the Court in *Askov* was that trial courts must balance a complex set of factors when determining whether an accused's right to be tried within a reasonable time is violated. These factors included the length of the delay, the specific reasons for the delay, whether the accused waived this right, and the degree of prejudice to the accused caused by the delay. Comparing systemic delays in judicial districts in several provinces, Justice Cory suggested that "a period of delay in a range of some six to eight months between committal and trial might be deemed to be the outside limit of what is reasonable."[19] Although Cory J. intended lower courts to apply this general balancing approach on a case-by-case basis rather than to follow the six- to eight-month standard strictly, lower courts missed this message and began staying proceedings that exceeded the eight-month limit. Crown counsel also began to dismiss or withdraw charges that exceeded this standard.

The key piece of extrinsic evidence in the case was an affidavit by Professor Carl Baar of Brock University, submitted on behalf of Askov. Professor Baar's affidavit reported three separate studies of court delays: two conducted in the context of preparing pre-*Charter* speedy trial legislation, and a third study conducted in 1987 of case dispositions in New Brunswick, six Ontario District Court jurisdictions, and two jurisdictions in British Columbia. In general, Baar's studies (which were the subject of extensive discussion during oral argument) indicated that the Brampton, Ontario District Court—from which *Askov* had originated—experienced significantly longer institutional delays than comparable jurisdictions.[20] Although the Baar affidavit had a narrow purpose—to demonstrate the unreasonableness of trial delays in a specific case and jurisdiction—the Court read it as a broader analysis of the general problem of trial delay. Although Baar's studies suggested that most Canadian jurisdictions could cope with a six- to eight-month standard, this was peripheral to the main argument of the affidavit. As Baar would later argue, "the Supreme Court went beyond the facts in *Askov*, and beyond the material presented in both affidavits, to establish principles of law not necessary for the decision in the case, principles founded on incomplete and incorrect analysis of the material before it."[21]

More importantly, although Justice Cory referred to Baar's analysis, he actually generated the six- to eight-month rule from data concerning trial lengths in three Montreal-area superior court jurisdictions. The time periods covered by the data also indicate that Justice Cory acquired the information *after* the Court had heard oral arguments in *Askov*.[22] According to Baar, the Court's use of legislative facts in this case suffered from two fatal flaws. First, by relying on evidence obtained through its own efforts, the Court avoided even the minimal critical review provided by the adversary process. Second, by using these data to invent a formula for determining unreasonable trial delays, the Court imposed a standard without taking any measure of its potential impact.[23] Indeed, the Court found itself compelled in *Morin*[24] to clarify that it had only intended to articulate general guidelines in *Askov*, and to illustrate the flexibility of those guidelines by accepting as constitutional a trial delay of fifteen months. Ironically, according to Baar, this clarification actually compounded the legislative fact errors the Court had made in *Askov*.[25]

Askov illustrates the difficulty that appellate courts have in evaluating and analyzing the "legislative facts" that are usually found in extrinsic evidence, even in areas where judicial expertise should be high. It also illustrates the difficulty of communicating expected consequences to individuals and institutions affected by their decisions.[26] One explanation for the initial miscommunication between the Supreme Court and lower trial courts is that the latter simply do not have the luxury of sufficient time to balance complex factors on a case-by-case basis. Given their workloads and resource constraints, the rational decision for lower court judges who want to avoid reversal on appeal is to err on the side of caution and follow that aspect of a judgment, in this case the six- to eight-month rule, with which compliance is easiest. As a result, Justice Cory badly miscalculated when he concluded that stays of proceedings "will be infrequently granted" as remedies for "unreasonable" trial delays.[27]

R. v. MARSHALL: MISINTERPRETATION, MIS-COMMUNICATION, OR MISCALCULATION?

At issue in *Marshall* was the validity of a conviction under several provisions of federal fishery regulations. The appellant, Donald Marshall, Jr., argued that his constitutionally protected treaty rights under section 35 of the *Constitution Act, 1982* exempted him from compliance with the regulations, and thereby rendered his conviction invalid. The Court agreed in a 5–2 judgment authored by Justice Ian Binnie. It held that a 1760 treaty affirmed "the right of the Mi'kmaq people to continue to provide for their own sustenance by taking the products of their hunting, fishing and other gathering activities, and trading for what in 1760 was termed 'necessaries.'"[28] In reaching this conclusion, the majority rejected a narrow interpretation of the treaty's language, in which the LaHave tribe of Mi'kmaqs promised not to "traffick, barter, or Exchange any Commodities in any manner but with such persons or the managers of such Truck houses as shall be appointed or Established by His Majesty's Governor at Lunenbourg or Elsewhere in Nova Scotia or Accadia."[29] Although the treaty obliged the British authorities to establish "Truck houses," a literal reading of its language appears to restrict the tribe's trading opportunities rather than to establish a positive guarantee of trading rights. Indeed, while titled a "Treaty of Peace and Friendship," the document reads more like a treaty of surrender. With the exception of the "Truck house" clause, the treaty consists of a list of promises by the Mi'kmaq not to interfere with "the jurisdiction and Dominion of His Majesty George the Second over the Territories of Nova Scotia or Accadia."[30] The one-sided nature of the treaty is perhaps best illustrated by the tribe's agreement to surrender "two prisoners . . . as Hostages" to ensure "the more effectual security of the due performance of this Treaty."[31] Contrary to the majority's conclusion that the "subtext of the Mi'kmaq treaties was reconciliation and mutual advantage,"[32] the language of the 1760 treaty appears instead to suggest a subtext of subjugation.

By taking a broad approach to extrinsic evidence, the majority determined that the written text of the treaty was incomplete, and that its terms had to be ascertained by reference to the "fragmentary historical record" and "the political and economic context."[33] Nineteen of the majority judgment's sixty-seven paragraphs are thus devoted to reviewing the documentary record and expert evidence. The majority placed particular emphasis on testimony by the Crown's expert, Dr. Stephen Patterson, to the effect that the British had recognized that the Mi'kmaq enjoyed "a right to live in Nova Scotia in their traditional ways," and that this encompassed hunting, fishing, and trading for "necessaries."[34] Like Carl Baar, Patterson would later criticize the Court's use of his evidence.[35] Speaking about six weeks after the judgment, Patterson argued that the Court seriously distorted his evidence by taking it out of context and using it selectively. Whether Patterson meant him to or not, Justice Binnie interpreted his testimony as supporting the proposition that the written document of 1760 did not exhaust the "enforceable treaty obligations" undertaken by the Crown.[36] In the final analysis, according to Justice Binnie, the evidence pointed to "a treaty right to continue to obtain necessaries through hunting and fishing by trading the products of those traditional activities," subject only to justifiable restrictions.[37]

Responding to Crown concerns that recognition of this right "would open the floodgates to uncontrollable and excessive exploitation of the natural resources," Justice Binnie asserted that this "fear (or hope) is based on a misunderstanding of the narrow ambit and extent of the treaty right."[38] Unfortunately, "fear," "hope," and "misunderstanding" are precisely what followed the judgment. A lawyer for the Mi'kmaq told CBC News one day after the decision that it had "implications that go far beyond the right to catch and sell fish. . . . It's about natural resource exploitation . . . fishery . . . trapping . . . animals . . . forestry."[39] Most of the conflict, however, involved lobster fishing, with Native fishers relying on *Marshall* to set out-of-season traps by early October of 1999. The conflict escalated into violence and continued throughout the summer and autumn of 2000. It probably reached its most critical point in August 2000, when Native protesters blockaded a provincial highway to protest raids by the Department of Fisheries and Oceans against their lobster traps.

Part of the confusion surrounding the September decision flowed from Justice Binnie's unqualified references to "hunting" and "fishing" throughout his reasons for judgment. More crucially, however, his initial definition of the treaty right protected under section 35 of the *Constitution Act, 1982* included a reference to "other gathering activities."[40] Justice Binnie attempted to narrow the right's scope by defining its purpose as securing "a moderate livelihood" rather than permitting "the open-ended accumulation of wealth."[41] Moreover, his final statement of the right referred only to hunting and fishing.[42] Nevertheless, it is hardly surprising that interested parties would attach a generous interpretation to Justice Binnie's language. Indeed, almost eighteen months after the judgment, the federal minister of Fisheries and Oceans still insisted that the "treaty right affirmed and upheld in *Marshall* applies to hunting, fishing and gathering more broadly."[43]

The confrontations that began in 1999 and continued throughout 2000, as well as the Fisheries minister's statements early in 2001, all indicate that the Supreme Court's own efforts to mitigate the consequences of the decision failed. On November 17, 1999 the Court took the unusual step of "clarifying" its September judgment in the course of denying a motion for rehearing and stay by one of the non-Aboriginal interveners in the case. In denying the motion, the Court stressed in several places the limited nature of its original judgment in several places. According to this clarification, the September judgment "did not hold . . . that the Mi'kmaq are guaranteed an open season in the fisheries."[44] The decision was "authority only for the matters adjudicated upon,"[45] which "related only to the closed season in the eel fishery."[46] According to the Court, any further extension of the treaty right, or justification for limiting treaty rights, would have to occur on a case-by-case, resource-by-resource, "species-by-species" basis.[47] However, the Court explicitly discouraged litigation as the appropriate vehicle for resolving the complex issues unleashed by the September judgment, stressing instead the importance of "consultation and negotiation."[48]

As in *Askov*, where Justice Cory criticized the rigid interpretation adopted by lower courts,[49] the *Marshall II* Court blamed misinterpretation rather than miscommunication for the unintended consequences that followed *Marshall I*. But there is a third possible explanation for those consequences: miscalculation. To be more precise, one can make a reasonable argument that the Court in fact intended to settle broader treaty rights issues and simply failed to anticipate the actual impact of its judgment. The basis for this argument is that *Marshall I* did not come to the Court as an appeal by right: a panel of Chief Justice Lamer and Justices Gonthier and Major granted leave to appeal on October 16, 1997. Less than 20 percent of all applications for leave to appeal are granted, with "public importance" serving as the key criterion for granting leave.[50] The Court must have believed that resolving the "issues necessary to dispose of [Marshall's] . . . guilt or innocence"[51] served some public purpose beyond simply correcting lower court errors in a local prosecution. Thus, in some sense the Court's broader intention was implicit in its decision to grant leave to appeal. The fact that the Attorney General of New Brunswick (where most of the subsequent confrontations occurred) and three nongovernmental organizations would expend the resources necessary to intervene in the appeal also indicates a perception, even prior to the judgment, that *Marshall I* would have a broad impact. At a minimum, the Court generated expectations of a broad ruling, which were not specifically contradicted by the language used by Justice Binnie. One can hardly fault the relevant parties for reacting in a manner consistent with those expectations.

In *Marshall*, the Court injected a murky 240-year-old treaty right, which had been in disuse for almost 220 years, into a volatile and thoroughly modern mixture of Aboriginal claims to self-government, resource conservation, and economic self-interest on the part of both Aboriginal and non-Aboriginal peoples. In this circumstance, miscommunication and misinterpretation can serve only as partial explanations for the chaos that followed the *Marshall I* judgment. Although federal government paralysis also played a role, the Court must share at least some of the responsibility. Yet this responsibility is not wholly the product of individual judicial error. Like *Askov*, it is symptomatic of broader constraints on the Court's policy-making capacity.

JUDICIAL CAPACITY AND LESSONS NOT LEARNED

The *Marshall* incident repeated at least four of the worst features of *Askov*: (1) questionable use of expert evidence; (2) confident predictions of limited impact that proved to be terribly inaccurate; (3) denial of judicial responsibility for the consequences; and (4) a follow-up judgment designed to clarify and ameliorate matters. Both incidents illustrate the perils of using rights-based judicial review to resolve complex and multi-faceted policy problems. As Alexander Bickel—whom the Court cited favourably in one of its most controversial decisions—argued thirty years ago, the judicial process

> . . . is too principle-prone and principle-bound . . . is . . . too remote from conditions, and deals, case by case, with too narrow a slice of reality . . . has difficulty controlling the stages by which it approaches a problem . . . rushes forward too fast, or it lags. . . . For all these reasons, it is, in a vast, complex, changeable society, a most unsuitable instrument for the formation of policy.[52]

Adjudication emphasizes rights and duties over costs and benefits. It focuses on static historical events rather than dynamic causal relationships. Finally, as both *Askov* and *Marshall* attest, adjudication provides only very clumsy policy review mechanisms. Judicial techniques of information-gathering, -processing, and -evaluating were developed in the context of an institution charged with resolving concrete private disputes. The suitability of those techniques to more complicated problems of broad social significance is less than obvious.[53]

Other than asking courts to be more careful about their use of extrinsic evidence, are there ways to avoid the problems evident in *Marshall* and *Askov*? Observers of similar phenomena in the United States have suggested that the United States Supreme Court appoint a panel of social scientists to assist in its evaluation of legislative facts, remand complicated cases to trial courts for proper adjudication of legislative fact assertions, and promulgate specific rules to govern the practice of taking judicial notice of social facts not contained in case materials.[54] Other American commentators, along with most judges, have embraced the idea of relying on "special masters" as expert advisors in formulating complex remedial decrees, as well as in providing ongoing supervision of the implementation of these decrees.

Each of these suggestions could be transplanted into the Canadian context. Indeed, former Justice Bertha Wilson advocated similar reforms while serving on the Supreme Court.[55] In her view, two changes were particularly necessary: expanding the number of parties involved in *Charter* litigation by liberalizing intervention rules, and resolving important problems of proof by enlarging the base of admissible evidence in *Charter* cases. Dale Gibson has also proposed reforms in this vein, arguing that there be greater reliance on social-science experts and public-opinion polls, that the size of the Court be increased, that the justices be provided better research staffs, and that law reform commissions develop law reform proposals that can be implemented by courts without legislative action.[56]

The decision-making reforms advocated by Miller and Barron in the United States, and by Gibson and Wilson in the Canadian context, would undoubtedly enhance the policy-making capacity of judicial institutions. However, these reforms would significantly transform the institutional character of courts as these bodies are understood in the common law world. To be more precise, they would further erode the institutional differences between courts and the legislative and executive bodies whose decisions judges are charged with reviewing.[57]

CONCLUSION

As the *Marshall* incident suggests, the Court is only weakly aware of its own policy-making limitations, although this awareness appears to be increasing.[58] Indeed, in several Aboriginal matters that came before it after *Marshall,* the Court appeared to step back from the broad approach it took in that case. In *Simon v. Oka,* the Court denied leave to appeal from a Quebec Court of Appeal decision that featured express disagreement on a division of powers issue with an earlier judgment of the British Columbia Court of Appeal; in denying leave to appeal in *Chippewas of Sarnia v. A.-G. Canada*, it declined an opportunity to consider the relationship between non-Aboriginal and unextinguished Aboriginal interests in the same land.[59] Moreover, in *Mitchell v. M.N.R.*, the Court refused to recognize an Aboriginal right to be exempt from paying duty on goods purchased in the United States.[60] Although the Court recognized the need for flexible application of the rules of evidence in Aboriginal rights cases, it concluded that the evidence in this case did not support the claimed right. The chief justice appears to have heeded her own advice in her *Marshall* dissent to approach the evidence flexibly but cautiously.

Nevertheless, the eighteenth-century rhetoric of democratic humility so frequently used by the Court's justices to describe their function limits the degree to which they are aware of the limits on their institutional capacity. They are particularly prone to the "guardian myth," which views the Court as protecting "basic constitutional values" that exist independently of judicial interpretation.[61] This myth assumes that constitutional interpretation is a legal exercise. As the chief justice has said: "There must be a body that determines whether the legislature is acting within its powers under the constitution. That body must be judicial, since the issue is a legal one."[62] The Court, according to this view, is simply "an agency to monitor compliance" with constitutional rules.[63]

These characterizations of judicial power are extremely problematic from the disciplinary perspective of political science, which for more than fifty years has rejected the view that judicial decision making in final courts of appeal is driven by legal considerations.[64] From the perspective of political science, the Supreme Court is, first and foremost, a political institution: it makes policy not as an accidental by-product of performing its legal function, but because its members believe that certain rules will be socially beneficial. The constitutional amendments of 1982, including the entrenchment of Aboriginal and treaty rights in section 35, increased judicial policy-making power by expanding the range of social and political issues subject to the Court's jurisdiction. When the Court decided to review Donald Marshall, Jr.'s eel-fishing conviction, it became a central, rather than peripheral, player in Atlantic Canada resource-management policy. It identified an unresolved policy issue, used section 35 to assert jurisdiction over that issue, and articulated its preferred resolution.

Although rights-based judicial review serves a crucial function in constitutional democracies, it is a very imprecise policy-making instrument. By changing the institutional constraints within which other political actors operate, it alters the status quo in unpredictable ways. The consequences that followed *Marshall I* were obviously unintended, but they should not have been unexpected under the circumstances. Nor is the Court's complete denial of responsibility in *Marshall II* credible or persuasive. The *Marshall* litigation was not just about eel fishing, and the Court knew that from the beginning.

NOTES

[1] James B. Kelly, "The *Charter of Rights and Freedoms* and the Rebalancing of Liberal Constitutionalism in Canada, 1982–1997" (1999) 37 Osgoode Hall L.J. 625 at 659.

[2] Schedule B to the *Canada Act 1982* (U.K.), 1982, c. 11. The eight cases are: *R. v. Badger*, [1996] 1 S.C.R. 771 [*Badger*]; *R. v. Pamajewon*, [1996] 2 S.C.R. 821; *R. v. Côté*, [1996] 3 S.C.R. 139 [*Côté*]; *R. v. Van der Peet*, [1996] 2 S.C.R. 507; *R. v. Gladstone*, [1996] 2 S.C.R. 723; *R. v. N.T.C. Smokehouse Ltd.*, [1996] 2 S.C.R. 672; *R. v. Adams*, [1996] 3 S.C.R. 101 [*Adams*]; and *R. v. Nikal*, [1996] 1 S.C.R. 1013 [*Nikal*].

[3] *Wildlife Act*, S.A. 1984, c. W-9.1, ss. 26(1), 27(1); *British Columbia Fishery (General) Regulations*, S.O.R./84-248, s. 4(1); *Quebec Fishery Regulations*, C.R.C., c. 852, ss. 4(1), 5(9).

[4] [1997] 3 SCR 1010 [*Delgamuukw*].

[5] For various comments on the *Delgamuukw* judgment, see John Borrows, "Sovereignty's Alchemy: An Analysis of *Delgamuukw v. British Columbia*" (1999) 37 Osgoode Hall L.J. 537; Kent McNeil, *Defining Aboriginal Title in the 90s: Has the Supreme Court Finally Got it Right?* (Toronto: Robarts Centre for Canadian Studies, York University, 1998); Brian Donovan, "The Evolution and Present Status of Common Law Aboriginal Title in Canada: The Law's Crooked Path and the Hollow Promise of *Delgamuukw*" (2001) 35 U.B.C. L. Rev. 43; Brent Olthuis, "Defrosting *Delgamuukw* (or 'how to reject a frozen rights interpretation of Aboriginal title in Canada')" (2001) 12 N.J.C.L. 385.

[6] [1999] 3 S.C.R 456 [*Marshall* or *Marshall I*], clarified [1999] 3 S.C.R. 533 [*Marshall II*]. The phrase "political thicket" was coined by United States Supreme Court Justice Felix Frankfurter to describe legislative reapportionment. See *Colegrove v. Green*, 328 U.S. 549 (1946) at 556.

[7] *Marshall*, *ibid.*

[8] Stephen Handelman, "Canadian Supreme Court" *Time* (Canadian Edition) (27 December 1999) 110.

[9] *Marshall II*, *supra* note 6.

[10] Right Honourable Beverley McLachlin, "Judicial Power and Democracy" (Speech to the Singapore Academy of Law, 14 September 2000), online: Singapore Academy of Law <http:www.sal.org.sg/media_speeches_al2000.htm>.

[11] *R. v. Askov*, [1990] 2 S.C.R. 1199 [*Askov*].

[12] *Ibid.* at 1247.

[13] Carl Baar, "Criminal Court Delay and the *Charter*: The Use and Misuse of Social Facts in Judicial Policy Making" (1993) 72 Can. Bar Rev. 305 at 314.

[14] Canadian Press "Hampton Calls for Review of Ruling in Askov Case" *Globe and Mail* (17 July 1991) A5.

[15] *R. v. Morin*, [1992] 1 S.C.R. 771 [*Morin*]. In this judgment, the Court emphasized the flexibility inherent in the *Askov* guidelines by accepting a trial delay of almost fifteen months. Interestingly, Justice Cory was not a member of the panel hearing this case.

[16] Donald L. Horowitz, *The Courts and Social Policy* (Washington, D.C.: Brookings, 1977) at 33–56. See also Paul Weiler, *In the Last Resort* (Toronto: Carswell, 1974).

[17] Horowitz, *ibid.* at 33.

[18] See *R. v. Mills*, [1986] 1 S.C.R. 863; *R. v. Rahey*, [1987] 1 S.C.R. 588; *R. v. Conway*, [1989] 1 S.C.R. 1659; and *R. v. Smith*, [1989] 2 S.C.R. 1120.

[19] *Askov*, *supra* note 11 at 1240.

[20] The evidence contained in the Baar affidavit is discussed by Justice Cory in *Askov*, *ibid.* at 1234–39.

[21] Baar, *supra* note 13 at 314.

[22] *Ibid.* at 315. Justice Cory's use of evidence obtained after oral argument would seem to stretch the

doctrine of judicial notice close to its limits. In this sense, his *Askov* judgment may have foreshadowed some important developments in this area of evidentiary law. See Lorne H. Wolfson, Daniel S. Melamed & Sandy J. Morris, "The Use of Judicial Notice in the Wake of *Moge v. Moge*" (1994) 11 Can. Fam. L.Q. 159; Justice Claire L'Heureux-Dubé, "Re-examining the Doctrine of Judicial Notice in the Family Law Context" (1994) 26 Ottawa L.R. 551.

[23] Baar, *supra* note 13 at 316–17.
[24] *Morin, supra* note 15.
[25] Baar, *supra* note 13 at 321–30. In *R. v. Bennett*, [1992] 2 S.C.R. 168, the Court apparently gave up trying to understand the social science of trial delays altogether. See Baar, *ibid.* at 331.
[26] For American views on these problems, see *e.g.* Peggy C. Davis, "'There is a Book Out . . .': An Analysis of Judicial Absorption of Legislative Facts" (1987) 100 Harv. L. Rev. 1539; Arthur Selwyn Miller & Jerome A. Barron, "The Supreme Court, the Adversary System, and the Flow of Information to the Justices: A Preliminary Inquiry" (1975) 61 Va. L. Rev. 1187 at 1222. Similar difficulties have been noted in the Canadian context. See Weiler, *supra* note 16; John Hagan, "Can Social Science Save Us? The Problems and Prospects of Social Science Evidence in Constitutional Litigation" and Brian G. Morgan, "Proof of Facts in Charter Litigation," both in Robert J. Sharpe, ed., *Charter Litigation* (Toronto: Butterworths, 1987) 213 and 159, respectively; Christopher P. Manfredi, "Adjudication, Policy-Making and the Supreme Court of Canada: Lessons from the Experience of the United States" (1989) 22 Can. J. Pol. Sci. 313; Katherine E. Swinton, *The Supreme Court and Canadian Federalism: The Laskin-Dickson Years* (Toronto: Carswell, 1990) at 137–58; Danielle Pinard, "Charter and Context: The Facts for Which We Need Evidence, and the Mysterious Other Ones" (2001) 14 Sup. Ct. L. Rev. 163.
[27] *Askov, supra* note 11 at 1247.
[28] *Marshall I, supra* note 6 at para. 4.
[29] *Ibid.* at para 5.
[30] *Ibid.*
[31] See *ibid.* at para. 5.
[32] *Ibid.* at para. 3.
[33] *Ibid.* at para. 41.
[34] *Ibid.* at para. 38.
[35] Robert Fife "High Court Accused of 'Distorting' History" *National Post* (28 October 1999) A1.
[36] *Marshall I, supra* note 6 at para. 40.
[37] *Ibid.* at para. 56.
[38] *Ibid.* at para. 57.
[39] "Nova Scotia worried about reaction to Mi'kmaq ruling" CBC News (18 September 1999), online <http://cbc.ca/cgi-bin/templates/view.cgi?/news/1999/09/18/nsfish990918>.
[40] *Marshall I, supra* note 6 at para. 4.
[41] *Ibid.* at para. 7.
[42] *Ibid.* at para. 56.
[43] Herb Dhaliwal, Minister of Fisheries and Oceans, "It's Not Just About Eels," Letter to the Editor, *National Post* (20 February 2001) A15.
[44] *Marshall II, supra* note 6 at para. 2.
[45] *Ibid.* at para. 23.
[46] *Ibid.* at para. 30.
[47] *Ibid.* at para. 21.
[48] *Ibid.* at para. 22.
[49] Canadian Press, *supra* note 14.
[50] See Supreme Court of Canada, *Bulletin of Proceedings: Special Edition, Statistics 1988–1998*, (1999). The rule is stated in s. 40(1) of the *Supreme Court Act*, R.S.C. 1985, c. S-26.
[51] *Marshall II, supra* note 6 at para. 11.
[52] Alexander M. Bickel, *The Supreme Court and the Idea of Progress*, 1st ed. (New York: Harper & Row, 1970) at 175. See *Vriend v. Alberta*, [1998] 1 S.C.R. 493 at para. 133, where the Court described

Bickel's argument about the dangers of judicial review as "eloquent."

[53] See generally Christopher P. Manfredi, *Judicial Power and the Charter: Canada and the Paradox of Liberal Constitutionalism,* 2nd ed. (Toronto: Oxford University Press, 2001) at 153–63ff.

[54] Miller & Barron, *supra* note 26 at 1233–44.

[55] Bertha Wilson, "Decision-Making in the Supreme Court" (1986) 36 U.T.L.J. 227 at 242–44.

[56] Dale Gibson, "Judges As Legislators: Not Whether But How" (1987) 25 Alta. L. Rev. 249 at 261–63.

[57] This point is made by Horowitz, *supra* note 16 at 298.

[58] McLachlin, *supra* note 10 at 6.

[59] *Oka (Municipalité) c. Simon*, [1998] R.J.Q. 108 (C.A.), leave to appeal to S.C.C. refused; *Chippewas of Sarnia Band v. Canada (A.G.)* (2000), 51 O.R. (3d) 641 (C.A.), leave to appeal to S.C.C. refused.

[60] *Mitchell v. M.N.R.*, [2001] 1 S.C.R. 911.

[61] See *United States v. Burns*, [2001] 1 S.C.R. 283 at para. 35 (". . . the Court is the guardian of the Constitution . . .").

[62] McLachlin, *supra* note 10 at 7.

[63] Hon. Bertha Wilson, "We Didn't Volunteer" (April 1999) 20:3 Policy Options 8 at 10.

[64] See Lawrence Baum, *The Puzzle of Judicial Behavior* (Ann Arbor: University of Michigan Press, 1997) at 57.

"LET US FACE IT, WE ARE ALL HERE TO STAY"

But Do We Negotiate or Litigate?

Leonard I. Rotman

Reconciling the Crown's[1] claim to sovereignty over Canada with the pre-existing rights of Aboriginal peoples has been a primary goal of the Supreme Court of Canada since its judgments in *R. v. Van der Peet*[2] and *Delgamuukw v. British Columbia*.[3] In *Van der Peet*, Chief Justice Lamer found a mandate for such reconciliation in section 35(1) of the *Constitution Act, 1982*:[4]

> [W]hat s. 35(1) does is provide the constitutional framework through which the fact that aboriginals lived on the land in distinctive societies, with their own practices, traditions and cultures, is acknowledged and reconciled with the sovereignty of the Crown. The substantive rights which fall within the provision must be defined in light of this purpose.[5]

This goal of reconciliation, subsequently reaffirmed in decisions such as *Delgamuukw*, is, and will continue to be, problematic. Even assuming, however, that it is both possible and legitimate, it cannot properly take place without the prior resolution of existing Aboriginal and treaty rights disputes. But by what means should these disputes be resolved? Should Aboriginal peoples claiming Aboriginal or treaty rights seek to negotiate these matters with the Crown, or should they be focusing their attention upon litigation?[6]

This question is not without its own difficulties; it yields no immediately correct or incorrect response. Instead, it requires reflection on the history of each of these ways of resolving Aboriginal and treaty rights disputes.

The quotation excerpted in the title of this paper, taken from Lamer C.J.'s majority judgment in *Delgamuukw*,[7] serves as a backdrop for deliberation over how Aboriginal peoples should seek to resolve such disputes. As the former chief justice said, Aboriginal and non-Aboriginal peoples have co-existed in Canada for quite some time and will continue to do so. This fact alone provides reason, separate from the Court's stated goal of reconciliation, for resolving outstanding disputes over the nature and extent of Aboriginal and treaty rights. Traditionally, negotiation and litigation have been viewed as alternative processes rather than being somehow related or complementary. It will be suggested that this vision is not entirely accurate and that, at least in the context of Aboriginal and treaty rights disputes, a direct relationship between negotiation and litigation has existed for quite some time. The history of Canadian Aboriginal and treaty rights jurisprudence illustrates how Aboriginal and treaty rights litigation begets negotiation and that negotiation pertaining to such matters becomes meaningful and effective only with the concomitant presence, or threat, of litigation.

The inquiry complicates further when consideration is given to two recent events involving Supreme Court of Canada justices: a media interview by Justice Michel Bastarache in January 2001[8] in which he made controversial comments about the use of litigation to resolve Aboriginal legal issues, and the controversy over Justice Ian Binnie's involvement in the case of *Wewaykum Indian Band v. Canada*[9] prior to his appointment to the bench. Although subsequent findings have exonerated those judges of any wrongful or improper conduct,[10] it is nonetheless suggested that these events bring into question Aboriginal peoples' ability to receive fair treatment when placing their disputes before Canadian courts and, consequently, the efficacy of litigation as an effective means of resolving, or encouraging negotiation of, their claims.[11] Certainly, the choice of vehicle for Aboriginal peoples to resolve their disputes is entirely theirs. This paper considers whether that choice is genuine or illusory.

The traditional debate as to whether Aboriginal and treaty rights disputes are best addressed via negotiation or litigation ignores the symbiotic relationship between these processes indicated above.[12] Each process, it will be suggested, has definite effects upon the other. The history of Aboriginal and treaty rights jurisprudence in Canada bears out this assertion. Although it is not possible here to canvass the entire history of Canadian Aboriginal and treaty rights jurisprudence, some selected examples should demonstrate the point.

NEGOTIATION, LITIGATION, AND CANADIAN ABORIGINAL AND TREATY RIGHTS JURISPRUDENCE

For the most part, the federal Crown perceived little reason, prior to the enactment of the *Constitution Act, 1982*, to negotiate with Aboriginal peoples regarding their rights.[13] Not only were there no constitutional safeguards for those rights, there was little protection afforded to them by Canadian courts. A statement made by Taschereau J. in the Supreme Court of Canada's decision in *St. Catherine's Milling and Lumber Co. v. The Queen* is indicative of this situation:

> The Indians must in the future . . . be treated with the same consideration for their just claims and demands that they have received in the past, but, as in the past, it will not be because of any legal obligation to do so, but as a sacred political obligation, in the execution of which the state must be free from judicial control.[14]

At about the same time, Lord Watson made a similar statement regarding treaty rights in the Privy Council's judgment in the so-called Robinson Annuities reference:

> Their Lordships have had no difficulty in coming to the conclusion that, under the treaties, the Indians obtained no right to their annuities . . . beyond a promise and agreement, which was nothing more than a personal obligation by its governor. . . ."[15]

As a result of the lack of legal recognition of, or protection for, Aboriginal and treaty rights, there was little pressure imposed on the federal Crown to negotiate disputes with Aboriginal peoples or to deal voluntarily with those rights. This situation was inherited upon Confederation, but had existed since the early part of the nineteenth century, when Britain ceased to rely on, or need, its earlier political and military alliances with North American Aboriginal peoples. Once Aboriginal peoples lost the leverage they had had to force Britain to fulfill its historical commitments to them, many treaty promises were neglected and other Aboriginal claims often ignored altogether.

Aboriginal groups continued to make representations to Britain—and later to Canada—about infringements upon and the non-fulfilment of Aboriginal and treaty rights, but to no avail. With the elimination of political and military threats, and in the absence of the judicial pressure facilitated by Aboriginal success in litigation, the "sacred political obligation" Justice Taschereau described remained largely unfulfilled. It was not until the twentieth century that Aboriginal and treaty rights claims began to be litigated in any significant numbers. For the most part, these early claims proved fruitless, as the rights claimed were either denied by the courts or found to have been extinguished.[16] In those days, Aboriginal and treaty rights were viewed by the courts as extinguishable whenever the federal Crown had either the desire or a perceived need to extinguish them, as long as the federal Crown's intention to extinguish the right was "clear and plain."[17]

Although the clear and plain test was first articulated in this form by Hall J. in *Calder v. British Columbia (A.G.)*,[18] and was later affirmed in *R. v. Sparrow*,[19] it had arguably been a part of Canadian common law long before its enunciation in those cases. The clear and plain test may be seen to be premised upon the application of what is generally called the "doctrine of continuity"[20] to the legal conflict between pre-existing Aboriginal legal systems and Britain's assertion of sovereignty over Canada.[21] Under this doctrine, pre-existing Aboriginal laws continued to exist and became a part of the common law in the absence of conflict with British sovereignty or with the British Crown's demonstrated intention to extinguish them upon its assertion of sovereignty. This principle was articulated in the celebrated case of *Campbell v. Hall* in 1774[22] and reflected in Canadian jurisprudence prior to the commencement of the twentieth century.[23] Put another way, Crown intent, at least in the context of extinguishing Aboriginal or treaty rights, could not be lightly implied.

Although the clear and plain test instituted a significant restriction upon the Crown's ability to extinguish Aboriginal customary laws and rights, this restriction was neither always enforced nor even well understood. For this reason, Aboriginal attempts to enforce their rights in the face of competing enactments were generally unsuccessful, even where those enactments did not evidence a clear and plain intent to extinguish the rights in question. The reason for this is that the question of what constitutes clear and plain intent was—and, in many ways, still is—a matter of great uncertainty.

Although the onus of demonstrating clear and plain intent rests upon the party seeking to extinguish rights,[24] debate over what constitutes clear and plain intent remains. Thus, for example, in his majority judgment in *Delgamuukw*, Lamer C.J. said:

> Although the latter types of laws may have been "necessarily inconsistent" with the continued exercise of aboriginal rights, they could not extinguish those rights. While the requirement of clear and plain intent does not, perhaps, require that the Crown "use language which refers expressly to its extinguishment of aboriginal rights" (*Gladstone*, *supra*, at para. 34), the standard is still quite high.[25]

Precisely how high the standard is was not articulated in *Delgamuukw*, although, as seen in the above quotation, the "necessarily inconsistent" argument put forward by the provincial Crown was rejected in that case as insufficient.

Although there were discrepancies between federal Crown practice and the requirements for extinguishing Aboriginal and treaty rights, when it came to regulating those rights, the federal Crown was deemed to possess unlimited discretion pursuant to its jurisdiction over "Indians, and Lands reserved for the Indians" under section 91(24) of the *Constitution Act, 1867*. Either way, without judicial enforcement, Aboriginal peoples' treaty rights were overwhelmingly ignored or regarded as trifling annoyances; Aboriginal rights, meanwhile, were simply not accounted for because they were generally not believed to exist.

This latter understanding first began to change with the recognition of Aboriginal title in *Calder* in 1973.[26] As a direct result of the recognition of Aboriginal title in *Calder*, the federal Crown established a policy meant as an alternative to litigation for Aboriginal peoples with certain kinds of land claims.[27] However, for a band to obtain a land claims settlement pursuant to this process, the federal Crown required a complete surrender of any and all existing Aboriginal rights in exchange for the rights granted in the settlement. Not surprisingly, many Aboriginal groups balked at relinquishing their traditional rights in exchange for delegated rights.[28] This requirement was later eased to allow for the cession of Aboriginal rights and surrender of title only in non-reserved areas while allowing title in reserves to continue. This alternative process proved, however, to be rather unsuccessful.

The federal Crown's process for resolving Aboriginal land claims through negotiation has proven to be lengthy and generally ineffective and has resolved few disputes. As a result, the tide turned back towards litigation to resolve these and other Aboriginal claims. This tide rose with the constitutionalization of Aboriginal and treaty rights in section 35(1) of the *Constitution Act, 1982* and the judicial recognition of the federal Crown's fiduciary duty to Aboriginal peoples articulated in *Guerin*.[29] It then became a full-fledged wave with the Supreme Court of Canada's first attempt to give shape to section 35(1) in *Sparrow* in 1990.[30]

THE CONSTITUTIONALIZATION OF ABORIGINAL AND TREATY RIGHTS AND THE *SPARROW* CASE

The *Sparrow* Decision

The inclusion of section 35(1) in the *Constitution Act, 1982* provided special recognition of and protection for Aboriginal and treaty rights. After section 35(1) came into effect on 17 April 1982, Aboriginal and treaty rights existing on that date could no longer be extinguished without the consent of the Aboriginal peoples in question or via constitutional amendment.[31] However, the contemporary, enlarged understanding of the effects of section 35(1) may be traced only as far back as the *Sparrow* judgment in 1990. In *Sparrow*, the Supreme Court sought to shift the means of resolving Crown–Native disputes away from litigation to the negotiating table. It endeavoured to do this by emphasizing the importance of section 35(1) and its effect on Crown–Native relations.

In providing a framework for the application of section 35(1) rights, *Sparrow* recognized the failures of the past and attempted to provide a more appropriate foundation that would recognize those rights as well as the effect upon them of the special fiduciary relationship between the Crown and Aboriginal peoples. The Supreme Court acknowledged that "there can be no doubt that over the years the rights of the Indians were often honoured in the breach,"[32] then declared that the enactment of section 35(1) "at the least, provides a solid constitutional base upon which subsequent negotiations can take place."[33] By this, the Court turned on its ear the Crown's pre-existing method of dealing with those rights. In support of this change, it quoted with approval Professor Lyon's characterization of the purpose and function of section 35(1):

> ... [T]he context of 1982 is surely enough to tell us that this is not just a codification of the case law on aboriginal rights that had accumulated by 1982. Section 35 calls for a just settlement for aboriginal peoples. It renounces the old rules of the game under which the Crown established courts of law and denied those courts the authority to question sovereign claims made by the Crown.[34]

The Supreme Court's judgment in *Sparrow* indicated that section 35(1) was a far more significant point in Crown–Native relations than may previously have been envisaged. This aspect of the judgment can be divided into three components. First, the Court recognized that some means was required to compel the Crown to negotiate with Aboriginal peoples regarding disputes over the latter's rights. It then affirmed that, aside from the limited effects of the *Calder* decision, there was no sustained pressure placed on the Crown to negotiate with Aboriginal peoples prior to 1982. Finally, the Court held that section 35(1) itself, put into its proper historical, political, and legal contexts, provides that missing element of coercion: it recognizes and affirms the rights; it incorporates the Crown–Native fiduciary relationship; and it limits federal legislative powers under section 91(24) of the *Constitution Act, 1867* as well as any ancillary provincial jurisdiction.[35]

With the entrenchment of section 35(1) and its elaboration in *Sparrow*, which included articulation of a justificatory test for legislative initiatives that derogated from Aboriginal rights,[36] the Crown no longer possessed unlimited powers to regulate those rights.[37] As the Court explained:

> Federal legislative powers continue, including, of course, the right to legislate with respect to Indians pursuant to s. 91(24) of the *Constitution Act, 1867*. These powers must, however, now be read together with section 35(1). In other words, federal power must be reconciled with federal duty and the best way to achieve that reconciliation is to demand the justification of any governmental regulation that infringes upon or denies aboriginal rights. Such scrutiny is in keeping with the liberal interpretive principle enunciated in *Nowegijick* . . . and the concept of holding the Crown to a high standard of honourable dealing with respect to the aboriginal peoples of Canada as suggested by *Guerin*. . . .[38]

Section 35(1) also circumscribed provincial legislative powers:

> Section 35(1), at the least, provides a solid constitutional base upon which subsequent negotiations can take place. It also affords aboriginal peoples constitutional protection against provincial legislative power.[39]

The Federal Response

The Indian Claims Commission

Following *Sparrow*, Canadian courts began giving greater recognition to Aboriginal and treaty rights, scrutinizing closely any regulation of those rights pursuant to the requirements of the *Sparrow* justificatory test. Legislative bodies were now far more constrained than ever before in their ability to deal with Aboriginal and treaty rights. This change prompted the federal Crown to facilitate negotiation with Aboriginal peoples rather than submit to the uncertainty of litigation, particularly now that courts were clearly becoming more receptive to Aboriginal claims. Shortly after *Sparrow*, and as a result of the Oka crisis of 1990, it created the federal Indian Claims Commission (ICC)[40] with the goal of enhancing negotiations with

Aboriginal peoples, and providing a viable alternative to litigation of disputes,[41] regarding "specific claims."[42] The ICC mandate included processes of inquiry[43] and mediation.[44]

This initiative led to frustration on the part of the many bands that received no satisfaction from the federal Crown despite obtaining findings against it of "lawful obligation"[45] as a result of ICC inquiries.[46] The failure of an ICC finding of lawful obligation to generate positive action by the federal Crown to rectify its failure to live up to its legal duties reveals the primary problem with the ICC—it does not have the ability to bind the parties, but merely issues reports and makes recommendations. Although bringing a dispute before the ICC is usually quicker and less formal than litigation—the time lapse may be as little as one to two years from initial request to final report—it does not guarantee a satisfactory conclusion even where a band's claim is upheld. The lack of adequate, or sometimes any, federal response to ICC findings in favour of Aboriginal groups has frustrated not only the Aboriginal claimants but the ICC itself. In its 1999–2000 annual report, the ICC resolved, for the first time, not to make any new recommendations to the federal Crown. Instead it preferred, in its own words, to "reiterate the recommendations we have offered since our inception" since they were "as valid now as they were when they were first crafted and, for the most part, have yet to be implemented."[47] For quite some time, the ICC has urged the creation of an independent, binding claims adjudication body.[48] In doing so, it has echoed the recommendations of various parliamentary committees, which have sought creation of just such a body for more than fifty years now.[49] The federal *Specific Claims Resolution Act*,[50] discussed below, is a very recent response to such representations.

Despite the manifest problems with the existing ICC process, it is, at least, an attempt to provide a means to deal with First Nations' specific claims that the federal Crown has rejected on the advice of its Department of Justice (DOJ).[51] No analogous process is now in place, or even contemplated, for rejected "comprehensive claims."[52] The ICC's limited mandate is not the only problem afflicting the current federal process for resolving specific claims. In addition, the federal government's definition of "lawful obligation," which grounds its specific claims process,[53] is dramatically underinclusive. What is conspicuously absent from the definition is the action for breach of fiduciary duty owed to an Indian band by the federal Crown, which underlies a significant number of Aboriginal claims.[54] The overly restrictive definition of "lawful obligation" was highlighted by the Royal Commission on Aboriginal Peoples (RCAP), which stated that

> a narrow and restrictive reading of the [specific claims] policy leads to the exclusion of many claims based on non-fulfilment of treaty obligations. Assertions of the right to exercise hunting and fishing rights, for example, or of rights to education, health

and other benefits, are not seen by government as coming within the policy even though they are justiciable rights.[55]

In sum, RCAP determined that the federal Crown's claims processes are plagued by restrictive interpretations of claims, overly rigid applications of claims process criteria, and exclusive reliance on common law conceptions of land. Thus, these "alternative" processes essentially replicate many of the problems that exist in Aboriginal title litigation.[56]

For these reasons, litigation is often perceived by Aboriginal peoples as a better avenue than the ICC for achieving results. While litigation too has its warts, including significant expenditures of time and expense, it is not as restrictive and, most importantly, provides binding results. If alternative claims processes, such as the ICC, are to be regarded as meaningful alternatives to litigation, they require modification so that they account for both common law and Aboriginal understandings of rights. Further, they must also shed the restrictions imposed by the litigation process to be regarded as true alternatives to litigation.

The Specific Claims Resolution Act

The *Specific Claims Resolution Act* addresses some of the problems arising from the Crown's current specific claims process: it defines "specific claim" to include claims alleging breach of Crown fiduciary obligation,[57] and it provides a mechanism, where negotiations fail, for binding adjudication of, and for binding compensation awards in respect of, specific claims.[58] The Act's other features, however, render it incapable of offering significant improvement.

There is, to begin with, reason to question the independence of the new bodies[59] established under the Act. All its members are to be appointed by the Governor in Council on the recommendation of the Minister of Indian Affairs. First Nations have no direct role in appointments, although the minister may consult with them informally. (This despite the ICC's own warnings about the importance of consultation with First Nation representatives on appointments[60] and the precedent of formal consultation established in 1992 with the appointment of the first ICC commissioners.) Finally, all members, whatever their functions, are subject to removal for cause by the Governor in Council, not by a body independent of government.[61]

The minister, however, has the power to recommend more than just the names of all the new scheme's prospective appointees. He or she will also have the power to prescribe, subject to Treasury Board approval, the maximum amount of compensation that the new tribunal may award (to all its claimants) and, apparently, the maximum number of compensation-related claims that the tribunal may entertain, in a given fiscal year.[62] This same minister, meanwhile, will continue to represent the federal Crown, as respondent, in all proceedings brought pursuant to the Act. In that latter capacity, he or she will have significant control over the process under the Act. The new commission's efforts to arrange claims resolution must await written confirmation as to whether the Minister will negotiate a claim.[63] The commission will not be able to refer a claim, or a compensation issue, to the new tribunal without first satisfying itself that the minister has considered the basis of the claim and all the relevant issues of fact and law that it poses.[64] In addition, it will have no power to compel the minister to respond in a timely manner to a claim or to a claimant.

Other features of the scheme cast doubt on both its accessibility and its relevance to substantial numbers of potential Aboriginal claimants. It will exclude, for example, claims based on events occurring within the fifteen years immediately preceding the date of the claim and claims based on, or alleging, Aboriginal rights or Aboriginal title.[65] It will empower the commission to administer and allocate funding for claims research and preparation, but only in accordance with such appropriations as the government may choose to make for this purpose.[66] It guarantees neither funding nor any claimant's entitlement to funding, thereby limiting access to the scheme in cases where First Nations cannot completely self-fund their participation. It establishes an upper compensation limit of $7 million per claim[67] (an amount well below what may be owing for some claims that would otherwise be eligible for the scheme), precludes awards of punitive or exemplary damages (even when warranted by the facts),[68] and, again, provides for caps on the total number of compensation-related arbitrations and the total amount of compensation that may be awarded in a given year.[69]

The *Specific Claims Resolution Act*, in other words, replicates some of the problems of the existing ICC and specific claims processes, but also introduces some new ones of its own. If the goal is to provide a more independent, less restrictive process that is adequate to both federal and First Nation concerns, these and other issues will require reconsideration.

Other Problems with the Federal Response

Limitations in scope and design and a lack of satisfactory results are not the only problems with these federally created alternatives to litigation. A pervasive problem is the method by which the initial determination of federal obligation is made. The federal Department of Justice, the in-house counsel of the federal Crown, makes its own determination of the merit, or lack thereof, of claims submitted through these processes and advises the federal Crown whether it believes any legal obligation exists. This opinion provides the basis for the Crown's ultimate determination of a First Nation's claim; in practice, DOJ's advice is almost always followed. When one considers that DOJ's function is to defend the federal Crown against claims adverse to the latter's interest—including those involving payment of monetary damages or loss of Crown land holdings—the DOJ is hardly in a position of neutrality when it considers the existence of that Crown's obligations to Aboriginal peoples.[70] Owing to its position and function, there is no reason why DOJ should be neutral on these matters—its duty is to the federal Crown, not to Aboriginal peoples. That being the case, it is clearly inappropriate to delegate to the DOJ, rather than to an independent body, the function of essentially determining whether the federal Crown owes lawful obligations to Aboriginal claimants. The DOJ's role here demonstrates the degree of federal Crown control over the existing process. Such control is inimical to achieving resolutions of outstanding Aboriginal claims.

Clearly, DOJ's role as both investigator and arbiter of a claim's merits creates a conflict of interest. Compounding the conflict is the fact that it will be DOJ, on behalf of the federal Crown, that resists the band's claim before the ICC or in litigation if it determines that no federal duty exists. Furthermore, in its role as defender of the claim, the DOJ is immediately at a distinct advantage vis-à-vis the Aboriginal claimant because it has in its arsenal its own report on the claim's merits, a report that makes use of information disclosed by the band to support its claim, as required under the specific claims process. Meanwhile, the DOJ refuses to share these reports, insisting that they are subject to solicitor-client privilege.[71]

Another, related problem is that, in practice, DOJ determines the existence of alleged federal Crown obligation in accordance with its own assessment of a claim's likelihood of success in litigation. In other words, the existence of a lawful obligation is based not solely upon the facts in issue or the criteria established by the process, but upon whether DOJ believes it can successfully defend against the claim in court. If the DOJ, as arbiter of fact, uses a perceived litigation result as a basis for negotiation, there is little incentive for a band to proceed through one of these alternative processes.[72] Given its various functions and practices, is it entirely inconceivable for DOJ to conclude that a particular claim demonstrates a federal legal obligation but to choose to deny the claim because it believes it could resist it successfully in litigation?[73] The mere possibility is inconsistent with the federal Crown's fiduciary duty to Aboriginal peoples (since, of course, the DOJ is an arm of the federal Crown).[74] It is for reasons such as these that an independent claims arbitration body has been suggested to replace the ICC.[75]

The Supreme Court's Aboriginal Rights Jurisprudence Since *Sparrow*
Largely because alternatives have not been found propitious, litigation has remained the predominant vehicle through which Aboriginal groups press forward their claims. Partly due to this phenomenon, the Supreme Court of Canada has in recent years heard and decided record numbers of Aboriginal disputes. From April 1996 through June 1997, the Court rendered twelve Aboriginal law judgments.[76]

From the 1997–98 term to the time that this paper was last revised at the end of the 2003–04 term, the Court issued twenty-two more decisions.[77] Although not all of these cases concern Aboriginal- or treaty-rights matters, these numbers indicate the prominence of Aboriginal issues in contemporary Canadian jurisprudence and the frequency with which litigation is used to resolve them.

A number of the judgments included in this recent deluge have diminished the initial promise suggested by cases such as *Guerin*,[78] *R. v. Sioui*,[79] and *Sparrow*.[80] For instance, in *Van der Peet*, the Supreme Court's majority judgment restricted the scope of constitutionally protected Aboriginal rights to those elements of a practice, custom, or tradition integral to the distinctive culture of the Aboriginal group claiming the right and traceable prior to contact.[81] The majority also distinguished between what it described as practices, customs, or traditions that were "integral" and those that were "incidental," protecting only the former, even where the latter may be necessary to the meaningful use of the former.[82] The result of this finding is, potentially, a situation where an Aboriginal right is protected but cannot be meaningfully exercised because actions associated with and necessary to its use are not protected.[83]

Meanwhile, in *Gladstone*, the justificatory standard that was developed in *Sparrow* was enlarged to allow the Crown greater scope to restrict Aboriginal rights based on broad and unarticulated notions of "public interest," a matter specifically held to be unacceptable in *Sparrow*.[84] There, the Court held that the Heiltsuk band possessed an Aboriginal right, uncircumscribed by internal limits, to fish commercially; that right, however, could be limited by government measures sensitive to the interests of non-Aboriginal fishers in access to the same resources (albeit not to the same degree). In the Court's view, the reconciliation imperative made it necessary to allow for the non-constitutionally protected interests of non-Aboriginal peoples to compete on par with constitutionally protected Aboriginal rights and even to limit the latter's scope. As it explained, "such objectives are in the interest of all Canadians and, more importantly, the reconciliation of Aboriginal societies with the rest of Canadian society may well depend on their successful attainment."[85] Even apart from doubts about the soundness of these conclusions, the *Gladstone* judgment is troublesome in that it eliminated an important restriction on the Crown's ability to regulate those rights, without acknowledging that it was, effectively, overturning *Sparrow* on this point.

Finally, in the Supreme Court's decision in *Mitchell v. M.N.R.*,[86] Binnie J.'s concurring judgment stepped back from the proposition, advanced in *Sparrow*, that section 35(1) "renounces the old rules of the game,"[87] substituting instead the lesser notion that section 35(1) "ushered in a new chapter ... it did not start a new book."[88] This characterization is consistent with his insistence on what he described as "the reality of Canadian sovereignty,"[89] a long-standing topic of concern among Aboriginal legal scholars, which has become firmly entrenched in Canadian jurisprudence despite having never undergone serious scrutiny, nor having been subjected to the same method of inquiry as Aboriginal title claims.[90] Justice Binnie's understanding of Canadian sovereignty was echoed by McLachlin C.J.'s majority judgment in *Mitchell*:

> English law, which ultimately came to govern aboriginal rights, accepted that the aboriginal peoples possessed pre-existing laws and interests, and recognized their continuance in the absence of extinguishment, by cession, conquest, or legislation . . . however, the Crown asserted that sovereignty over the land, and ownership of its underlying title, vested in the Crown. . . .[91]

Of course, both of these statements in *Mitchell* affirmed the Court's unanimous observation, in *Sparrow*, that

> while British policy towards the native population was based on respect for their right to occupy their traditional lands, a proposition to which the Royal Proclamation of 1763 bears witness, there was from the outset never any doubt that sovereignty and legislative power, and indeed the underlying title, to such lands vested in the Crown. . . .[92]

Perhaps as a result of its increased caseload, the Supreme Court continued to emphasize that negotiation was the better way to resolve outstanding Aboriginal and treaty rights claims even as it was entertaining greater numbers of Aboriginal law cases. Such sentiments are seen most prominently in judicial remarks in *Delgamuukw* and *Marshall*.

In *Delgamuukw*, La Forest J., concurring, stated that "the best approach in these types of cases is a process of negotiation and reconciliation that properly considers the complex and competing interests at stake."[93] In that same case, Chief Justice Lamer more famously said that

> [u]ltimately, it is through negotiated settlements, with good faith and give and take on all sides, reinforced by the judgments of this Court, that we will achieve what I stated in *Van der Peet* . . . to be a basic purpose of s. 35(1)—"the reconciliation of the pre-existence of aboriginal societies with the sovereignty of the Crown". Let us face it, we are all here to stay.[94]

In *Marshall II*, the Supreme Court again indicated its preference of negotiation over litigation in Crown–Native disputes:

> As this and other courts have pointed out on many occasions, the process of accommodation of the treaty right may best be resolved by consultation and negotiation of a modern agreement for participation in specified resources by the Mi'kmaq rather than by litigation.[95]

This passage affirms that consultation forms an equally important part of the non-adversarial resolution of disputes between the Crown and Aboriginal peoples.

The importance of consultation was established in *Sparrow*, where the Court held that in the process of justifying a limit on an Aboriginal right, the Crown had a duty to consult with the Aboriginal peoples affected.[96]

Sparrow's emphasis on the importance of consultation reinforced the Supreme Court's findings in *Guerin* on the need for consultation in situations where Aboriginal peoples' interests could potentially be adversely affected. In *Guerin*, the Court further found that where the Crown had properly consulted with a band about acceptable terms in the context of negotiating a surrender of reserve lands for lease, it could not ignore those terms when it negotiated the lease with a third party.[97] In the words of Justice Wilson, once oral terms had been established by the band and agreed to by the federal Crown and the surrender executed, "[t]he Crown was no longer free to decide that a lease on some other terms would do. Its hands were tied."[98] Thus, the requirement to consult is not satisfied merely by advising of actions taken.

In other respects, the nature and extent of the Crown's duty to consult remains a source of contention.[99] What is clear from *Delgamuukw* is that "[t]he nature and scope of the duty of consultation will vary with the circumstances."[100] For its part, *Marshall II* has affirmed that where consultation does not produce an agreement in the context of justifying limits on Aboriginal or treaty rights, "the adequacy of the justification of the government's initiative will have to be litigated in the courts."[101] Here, the process of consultation takes on a role akin to that of negotiation. Given the nature of the Crown–Native fiduciary relationship, consultation is not only necessary, it is also a useful tool to avoid disputes and facilitate the balancing of Aboriginal and non-Aboriginal interests. However, where the parties' disagreement persists after such consultation, the need to litigate remains and has been recognized by the courts.

Summary

Because of the several limitations endemic to the federal Crown's comprehensive and specific claims processes,[102] and because of the inability or unwillingness of the federal and/or Aboriginal parties to resolve Aboriginal and treaty rights disputes through negotiation, a considerable number of such disputes are dealt with through litigation. Although the Supreme Court of Canada has indicated, as illustrated above, that such disputes are better addressed through negotiation, it recognizes that litigation is a necessary alternative should consultation or negotiation fail. In addition, litigation may coerce the parties to work towards achieving lasting settlements. Certainly, as illustrated, Aboriginal peoples' success in the courts has prompted the Crown to create alternative processes, albeit ones that provide it with a greater measure of control over the process and its outcome.[103] Litigation, however, is effective as a coercive measure only when there is some potential for judicial decisions favourable to Aboriginal and treaty rights. That requires that courts give proper consideration to Aboriginal claims and not dismiss them perfunctorily.

THE ISSUE OF PERCEIVED JUDICIAL BIAS

Recent (post-*Calder*) Aboriginal and treaty rights jurisprudence demonstrates that Canadian courts have grown increasingly dependent upon the Supreme Court of Canada for legal tests and approaches to assist in determining the merits of such claims because of the difficulty of these issues and the growing complexity of litigation surrounding them. Such exceptional reliance subjects the Supreme Court's statements and actions to even greater scrutiny than they would routinely face by reason of being binding on lower courts. Given this reality, perceptions of bias among Supreme Court members give increased cause for concern about courts' ability generally to appraise the merits of Aboriginal and treaty rights claims. Two separate events, involving Justices Bastarache and Binnie, respectively, have raised this concern; they, in turn, bring into question the efficacy of litigation as an alternative to negotiation or as a coercive means to spur the Crown to negotiation.

Justice Bastarache's 2001 Newspaper Interview

In a newspaper interview, Justice Bastarache made a number of comments about the Supreme Court's handling of Aboriginal and treaty rights disputes, which raised the spectre of bias. He said, "I think the [Supreme] court is not the right forum for determining how the native rights will blend in with other rights of citizens in the country, and with citizenship and all of those other issues,"[104] and expressed the desire that "most of these things could be determined through negotiation, . . . [because] I don't really believe the court is going to be able to be the final arbitrator in that area."[105] He also expressed disagreement with the majority's decision in *Marshall*,[106] as well as serious concern over the public's reaction to the judgment:

> The first reaction of the public, especially in the Maritimes, is that the court was very result-oriented and was inventing rights that weren't even in the treaties that were brought before the court in that case."[107]

He later added that "the court was maybe seen as being unduly favourable to the native position in all cases, and that it sort of has an agenda for extending these [Aboriginal] rights, and that it has no concern for the rights of others."[108]

The Canadian Judicial Council investigated complaints about Justice Bastarache's remarks and cleared him of any impropriety.[109] Even so, his comments about Aboriginal and treaty rights generally, and the *Marshall* case specifically, make it legitimate to question whether Aboriginal peoples may receive a fair and impartial hearing before him or before a court of which he is a member and on which he wields influence. If Justice Bastarache truly believes that the Supreme Court should keep out of Aboriginal and treaty rights matters, it may be difficult to perceive him to be objective or fair to an Indian band arguing in front of him. Unless he publicly retracts his statements or recuses himself from Aboriginal legal disputes brought before the Supreme Court of Canada, the Court itself, fairly or unfairly, may be coloured with the same apprehension. Continuing involvement in such matters makes Justice Bastarache an active participant in all aspects of the Court's investigatory and decision-making functions, thus potentially tainting the public's perception of the Court's objectivity. The fact that he is only one of a number of judges on a given panel does not diminish the possibility that his questions or observations might influence his fellow judges' perception of a case.[110] Discussion of the merits of the case at the Court's post-hearing conferences may afford him opportunities to influence the other judges on the panel. Whether he would seek to do so is ultimately immaterial to the perception of bias; the fact that he has the ability to do so is what is paramount.

The mere perception that Justice Bastarache may be biased against judicial resolution of Aboriginal and treaty rights disputes creates a significant disincentive for Aboriginal peoples to bring their claims before Canadian courts. Intimations from a sitting judge, particularly one serving on the country's highest court, that Aboriginal legal issues are best left to negotiation are more likely than similar comments made by others to affect the public's perception—not to mention that of any Aboriginal group considering litigation—of the likelihood of success of such claims before the courts. Such apprehension also affects Aboriginal peoples' ability to use negotiation successfully; as indicated above, it has taken external pressure, such as that generated by the (actual or perceived) threat of litigation and of success in its use, to coerce the Crown into negotiations. Without this threat or something comparable emanating from some other external event, such as the Oka crisis of 1990, the Crown's participation in the negotiation of Aboriginal and treaty rights disputes is entirely at its own discretion.

Justice Binnie and *Wewaykum*

In *Wewaykum*,[111] clerical errors in a federal schedule of British Columbia reserves had led to confusion about the interests the Wewaykum and Wewaikai bands each had in their own and in one another's reserves. Both bands sought compensation from the federal Crown for breach of fiduciary duty alleged to result from these clerical errors. The Supreme Court dismissed both bands' appeals unanimously. Justice Binnie, who wrote for the Court, held that the clerical error did not amount to a breach of federal fiduciary obligations[112] and that the bands' claims could not have succeeded in any event because of limitations, laches, and acquiescence defences.[113]

The problem was that, in the mid-1980s, when the Wewaykum Band's claim first came to the federal Crown's attention, Binnie[114] had been Associate Deputy Attorney General for Canada, with supervisory responsibility for Native law in the federal DOJ. Shortly after the Supreme Court dismissed the *Wewaykum* appeal, the Wewaykum Band invoked the federal *Access to Information Act*[115] to ascertain what involvement, if any, Binnie might have had in the matter while at DOJ.[116] It developed that he had indeed received correspondence from, and had attended a meeting with, DOJ counsel involving *Wewaykum* in the early days of the claim, before the band had filed its statement of claim. Subsequently, counsel preparing Canada's defence had relied on advice that Binnie provided in those encounters.[117]

DOJ considered this information sufficiently significant to warrant waiving solicitor–client privilege in respect of it (so that the Wewaykum could obtain the relevant documents) and to seek directions from the Supreme Court about what further steps, if any, it might warrant.[118] On receipt of the motion for directions, Justice Binnie recused himself from further involvement in the case and filed a statement advising the Supreme Court registrar that he had no recollection of his involvement in the *Wewaykum* defence and that he had, at the time, been responsible for providing guidance to DOJ lawyers in literally thousands of cases.[119]

In argument before the Supreme Court of Canada on the motion,[120] both the federal Crown and the Attorney General of British Columbia argued that the *Wewaykum* decision ought not to be disturbed. The federal Crown emphasized the seventeen-year passage of time between Binnie's initial involvement and his participation in the appeal, the fact that Justice Binnie had no recollection of his earlier involvement, and the fact that every judge, at every level, had held the bands' claims to be without merit. Counsel for British Columbia observed that Binnie's earlier role in *Wewaykum* had been purely administrative and supervisory and argued that the Supreme Court's unanimity in the result made it difficult to maintain that Justice Binnie's participation had tainted the decision.[121]

Not surprisingly, the bands saw the matter differently. The Wewaykum, the Wewaikai, and three intervener B.C. bands all sought orders vacating the judgment.[122] Counsel for the various bands emphasized the fundamental importance of preserving the Court's integrity and of maintaining the appearance, as well as the reality, of justice being done. They argued that a reasonable apprehension of bias arises whenever a judge takes part in a case in which he or she has had prior involvement and that Justice Binnie had acted as counsel for the federal Crown in *Wewaykum*. The concurrence of the eight other judges in his opinion on the case did not, in their view, remove the taint of bias. They called attention to Binnie's special interest in Aboriginal matters and to his involvement as counsel for the Crown in previous Aboriginal cases; they also alleged that, while at DOJ, Binnie had been actively involved in risk analysis and the development of litigation strategy.[123] Outside the courtroom, Wewaykum Chief Aubrey Roberts commented that "[i]t would be nice to have our own judge sitting there deciding for us. As far as I'm concerned, those nine judges are like a jury. If someone taints a juror, it taints the whole jury."[124]

On 26 September 2003, the Supreme Court released its judgment on these motions. It held that *Wewaykum* ought to stand: that there was no reasonable apprehension of bias. A claim based on such apprehension, the Court said,

> can only succeed if it is established that reasonable, right-minded and properly informed persons would think that Binnie J. was consciously or unconsciously influenced in an inappropriate manner by his participation in this case over 15 years before he heard it here in the Supreme Court of Canada.[125]

It was for the bands to establish this, and, in the Court's view, they had not done so.

The Court acknowledged that Justice Binnie's prior involvement in *Wewaykum* "exceeded *pro forma* management of the files,"[126] but held nonetheless that the facts about it "would convince a reasonable person that his role was of a limited supervisory and administrative nature."[127] It emphasized that Binnie never was counsel to the federal Crown in *Wewaykum* and that he had advised only on the negotiation of the matter, not its litigation.[128] Another "significant factor," the Court said, in weighing apprehension of bias is the passage of time.[129] In its judgment, the significant interval between Binnie's involvement in *Wewaykum* as associate deputy minister and his involvement as a judge sitting on the final appeal of the matter rendered it "improbable" that a reasonable person would conclude that bias tainted his participation at the hearing.[130] The Court did not offer reasons for this conclusion.

Despite the Court's salutary insistence in *Wewaykum II* that "public confidence in our legal system is rooted in the fundamental belief that those who adjudicate in law must always do so without bias or prejudice and must be perceived to do so"[131] and that impartiality, and the public's confidence in it, "is the fundamental qualification of a judge and the core attribute of the judiciary,"[132] its decision is unlikely, for several reasons, to reassure the Wewaykum, who had sought the information on Binnie's prior involvement, or the other Aboriginal parties who had supported their position on the motion.

First, there is reason to doubt the completeness of the documentary record available to the Court.[133] It includes, for example, a memo from Binnie thanking a Vancouver DOJ colleague for an earlier note, but does not include the earlier note.[134] And it includes no items at all from the last four months of Binnie's tenure at DOJ in 1986. One can only wonder what impact any additional relevant material might have had on the result.

Second, the Court may well have erred in concluding that all of Binnie's involvement predated the litigation stage of the claim. For one thing, the record shows that DOJ Vancouver colleagues had sent Binnie copies of both the Wewaykum Band's statement of claim and the federal Crown's statement of defence.[135] But even if this had not been the case, the line being drawn here would have been problematic. The *Wewaykum* claim was subject to the federal specific claims process; as noted above,[136] that process tests bands' allegations against a standard of "lawful obligation," based on a DOJ assessment of the claims' likelihood of success in litigation. Binnie's advice on *Wewaykum*, in other words, would have been just as relevant in litigating the claim as in negotiating it, and the DOJ lawyers would have known that.

These same facts cast doubt on the Court's characterization of Binnie's involvement in the file as "limited supervisory and administrative" in nature.[137] Even though he was not Crown counsel of record in the case and may not have been directly involved in planning its litigation strategy, it is clear that Binnie offered advice on the claim, that he expected DOJ counsel of record to rely on it, that they were aware of that advice and attempted to follow it, and that they kept him informed about the progress of the matter even after the claim became a litigation file.[138] He was the DOJ official responsible for Aboriginal law in civil matters: the one to whom the DOJ staff who did serve as counsel reported. Why ought this prompt less concern about his capacity for impartiality in respect of this case than if he had served as counsel himself for a similar length of time?

No less troubling is the way in which the Court transformed the broader inquiry into reasonable apprehension of bias—an inquiry it rightly characterized as "the manifestation of a broader preoccupation about the image of justice"[139]—into a focused consideration of "the judge's state of mind, albeit viewed from the objective perspective of the reasonable person."[140] Only on this narrower view may the time lapse between the date of first involvement and the date of the hearing in which Justice Binnie took part assume the importance the Court ascribed to it. But if the public perception—the image of justice—were indeed what needed preserving, then one would have expected a judicial inquiry into the risk of bias to be based on all the relevant circumstances from which the *Wewaykum* decision emerged. These may or may not have been restricted to Justice Binnie's state of mind. The mere fact of his previous involvement in the matter might well have been enough to prompt some reasonably-minded members of the public, acting objectively, to question his capacity to decide the case impartially.

Finally, it gives some pause that the Court was content in *Wewaykum II* to hold that a reasonable apprehension of bias was on these facts "improbable."[141] One might have hoped that the Court would seek to dispel altogether such apprehension. "Improbable" is more akin to "unlikely" than to "never."

The Effects of These Incidents
Although the actions of Justices Bastarache and Binnie pose different problems, both give rise to perceptions of bias vis-à-vis the resolution in the Supreme Court of Canada of Aboriginal and treaty rights claims. If Aboriginal peoples and other members of the public lose confidence in the Supreme Court's ability to make unbiased pronouncements, the effects reach across the country and down to courts of first instance. This may have a chilling effect on the use of both negotiation and litigation for the resolution of Aboriginal claims.

The importance of maintaining confidence in the administration of justice is one of the fundamental requirements of the application of law in democratic societies. Justice Sopinka's majority judgment in *MacDonald Estate v. Martin*[142] underscores the importance of maintaining confidence in the justice system. In that case, a potential conflict of interest involving a risk of improper sharing of confidential information arose because a lawyer shifted her employment from a firm acting on one side of a legal dispute to the firm representing the other side. In considering whether the lawyer's new firm could continue to represent its client in that dispute, Sopinka J. placed primary emphasis upon the importance of maintaining confidence in the administration of justice:

> The legal profession has historically struggled to maintain the respect of the public. This has been so notwithstanding the high standards that, generally, have been maintained. When the management, size of law firms and many of the practices of the legal profession are indistinguishable from those of business, it is important that the fundamental professional standards be maintained and indeed improved. This is essential if the confidence of the public that the law is a profession is to be preserved and hopefully strengthened. Nothing is more important to the preservation of this relationship than the confidentiality of information passing between a solicitor and his or her client. The legal profession has distinguished itself from other professions by the sanctity with which these communications are treated. The law, too, perhaps unduly, has protected solicitor and client exchanges while denying the same protection to others. This tradition assumes particular importance when a client bares his or her soul in civil or criminal litigation. Clients do this in the justifiable belief that nothing they say will be used against them and to the advantage of the adversary. Loss of this confidence would deliver a serious blow to the integrity of the profession and to the public's confidence in the administration of justice.[143]

More recently, in *R. v. Neil*,[144] the Supreme Court's unanimous judgment—delivered by Justice Binnie—warned about conflicts of interest that could damage the interests of lawyers' former clients. Speaking for the court, Binnie J. said:

> [I]t is essential to the integrity of the administration of justice and it is of high public

importance that public confidence in that integrity be maintained: *MacDonald Estate v. Martin*, [1990] 3 S.C.R. 1235, at pp. 1243 and 1265, and *Tanny v. Gurman*, [1994] R.D.J. 10 (Que. C.A.). Unless a litigant is assured of the undivided loyalty of the lawyer, neither the public nor the litigant will have confidence that the legal system, which may appear to them to be a hostile and hideously complicated environment, is a reliable and trustworthy means of resolving their disputes and controversies. . . .[145]

He added that

[t]he value of an independent bar is diminished unless the lawyer is free from conflicting interests. Loyalty, in that sense, promotes effective representation, on which the problem-solving capability of an adversarial system rests.[146]

The role of the judge—and, indeed, the presumptions surrounding that judge—is even more vital to the administration of justice than that of the lawyer. If the Supreme Court was correct, in *Neil* and in *MacDonald Estate*, to be concerned that the potential for lawyers' conflicts of interest would adversely affect public confidence in the administration of justice, certainly it would have been reasonable to anticipate still greater concern about actions by the Court's own members that might credibly be regarded as instances of judicial partiality. This is so despite the contrary findings in the Bastarache and Binnie incidents by the Canadian Judicial Council[147] and the Supreme Court in *Wewaykum II*,[148] respectively. The law has always been wary of the impact of perceptions affecting the administration of justice and the public's confidence in it—and rightly so. In the familiar words of Lord Hewart C.J. in *The King v. Sussex Justices*, "justice should not only be done, but should manifestly and undoubtedly be seen to be done."[149] The test for bias in administrative law, which considers whether a "reasonable apprehension of bias" (with or without demonstrable bias) exists, is just one manifestation of law's desire to maintain the perception, as well as the reality, that justice is being done. This test, as established by de Grandpré J.'s dissenting judgment in *Committee for Justice and Liberty v. National Energy Board*, requires that

the apprehension of bias must be a reasonable one held by reasonable and right-minded persons, applying themselves to the question and obtaining thereon the required information. . . . [T]hat test is "what would an informed person, viewing the matter realistically and practically—and having thought the matter through—conclude. Would he think that it is more likely than not that [the decision-maker], whether consciously or unconsciously, would not decide fairly."[150]

As members of the bench who have assumed duties to carry out the law, Justices Bastarache and Binnie occupy vital roles in the administration of justice. As the American jurist Learned Hand once observed, "Justice does not depend upon legal dialectics so much as upon the atmosphere of the courtroom, and that in the end depends primarily upon the judge."[151] In another case, Lord Denning said that, in considering whether bias exists, a court

> looks at the impression which would be given to other people. Even if [the judge] was as impartial as could be, nevertheless, if right-minded persons would think that, in the circumstances, there was a real likelihood of bias on his part, then he should not sit. And if he does sit, his decision cannot stand.... The reason is plain enough. Justice must be rooted in confidence: and confidence is destroyed when right-minded people go away thinking: "The judge was biased."[152]

Although the mere appearance of bias need not, and may not, indicate actual bias, public perception and confidence is integral to the efficacy of the judicial system in a democratic society.[153] Appreciating this notion is essential to understanding the rationale behind the House of Lords decision in *Pinochet (No. 2)*.[154] That decision vacated, because of concern about an apprehension of bias, its own earlier high-profile judgment (*Pinochet (No. 1)*) denying diplomatic immunity to the former Chilean dictator in respect of crimes against humanity he allegedly committed while serving as Chile's head of state.[155] The sole problem there was that Lord Hoffman, one of the five judges who had decided *Pinochet (No. 1)*, had failed to disclose that he was an unpaid director and chairperson of Amnesty International Charity Limited, an organization established and controlled by Amnesty International (AI), a non-profit humanitarian organization, and that his wife was employed by AI.

Are the situations involving Justices Bastarache and Binnie similar to that in *Pinochet (No. 1)*? Alan Gold, then-president of the Criminal Lawyers' Association, a group that had filed a complaint against Justice Bastarache to the Canadian Judicial Council, alleged that Justice Bastarache's actions were worse than Lord Hoffman's lack of disclosure in *Pinochet (No. 1)*, calling the latter "... a drop in the bucket compared to here, where you have a judge actually expressing preconceived views."[156] Meanwhile, then–Grand Chief Matthew Coon Come of the Assembly of First Nations argued that Justice Bastarache had "brought the judiciary into disrepute by questioning the outcome of a case before the Supreme Court—his own court—where he had not even been present to hear arguments."[157] The Judicial Conduct Committee of the Canadian Judicial Council did not feel that Justice Bastarache's statements indicated a prevailing bias on Aboriginal legal issues, but it specifically made "no observation" as to whether Justice Bastarache's recusal from any case "may be desirable in the future."[158] Since then, Justice Bastarache appears to have reconsidered his earlier openness; at a Canadian Bar Association conference on the issue in August 2003, he advocated that judges refrain from commenting on public issues outside the courtroom. "I personally believe," he said, that "there is a price to pay for exercising the judicial role. Reticence, it seems to me, is a small price to pay to assure judicial independence."[159]

Justice Binnie's situation seems even more akin to the *Pinochet (No. 1)* scenario. Whether or not he recalled having advised on *Wewaykum*, surely he ought to have recognized that he could have done so because of his position at the time and his responsibility for Aboriginal legal matters. Unless he was able to satisfy himself that he had not had any consequential involvement in the *Wewaykum* matter, he ought to have recused himself from *Wewaykum* in order to avoid the very problems that arose in *Pinochet (No. 1)*. Interestingly, in *Wewaykum II*,[160] the Supreme Court distinguished *Pinochet (No. 1)* on the basis that Justice Binnie had neither financial nor any other interest in *Wewaykum* that could have put him in the position of a party to the cause.[161]

The idea of a Supreme Court judge recusing himself/herself from a case is unusual but not unheard of. Justice John Sopinka recused himself when the Supreme Court heard the appeal in *Ontario (A.G.) v. Bear Island Foundation*[162] because, while still in practice, he had discussed the case with the Aboriginal litigants, who had approached him to undertake their appeal of the trial judgment in that matter.[163] More recently, Justice Iacobucci recused himself from the appeal in *Authorson v. Canada (A.G.)*,[164] a class action by war veterans concerned about the federal government's administration of interest payments on funds it held for them, because of his former role as federal Deputy Minister of Justice.[165]

Because of the Supreme Court's unavoidable leadership role in Canadian Aboriginal and treaty rights jurisprudence, concerns about bias or conflict of interest on the part of Supreme Court judges cast doubt upon the effectiveness of litigation. Such doubts may also compromise Aboriginal peoples' ability to use negotiation to resolve their Aboriginal and treaty rights claims. As suggested earlier, Aboriginal peoples have repeatedly needed successes in litigation (or other forms of external pressure) to coerce the Crown into negotiating their claims.

Given all the emphasis in *Wewaykum II* on the reasonable person's perspective on the bias issue, it would be interesting to consider whether a reasonable and informed Aboriginal person viewing Justice Binnie's prior involvement in *Wewaykum* would come to the same conclusion as the Court. A negative answer would seem to buttress the claims made herein about the effects of Justice Binnie's conflict of interest in *Wewaykum*—if not also the potential bias of Justice Bastarache—upon Aboriginal peoples' use of litigation as a means to address their disputes with the Crown.

PUTTING IT ALL TOGETHER

As Justice Learned Hand observed, the perception of justice in a democratic society is more dependent upon the light in which its judges are perceived than upon its dialectics.[166] However, even an appearance of impropriety may take on greater significance than usual in the context of the legal and political controversies surrounding the resolution of outstanding Aboriginal issues in

Canada. For this reason, the questionable nature of Justice Bastarache's comments and the dubiousness of Justice Binnie's decision not to recuse himself, even as a precautionary measure, from *Wewaykum* may well substantially affect Aboriginal peoples' choice between negotiation and litigation as means to resolve their claims.

Canadian courts' ability to adjudicate difficult Aboriginal law issues is enough of a concern even without having to factor in apprehensions about judicial bias or indiscretion. Few judges are familiar with, much less expert in, the complex issues they face in Aboriginal and treaty rights cases. In this respect, the specialized nature of Aboriginal law resembles other discrete areas of practice, such as securities regulation or labour relations, in which generalists have difficulty. In those latter contexts, specialized adjudicative tribunals provide the expertise necessary to deal authoritatively with, and make binding pronouncements upon, the complex issues that regularly arise. Again, no similar arrangement now exists with respect to Aboriginal legal issues.

The complexity of Aboriginal and treaty rights disputes becomes more apparent with the realization—only relatively recently achieved by Canadian courts—that these matters transcend strictly legal considerations. They involve wading through historical documents and properly contextualizing the nature of Crown representations and the understanding of those representations by Aboriginal peoples who could not read English. Judges must be conscious of the need to give appropriate weight to Aboriginal oral histories[167] and to rationalize the different worldviews held by the Crown's representatives and the Aboriginal leaders, particularly when dealing with transactions involving Aboriginal lands and their surrender under treaty or deed. Justice Bastarache, speaking extra-curially in 1998 about the *Delgamuukw* case, expressed the difficulty of addressing such transactions:

> . . . [T]he Court concluded that "traditional real property rules" could not appropriately describe the content of aboriginal title and proceeded to describe a type of property right which gives effect to the unique nature of aboriginal presence on land over hundreds of years. Not surprisingly, that *sui generis* property right is a novel creation and one which will no doubt require many cycles of trial and appeal before its precise character is fully fleshed out. In the meantime, the tapestry of property law has a piece missing of indeterminate size which places considerable strain on the coherence of the structure. And yet, can there be any doubt that aboriginal interest in lands, which they have used since time immemorial, must be recognized and protected under our law? The difficulty is in accommodating, adjudicating, and vindicating that obvious reality when it doesn't quite fit into the conventional paradigms of property law. And where will these *sui generis* property rights fit in with the rest of our hierarchy of legal rights? We have embarked on the road of refashioning our legal tools. Time will tell whether aboriginal aspirations, and realities, of land occupation can be successfully and sensitively recognized by

our law. The livelihoods and sense of identity of millions of people are at stake, and there can be no doubt that this difficult—perhaps even defining—issue will be with us for many years to come.[168]

In his newspaper interview, Bastarache J. characterized the situation in this manner:

> When we come to land claims, and to rights that are very ill-defined in very old documents which were set in an historical context that certainly doesn't exist now, and where you try to determine the impact of these kinds of decisions on government policy and on the rights of other people who are affected, I don't know how we will come to a determination. If we have to, we will, obviously.[169]

Ironically, Justice Bastarache's comments about the difficulty of interpreting historical actions and documents are similar to Binnie J.'s remarks in his majority judgment in *Marshall*.[170] Speaking about the Court's task of interpreting a 238-year-old treaty, Justice Binnie commented that "[f]rom this distance, across more than two centuries, events are necessarily seen as 'through a glass, darkly.'"[171] Nonetheless, in spite of the difficulty in resolving disputes arising out of ancient documents and their subjective interpretations, Justice Binnie was able to use the Supreme Court's canons of treaty interpretation to assist in the very task of getting to the heart of such challenging and controversial disputes.[172] His judgment indicates that the methodology he employed to discover the appropriate meaning of the relevant clause in dispute (the "truckhouse" clause)[173] was not based on some "vague sense of after-the-fact largesse."[174] Rather, the rules of interpretation he used were required to overcome what he described as the "special difficulties," including the lack of a written Aboriginal account, involved in determining what had transpired.[175]

For the most part, Justice Binnie's majority judgment in *Marshall* demonstrates that adoption of a contextual approach can address adequately the difficulties arising in Aboriginal and treaty rights disputes. The Supreme Court has shown—albeit all too rarely—that it is capable of constructing a contextual framework for understanding Aboriginal and treaty rights (or, at the very least, of working within a framework constructed by others).[176] The Supreme Court's use of the canons of treaty interpretation provides a prime example of its ability to adapt its interpretive function to the unique circumstances of Crown–Native relations, even if the judgments in *Marshall* were not always consistent with this approach.[177]

Adoption of a suitably contextual approach is necessary to the proper resolution of Aboriginal legal issues, whether in negotiation or in litigation, but so is an understanding of the reasons for using such an approach. For instance, in the context of a treaty rights claim, a negotiator or adjudicator must be able to recognize and appreciate the significance of certain fundamental points. Among them are: the Crown's historic wrongs against Aboriginal peoples and the resultant benefit that flowed to the Crown at the Aboriginals' expense; the problems of treaty interpretation as a result of differences in language and worldviews; and the way in which the canons of treaty interpretation attempt to address these issues. The ability of an individual or a tribunal to recognize and appreciate these details plays a vital role in whether the canons of treaty interpretation are engaged as a purposive device or simply as a rhetorical tool (i.e., articulated, but not given practical effect). The use of rhetoric unaccompanied by a commitment to its subsequent implementation and enforcement is disingenuous; ultimately, it renders meaningless any judgment containing such empty rhetoric. Indeed, the distinction between purposive applications and rhetoric is one of the primary ways to differentiate between the majority and minority judgments in *Marshall*.[178]

The fact that the Supreme Court of Canada has demonstrated, even if only intermittently,[179] the ability to contextualize Aboriginal and treaty rights disputes properly suggests that it can be an appropriate forum in which to resolve such matters. This does not mean that litigation is the only method for resolution of these issues. However, given the current political climate in Canada, courts are indispensable to the process of resolving Aboriginal law disputes.

The Indian Claims Commission experience, discussed earlier, demonstrates this. Insofar as the federal Crown retains the discretion to accept, reject, or simply shelve without consequence the ICC's recommendations, the time, expense, and effort involved in bringing a claim before the ICC may not yield any practical benefit for the Aboriginal claimants. When alternative processes such as this fail to generate satisfactory results, they effectively force Aboriginal peoples to resort to litigation. Reliance on litigation, however, is inconsistent with their understanding of their relationship with the Crown as one based on peace, friendship, and respect, cardinal principles of Crown–Native relations since at least the *Treaty of Albany, 1664*.[180] The adversarial nature of litigation is inimical to the maintenance of peaceful, friendly, and respectful relations between peoples. If, however, litigation ceases to be a meaningful alternative, Aboriginal peoples will be left without any satisfactory method of addressing their claims without the voluntary cooperation of the Crown.

The history of Crown treatment of Aboriginal claims prior to the litigation successes in *Calder* and *Guerin*—and its more recent history, except when faced with direct and significant threats, such as the Oka crisis—makes it appear unlikely that the Crown will negotiate Aboriginal peoples' claims on fairer terms than at present without the threat of litigation. From a purely self-interested Crown perspective, the costs[181] associated with the resolution of Aboriginal and treaty rights claims, and the potential public backlash against the expenditures associated with resolving those claims, far outweigh the political benefits to be obtained from such resolution. Accordingly, it is generally against the Crown's interests to settle, or indeed to negotiate, Aboriginal and treaty rights claims voluntarily.

Positive litigation results for Aboriginal peoples, however, create uncertainty for the Crown. This uncertainty provides an impetus for the Crown to renew attempts at negotiation, in order to foster greater certainty over the outcome of the process and to maximize its control over the process of resolution. The *Calder* decision is the first modern example. However, a vicious circle has emerged from federal Crown-controlled alternative processes. Their ineffectiveness has repeatedly led Aboriginal peoples to hasten back to litigation; this, in turn, has led to yet further federal Crown attempts to create litigation alternatives. The courts, in other words, have been a necessary component of the process of addressing Aboriginal claims; ultimately, they are the catalyst for the resolution of Crown–Aboriginal disputes. This situation will certainly continue unless and until negotiation becomes a meaningful alternative to litigation in its own right. That will require mechanisms capable of ensuring fair, timely, and binding resolution of such disputes outside of court.

CONCLUSION

After all this, are we any closer to resolving the negotiation versus litigation debate? Probably not. However, it should now be clear that the question is not as simple as asking whether Aboriginal disputes should be negotiated or litigated. Given the complexity and controversy–both legal and political–surrounding Aboriginal and treaty rights, not to mention the uncertain impact of their recognition on non-Aboriginal interests, it should not be surprising that the "answer" to the question posed by the title to this paper produces not a solution, but only further and more complex questions.

It has been suggested here that Aboriginal and treaty rights litigation begets negotiation and that negotiation becomes meaningful and effective only with the continued presence, or threat, of litigation. So understood, litigation is akin to the sword of Damocles, precariously hanging over the head of the Crown, which never knows when it may drop. Of course, when actions such as those of Justices Bastarache and Binnie prompt Aboriginal peoples to doubt the efficacy of litigation, the sword appears more firmly anchored than it would otherwise seem.

This paper has purposely not suggested a preference for either negotiation or litigation to resolve Aboriginal and treaty rights issues. That choice belongs entirely to Aboriginal claimants. There are, however, some concluding observations that can be made.

In many ways, negotiation seems preferable to litigation. The Crown–Native fiduciary relationship, which the Supreme Court described in *Sparrow* as "trust-like, rather than adversarial,"[182] is consistent only with negotiated settlement of outstanding issues, not with adversarial litigation. Although negotiation may be a vehicle to resolve Aboriginal and treaty rights disputes while maintaining the fiduciary nature of Crown–Native relations, it has been shown to be effective only where there is either a will to negotiate in good faith or a compulsion to do so. For the most part, the federal government has lacked sufficient political will to negotiate Aboriginal claims. Further, the lack of independent and effective negotiation processes to date has left Aboriginal peoples at a distinct disadvantage. Consequently, litigation is still necessary, even if it is a necessary evil. Therefore, the negotiation-versus-litigation debate will likely continue for some time yet.

Some recent judicial statements have emphasized that negotiation is preferable to litigation for the resolution of outstanding Aboriginal and treaty rights claims.[183] What has not yet been acknowledged, however—and what has been largely ignored by those favouring the removal of such claims from Canadian courts—is that these statements are often accompanied by rather equivocal commentary. In *Delgamuukw*, Lamer C.J.C. said clearly that negotiated settlements, not litigation, would achieve the important goal of reconciling the pre-existence of Aboriginal societies with Crown sovereignty. However, he also stated that the Crown "is under a moral, if not a legal, duty to enter into and conduct those negotiations in good faith."[184] Is he saying that the duty is moral, legal, or both? His choice of words here implies that a moral duty definitely exists and that a legal duty might exist, but that he is unwilling to pronounce upon the matter. To state the obvious, there is a tremendous distinction between moral duties and those that may be enforced in courts of law.[185]

Similar ambiguity may be seen in the statements of federal Crown representatives on Native rights and on the federal Crown's intention to honour its commitments to Aboriginal peoples. A case in point is a statement made by former Minister of Indian Affairs Robert Nault, who said, in relation to the proposed federal estimate of $2 billion to settle residential school lawsuits:

> I'm not as interested in what the courts say or don't say, because I think it is important for governments to create policies based on what is the right thing to do. ... Sometimes, just because you have a legal opinion on something, that doesn't mean you have to follow that to a T.[186]

Does this statement mean that the minister will do what rightfully should be done to benefit Aboriginal peoples, regardless of what legal opinions dictate, or does it mean that the federal Crown will not be bound by judicial determinations on the nature of its obligations to Aboriginal peoples if it does not believe that following those determinations is the "right thing to do"?

As former Chief Justice Lamer stated in *Delgamuukw*, "we are all here to stay."[187] As he recognized, this reality requires a significant degree of reconciliation.

However, there is not only a need to reconcile "the fact that aboriginals lived on the land in distinctive societies, with their own practices, traditions and cultures ... with the sovereignty of the Crown," as expressed in *Van der Peet*.[188] The entrenchment of Aboriginal and treaty rights in section 35(1) of the *Constitution Act, 1982* also necessitates reconciling the co-existence of Aboriginal and Canadian societies with the historic, sovereign injustices perpetrated against Aboriginal peoples by the British, and later Canadian, Crowns through their self-interested actions. Although these various forms of reconciliation may be achieved—at least in a legal sense—by litigation, they can be obtained in a literal sense only through a more conciliatory and participatory process such as negotiation. Furthermore, because of the historical relationship between the parties built upon the principles of peace, friendship and respect, the constitutional recognition of Aboriginal interests, and the restrictions upon governmental derogation from those interests, a true and lasting reconciliation is best achieved through negotiation rather than litigation.

Where all of this leaves the present situation is uncertain. This paper has attempted to demonstrate that the pressure of litigation does provide tangible benefits to Aboriginal peoples, beyond their successes in individual judgments, by increasing the Crown's willingness to engage in meaningful negotiation. Such benefits will be fleeting, however, if litigation ceases to be a meaningful option for resolution of Aboriginal and treaty rights disputes. Perceptions that the deck is stacked against Aboriginal interests can diminish, or even eliminate, Aboriginal peoples' faith in the efficacy of litigation. Incidents such as those involving Justices Bastarache and Binnie buttress such perceptions. The manner in which the Supreme Court dealt with Justice Binnie's conflict of interest in *Wewaykum II* has certainly done nothing to alleviate them. If anything, the Court's response has only fanned the flames of Aboriginal discontent and further discouraged Aboriginal peoples from using litigation to resolve their disputes with the Crown.

The various problems with the *Specific Claims Resolution Act*—the cap it imposes on claims compensation, the questionable independence of its investigative and adjudicative bodies, and the potential for conflicts of interest inherent in the powers it would reserve to the Minister of Indian Affairs—replicate existing conflicts of interest in a scheme that should be striving to remove such conflicts. Although the future may be geared increasingly away from current litigation and negotiation practices and towards a binding and more specialized tribunal process, the problems associated with the new scheme demonstrate that we are not there yet.

NOTES

[1] The term "the Crown" is used here and throughout this paper to denote both the Canadian federal

230   LEONARD I. ROTMAN

and provincial Crowns, unless only one or the other is specified in the text.
[2] [1996] 2 S.C.R. 507 [*Van der Peet*].
[3] [1997] 3 S.C.R. 1010 [*Delgamuukw*].
[4] *Constitution Act, 1982*, being Schedule B to the *Canada Act 1982* (U.K.), 1982, c. 11.
[5] *Van der Peet*, *supra* note 2 at para. 31.
[6] Whether Aboriginal peoples ought to seek international methods of dispute resolution is another issue, but one beyond the ambition of this paper.
[7] *Delgamuukw*, *supra* note 3 at para. 186.
[8] Cristin Schmitz, "SCC Wrong Forum for Native Land Claims: Bastarache" *Lawyers Weekly* (19 January 2001). See also Cristin Schmitz, "Bastarache Explains Dissents in One-third of SCC Decisions" *Lawyers Weekly* (19 January 2001) 1, 7 [Schmitz, "Bastarache Explains"]. Excerpts from the interview were reproduced in general-circulation newspapers, including the *National Post* and the *Ottawa Citizen*. Justice Bastarache also commented on a number of criminal law cases and issues, but they will not be addressed in this paper.
[9] [2002] 4 S.C.R. 245, 2002 SCC 79 [*Wewaykum*].
[10] See Letter from Chief Justice R.J. Scott, Chairperson of the Judicial Conduct Committee of the Canadian Judicial Council, to Hon. M. Bastarache (15 March 2001), online: Canadian Judicial Council <http://www.cjc-ccm.gc.ca/english/news_releases/2001_03_16.htm> ["Letter from Chief Justice R.J. Scott"], and *Wewaykum Indian Band v. Canada*, [2003] 2 S.C.R. 259, 2003 SCC 45 [*Wewaykum II*].
[11] This paper is not intended to be an indictment of Justices Bastarache or Binnie; rather, it attempts to demonstrate the profound effects their actions—whether positive (Bastarache) or passive (Binnie)—may have on the resolution of Aboriginal and treaty rights disputes in Canada.
[12] Whether or not it recognizes this symbiosis, the Supreme Court of Canada stated in *R. v. Powley*, [2003] 2 S.C.R. 207, 2003 SCC 43 at para. 50 [*Powley*] that "a combination of negotiation and judicial settlement will more clearly define the contours of the Métis right to hunt. . . ."
[13] Treaties are an obvious exception to this general statement, although the Crown's negotiation of treaties also reflects the point to be made in this paper: that the Crown generally negotiates with Aboriginal peoples only where it is compelled to do so by extraneous pressures, including concern over perceived litigation results, the effects of constitutional enactments, political and economic pressures, or, in the case of historic treaties, the desire (at different times) to obtain Aboriginal military and political alliances or to obtain surrenders of Aboriginal lands.
[14] (1887), 13 S.C.R. 577 at 649. More recently, the idea that the Crown's obligations are political, rather than legal, appeared in the Federal Court of Appeal's judgment in *Guerin v. The Queen* (1983), 143 D.L.R. (3d) 416 (F.C.A.), rev'd [1984] 2 S.C.R. 335 [*Guerin* (C.A.)]. At the Federal Court of Appeal, Le Dain J. dismissed the Musqueam Band's claim against the Crown for the latter's mishandling of a lease of some of the band's reserve lands, holding that the Crown's only duty was a non-justiciable political trust, or "trust in a higher sense," which resulted in no federal Crown liability. Upon appeal, the Supreme Court of Canada determined that the Crown owed, and had breached, a legally binding fiduciary obligation to the band and was liable for $10 million in damages.
[15] *Canada (A.G.) v. Ontario (A.G.)*, [1897] A.C. 199 (P.C.) at 213. This statement was later cited, with approval, in *R. v. Wesley*, [1932] 4 D.L.R. 774 (Alta. C.A.) at 788: "In Canada the Indian treaties appear to have been judicially interpreted as being mere promises and agreements. See *A.-G. Can. v. A.-G. Ont.* (Indian Annuities case), [1897] A.C. 199 at 213." See also *R. v. Sikyea* (1964), 43 D.L.R. (2d) 150 (N.W.T.C.A.) at 154 [*Sikyea*]: "While this [Lord Watson's statement in the *Re Indian Claims* case] refers only to the annuities payable under the treaties, it is difficult to see that the other covenants in the treaties, including the ones we are here concerned with, can stand on any higher footing."
[16] As, for example, in cases such as *Sikyea, ibid.* or some pre–fiduciary duty cases, including *Miller v. The King*, [1950] S.C.R. 168 and *St. Ann's Island Shooting and Fishing Club Ltd. v. The King*, [1950] S.C.R. 211.
[17] Provincial Crowns, as indicated in *Delgamuukw*, *supra* note 3 at paras. 172–83, could not extinguish these rights because they could not display the requisite clear and plain intention to do so, without

intruding upon the federal Crown's exclusive legislative jurisdiction over "Indians, and Lands reserved for the Indians" under section 91(24) of the *Constitution Act, 1867* (U.K.), 30 & 31 Vict., c. 3, reprinted in R.S.C. 1985, App. II, No. 5.

[18] [1973] S.C.R. 313 [*Calder*].

[19] [1990] 1 S.C.R. 1075 [*Sparrow*].

[20] Also known as the doctrine of reception.

[21] Thus, it may be seen that Lamer C.J.'s notion of reconciling the Crown's assertion of sovereignty and pre-existing Aboriginal rights (see *supra* note 5 and accompanying text) was not the first time that the law has addressed the intersection of these issues.

[22] (1774), 1 Cowp. 204 at 209, 98 E.R. 1045 (K.B.) at 1047–48. See also Brian Slattery, "The Doctrine of Continuity" in Brian Slattery, *Ancestral Lands, Alien Laws: Judicial Perspectives on Aboriginal Title* (Saskatoon: University of Saskatchewan Native Law Centre, 1983), c. 4.

[23] See for example *Connolly v. Woolrich* (1867), 17 R.J.R.Q. 75 (Qc. S.C.), aff'd *sub nom. Johnstone v. Connolly* (1869), 17 R.J.R.Q. 266 (Que. C.A.); *R. v. Nan-e-quis-a-ka* (1889), 1 Terr. L.R. 211 (N.W.T.S.C.); and *R. v. Bear's Shin Bone* (1899), 3 C.C.C. 329 (N.W.T.S.C.), all of which recognized the effect of Aboriginal customary laws.

[24] Note, for example, *Simon v. The Queen*, [1985] 2 S.C.R. 387 at 406:
> Given the serious and far-reaching consequences of a finding that a treaty right has been extinguished, it seems appropriate to demand strict proof of the fact of extinguishment in each case where the issue arises. As Douglas J. said in *United States v. Santa Fe Pacific R. Co.*, *supra*, at p. 354, "extinguishment cannot be lightly implied."

[25] *Delgamuukw*, *supra* note 3 at para. 180.

[26] *Supra* note 18.

[27] Canada, Department of Indian Affairs and Northern Development, *Statement on Claims of Indian and Inuit People* (Ottawa: Queen's Printer, 1973).

[28] If the rights delegated from the federal Crown were the same as the rights to be relinquished, as the federal Crown often represented to bands, what was the rationale for requiring this swap? Clearly, while the rights may have been similar at the time the comprehensive claims process was devised, the federal Crown was concerned about the judicial interpretation and possible enlargement of those rights, which would deny the federal Crown the certainty that it sought in settling land claims. See the discussion of comprehensive claims in note 42, *infra*.

[29] *Supra* note 14.

[30] *Supra* note 19.

[31] See for example *Van der Peet*, *supra* note 2 at para. 28, Lamer C.J.C. Compare McLachlin J., dissenting *ibid.* at para. 315.

[32] *Sparrow*, *supra* note 19 at 1103.

[33] *Ibid.* at 1105.

[34] Noel Lyon, "An Essay on Constitutional Interpretation" (1988) 26 Osgoode Hall L.J. 95 at 100, cited with approval in *Sparrow*, *ibid.* at 1106.

[35] See quotations in text at note 38–39, *infra*.

[36] This test, in brief, requires that Crown legislative objectives be reasonable, not impose undue hardship on the Aboriginal peoples to be affected, and not deny Aboriginals their preferred means of exercising their section 35(1) rights. Other requirements are that the legislative goal be consistent with the Crown's fiduciary obligations, that it minimally infringe the rights in question in order to effect the desired result, and that the Crown engage in consultation with Aboriginal peoples regarding the legislative initiative and, where appropriate, offer fair compensation for its legislative infringement of section 35(1) rights. See generally *Sparrow*, *supra* note 19 at 1109–10, 1113–19.

[37] There is a need here to qualify the author's perspective on this statement. Although *Sparrow*, *ibid.* created a justificatory framework for the regulation of Aboriginal rights, a framework adopted vis-à-vis treaty rights in *R. v. Badger*, [1996] 1 S.C.R. 771 [*Badger*] and in *R. v. Marshall*, [1999] 3 S.C.R. 456 [*Marshall*] and *R. v. Marshall*, [1999] 3 S.C.R. 533 [*Marshall II*], this author has suggested that application of the *Sparrow* test to treaty rights is inappropriate because of the important distinctions between the two kinds of rights: see Leonard I. Rotman, "Defining Parameters: Aboriginal Rights,

Treaty Rights, and the *Sparrow* Justificatory Test" (1997) 36 Alta. L. Rev. 149.

[38] *Sparrow, ibid.* at 1109.

[39] *Ibid.* at 1105.

[40] The ICC was created in August 1991 and continued on 1 September 1992, both pursuant to federal Orders in Council: P.C. 1991-1329 (15 July 1991) and P.C. 1992-1730 (27 July 1992), respectively.

[41] A band pursuing the resolution of a dispute through the ICC is theoretically not prevented from initiating litigation on the matter, or continuing litigation already in progress, while submitting to the ICC process, but concurrent litigation would, in all likelihood, result in the breakdown of the process from the Crown's end. An example of this is the ICC's Mi'kmaqs of Gesgapegiag Inquiry report of December 1994, which the Crown acknowledged having received but put in abeyance pending the outcome of the litigation related to the claim. (A copy of this report is available from the ICC, online: Indian Claims Commission <http://www.indianclaims.ca/english/pub/claimsreports.html>.) Certainly a band is not barred from commencing future litigation after completion of the ICC process.

[42] The term "specific claims," as explained in the *Indian Claims Commission Information Guide* (Ottawa: Minister of Supply and Services, 1997) at 3, refers to "the breach or non-fulfilment of government obligations found in treaties, agreements or statutes." This is to be distinguished from "comprehensive claims," which pertain to claims based on unextinguished Aboriginal title where no treaty has been signed. The federal government's definitions of these types of claims are to be found, respectively, in: Department of Indian Affairs and Northern Development, "Outstanding Business: A Native Claims Policy" (Ottawa: Supply and Services Canada, 1982) [*Outstanding Business*], and Indian and Northern Affairs, "In All Fairness: A Native Claims Policy" (Ottawa: Supply and Services Canada, 1981).

[43] Inquiries may be commenced by request of the band only where: (1) the Department of Indian Affairs and Northern Development has rejected the band's claim under the federal specific claims process, or (2) the minister has accepted the claim for negotiation, but a dispute has arisen over the compensation criteria being used. See "The Claims Process," online: Indian Claims Commission <http://www.indianclaims.ca/english/about/claimsprocess.html>.

[44] Mediation may encompass a variety of dispute-resolution techniques where there is mutual agreement of the parties to submit to such a process. For more information, see "Mediation Services," online: Indian Claims Commission <http://www.indianclaims.ca/english/about/mediation.html>.

[45] Under the specific claims process, the federal government is obliged only to discharge "lawful obligations." The notion of lawful obligation, which is found in "Outstanding Business," *supra* note 42 at 2, includes an obligation derived from law that may arise from any of the following circumstances:
1. The non-fulfilment of a treaty or agreement between Indians and the Crown
2. A breach of obligation arising out of the *Indian Act* or other statutes pertaining to Indians and the regulations thereunder
3. A breach of an obligation arising out of government administration of Indian funds or other assets
4. An illegal disposition of Indian land.

[46] One example of an ICC inquiry in which an unequivocal finding of a lawful obligation was made but no governmental action was taken within a reasonable period of time is the Athabasca Chipewyan First Nation Inquiry. The March 1998 ICC report found that the federal Crown had breached its fiduciary duty to the First Nation by not taking adequate steps to prevent or mitigate damages or to seek compensation for unjustified infringements of the First Nation's treaty rights and for environmental damages caused to its reserve by the construction and operation of the W.A.C. Bennett dam. The federal government eventually responded to the ICC's recommendations in April, 2001 and rejected them outright. The matter is now in litigation. A copy of this report is available from the ICC, "Completed Claims Reports," online: Indian Claims Commission <http://www.indianclaims.ca/english/pub/claimsreports.html>.

As of March 2003, four ICC reports that have made positive recommendations in favour of the Aboriginal claimants have yet to be responded to; one of them dates from June 1994: see Indian Claims Commission, *Annual Report, 2001–2002* (Ottawa: Minister of Public Works and Government

Services Canada, 2003) at 8–22.

As indicated in the Indian Claims Commission's latest annual report, *ibid.* at 1, of fifty-five claims investigated by the ICC since 1991, twenty-five have been settled or accepted for negotiation; fifteen claims recommended for negotiation by the ICC were rejected by the federal government.

[47] See Indian Claims Commission, *Annual Report, 1999–2000* (Ottawa: Minister of Public Works and Government Services Canada, 2001) at 1.

[48] See Daniel J. Bellegarde, Notes for an Address (Paper Presented to the Aboriginal Law Conference of the Continuing Legal Education Society of British Columbia, March 2002), online: Indian Claims Commission <http://www.indianclaims.ca/english/about/bellegardeeng.html> ["Commissioner Bellegarde's Remarks"]:

> Every Commission report dating back to 1994 has called for the creation of an independent claims body with the legislative authority to make binding decisions with regard to the Crown's lawful obligations towards First Nations and the fair compensation when those obligations have been breached.

[49] *Ibid.*:

> For as long as I can remember, there has been continual, unabated pressure on the Government of Canada to reform the specific claims process and establish an independent claims body. Virtually every respected academic, jurist and public policy commentator who has examined this area since 1947 has come to the same conclusion. Yet, as of today, this has not happened.

See also Indian Claims Commission, "Bill C-6, An Act to establish the Canadian Centre for the Independent Resolution of First Nations Specific Claims" (Brief Presentation to the House of Commons Standing Committee on Aboriginal Affairs, November 2002), online: Indian Claims Commission <http://www.indianclaims.ca/download/StandingCtteeBillC6Nov262002Eng.pdf>; Indian Claims Commission, "Bill C-6, An Act to establish the Canadian Centre for the Independent Resolution of First Nations Specific Claims" (Presentation to the Standing Senate Committee on Aboriginal Peoples, June 2003), online: Indian Claims Commission <http://www.indianclaims.ca/download/ICC_Bill%20C-6_Senate%20Cttee%20Presentation_June%202003_Eng.pdf>.

[50] See the *Specific Claims Resolution Act*, S.C. 2003, c. 23.

[51] See the discussion of this point in the text below.

[52] See *supra* note 42 for the federal distinction between specific and comprehensive claims. As its name suggests, the new *Specific Claims Resolution Act, supra* note 50, will apply only to specific claims.

[53] See *supra* note 45.

[54] Interestingly, in Appendix "C" of Indian Claims Commission, "Human Rights, Justice and the Need for an Independent Claims Body in Canada" (Brief Presentation to the House of Commons Standing Committee on Aboriginal Affairs, May 2001), online: Indian Claims Commission <http://www.indianclaims.ca/download/sceng.pdf>, then–commission co-chairs Daniel Bellegarde and James Prentice indicate that, of the nine ICC reports at the time whose recommendations had been rejected by the federal government, five featured findings based on a fiduciary duty analysis. See the discussion in note 57, *infra* and accompanying text.

[55] *Report of the Royal Commission on Aboriginal Peoples: Restructuring the Relationship*, vol. 4 (Ottawa: Supply and Services Canada, 1996) at 545 [RCAP].

[56] As the RCAP stated, *ibid.* at 556, "federal claims policies continue to perpetuate procedures that are dilatory, adversarial and unsatisfactory to all concerned."

[57] Section 26 of the *Specific Claims Resolution Act, supra* note 50, defines the scope of admissible claims as including:

> (a) breach of—or failure to fulfil—a legal obligation of the Crown, including a fiduciary obligation. . . .

[58] See *e.g. ibid.*, ss. 44–46.

[59] The Act creates a permanent body, to be called the Canadian Centre for Independent Resolution of First Nations Specific Claims. The centre will comprise a commission, whose function is to facilitate the negotiation of settlements (see *ibid.*, ss. 23–24), and a tribunal, empowered to make binding decisions

on validity and compensation where other forms of dispute resolution fail (see *ibid.*, ss. 44–46).

[60] In its 26 November 2002 submission about this bill to the House of Commons Standing Committee on Aboriginal Affairs, *supra* note 49, the ICC observed (at 16) that "a consultative process to appointments which involves representatives of the First Nations . . . is key to minimizing problems associated with independence in the new body."

[61] *Specific Claims Resolution Act*, *supra* note 50, ss. 20(4)–(5), 41(5)–(6).

[62] *Ibid.* s. 35(1)(e).

[63] *Ibid.* s. 30(1).

[64] *Ibid.* ss. 32(1)(a), 35(1)(a).

[65] *Ibid.* s. 26(2)(a), (f). Subsections (b)–(e) establish other restrictions.

[66] *Ibid.* ss. 23(a), 24(a).

[67] *Ibid.* s. 56(1)(a).

[68] *Ibid.* s. 56(1)(b).

[69] See *supra* note 62 and accompanying text.

[70] See Leonard Ian Rotman, *Parallel Paths: Fiduciary Doctrine and the Crown–Native Relationship in Canada* (Toronto: University of Toronto Press, 1996) at 266 [Rotman, *Parallel Paths*] concerning the conflict of interest of the Department of Indian Affairs and the Department of Justice in relation to Aboriginal claims:

> How is it then possible that these departments may impartially decide on the merits of a particular Indian claim which seeks to reclaim revenue-generating lands from the federal Crown whose best interests the departments both represent and seek to protect? Quite simply, it is not possible.

See also "Commissioner Bellegarde's Remarks," *supra* note 48, which describes the process as follows:

> The Indian Claims Commission believes that history will judge the current specific claims process very harshly. There is no other area of public policy in this country, or perhaps in any other western democracy, that operates in this manner.
>
> Picture it: a claimant First Nation, which is typically underfunded and existing in impoverished circumstances on the fringes of society, advances a claim based upon outstanding lawful obligation by the Government of Canada.
>
> The government is not only the defendant of that claim but also the judge of the legitimacy of the claim. The government judges the claim based upon legal advice which it obtains from its own lawyers.
>
> The government then renders a decision based upon that legal advice but refuses to share the legal opinion with the claimant First Nation, on the basis that the opinion is subject to solicitor/client privilege.

[71] "Commissioner Bellegarde's Remarks," *ibid.*

[72] As indicated earlier, cost considerations and the length of the process are factors a First Nation might consider here. In addition, because the DOJ could be wrong in its assessment of the likely outcome in court of the claim, a band should not rely solely on a DOJ determination of a claim's merits when deciding whether to litigate it.

[73] A possible example of such an occurrence is the ICC report on the Chippewas of Kettle and Stony Point 1927 land surrender, dated March 1997, which recommended that the claim be negotiated. The matter ultimately proceeded through litigation. The Supreme Court of Canada dismissed the action in 1998, agreeing with the Ontario Court of Appeal that the surrender was valid, although the Crown's fiduciary duty was not in issue before it: see *Chippewas of Kettle and Stony Point v. Canada (A.G.)*, [1998] 1 S.C.R. 756.

[74] It would, for example, be a breach of fiduciary duty for the Crown, through its DOJ, to deny legitimate claims simply to force a First Nation to submit to litigation, because the Crown, in litigation, could use its superior resources to subdue the Aboriginal claimant by exhausting the latter's comparatively meagre resources. The use of litigation procedures to subdue financially weaker opponents is a well-known "defence" to claims, used successfully by various lawyers, not only (or necessarily) the Crown.

[75] Of course, the most recent is the *Specific Claims Resolution Act*, *supra* note 50.

[76] *Badger*, supra note 37; *R. v. Lewis*, [1996] 1 S.C.R. 921; *R. v. Nikal*, [1996] 1 S.C.R. 1013; *Van der Peet*, supra note 2; *R. v. Gladstone*, [1996] 2 S.C.R. 723 [*Gladstone*]; *R. v. N.T.C. Smokehouse Ltd.*, [1996] 2 S.C.R. 672; *R. v. Pamajewon*, [1996] 2 S.C.R. 821; *R. v. Adams*, [1996] 3 S.C.R. 101; *R. v. Côté*, [1993] 3 S.C.R. 139 [*Côté*]; *Goodswimmer v. Canada (Minister of Indian Affairs and Northern Development)*, [1997] 1 S.C.R. 309; *Opetchesaht Indian Band v. Canada*, [1997] 2 S.C.R. 119; and *St. Mary's Indian Band v. Cranbrook (City)*, [1997] 2 S.C.R. 657.

[77] *Delgamuukw*, supra note 3; *Marshall*, supra note 37; *Marshall II*, supra note 37; *Union of New Brunswick Indians v. New Brunswick (Minister of Finance)*, [1998] 1 S.C.R. 1161; *R. v. Williams*, [1998] 1 S.C.R. 1128; *R. v. Sundown*, [1999] 1 S.C.R. 393; *R. v. Gladue*, [1999] 1 S.C.R. 688; *Corbiere v. Canada (Minister of Indian and Northern Affairs)*, [1999] 2 S.C.R. 203; *R. v. Wells*, [2000] 1 S.C.R. 207; *Westbank First Nation v. British Columbia Hydro and Power Authority*, [1999] 3 S.C.R. 134; *Lovelace v. Ontario*, [2000] 1 S.C.R. 950; *Musqueam Indian Band v. Glass*, [2000] 2 S.C.R. 633; *Mitchell v. M.N.R.*, [2001] 1 S.C.R. 911 [*Mitchell*]; *Osoyoos Indian Band v. Oliver (Town)*, [2001] 3 S.C.R. 746; *Ross River Dena Council Band v. Canada*, [2002] 2 S.C.R. 816; *Kitkatla Band v. British Columbia (Minister of Small Business, Tourism and Culture)*, [2002] 2 S.C.R. 146 [*Kitkatla*]; *Wewaykum*, supra note 9; *Powley*, supra note 12; *R. v. Blais*, [2003] 2 S.C.R. 236, 2003 SCC 44; *Wewaykum II*, supra note 10; *Paul v. British Columbia (Forest Appeals Commission)*, [2003] 2 S.C.R. 585, 2003 SCC 55; *British Columbia (Minister of Forests) v. Okanagan Indian Band*, [2003] 3 S.C.R. 371, 2003 SCC 71.

[78] *Supra* note 14.

[79] *R. v. Sioui*, [1990] 1 S.C.R. 1025.

[80] *Supra* note 19. Although it has been suggested that the Supreme Court has departed from the initial promise of cases like *Sparrow*, one must remember that the statements made in that case were not unqualified. Despite the judgment's affirmation of the constitutional status of Aboriginal and treaty rights, its foundation rests on its statement, that "while British policy towards the native population was based on respect for their right to occupy their traditional lands, . . . there was from the outset never any doubt that sovereignty and legislative power, and indeed the underlying title, to such lands vested in the Crown . . ." (*ibid.* at 1103).

Here, the Court articulated, in clear and concise language, its view of the subordinate position of Aboriginal legal interests in Canadian law. Thus, although the rights themselves are still the subject of negotiation and litigation, *Sparrow* made unequivocal their subordination to Canadian sovereignty. Nothing suggests that this has changed since 1990. For a thoughtful analysis of the impact of the *Sparrow* judgment on the place of Aboriginal legal rights in Canadian law, see Michael Asch & Patrick Macklem, "Aboriginal Rights and Canadian Sovereignty: An Essay on *R. v. Sparrow*" (1991) 29 Alta. L. Rev. 498.

[81] *Van der Peet*, supra note 2 at paras. 44–46.

[82] *Ibid.* at paras. 56, 70.

[83] *Côté*, supra note 76, is a notable exception. At para. 56, the Court held that an Aboriginal right to fish for subsistence included the incidental practice of educating younger band members in traditional fishing practices to ensure their continuity.

[84] *Gladstone*, supra note 76 at paras. 73–75. In *Sparrow*, supra note 19, the Court expressly stated (at 1113) that "We find the 'public interest' justification to be so vague as to provide no meaningful guidance and so broad as to be unworkable as a test for the justification of a limitation on constitutional rights." For further commentary on this point, see Kent McNeil, "How Can Infringements of the Constitutional Rights of Aboriginal Peoples Be Justified?" (1997) 8 Const. Forum Const. 33; Leonard I. Rotman, "'My Hovercraft is Full of Eels': Smoking Out the Message in *R. v. Marshall*" (2000) 63 Sask. L. Rev. 617 at 637–38. The *Gladstone* form of justification was expressly affirmed in *Delgamuukw*, supra note 3 at paras 161–71.

[85] *Ibid.* at para. 75.

[86] *Mitchell*, supra note 77.

[87] See *supra* note 34 and accompanying text.

[88] *Mitchell*, supra note 77 at para. 115.

⁸⁹ *Ibid.* at para. 70.

⁹⁰ Binnie J.'s judgment in *Mitchell, ibid.* does clear up the confusion created in *Sparrow, supra* note 19, where the Court put forward a strong vision of section 35(1), yet accepted the existence of Canadian sovereignty and title to land: see note 80, *supra* and accompanying text.

⁹¹ *Ibid.* at para. 9.

⁹² *Sparrow, supra* note 19 at 1103.

⁹³ *Delgamuukw, supra* note 3 at para. 207.

⁹⁴ *Ibid.* at para. 186.

⁹⁵ *Marshall II, supra* note 37 at para. 22.

⁹⁶ *Sparrow, supra* note 19 at 1119; the duty to consult was also prominent in *Delgamuukw, supra* note 3, especially at para. 168.

⁹⁷ Under the terms of the federal *Indian Act*, a band is prohibited from alienating its interest in reserve lands directly to third parties; it may do so only by first surrendering its interests to the federal Crown, which may then negotiate with a third party on the band's behalf. As a result of *Guerin, supra* note 14, the Crown is now understood to owe a fiduciary duty to act in a band's best interests when it obtains a surrender of reserve lands for the purposes of sale or lease to a third party.

⁹⁸ *Guerin, supra* note 14 at 355. Note also the comments of Dickson J., as he then was, *ibid.* at 385:
> When, as here, an Indian Band surrenders its interest to the Crown, a fiduciary obligation takes hold to regulate the manner in which the Crown exercises its discretion in dealing with the land on the Indians' behalf.

⁹⁹ This issue is a primary basis of the appeals in *Taku River Tlingit First Nation v. British Columbia (Project Assessment Director)*, [2002] 2 C.N.L.R. 312 (B.C.C.A.), leave to appeal to S.C.C. granted, [2002] S.C.C.A. No. 148 and in *Haida Nation v. British Columbia (Minister of Forests)*, [2002] 2 C.N.L.R. 121 (B.C.C.A.), leave to appeal to S.C.C. granted, [2002] S.C.C.A. No. 417. For further discussion of the duty to consult, see Richard F. Devlin & Ronalda Murphy, "Contextualizing the Duty to Consult: Clarification or Transformation?" (2003) 14 N.J.C.L. 167; Sonia Lawrence & Patrick Macklem, "From Consultation to Reconciliation: Aboriginal Rights and the Crown's Duty to Consult" (2000) 79 Can. Bar Rev. 252.

¹⁰⁰ *Delgamuukw, supra* note 3 at para. 168, Lamer C.J.

¹⁰¹ *Marshall II, supra* note 37 at para. 43.

¹⁰² Full discussion of these limitations is beyond the ambit of this paper. For present purposes, it is sufficient to note that they require Aboriginal claimants to tailor their claims to the requirements unilaterally established by the federal Crown, and do not always account for Aboriginal perspectives or concerns on these matters.

¹⁰³ As seen, for example, in the *Specific Claims Resolution Act, supra* note 50.

¹⁰⁴ Schmitz, "SCC Wrong Forum," *supra* note 8 at 20.

¹⁰⁵ *Ibid.*

¹⁰⁶ *Supra* note 37.

¹⁰⁷ Schmitz, "SCC Wrong Forum," *supra* note 8 at 20.

¹⁰⁸ *Ibid.*

¹⁰⁹ See note 158 *infra* and accompanying text.

¹¹⁰ But see *Wewaykum II, supra* note 10 at paras. 92–93, in particular the following statement at para. 93:
> [E]ven if it were found that the involvement of a single judge gave rise to a reasonable apprehension of bias, no reasonable person informed of the decision-making process of the Court, and viewing it realistically, could conclude that it was likely that the eight other judges were biased, or somehow tainted, by the apprehended bias affecting the ninth judge.

Although there is opportunity for each member of the Supreme Court to express his or her opinions independently, the collegial nature of the process, emphasized by the Court, *ibid.* at para. 56, creates opportunity for one judge to try to influence the others.

¹¹¹ *Wewaykum, supra* note 9.

¹¹² See *ibid.* at paras. 86–106.

"LET US FACE IT, WE ARE ALL HERE TO STAY"   237

[113] *Ibid.* at paras. 111–12 (laches and acquiescence), 113–36 (limitations).

[114] For greater clarity, I have used "Binnie" to refer to Justice Binnie in respect of times before his appointment to the bench.

[115] R.S.C. 1985, c. A-1.

[116] The request sought
> copies of all records, including letters, correspondence and internal memoranda to, from or which make reference to Mr. William Binnie (Ian Binnie) [now Mr. Justice Binnie] in the matter of the claim against Canada by the Wewaykum (or Campbell River) Indian Band and the Wewaikai (or Cape Mudge) Indian Band for Quinsam IR 12 and Campbell River IR 11 between the years 1982 and 1986:

Wewaykum II, supra note 10 at para. 15.

[117] Binnie's advice had been that Canada not seek in *Wewaykum* to "go behind" the report of the McKenna-McBride Commission, a federal-provincial body charged in the early part of the twentieth century with resolving the outstanding issues concerning land for Indian reserves in British Columbia. Memoranda dated 25 February 1986 (Mary Temple to Bill Scarth), 27 February 1986 (Temple to Carol Pepper) and 3 March 1986 (Scarth to Binnie himself) all acknowledge that Binnie had given this advice. The first sought to ensure that Binnie was made aware that DOJ was considering a different approach; the latter two reported that Binnie's own preferred approach, in the end, prevailed. These and the other memoranda obtained from DOJ appear in an appendix to the decision in *Wewaykum II, ibid.*

[118] *Wewaykum II, ibid.* at para. 20. Lawyer Vincent O'Donnell, representing the DOJ, acknowledged that DOJ lawyers had recalled, while preparing their briefs for the *Wewaykum* appeal, that Binnie had worked for the department, and that they had questioned whether he had been involved in the case, but had not followed up. In his words, "Counsel did not conduct a thorough examination of the files (with a focus on this question)."

[119] In his words, "I had no recollection of personal involvement 17 years earlier at the commencement of this particular file, which was handled by departmental counsel in the Vancouver Regional Office": *ibid.* at para. 23.

[120] For news reports about the incident and the hearing of the motion, see Jim Brown "Judge's Past Work Could Taint Top Court's Ruling" *Canadian Press* (30 May 2003), online: <http://www.macon.com/mld/philly/news/5981804.htm> . See also Kirk Makin, "Judge Seen as Absolved of Any Bias," *Globe and Mail* (31 May 2003) A6; Jim Brown, "Top Court Asked to Overturn Land Claim Judgment over Possible Binnie Conflict," *CNEWS* (23 June 2003), online: CNEWS <http://cnews.canoe.ca/CNEWS/Law?2003?05/30/99650-cp.html>; Mark Bourne "Top Court to Decide on Vacating Judgment," *Law Times* (30 June 2003) at 3.

[121] See *Wewaykum II, supra* note 10 at paras. 52–56.

[122] *Ibid.* at paras. 24–25.

[123] *Ibid.* at paras. 47–51.

[124] Kirk Makin, "Judges' Conflict Mars Supreme Court Ruling" *Globe and Mail* (30 May 2003) A1. Compare the words of Bob Duncan, economic development officer with the Wewaykum Band, who wrote on 29 May 2003 to Vancouver Island North MP John Duncan that his band "feels very strongly that we didn't receive a fair trial in the highest court of the land; what is the alternative for justice in this case given the circumstance?": "Native Land Case Ruling in Jeopardy" *Campbell River Mirror* (4 June 2003), online: BCFN News <http://www.bcfn.org/news060403.htm>.

[125] *Wewaykum II, supra* note 10 at para. 73. The Court rephrased the question at para. 74, as follows:
> What would an informed person, viewing the matter realistically and practically—and having thought the matter through—conclude? Would this person think that it is more likely than not that Binnie J., whether consciously or unconsciously, did not decide fairly?

[126] *Ibid.* at para. 83.

[127] *Ibid.* at para. 82.

[128] *Ibid.* at paras. 81–82. Compare *ibid.* at para. 71:
> [T]he rule of automatic disqualification [of a judge] does not apply to the situation in which

the decision-maker was somehow involved in the litigation or linked to counsel at an earlier stage, as is argued here.

[129] *Ibid.* at para. 85.

[130] *Ibid.* at para. 89.

[131] *Ibid.* at para. 57.

[132] *Ibid.* at para. 59, quoting *Ethical Principles for Judges* (Ottawa: Canadian Judicial Council, 1998) at 30.

[133] All parties had accepted that the documents produced by the Crown had disclosed the full extent of Binnie's involvement in the *Wewaykum* matter in 1985–86. The Court had proceeded on that assumption: see *Wewaykum II, ibid.* at para. 44.

[134] On 15 January 1986, Binnie had written to thank Harry Wruck of DOJ's Vancouver Regional Office, for his note of "January 16, 1985." This date may have been ascribed in error to Wruck's note, but the record provided to the Court includes no such note—of any date—from Wruck. See *Wewaykum II, ibid.*, appendix.

[135] See memoranda nos. 9 (Mary Temple to Binnie: statement of claim) and 12 (Bill Scarth to Binnie, 3 March 1986: statement of defence) in the appendix to *Wewaykum II, ibid.*

[136] See *supra* notes 71–75 and accompanying text.

[137] *Wewaykum II, supra* note 10 at para. 82. Compare at paras. 89–90, where the Court described Justice Binnie has having had "a limited administrative and supervisory role . . ."

[138] See, in addition to the references listed *supra* at notes 117 and 134–35, the memo dated 3 February 1988, in which Bill Scarth tells Binnie's successor at DOJ that he had followed Binnie's advice regarding the report of the McKenna–McBride Commission: *Wewaykum II, ibid.*, appendix.

[139] *Wewaykum II, ibid.* at para. 66.

[140] *Ibid.* at para. 67.

[141] See *ibid.* at para. 89.

[142] *MacDonald Estate v. Martin*, [1990] 3 S.C.R. 1235 [*MacDonald Estate*]. This case is sometimes referred to as *Martin v. Gray*.

[143] *Ibid.* at 1244. In his minority judgment, Cory J. likewise concluded, at 1265, that:
Neither the merger of law firms nor the mobility of lawyers can be permitted to affect adversely the public's confidence in the judicial system. . . . [I]t is fundamentally important that justice not only be done, but appear to be done in the eyes of the public.

[144] [2002] 3 S.C.R. 631, 2002 SCC 70.

[145] *Ibid.* at para. 12.

[146] *Ibid.* at para. 13.

[147] See "Letter from Chief Justice R. J. Scott," *supra* note 10.

[148] See *Wewaykum II, supra* note 10.

[149] *The King v. Sussex Justices*, [1924] 1 K.B. 256 at 259.

[150] [1978] 1 S.C.R. 369 at 394–95. The full Supreme Court has since affirmed this test: see *e.g. Valente v. The Queen*, [1985] 2 S.C.R. 673, and *R. v. S.(R.D.)*, [1997] 3 S.C.R. 484 (both specifically concerned with the actions of judges), and *Wewaykum II, supra* note 10.

[151] *Brown v. Walter*, 62 F.2d 798 at 799–800 (2d Cir. 1933).

[152] *Metropolitan Properties Co. v. Lennon*, [1969] 1 Q.B. 577 (C.A.) at 599.

[153] The Supreme Court of Canada recognized this in *Re Therrien*, [2001] 2 S.C.R. 3 at para. 147:
The public's invaluable confidence in its justice system, which every judge must strive to preserve, is at the very heart of this case. The issue of confidence governs every aspect of this case, and ultimately dictates the result. Thus, before making a recommendation that a judge be removed, the question to be asked is whether the conduct for which he or she is blamed is so manifestly and totally contrary to the impartiality, integrity and independence of the judiciary that the confidence of individuals appearing before the judge, or of the public in its justice system, would be undermined, rendering the judge incapable of performing the duties of his office.

[154] *R. v. Bow Street Metropolitan Stipendiary Magistrate and others ex parte Pinochet Ugarte (No. 2)*, [2000] 1 A.C. 119 (H.L.) [*Pinochet (No. 2)*].

"LET US FACE IT, WE ARE ALL HERE TO STAY" 239

[155] *R. v. Bow Street Metropolitan Stipendiary Magistrate and others ex parte Pinochet Ugarte*, [2000] 1 A.C. 61 (H.L.) [*Pinochet (No. 1)*]. On rehearing, [2000] 1 A.C. 147 (H.L.) [*Pinochet (No. 3)*], the majority of a differently constituted House of Lords panel reaffirmed, but narrowed the scope of, its earlier denial of diplomatic immunity to Pinochet.

[156] Kirk Makin, "Judge's Comments Assailed" *Globe and Mail* (8 February 2001) A3.

[157] *Ibid*. Justice Bastarache, in his press interview, had commented on *Marshall*, *supra* note 37, despite not having been part of the panel hearing the case. See notes 104–7, *supra* and accompanying text.

[158] See "Letter from Chief Justice R.J. Scott," *supra* note 10.

[159] David Gambrill "Judges Butt Heads on Freedom to Speak" *Law Times* (25 August 2003) at 2.

[160] *Wewaykum II*, *supra* note 10 at paras. 71–72.

[161] *Ibid.* at para. 72.

[162] [1991] 2 S.C.R. 570.

[163] *Ontario (A.G.) v. Bear Island Foundation* (1984), 15 D.L.R. (4th) 321 (Ont. H.C.).

[164] [2003] 2 S.C.R. 40, 2003 SCC 39.

[165] Indeed, Justice Iacobucci was Deputy Minister of Justice while Binnie was Associate Deputy Minister, but nothing is known at present of his previous involvement, if any, in *Wewaykum*.

[166] See *supra* note 151 and accompanying text.

[167] Recent jurisprudence on this point includes *Delgamuukw*, *supra* note 3, *Mitchell*, *supra* note 77, and *Kitkatla*, *supra* note 77.

[168] The Honourable Michel Bastarache, "The Challenge of the Law in the New Millennium" (1998) 25 Man. L.J. 411 at 413.

[169] Schmitz, "SCC Wrong Forum," *supra* note 8.

[170] *Marshall*, *supra* note 37.

[171] *Ibid.* at para. 3.

[172] For an itemized list of the existing canons of interpretation, see McLachlin J.'s dissenting judgment in *Marshall*, *ibid.* at para. 78. For further discussion of some of these canons and why they exist, see Leonard I. Rotman, "Taking Aim at the Canons of Treaty Interpretation in Canadian Aboriginal Rights Jurisprudence" (1997) 46 U.N.B.L.J. 11.

[173] The clause in question promised the ability to trade at "truck houses," which were trading posts established by the British for trade with Aboriginal peoples in the Maritimes.

[174] *Marshall*, *supra* note 37 at para. 14.

[175] *Ibid*. Justice Binnie stressed, however (at para. 43), that courts read implied terms even into written agreements prepared by sophisticated commercial actors and their legal advisors, in order to ensure the efficacy of those contracts; the practice is not restricted to Crown–Native treaties.

[176] The only hesitation here concerns the lack of consistency in the Court's approach to Aboriginal legal issues from case to case. Some decisions seem much more sensitive to these issues than others.

[177] A case in point is the majority's finding that the Mi'kmaq treaty right to fish was limited to the "right to trade for necessaries," which it equated with a modern-day moderate livelihood: *Marshall*, *supra* note 37 at para. 60.

[178] For further discussion of this distinction, see Leonard Rotman, "Marshalling Principles from the *Marshall* Morass" (2000) 23 Dal. L.J. 5.

[179] This is true even within individual judgments. A prime example of this is *Sparrow*, *supra* note 19, which expressly recognized the importance of s. 35(1) of the *Constitution Act, 1982* and past failures to recognize the rights entrenched within it ("there can be no doubt that over the years the rights of the Indians were often honoured in the breach": *ibid.* at 1103), that enactment of s. 35(1) "at the least, provides a solid constitutional base upon which subsequent negotiations can take place": *ibid.* at 1105, and that the Crown must be held "to a high standard of honourable dealing with respect to the aboriginal peoples of Canada as suggested by *Guerin* . . .": *ibid.* at 1109. However, underscoring all these positives—and effectively deflating their importance—was the Court's statement, *ibid.* at 1103, that

> while British policy towards the native population was based on respect for their right to occupy their traditional lands . . . there was from the outset never any doubt that sovereignty and

legislative power, and indeed the underlying title, to such lands vested in the Crown. . . .

Thus, in spite of the Court's ability in most of *Sparrow* to place Aboriginal rights and s. 35(1) within an appropriate contextual framework, it was unable to sustain that focus throughout the entire decision.

[180] "Articles Between Col. Cartwright and the New York Indians" in E.B. O'Callaghan, ed., *Documents Relative to the Colonial History of the State of New York* (Albany: Weed, Parsons, 1853), vol. 3, 67. The *Treaty of Albany, 1664* was the first formal treaty between the British and Aboriginal peoples in North America. It was recorded both on parchment and in a wampum belt, known as the Two-Row Wampum. For further discussion of both, see Rotman, *Parallel Paths, supra* note 70.

[181] In documents released by the Finance Department in late 1999, the federal government estimated that the cost of resolving the bulk of the Aboriginal peoples' outstanding claims, based on what was then being claimed through litigation and alternative processes, stood at $200 billion: see Madelaine Drohan "Bill for Colonial Past Comes Due" *Globe and Mail* (22 October 1999) B2; Heather Scoffield "Ottawa Prices Native Demands at $200-Billion" *Globe and Mail* (26 October 1999) A3; Erin Anderssen & Heather Scoffield "The Legal Logjam That Has Ottawa Spooked" *Globe and Mail* (30 October 1999) A19. According to the second of these articles, a contemporaneous assessment by the Department of Indian Affairs estimated the exposure at a far lower $11.8 billion.

Both figures are, of course, highly speculative; it is unclear whether either accounts for the likelihood of success of claims or for any provincial or territorial liability arising out of Aboriginal claims. These estimates may also have failed to account for issues such as pre-judgment interest on damage awards, which can easily comprise a major portion of any successfully litigated Aboriginal claim. Nevertheless, these figures, though widely divergent, are significant. What is curious is why these estimates are so far apart.

[182] *Sparrow, supra* note 19 at 1109.

[183] See for example notes 93–95, *supra,* and accompanying text.

[184] *Delgamuukw, supra* note 3 at para. 186.

[185] To see this difference, one need only compare the Federal Court of Appeal's judgment in *Guerin* (C.A.), discussed *supra* at note 14, with the Supreme Court's decision in the same case.

[186] Richard Foot and Justine Hunter "Ottawa Guessing at Liability in Abuse Bailout" *National Post* (1 February 2001) A4.

[187] *Delgamuukw, supra* note 3 at para. 186.

[188] *Van der Peet, supra* note 2 at para. 31.

ABORIGINAL RESOURCE RIGHTS AFTER *DELGAMUUKW* AND *MARSHALL*

Gordon Christie

While many Aboriginal people think of greater access to lands and resources in terms of the economic opportunities this may generate for both communities and individuals, for others greater access is vitally important for quite different reasons. For many Aboriginal people, lands and resources are thought of as inextricably connected to the people; indeed, this connection can be so strong, and of such a nature, that it goes into forming collective and individual identities. For some Aboriginal people, greater access to lands and resources is necessary for the ongoing project of strengthening culture and identity, an identity inextricably linked to the land and to its spirits. Emphasizing the economic implications of greater access to resources does not conflict directly with other, more spiritual or holistic visions of the relationship between land and people, but it does set up a tension, a tension that can exist between communities, within communities, and even within individuals.

In 1997 and 1999 the Supreme Court of Canada handed down two major decisions affecting Aboriginal peoples' access to resources. *Delgamuukw v. British Columbia*[1] set out basic principles surrounding Aboriginal title; *R. v. Marshall*[2] dealt with access to resources in relation to a treaty right to trade. This paper explores these decisions, examining the consequences of their pronouncements for the abilities of Aboriginal peoples to further their varied interests in resources. It works through several sets of disjunctive though intersecting considerations. It takes as a starting point the law as set out in seminal cases spanning the period from 1990 to 1996 (from *R. v. Sparrow*[3] in 1990 to *R. v. Van der Peet*[4] and *R. v. Gladstone*[5] in 1996), and explores the impact of *Delgamuukw* and *Marshall* on this jurisprudence, especially as it relates to access to resources. The analysis begins, however, with the establishment of a conceptual framework constructed around the various sorts of interests an Aboriginal community might have in gaining greater access to resources. Although these many and varied interests can coexist within a particular community (or even within an individual), they will be artificially compartmentalized to facilitate discussion and analysis. With this structure in place, the Supreme Court decisions can more fruitfully be dissected. The discussion will conclude with an analysis of the implications of these decisions for satisfaction of these compartmentalized interests, and a consideration of possible strategies that have potential to move Aboriginal communities toward their greater satisfaction.

INTERESTS IN, AND CONCEPTUALIZATIONS OF, LANDS AND RESOURCES

A certain degree of artificiality and superficiality surrounds any attempt at conceptualizing and structuring the types of interests Aboriginal peoples may have in land and resources. Nevertheless, doing so furthers the legal analysis attempted in this work; it allows for clear and concise treatment of the case law when considering how this jurisprudence does, or does not, move communities toward futures wherein their interests are more satisfactorily met.

As noted above, within the diverse set of communities and individuals comprising the class of "Aboriginal peoples," we find those with an interest in gaining greater access to their traditional lands and resources in furtherance of what one might term "traditional" livelihoods (where this is somewhat simplistically equated with strengthening culture and identity), as well as those with an interest in having access to all types and manners of resources drawn from their lands, in order to do nothing other than generate wealth and open up economic opportunities.[6]

The interaction between these interests and the law can be confusing, as those who wish access to lands and resources in furtherance of traditional ways of living (hunting, fishing, gathering, conducting ceremonies, and the like) may think of the land and its resources as "theirs,"[7] or they may carefully refrain from the language of ownership, instead framing their interests in terms of reciprocal and spiritual connections to the land. Similarly, those who wish access to lands and resources in order to generate wealth may justify their claims on the basis of ownership interests, or they may do so on the basis of belief in their right to continue to provide for their families and communities "from the land," where, in contemporary contexts, this amounts to a culling of resources in order to carve out livelihoods within a market economy.

To simplify matters, it is helpful to distinguish between the different ways in which the relationship between a people and their land can be self-conceptualized, and thereby vested with meaning. To focus discussion further, each side of this distinction is illustrated with a hypothetical scenario, allowing us to assess the impact of recent jurisprudence on two possible community projects, each aligned with one of the two very different sorts of interests that communities may have in achieving greater access to lands and resources.

On the one hand, an Aboriginal community may authenticate or validate its interest in the resources on its lands in a vision of a deep connection between itself and its land. This community will have an interest in using resources on its lands to meet its immediate needs, where this interest itself is grounded in a conceptualization of the connection between the land and the people as one of respect and reciprocity. This connection provides for them certain things, but also requires of them certain things. For this community, the land, properly respected, meets its immediate needs, whether those are understood entirely in terms of subsistence (in the furtherance of what one might term traditional livelihoods) or in terms of the provision of livelihoods in the contemporary world (through the culling of resources that can be used in the modern market economy). Regardless of what the land provides, it is regarded as doing so in return for the maintenance of a respectful position adopted by the community. People identified with the land in this way think of the land as theirs only in the sense that they have a strong sense of connection to the land. On this side of the distinction, a diverse set of interests in land and resources can be drawn together under what we can term, for simplicity's sake, a land–people vision.

On the other hand, another Aboriginal community may authenticate or validate its interests in land and resources in a vision of the land as a thing to be exploited. Here, the interest in the resources is represented as gaining access to that to which they have a claim, and is grounded in a conceptualization of the relationship between people and land as one of users and a thing to be used. An Aboriginal community thinking and acting from this standpoint will see the land as theirs exclusively in a property sense, for when unpacked, its conception yields nothing other than a sense that in relation to other people they have a claim that in some sense equals or supersedes other interests or claims. Under this conceptualization, there is no sense of identification with the land per se; one does not have this sort of relationship to a mere thing. For people who view the land in such a manner, only relationships within the community and with other people directly generate notions of identity. On this side of the distinction, then, a diverse set of interests in land and resources can be drawn together under what we can term a user–thing vision.

Although the land–people vision embodies a shared community interest in pursuing lives as culturally synchronized with traditional lives as is possible in the contemporary world, this vision also encompasses many possible sub-interests. As noted above, this vision may validate an interest in trading resources culled from the land for either money or other goods, the end sought being the meeting of personal and social needs. So long as the Aboriginal community in question observes and respects obligations entailed in the particular land–people relationship, the land provides sustenance in any number of ways, including some ways appropriate to contemporary circumstances.

The line between the land–people and user–thing conceptualizations of the relationship between land and people can best be understood through the concept of exploitation. The land–people vision understands resource acquisition, even for trade, as proof that the land is providing for the needs of the people: the land itself being thought of as a partner in the process. Under the user–thing vision, resource extraction for trade is simply a means by which the land is used. The land itself is not held to have any interest in the relationship, as it is not seen as a thing that has interests or that enters into relationships. Under this latter vision, humans think of the land and its resources as things there for the taking, the only concern being competition with other humans for access and control. Successful competition with other humans (on a legal as much as a physical level) is seen as the path to wealth creation.

To focus discussion further, imagine a community seeing the world though the lens of the land–people vision and desirous of a certain degree of control over its traditional territory and its resource wealth. Imagine that it wishes to undertake a community forestry operation. It wants control over its territory, coupled with access to the land and its resources, so that it may both manage how the land is treated by all potential users and maintain and foster respectful relations with the land. For such a community, it will most likely not be sufficient to have been allocated a percentage of the tree harvest envisioned by the province, just as it will most likely not suffice to have a shared-use agreement with whatever companies might have licences to harvest these lands. The community wants to harvest that number of trees which it feels is the fewest necessary to support itself,[8] all the while thinking ahead to the many future generations who will also need to have this land available with which to partner. Furthermore, in so thinking, it will necessarily be concerned about how other forestry operations on the land are functioning, for it will do little good for it to establish its operations under a land–people vision if others are engaged in exploitative and destructive operations over these same lands.

Alongside this first community, imagine another, an Aboriginal community also interested in entering into a forestry operation on its traditional territory, but one more in line with the sorts of operations currently in place, functioning under existing forestry licences and forest-practice codes. This community's interest is in finding a "fair" place within the current forestry regime, an interest that leaves little room for concern over, for example, how current forestry codes function to protect the land from over-exploitation.[9] It thinks of the land as a thing to be used, sees land over which it feels it has a valid claim being used by others, and so claims a right to be included in the current regime of exploitation.

With these two imagined communities in mind, we can now: (1) consider the state of the law around Aboriginal and treaty rights before *Delgamuukw* and *Marshall*; then (2) consider changes introduced by these two cases; and finally (3) focus on the impact these changes might have on real communities with interests and visions similar to these artificial constructions.

THE LAW PRIOR TO *DELGAMUUKW* AND *MARSHALL*

Limited Rights to Certain "Aboriginal" Activities

Canadian courts have generally accepted that, in the right circumstances, Aboriginal peoples have valid claims, under both Aboriginal and treaty rights, to hunt, fish, and gather in order to meet their personal or social needs.[10] These same authorities, however, have traditionally been reluctant to extend the validity of Aboriginal claims to cover rights to resources in the pursuit of commercial ends.[11] Because courts have crudely conflated under the rubric "commercial rights" such efforts as the sale of a few fish, irrespective of whether commercial activity is engaged in to meet personal and social needs in a changing economic environment or to advance exploitative ends, Aboriginal peoples, historically, have been severely restricted in relation to the varied interests they may have in using their land. Courts have accepted that game and fish may be taken for consumption or ceremonial purposes[12] but have been by and large unwilling to allow any trade in these goods, no matter the degree or level of trading.[13] The fear—historically prevalent, but still present today[14]—appears to be that this would condone trading in general, and so open the door to Aboriginal peoples exploiting their own lands and resources, a situation that would entail significant restrictions on non-Aboriginals' access to these same lands and resources.[15]

Fear of competitive exploitation by Aboriginal or treaty rights-holders does not explain, however, restrictions on the exercise of those Aboriginal or treaty rights that the law has recognized. The Aboriginal rights regime protects those practices, traditions, and customs integral to the distinctive identities of the people claiming such rights,[16] while treaty rights in relation to resources are generally rights to live "traditional" lives off the land. Exercise of these rights does not conflict directly with the exploitative ends of non-Aboriginal parties, yet their exercise has become heavily regulated and restricted.

The fear or concern within the law about these rights is twofold. First, their exercise demands access to lands and resources, and access rights can conflict with land use and resource exploitation. Second, the rights-holders would naturally expect other users of the subject lands to be respectful and to recognize the need at least to share the land with the rights-holders. This imparts a certain degree of control over land use and resource exploitation to Aboriginal and treaty rights-holders, even if the Crown might exercise such control on their behalf.

of Incidental or Implied Rights

...nd fears about the exercise of Aboriginal and treaty rights have been dealt with, by and large, by construing narrowly the nature and scope of these rights, by restricting the scope of the class of rights-holders, by regulating heavily the exercise of these rights, and by ignoring or denying the existence and power of incidental or implied rights. These incidental rights give the fundamental Aboriginal and treaty rights much of the force that generates fear and concern about their exercise.

Questions about the nature and status of incidental, implied, or indirect rights received insufficient judicial attention leading up to *Delgamuukw* and *Marshall*, a problem compounded by inconsistencies in the treatment such rights claims did receive. In relation to treaty rights, for example, the Supreme Court, in *Simon*, found that a community having a treaty right to hunt in an area removed from the reserve community must also, of necessity, have a right to travel with hunting equipment to that area.[17] On the other hand, the same court said in *Van der Peet* that incidental rights cannot simply piggyback on Aboriginal rights,[18] a result that suggests that a community may not have a right to travel with hunting equipment to the area over which its Aboriginal right to hunt can be exercised. The right to travel with equipment to the hunting location might have to be established independently as an Aboriginal right.

As inconsistent as these judicial ruminations about incidental rights might be, however, they focus on fairly insignificant implied activities. More troublesome has been the lack of attention paid to other incidental rights. Although some incidental rights may be relatively insignificant, other rights inextricably connected to rights contained in treaties or directly falling under Aboriginal rights could, as noted above, be as important to Aboriginal communities as the central rights themselves. For example, a treaty or Aboriginal right to hunt and fish as one's ancestors have done for countless generations requires for its exercise areas of land relatively untouched by modern development. Similarly, a treaty or Aboriginal right to gather or use resources drawn from the land will require access to traditional or treaty areas. Our exploration of the impact of *Delgamuukw* and *Marshall* must contemplate the status of incidental rights.

DELGAMUUKW ON ACCESS TO RESOURCES

The Nature of Aboriginal Title

The Supreme Court determined in *Delgamuukw* that Aboriginal title constituted a communal right to the land itself, not merely a bundle of rights to various uses of the land.[19] This right to land was found to be exclusive[20] and to carry a right to decide the uses to which the land might be put.[21] Finally, the right to the exclusive use and occupation of Aboriginal title lands was found to include such things as mineral rights, via an argument that clearly established that this right to land encompassed general rights to the resources both above and below the surface.[22]

Access to resources would seem, then, to be fairly straightforward, as Aboriginal titleholders would have a right to their land and to the resources on and below it: a right that could work to exclude others from the land and its resources; a right that includes the ability to decide the uses to which the lands would be put, including, presumably, the right to decide to harvest the land's resources.

The only limit explicitly attached to this form of title came from judicial perception of the need to conserve the land and its resources with an eye to future generations.[23] Lamer C.J. found that an Aboriginal titleholder was precluded from using its lands in such a way as to break the historic connection that formed a basis for the community's claims to these lands. This "inherent limit" would, for example, preclude a titleholder with historic ties to its hunting and gathering lands from strip-mining these lands, as that would render the lands useless for further hunting and gathering.[24]

Unfortunately, however, the picture is much more clouded than this overview suggests. Two notable factors must be considered, both of which cast into doubt the ability of titleholders to benefit from resources on their lands. First, those claiming the right to their lands and the resources on them must either prove the validity of their claims or enter into an appropriate agreement with the federal and provincial governments of Canada.[25] This must be accomplished prior to any legally sanctioned efforts at harvesting resources. Second, the ability to harvest resources will be measured against existing laws and regulations governing resource access and extraction. Although these laws and regulations may have to give way to the rights of a titleholder, it is still incumbent on a titleholder to show that these regimes unjustifiably infringe its rights to resource access and extraction.[26] We will consider these two factors in turn.

Proving a Claim of Aboriginal Title
Satisfying the following criteria validates a claim to title:

(1) the land must have been occupied prior to Crown sovereignty;

(2) if present occupation is relied on as proof of occupation pre-sovereignty, there must be continuity between present and pre-sovereignty occupation; and

(3) at sovereignty, that occupation must have been exclusive.[27]

Occupation may be shown by either: (a) demonstrating physical occupation (regular use of the land for hunting and gathering, for example), or (b) detailing an Aboriginal system of regulation historically in place over these lands (what would be termed in the common law a land tenure system, defining who had rights to what parcels of land, or aspects of land, at what times, under what conditions).[28]

Exclusivity, for its part, may be shown by demonstrating either: (a) the "factual reality" of exclusive occupation (the existence of physical efforts at excluding, and controlling, all but the titleholders), or (b) an "intention and capacity to retain exclusive control" (the existence, for example, of legal systems, including such things as trespass laws, designed to control and regulate the use of the land by others).[29]

There are two aspects surrounding this proof-structure that have the potential to restrict a community's ability to benefit from resources drawn from its lands. First, there is the simple hurdle of demonstrating title according to these criteria. Although the Court allows for two separate ways of showing both occupation and exclusivity, it nevertheless remains a daunting task to show either to the satisfaction of the law.[30]

In addition to these questions about the requisite standard of proof, there are also questions about the meaning of occupation and exclusivity in this context. In showing occupation, must the Aboriginal community demonstrate extensive use of the claimed lands, or merely some form of regular use?[31] Could a court go so far as to find that occasional use will suffice to ground title? In showing exclusivity, must the Aboriginal community demonstrate both positive and negative efforts at asserting control?[32]

These are unsettled questions, the determination of which will have an enormous impact on the extent of Aboriginal titleholdings in Canada. The result may well be that titleholders will be able to demonstrate title over only parts of their traditional lands, those they can show were historically occupied in such a manner as to preclude questions as to their presence and control.[33]

Second, it is only after expending a considerable amount of time and money constructing a case to show these elements of title, and then doing so successfully over and against efforts by the Crown to show otherwise, that an Aboriginal titleholder can safely begin to use its title-claim to access resources on its lands.

Two factors make the demonstration of title a requirement, practically speaking, for the prudent deployment of rights falling under that title. First, as was just noted, there are questions about the tests for occupation and exclusivity that make the use of title a risky endeavour. It would be difficult for an Aboriginal community to know beforehand clearly and definitively the lands to which it can validly claim title. Second, even over those lands to which it might have a clear sense of ownership, the use of title before its demonstration to the Crown's, or a court's, satisfaction will likely run into costly efforts at protection. Imagine an Aboriginal community that has yet to establish title in court, or to fix the extent and characteristics of its title by way of modern treaty. In a sense, there is nothing preventing it from acting according to its current assessment of the extent of the Aboriginal title it enjoys (especially when it does so over land for which clear title can most likely be shown—for example, around long-used village locations)—for once it does establish title, this will merely demonstrate the extent of title that always existed, thereby retrospectively protecting activities engaged in over title lands (so long as these activities were themselves acceptable under Aboriginal title). The Crown, however, does not recognize title yet to be shown. In fact, the Crown, by and large, acts as if there were no title. Attempts to act under this title prior to its being established in court or fixed in treaty will run into opposition from the Crown, likely leading to litigation (which operates to push parties toward negotiations).

How small and poor communities will be able to finance these activities, and maintain the structure and momentum of an organization dedicated to proving title, remains to be seen.[34]

The Supreme Court of Canada recently approved a bold lower court decision to award costs to an Aboriginal party at the outset of its litigation against the Crown,[35] but how this will affect Aboriginal peoples considering litigation as a means of proving title is unclear.[36] These communities will still have to weigh the risks of not meeting the Supreme Court's eligibility conditions for obtaining costs in advance.[37] Only time will tell whether this measure has a major impact on the problem of funding litigation to prove rights that the Crown often treats as inconsequential until definitively established.

Legislative Infringement

Once a community completes the onerous task of proving Aboriginal title to its lands, it must contend with the impact of extensive provincial (and federal) regulatory schemes that will most certainly govern the activities of getting to, and harvesting, resources.[38] For example, a valid claim to title does not automatically exempt the titleholder from having to regulate hunting activities in accord with provincial hunting laws, or from having to contend with provincial forestry codes and regimes.[39]

The interaction of Aboriginal title and these governmental systems is determined not through analysis of this form of title, but via analysis of the permissible scope for Crown infringement of Aboriginal title.[40] In certain cases, where the Crown can justify the impacts on title of its regulatory schemes, the rights of titleholders may have to give way to Crown power to control resource use; in other circumstances, these rights may force government(s) to accommodate the interests of titleholders in the resources on their lands. In very limited situations, the rights of titleholders might even prevail over government schemes.

To see how the Crown's legislative power to infringe title affects titleholders' ability to preserve access to their land and its resources, imagine that an Aboriginal community has, at enormous expense, successfully established title over lands in and around its current living areas. Then suppose that that community wishes to maintain access to resources on these lands, pursuant to the rights falling under its title. Whether it wishes to continue to hunt or to start up a community forestry operation, the Crown most certainly will have regulated the relevant activity, and will likely already have licensed non-Aboriginal parties to engage in it on this very land. How will the sovereign deal with the interest of the Aboriginal community?

Consider the regulatory scheme through which the Crown controls whatever activity the titleholders have decided to pursue, a regulatory scheme that most certainly includes both licensing/leasing requirements and standards regulating how this sort of activity will be carried out over these lands. The Crown most certainly will not simply permit the Aboriginal community to bypass this regulatory regime, if only because that course would appear to jeopardize its jurisdiction over these lands.[41] The Aboriginal community will have to choose whether to negotiate with the Crown (to arrive at some accommodation for its interest in using its lands in this manner) or, alternatively, to challenge the regulatory scheme in court (arguing that it infringes unjustifiably its rights to engage in this activity on its title lands).

Consider the route of litigation. Imagine infringement of title has been established.[42] The onus then shifts to the Crown to show that the infringement is justified. It is in settling the question of justification that the titleholders' access to their resources is addressed.

The very purpose for which the Crown has enacted a regulatory scheme must first itself be shown by the Crown to be sufficiently "compelling and substantial."[43] In relation to Aboriginal title, the Court has found that a broad and deep range of objectives satisfies this requirement, including such matters as "settling foreign populations" and all manner of economic development initiatives.[44]

Because the courts have said that practically any legislative undertaking can satisfy this requirement, the real concern is with the implementation of the relevant regulatory regime. Fiduciary doctrine governs the infringement of Aboriginal title in relation to laws and regulations developed under a particular "compelling and substantial" objective. This is so because of the Crown's discretionary power to make decisions affecting land interests of Aboriginal peoples. Strict rules regulating the use of this discretion are intended to guide the Crown in its treatment of the rights of Aboriginal titleholders.

Three aspects of Aboriginal title affect the fiduciary situation and generate fiduciary responsibilities: the exclusivity of Aboriginal title; the fact that this title carries with it the right to decide the uses to which the title lands may be put; and the economic component of Aboriginal title, which may force the Crown to compensate when it infringes the title.[45] The first two aspects require elaboration.

Before we get to this, a few remarks are in order about the grounding of Crown responsibilities in the nature of both the claimed Aboriginal right and the government action infringing this right.

A range of responsibilities assail the Crown, out of which emerge particular fiduciary duties, depending on the sort of Aboriginal title asserted and the nature of the government action affecting the title.[46] This means, for example, that when title is asserted to further the interest of maintaining traditional harvesting activities and the impugned Crown action stems from restrictions on such activities, the relevant Crown fiduciary responsibilities will crystallize accordingly. Where, on the other hand, the Crown's action is that of facilitating non-Aboriginal economic projects (*e.g.,* by issuing timber licences), the Crown's fiduciary responsibilities will likely take different shape, even if title is being used to protect the same sorts of community activities.

The same is true when the Aboriginal interest alters: when, for example, the interest is in using the land to sustain a community forestry operation rather than to hunt, fish, or gather in a traditional manner. A different range of responsibilities will then befall the Crown, depending, again, on whether the Crown is regulating forestry practices or acting to further the use of these lands for non-Aboriginal purposes (*e.g.,* for hydro-electric development).

Fiduciary Responsibilities and the Exclusivity of Aboriginal Title
First, the exclusivity of this form of title entails the application of the *Gladstone* modification of priorization. To understand the implications of this, we need to go back to the birth of the notion that fiduciary doctrine demands of the Crown that it justify its regulatory regimes in relation to resource access and use. This story begins in *Sparrow,* with the emergence of the notion that the Crown and Aboriginal peoples are locked in a fiduciary embrace, out of which emerges a framework situating Aboriginal interests in resources in relation to other interests in these same resources.[47] *Sparrow* places definite guidelines on how the Crown (as fiduciary in relation to Aboriginal peoples, but also as sole sovereign over lands within Canada) is to go about its business of regulating access to, and harvesting of, resources.[48] The Court required that the Crown give priority to Aboriginal rights in relation to other interests in a resource (such as conservation and various non-Aboriginal uses). The Court deemed the right claimed in *Sparrow* (to fish for food and ceremonial purposes) to be such as to require the Crown to rank this interest immediately after conservation needs, and before such non-Aboriginal interests as sport and commercial fishing.[49]

In *Gladstone*, however, the Court was faced with a situation wherein simple prioritization of the Aboriginal right could exclude non-Aboriginals from using and harvesting the resource in question. In *Gladstone*, the Aboriginal party was found to have that rarest of entitlements, an Aboriginal right to fish on a commercial scale.[50] Requiring simple priority for this right ahead of non-Aboriginal interests could seriously threaten non-Aboriginal fisheries. The response from the Court was to modify the Crown's fiduciary obligations when faced with an Aboriginal right that lacks an internal limit.[51] While the claimed right in *Sparrow* had such a limit (as the right to fish for food or ceremonial purposes would be satisfied with sufficient fish to meet these needs), the right claimed in *Gladstone* did not (as the right to fish commercially could extend indefinitely, limited only by such external constraints as the marketplace and the supply of fish).

Under the modified priority approach, the Crown is generally held to the much lower requirement that it merely respect the prior Aboriginal right.[52] The reader should bear in mind the consequences of this in the context of Aboriginal title, for an exclusive right to use and occupy land has a similar potential to threaten the use and enjoyment of title lands by non-Aboriginal parties. The Crown, acting in its capacity as sovereign over these lands, making decisions about the allocation of resources to be drawn from these lands, is required as fiduciary to Aboriginal titleholders only to respect the prior presence of the Aboriginal people on these lands. The Court in *Delgamuukw*, then, not only upheld the power of the Crown to authorize non-Aboriginals to exploit Aboriginal title lands; it also required of the Crown only that it respectfully bear in mind the interests of Aboriginal titleholders while authorizing such exploitation.

Fiduciary Responsibilities and the Right to Decide the Uses to Which Land May Be Put
The second aspect of Aboriginal title affecting the Crown's fiduciary obligations is the right it confers to decide the uses to which title lands are put.[53] This aspect of title requires that the Crown endeavour to involve the titleholder in its decision-making processes.[54] This obligation on the Crown manifests into a range of possible duties, from consulting with the affected Aboriginal people to seeking their consent.[55]

This range of fiduciary responsibilities, and its basis in the sort of Aboriginal interest at issue in relation to the impugned Crown activity, can be seen when the Court considers the sorts of titleholder involvement that could be required in Crown deliberations. The range stretches from the possibility of there being no duty on the Crown (where the impact is so slight as not to require the Crown to involve the titleholders in its decision making),[56] to a duty to consult (which the Court remarks is always to be one of "good faith" consultation), to a duty to obtain the consent of the titleholder affected.

At one end of the scale are situations in which the Crown activity is minor and the titleholder interest is not considered important. There, titleholder involvement in decision making is not required. At the other end are situations in which the Crown may have to seek titleholders' consent in relation to its action, in order to satisfy the requirement that it involve titleholders in its decision making vis-à-vis the lands. The only example the Court provides of the latter—imposition of hunting and fishing regulations—points to an onerous set of duties befalling the Crown when a titleholder asserts an Aboriginal right to engage in these subsistence forms of activities on its lands and the Crown attempts to regulate these very same activities.

We are now in a position to undertake close examination of the interaction between Aboriginal interests in access to resources and Crown power to control such access. This examination will reveal how much access to resources Aboriginal titleholders may come to enjoy as a result of *Delgamuukw*.

ACCESS TO LAND AND RESOURCES

Under a Land–People Vision

Consider first the question of access to resources for traditional activities under the general umbrella of Aboriginal rights.[57] Under an Aboriginal rights claim, established traditional cultural practices meeting the *Van der Peet* test trigger generally onerous requirements on the Crown. The requirements are generally onerous because the activities are, in most cases, in themselves, internally limited. Whether or not an activity is internally limited determines the divide between the *Sparrow* approach to Crown fiduciary duties and the modified *Gladstone* approach. When a claimed Aboriginal right is internally limited (as, for example, when the right claimed is to fish for food or ceremonial purposes only, as in *Sparrow*), it may require of the Crown a simple form of prioritization (placing these interests after only such clearly overarching concerns as conservation and safety). But when the claimed right lacks an internal limit (as, for example, in *Gladstone*, where the right claimed was to a commercial fishery, which would be limited only by the demands of the marketplace and the overall supply of fish), the sorts of duties on the Crown drastically alter. In such circumstances, it must concern itself with allocating resources between the Aboriginal claimants and other historic users, an act that the Court describes as balancing rights.

This reveals a startling aspect of Aboriginal title, which is at its most startling when title is used to protect such traditional activities as hunting, fishing, and gathering for personal or social needs. Although the Crown's fiduciary obligations vary, depending at least in part on the sort of activity for which protection is sought under the claim to title, it cannot be forgotten that the general right claimed is that to land itself. The Court found in *Gladstone* that a right to sell fish cannot attract the same degree of priority as a right to fish for food would enjoy because of its potential to be exclusive. Assigning it such priority would threaten the interests of all other users of the resource. The right to land, even when that right is used only to assert a claim to use the land for traditional (and thereby internally limited) purposes, has similar potential to exclude all other users, and so will trigger the modified *Gladstone* approach.[58] Therefore, even though the actual land use intended could co-exist with other resource users and uses, it will not be as well protected as an aspect of Aboriginal title as it might be if asserted as a simple Aboriginal right, not tied to a claim to land.[59] The former would require the Crown (within the range of responsibilities befalling it) only to take seriously titleholders' interests; the latter would require the Crown to give the Aboriginal use priority.

We can see this most clearly when we consider, not the impact of hunting and fishing regulations on the claimed interest in subsistence activities, but the impact of Crown efforts to facilitate the other sorts of endeavours the Court considered to qualify as compelling and substantial objectives. To illustrate this point, consider Crown efforts to support non-Aboriginal forestry operations on Aboriginal title lands.

Although the titleholder may assert title in an effort to protect its access to traditional resources for traditional purposes, its interest in such access will attract less protection than might otherwise be available because the claim is being made under title, which threatens the interests of non-Aboriginals (in this case, primarily the interests of multinational forestry corporations and their employees). The Crown needs to respect the title asserted, but what it must do is remarkable, in light of the nature of the interests that the titleholder is advancing. For one, the Crown would seem enjoined to work toward involving the titleholder in the forestry operations it wishes to promote.[60] For another, it would seem required to consult with the titleholder in relation to its decision to promote forestry operations on the title lands.[61] Finally, should the forestry operations go ahead against the wishes of the titleholder and without an agreement, compensation may be required.[62] Aboriginal interests in maintaining traditional ways could be exchanged unilaterally for money. In effect, then, an Aboriginal community operating under a land–people vision, interested in undertaking a forestry operation on its lands, will find itself pressured into adopting the sort of operation that fits under a user–thing vision.

This is not to say that the use of a title claim to protect an interest in using resources for respectful purposes is not an option to be explored. Titleholders should be aware, however, of the radical shortcomings of this legal avenue, in that such interests will be forever threatened by the power of the Crown to facilitate the use of their lands by non-Aboriginal parties. The most that is likely to emerge from efforts to protect traditional uses of title lands is an argument that some measure of undisturbed (or fairly undisturbed) land is essential to a minimal continuation of traditional activities. The protection accorded traditional activities, then, will likely not extend as far as Aboriginal peoples would want, but will rather be constricted to the narrowest extent possible. This constriction, carried out in light of the interests of non-Aboriginals in using title lands, will likely extend as far as the Crown and courts think the noose can be tightened without making this exercise of the right completely impossible. This approach would therefore have to be supplemented with arguments asserting other, incidental rights.

Under a User–Thing Vision

What, then, of the use of Aboriginal title to protect access to resources in efforts to create wealth? What of efforts to create a forestry operation under a user–thing vision? We first come, again, to the reality of legislative control, and to the need to examine this control through the requirements of fiduciary doctrine. Some accommodation of the interest in undertaking a forestry operation must be made, given the regulatory scheme in place.

As has been argued above, "advancement" is more than likely under this vision. It is not only that the Crown's fiduciary responsibilities fall in line with this sort of vision, but also that the Crown's activity in fulfilment of these obligations will have all the appearance of being progressive, because Aboriginal peoples, historically, have been denied opportunities to develop economic projects on their traditional territories. Bearing in mind that the Crown need not simply prioritize this interest, it must nonetheless work to find a place in the current legal/economic landscape for interests falling under the user–thing vision. We must ask of the regulatory framework in place, can

> ... the government demonstrate "both that the process by which it allocated the resource and the actual allocation of the resource which results from the process reflect[s] the prior interest" of the holders of Aboriginal title in the land?[63]

Properly reflecting this prior interest

> ... might entail, for example, that governments accommodate the participation of Aboriginal peoples in the development of the resources of British Columbia, that the conferral of fee simples for agriculture, and of leases and licences for forestry and mining reflect the prior occupation of Aboriginal title lands, that economic barriers to Aboriginal uses of their lands (e.g. licensing fees) be somewhat reduced.[64]

For example, faced with a challenge to its control of forestry operations by an Aboriginal titleholder intent on establishing a sustainable forestry operation on title lands (a challenge to how it regulates activities and issues licences), the Crown must work toward fitting this interest into the contemporary situation. Just as clearly, however, this does not simply mean working with the titleholder to establish this operation according to the titleholder's desires and plans. If the land is already heavily exploited by non-Aboriginal forestry operations, for instance, a new operation will not simply be approved and put in place, no matter how onerous the fiduciary responsibilities on the Crown may be. The Court has instructed the Crown to respect the interests Aboriginal titleholders might have in access to resources on their lands, and this is to be done in accordance with the *Gladstone* approach to justifying the interaction of Crown action and Aboriginal interests.

Clearly, then, the advent of the doctrine of Aboriginal title in *Delgamuukw* promises a new world of Aboriginal economic development. The Crown, as fiduciary in relation to Aboriginal peoples and their lands, must endeavour to accommodate interests Aboriginal titleholders might have in using their lands and resources in exploitative fashions.

MARSHALL ON ACCESS TO RESOURCES

We now turn to the effect of *Marshall*[65] on treaty rights-holders' access to resources on treaty lands. It should be noted at the outset that most treaties do not have the sort of provision contained in the Treaty of 1760 that led to the result in *Marshall*. The Supreme Court has been accused of creating treaty rights in *Marshall*,[66] but unquestionably the Court's conclusions rested on treaty clauses that could plausibly be extended to protect a Mi'kmaq right of access to resources.[67]

The treaty in this case contained a "Truck house" clause, purportedly creating a treaty obligation on the Crown to facilitate a trading regime with the Mi'kmaq.[68] Given this clause, and employing principles of treaty interpretation developed over the last thirty years (including an innovative use of the principle of efficacy, drawn from contract law), the Court was able to find an incidental right to gather goods to trade.[69] This right was not open-ended, but rather found to be subject both to restrictions contained within the treaty and to those imposed through the reasonable use of legislative authority.[70]

Most treaties in Canada, especially those that cover vast expanses of land, west from Quebec to the Rocky Mountains, north roughly to the tree line, do not contain such trading clauses, or clauses that could be similarly used to buttress treaty rights to resources. There is, however, one conventional treaty right to resources, found in the commonly incorporated promise to Aboriginal signatories of "the right to pursue their usual vocations of hunting, trapping and fishing."[71] This right is seen to protect an Aboriginal way of life, with fish and game being taken to support subsistence needs. Grounded as it is in the protection of historic practices tied to living off the land, such a right commonly extends only to the protection of such low-scale commercial activities as the exchange of trapped furs.

As *Badger* established and *Marshall* illustrates, this sort of treaty right can be commonly subject to restrictions from both within and without. The typical treaty right to hunt, fish, and trap as usual is commonly subject to two forms of internal limits: geographic restrictions and regulatory restrictions. For example, Treaty No. 8—the treaty under consideration in *Badger*—contemplates the "taking up" of land for "settlement, mining, lumbering, trading or other purposes"[72] (land over which, insofar as it was put to a visible, incompatible use, the right to hunt, fish, and trap as usual would no longer be exercisable). The Court in *Badger* characterized this as a geographic limitation. This same treaty also provides for the right to be "subject to such regulations as may from time to time be made by the Government of the country."[73] The Court in *Badger* characterized this as a regulatory restriction.

Furthermore, treaty rights in Canada are subject to "reasonable" infringement from without, measured according to the *Sparrow* test and applied in *Badger* to the treaty rights arena. This point was stressed in *Marshall*, especially in the motion for re-hearing (*Marshall II*),[74] a "clarification" of the original judgment that (disturbingly) seemed to be issued in light of concern voiced by non-Aboriginal fishers and the general Canadian public.[75]

Although *Marshall* was concerned with a particular sort of "unique" treaty right, it nevertheless has something to say about the nature of treaty rights in general, something that affects the utility they may possess in future negotiations.[76] What must be taken from *Marshall* are not points concerning the treaty of 1760, but principles to be applied in the context of other treaty rights.[77]

The Court in *Marshall* paid particular heed to the principle that treaties are to be understood in light of the vital need to uphold the honour, integrity, and dignity of the Crown.[78] In particular, the Court spoke of the need to ensure that treaties are interpreted in such a manner as to uphold the Crown's honour.[79] It was in looking at the treaty of 1760 with this concern in mind that the Court considered whether a treaty right to trade ought not be assumed to include an implied right to gather things with which to trade.[80] Although this right would not be distinct from the rights of others then living in the Maritimes to gather goods from the land to trade, as an implied right under this treaty it would now find itself constitutionally protected under s. 35 of the *Constitution Act, 1982*.[81]

In the context of common treaty rights, this approach suggests an argument that could bolster the bargaining position of treaty nations, should they be interested in attempting to challenge the Crown's compliance with the full terms of their treaties. In *Badger*, the Court recognized that "it is clear that for the Indians the guarantee that hunting, fishing and trapping rights would continue was the essential element which led to their signing of the treaties."[82] Insofar as the honour of the Crown informs the need to interpret the treaty with this motivation in mind, the outcome should be clear: the Crown is under an obligation to restrict both the taking up of land and the imposition of regulations so as to keep its promise that treaty nations would be able to continue to pursue their traditional livelihoods.

Although a number of cases have dealt with the imposition of regulations, little attention has been paid to the facilitation of settlement. A right to hunt, fish, or trap "as usual" can be given efficacy only with the protection of sufficient lands over which to carry out these activities. Accordingly, it is not enough to measure such settlement against the need to protect these activities; the treaty right ought also to be interpreted so as to be seen to include a right to the protection of these lands from over-development. A balance must be struck, then, between Aboriginal treaty rights to hunt, fish, and trap in the traditional sense and the rights acquired by the Crown under these agreements to facilitate the settlement of treaty lands.

This suggests that Aboriginal treaty communities interested in pursuing greater access to treaty lands and their resources—under either land–people or user–thing visions—have avenues to explore opened up by *Marshall*. Given that achieving this balance has not been a priority for the Crown over the last few generations, some may push this argument in treaty litigation, with the aim of better protecting treaty lands from uses incompatible with their vision of how their land should be treated; others might argue for a need to reach new agreements, with the aim of either better spelling out how the Crown must act to allow traditional uses to flourish or facilitating translation of the older treaty rights into contemporary rights to exploit treaty lands and resources.[83]

No matter the path suggested by *Marshall*, the general aim would be to push the Crown toward greater acknowledgement of, and attentiveness to, its fiduciary obligations under constitutionally protected treaty rights. Whether under the old treaties or new agreements, the Crown must be led to realize the responsibilities entailed in upholding its honour, dignity, and integrity in dealing with treaty nations. Whether new agreements are meant to supplement or to supplant the old treaties,[84] interested treaty nations should be able to achieve some progress in bargaining for harvesting rights more generous on treaty lands than those in the older clauses dealing with pursuit of the "usual vocations of hunting, fishing and trapping."

CONCLUSION: STRATEGIES OUT OF *DELGAMUUKW* AND *MARSHALL*

Strategies for Aboriginal peoples interested in greater access to lands and resources will vary depending on whether their claims are based on Aboriginal title or on treaty rights. This is so under either land–people or user–thing visions of the relationship between titleholders and their lands.

If a claim is based on Aboriginal title, it triggers the *Gladstone* approach to determining Crown fiduciary responsibilities; that regime circumscribes the range of fiduciary duties, for the Crown need only "respect" the prior interest of titleholders. Given that titleholders' resource-access aspirations must go through a legal matrix constructed by Crown legislative power and attendant Crown fiduciary obligations, and that justification of Crown interference with title may not be especially difficult, titleholders will need to consider the impact of such of interference on their plans to use and harvest resources.

If the claim is based on a treaty whose terms protect activities that draw resources from treaty lands, efforts must be made to emphasize those key promises that led Aboriginal nations into what many now consider to be constitutional agreements.[85] These promises must be understood in light of the honour of the Crown and the fiduciary position it now occupies in its dealings with Aboriginal treaty nations. Given the treaties' vulnerability to legislative infringement, it is clear that the protection of resource access and use under treaties can be assured only through renewed efforts at protecting not only rights of access to resources, but also the lands (and waters) over which such activities can take place.

To enlarge upon these general directions, consider again the two community forestry operations introduced earlier, appraising each in turn under, first, an Aboriginal title claim, then a treaty claim.

Harvesting Trees under a Land–People Vision

Operating under a vision of strong and deep connection to the land and to its spirits, our first Aboriginal community wants to undertake forestry operations over its lands in a respectful manner, but recognizes that it must do so while in possession of sufficient control over these lands to enable it to ensure that all potential users treat the land respectfully.

Under an Aboriginal title claim, the community would hope to demonstrate exclusive control over these lands. If successful in its claim, it would demonstrate title, which would recognize such exclusivity. On its face, this would equip the titleholders with the power to make decisions about the use of these lands, not just by the community itself, but also in relation to any other potential users.

We have seen, however, how Aboriginal title is not just tempered by but indeed conceptually and practically intertwined with extensive Crown powers. The first key point is that these title lands almost certainly will already be subject both to Crown-issued licences and leases and to the Crown's power to maintain and amplify its regulatory schemes in relation to these lands. The second key point is that the modified (*Gladstone*) approach would be engaged both to gauge the severity of Crown infringement and to determine measures the Crown would need to implement to justify this interference, because the community's power to make decisions would be exclusive in nature (as a component of its general title).

Quite clearly, this community would be forever under threat, its forestry operation continually in conflict with the sorts of structures provincial governments have in place to regulate forestry operations, and indeed with any further exercises of Crown power they can justify under the *Gladstone* approach.

The community could try to establish its forestry operation under a non-title Aboriginal right, but this option too poses risks. To establish such a right, it must link its enterprise closely with traditions, practices, and customs integral to the community at the time of European contact; having done so, it must fend off Crown interference with the exercise of this right. One advantage of this approach is the opportunity it presents to build an internal limit into the right claimed (to attract the more protective *Sparrow* approach to Crown infringement.)[86] Regardless of how it is defined, however, the right itself would only be to engage in an activity, not to exert over it the control necessary to further the sort of interest imagined. To control all access to the resource (by those inside and outside the community), it would need to establish, separately, a right best classified as a self-government right.[87]

The limited geographic range of the parallel self-government right may appear to attract to it the stricter *Sparrow* approach to Crown infringement, but this seems unlikely. The judiciary seems concerned whenever any Aboriginal right has the potential to interfere with the exercise of other (non-Aboriginal) rights and interests. Such concern will likely lead it to characterize as (potentially) exclusive a community's power to control the forestry operations over its traditional territory, and, accordingly, to require only that the Crown "respect" this right.

Besides enlarging the scope of permissible Crown infringement, courts have other means of limiting attempts at establishing rights to control forestry operations. The doctrine of sovereign incompatibility might serve to cut off communities' claims to such capacity before they can be considered as constitutionally protected Aboriginal rights. Under this doctrine, Aboriginal powers of self-determination incompatible with Crown sovereignty are deemed not to have survived the assertion of Crown sovereignty and cannot today be claimed in domestic courts as Aboriginal rights.[88] Whether the power to control forestry over traditional territories would be such an "originally" extinguished power would have to be determined.

The latitude accorded the Crown for permissible interference with Aboriginal rights (including title) creates potential for relentless assault upon such rights. At some point, therefore, this community may well have to consider treaty negotiations. One might argue that *Delgamuukw*, which seems to promise so much but frustrates opportunity by means of challenging proof requirements and the ever-present threat of justified Crown interference, is designed to do little more than pressure communities into negotiations.

There are two fundamental problems with the momentum (one might say Crown- and court-driven push) toward modern treaties and agreements from the standpoint of a community interested in maintaining respectful access to its resources. First, modern agreements are directed more toward promoting economic development through the enablement of partnerships between local Aboriginal communities and investors and resource companies than they are toward protection of ways of life informed by traditional values and principles. Second, the rights conferred in agreements between the Crown and Aboriginal peoples, even when constitutionalized pursuant to section 35(3) of the *Constitution Act, 1982*,[89] are open to justifiable Crown infringement. This, recall, was the import of *Badger*,[90] which transferred the doctrine of justifiable infringement developed in *Sparrow*[91] from the context of Aboriginal rights to that of treaty rights. Unless stronger protections can be built into the agreements themselves, these agreements will always offer less than sufficiently secure protection of interests that Aboriginal communities might want to have protected.[92]

Harvesting Trees under a User–Thing Vision
An Aboriginal community experiencing and making sense of the world through a user–thing vision values greater access to land and resources so as to produce economic opportunities. It hopes to establish a community forestry operation that generates both wealth and employment. For it, the land and its resources are nothing more than means to that end.

Under Aboriginal title, prospects for such an operation are good. The development of the law on Crown infringement seems designed to lead Aboriginal communities in this direction, for the law acts to foster this sort of underlying vision. Aboriginal communities interested in entering fully the modern world of resource exploitation will find they can both initiate their own operations and reap the benefits when the Crown attempts to interfere with the exercise of their title and its attendant rights. Unilateral pursuit of a forestry operation would likely bring such a community into conflict with the province, but there is no underlying incompatibility between the interests of the province and those animating the community. As a result, the parties could negotiate the community's involvement in the modern resource economy. Similarly, on those occasions when the Crown acted in such a manner as to infringe the community's title, the outcome of the ensuing dispute would be easily foreseeable; here too, the interests of Crown and community would run roughly parallel.

The same assessment applies if this community has treaty rights that may allow access to resources, but not on a scale or of a nature that would support establishment of commercial-scale forestry. Although furthering its interests in such an operation under its historic treaty rights would be difficult, substituting new treaty rights for old could be a viable option, as the Crown would likely be more than willing to put to rest rights that could slow the exploitation of lands and resources. The risk that treaty rights to "hunt and fish as usual" might protect, by implication, more or less undisturbed access to sufficient land suitable for hunting and fishing activity can only heighten the Crown's interest in laying such rights to rest.

This community would have less cause for concern about the regime for justification of Crown infringements of either historic or modern treaties. Its rights would likely have to be accommodated should the Crown act to infringe; such accommodation would likely fall in line with its own user–thing vision. Getting its fair share of the modern resource economy on its traditional lands is something this community can aim for, with hopes of achieving this end.

When we look, then, to the impact of *Delgamuukw* and *Marshall*, whether in relation to Aboriginal title or treaty rights, the repercussions seem remarkably clear. For those communities wrestling with the difficult task of reinvigorating their culture and identity, these two cases offer little by way of assistance. Indeed, they seem designed to thwart these struggles, pushing Aboriginal communities toward futures as little more than Canadian municipalities. In such a future, they might find themselves distinct from other municipalities, in that they may continue to hold particular and unique rights to lands and resources; if present doctrinal trends continue, however, such rights will be underlain by a vision of land as a thing to be exploited and of people as properly in competition for the right to be its exploiters. Those communities still operating under different visions of this relationship, and struggling to reassert their culture and identity, will be under constant assault unless and until they capitulate to the alternative, dominant vision.

NOTES

[1] *Delgamuukw v. British Columbia*, [1997] 3 S.C.R. 1010 [*Delgamuukw*].
[2] *R. v. Marshall*, [1999] 3 S.C.R. 456 [*Marshall*].
[3] *R. v. Sparrow*, [1990] 1 S.C.R. 1075 [*Sparrow*].
[4] *R. v. Van der Peet*, [1996] 2 S.C.R. 507 [*Van der Peet*].
[5] *R. v. Gladstone*, [1996] 2 S.C.R. 723 [*Gladstone*].
[6] Although one could certainly argue that generating wealth is not necessarily inconsistent with the project of reinvigorating culture and identity, when a particular community has an ancestral group identity inconsistent with a focus on wealth generation (where such a focus is to the detriment of other group aims and projects), one can say that that community, in having such a focus, is re-inventing itself and, in the process, moving away from its historic roots.
[7] With such language, this community may signal a self-conceptualization understandable within the common law, as they express what could be translated as some form of ownership claim. As the Supreme Court has required that Aboriginal rights be framed in such a way as to be cognizable within the common law (*Van der Peet*, *supra* note 4 at para. 49), such language may be necessary for legal claims to advance.

8 The "fewest necessary," in certain circumstances, might go so far as to mean that no trees were cut.

9 I do not believe there would be many, if any, communities along these imagined lines. Although current forestry operations over much of Canada are excessively exploitative, this is likely not the result of a lack of caring and responsible vision on the part of local communities, but because codes and policies are established by provincial governments that are: (a) located in cities far removed from the woods, (b) by and large under the sway (or even control) of large forestry companies, and (c) very much concerned with the need to boost provincial revenues through the licensing of forestry operations and the collection of stumpage fees, the province's taxes on tree removal. Whether forestry operations were more in control of local Aboriginal or local non-Aboriginal communities, the end result would likely be similar: forestry regimes would become more "sustainable." See, for example, N.G. Anderson & W. Horter, *Connecting Lands and People: Community Forests in British Columbia* (Victoria: Dogwood Initiative, 2002).

10 *Sparrow*, *supra* note 3, and *Van der Peet*, *supra* note 4, acknowledged this in relation to Aboriginal rights, while *Simon v. The Queen*, [1985] 2 S.C.R. 387 [*Simon*], *R. v. Adams*, [1996] 3 S.C.R. 101 [*Adams*], and *R. v. Badger*, [1996] 1 S.C.R. 771 [*Badger*] did so in relation to treaty rights. As Aboriginal rights are communal in nature, meeting "personal and social needs" involves meeting basic requirements for family and community.

11 See *Van der Peet*, *ibid.*, *Gladstone*, *supra* note 5, and, in an indirect fashion, *R. v. Pamajewon*, [1996] 2 S.C.R. 821. Leonard Rotman notes (in his "'My Hovercraft Is Full of Eels': Smoking Out the Message in *R. v. Marshall*" (2000) 63 Sask. L. Rev. 617 at 628 [Rotman, "My Hovercraft is Full"]) that "[t]he ability of treaty Indians to make use of treaty rights on a commercial basis has been the subject of contention for quite some time." See also *R. v. Horseman*, [1990] 1 S.C.R. 901 [*Horseman*]; *R. v. Gladue et al.* (1996), 178 A.R. 248 (C.A.); *R. v. Lamouche* (2000), 265 A.R. 332 (Q.B.).

12 *Sparrow*, *supra* note 3.

13 See for example *Van der Peet*, *supra* note 4. One might say that the exceptions to this proposition indicate its strength. In *R. v. Agawa* (1988), 65 O.R. (2d) 505, the Ontario Court of Appeal noted the existence of a treaty right to fish commercially, held pursuant to a provision in the Robinson-Huron Treaty of 1850 permitting the Aboriginal signatories to "fish in the waters thereof, as they have heretofore been in the habit of doing." To claim such a treaty right, however, the Aboriginal communities in question had to demonstrate that at the signing of the treaty they were already engaged in commercial fishing operations (i.e., that such operations would fall under "as they have heretofore been in the habit of doing"). Similarly, in *Gladstone*, *supra* note 5, the Heiltsuk had to demonstrate that at the time of contact with Europeans they were engaged in trading of fish to a degree recognizable today as capable of translation into a right to trade on a commercial scale, and that this trading practice was integral to their distinct culture (i.e., that it went into making the Heiltsuk the people they were and are). Finally, in *Horseman*, *supra* note 11, the Supreme Court acknowledged that Treaty No. 8 provided for a right to the treaty nations to "pursue their usual vocations of hunting, trapping and fishing," a right understood as encompassing a right to hunt in order to barter: in other words, a right to hunt on a commercial level. But paragraph 12 of the Natural Resource Transfer Agreement of 1930 (one of a number of such agreements transferring control of natural resources from the federal government to the prairie provinces) was found to have limited treaty rights to hunt, fish, and trap, and in particular to have eliminated the commercial dimension of any such rights.

14 For the historical picture, see Olive Dickason, *Canada's First Nations: A History of Founding Peoples from Earliest Times* (Toronto: McClelland and Stewart, 1992); for a particular narrative drawn from that larger historical drama, see Douglas C. Harris, *Fish, Law and Colonialism: The Legal Capture of Salmon in British Columbia* (Toronto: University of Toronto Press, 2001). On the contemporary scene, the fisheries disputes on both the east and west coasts illustrate the tension between Aboriginal- and treaty-rights claimants and non-Aboriginal resource users.

15 Though it may be tempting to suppose that this shows a concern for the well-being of Aboriginal culture, it is at least as probable that the aim in restricting Aboriginal exploitation of their lands was to keep potential competitors from an arena inhabited by non-Aboriginal exploiters. Canadian history,

post–fur trade, seems to tell this story.

[16] *Van der Peet, supra* note 4.

[17] *Simon, supra* note 10. See also *R. v. Côté*, [1996] 3 S.C.R. 139.

[18] *Van der Peet, supra* note 4 at para. 70.

[19] *Delgamuukw, supra* note 1 at para. 111. It should be noted as well, however, that Aboriginal title was found not to be on the order of fee simple title.

[20] *Ibid.* at para. 117.

[21] *Ibid.* at para. 168.

[22] *Ibid.* at paras. 120–22. Lamer C.J. began by noting that in *Guerin v. Canada*, [1984] 2 S.C.R. 335 [*Guerin*], Dickson J. had asserted (at 379) that "[t]he Indian interest in [reserve land and Aboriginal title land] is the same in both cases." Because the *Indian Oil and Gas Act*, R.S.C. 1985, c. I-6 ". . . presumes that the aboriginal interest in reserve land includes mineral rights . . . aboriginal title also encompass[es] mineral rights." The presumption would, of course, be general in scope, at least in relation to Aboriginal interests in reserve land.

[23] For critiques of this attached limit, see: John Borrows, "Sovereignty's Alchemy: An Analysis of *Delgamuukw v. The Queen*" (1999) 37 Osgoode Hall L.J. 537; Kent McNeil, *Defining Aboriginal Title in the 90's: Has the Supreme Court Finally Got It Right?* (Toronto: Robarts Centre for Canadian Studies, 1998) at 11–13 [McNeil, *Defining Aboriginal Title*]; William Flanagan, "Piercing the Veil of Real Property Law: *Delgamuukw v. British Columbia*" (1998) 24 Queen's L.J. 279; Taiaiake Alfred, *Peace, Power, Righteousness: An Indigenous Manifesto* (Toronto: Oxford University Press, 1999) at 120–21. In "Aboriginal Rights in Canada: From Title to Land to Territorial Sovereignty" (1998) 5 Tulsa J. Comp. & Int'l L. 253 at 270–71 [McNeil, "Territorial Sovereignty"], Kent McNeil questions how the inherent limit might operate if, for example, an Aboriginal community altered its culture. He then goes on to suggest, however, that it may not be such a great "barrier to changes in Aboriginal use," so long as the community maintains environmentally sustainable operations. McNeil presents a much less sympathetic portrayal of the potential impact of this limit in "The Post-*Delgamuukw* Nature and Content of Aboriginal Title" in his collection *Emerging Justice? Essays on Indigenous Rights in Canada and Australia* (Saskatoon: Native Law Centre, University of Saskatchewan, 2001) 102 at 116–22.

[24] *Delgamuukw, supra* note 1 at paras. 125–28.

[25] Further complicating this situation is the federal government's current insistence that, in entering negotiations, it is not admitting the existence of Aboriginal title over the lands in question. The federal position is that Aboriginal title is established only through litigation and that negotiations begin with no admission of title and end with the extinguishment of whatever title may have existed prior to the agreement. See the critique of this position (as adverse to the honour of the Crown and its fiduciary responsibilities, and as generally at odds with the Court's ruling in *Delgamuukw, ibid.*) in Algonquin Nation Secretariat, *Land Rights & Negotiations: Measuring Canada's 1986 Comprehensive Claims Policy Against the Supreme Court of Canada's 1997* Delgamuukw *Decision* (Ottawa, 1999), online: University of Saskatchewan <http://www.usask.ca/nativelaw/ANS.pdf>.

[26] It might be suggested that this formulation mistakenly reverses the onus of proof, for the Court presents the process as one of the Aboriginal titleholder showing title, and a diminution of its rights pursuant to this title by legislative infringement, followed by a shift to the Crown to justify the infringement. But the presumption still exists, notwithstanding this shift in the onus of proof, that the appropriate legislature has the authority to infringe the rights pursuant to title. Its only task is to show an appropriate objective and to ensure that it meets minimal requirements in relation to how it goes about pursuing that objective. In the larger picture, then, the Aboriginal titleholder quite clearly has the much larger task. It is in this sense that I say that it has to show the infringement is unjustified.

[27] *Delgamuukw, supra* note 1 at para. 143.

[28] *Ibid.* at paras. 148–49.

[29] *Ibid.* at para. 156.

[30] In *Van der Peet, supra* note 4, the Court held (at para. 68) that due to the special problems attendant on Aboriginal rights claims, ". . . a court should approach the rules of evidence, and interpret the evidence that exists, with a consciousness of the special nature of aboriginal claims, and of the

evidentiary difficulties in proving a right which originates in times where there were no written records of the practices, customs and traditions engaged in." In *Mitchell v. M.N.R.*, [2001] 1 S.C.R. 911 [*Mitchell*], however, McLachlin C.J. held (at para. 39) that ". . . the *Van der Peet* approach does not operate to amplify the cogency of evidence adduced in support of an aboriginal claim. . . . Claims must still be established on the basis of persuasive evidence demonstrating their validity on the balance of probabilities."

[31] For example, regular use might include seasonal rounds, as a seminomadic people move with the seasons from set location to set location.

[32] In *R. v. Bernard* (2003), 230 D.L.R. (4th) 57 (C.A.), 2003 NBCA 55 [*Bernard*], Daigle J.A. (at paras. 137–57) extracts this distinction from Lamer C.J.'s judgment in *Delgamuukw, supra* note 1. Although the trial judge in *Bernard* had seemed to require demonstration that the Miramichi Mi'kmaq historically had undertaken active measures to exclude others from the lands in question (negative efforts), Daigle J.A. concluded that exclusivity of occupation could also be shown, in instances where no others were attempting to intrude, by the mere act of using and occupying the land (positive efforts).

[33] For a narrow reading of "occupation" see *R. v. Marshall (Stephen)* (2001), 191 N.S.R. (2d) 323 (Prov. Ct.) [*Stephen Marshall*] wherein it was found, at para. 5, that:

. . . the Mi'kmaq of mainland Nova Scotia in the 18th century likely had aboriginal title to lands around some bays and rivers, but not to any of the cutting sites [inland], . . . the Mi'kmaq did not have aboriginal title to any part of Cape Breton Island, [and] . . . 18th century Mi'kmaq might have had some claim to coastal lands from Musquodoboit to the Strait of Canso and then along the Northumberland Strait to the New Brunswick border, but those lands did not include any of the cutting sites [again, inland].

As there was no substantial competition for these lands from other Aboriginal peoples, Curran J. did not find exclusivity to be an issue. However, "occupation," he found (*ibid.* at paras. 139–40), must be considered in terms of "sufficient occupancy," for this accords with the notion of a spectrum of Aboriginal rights in relation to lands. Using concepts and tests the Supreme Court borrowed from Professors Slattery and McNeil, Curran J. concluded (at para. 141) that "the line separating sufficient and insufficient occupancy for title seems to be between nomadic and irregular use of undefined lands on the one hand and regular use of defined lands on the other."

On the other hand, for a more relaxed reading of "occupation," see the Court of Appeal's decision in *R. v. Stephen Marshall*, (2003), 218 N.S.R. (2d) 78, 2003 NSCA 105, wherein Cromwell J.A. agreed with Professor Kent McNeil (*Common Law Aboriginal Title* (Oxford: Clarendon Press, 1989)) that the appropriate standard of occupation to apply to the question of Aboriginal title is the common law standard of the general occupant. This standard would require only ". . . an actual entry, and some act or acts from which an intention to occupy the land could be inferred" (*ibid.* at para. 136, quoting *Common Law Aboriginal Title, ibid.* at 198).

Along similar lines, Daigle J.A. in *Bernard, ibid.*, held (at para. 77) that the Court in *Delgamuukw* had tacitly accepted the position advanced by Professor McNeil (*Common Law Aboriginal Title, ibid.* at 202), to the effect that ". . . probably even outlying areas that were visited occasionally, and regarded as being under their exclusive control, would also be occupied by them in much the same way as the waste of a manor would be occupied by the lord. . . ." With this understanding of "occupation" in hand, he was able to find that ". . . [o]n the evidentiary record, I am satisfied that the Miramichi Mi'kmaq used and occupied the Northwest Miramichi watershed, including the Sevogle area, as their traditional territory during the pre-sovereignty period from contact unto the time of Crown assertion of sovereignty in 1759": *Bernard, ibid.* at para. 127.

[34] Patrick Macklem and Sonia Lawrence remark on the need to provide funding to Aboriginal peoples caught up in the consultation/negotiation process: see "From Consultation to Reconciliation: Aboriginal Rights and the Crown's Duty to Consult" (2000) 79 Can. Bar Rev. 252 at 272 [Macklem & Lawrence, "From Consultation to Reconciliation"]. Insofar as the process of showing Aboriginal title may be part of this process, a funding program should also be made available to those peoples trying to do so, even though the immediate use of such funds may be to aid in the pursuit of claims against the government(s) of Canada. Recent efforts at providing loans are questionable, given the fiduciary position the Crown occupies.

[35] *British Columbia (Minister of Forests) v. Okanagan Indian Band*, [2003] 3 S.C.R. 371, 2003 SCC 71 [*Okanagan*], aff'g (2001), 208 D.L.R. (4th) 301 (B.C.C.A.), 2001 BCCA 647.

[36] In *Okanagan, ibid.*, the Aboriginal party is the defendant. In *Tsilhqot'in Nation v. Canada (A.G.)*, [2002] B.C.J. No. 346 (QL), 2002 BCCA 122, on the other hand, Esson J.A. (in chambers) reversed a lower court order awarding the Tsilqot'in Nation costs in advance of the litigation, in part because it was the plaintiff in the action. The British Columbia Court of Appeal, however, restored the initial costs award ((2002), 3 B.C.L.R. (4th) 231, 2002 BCCA 434), finding no fault with the exercise of discretion in the court below and agreeing that the case seemed be a significant test case, one unlikely to go forward without this sort of funding order. On 13 January 2004, the Supreme Court of Canada, rather than hearing the Crown's appeal from the funding order, remanded the matter to the trial court for reconsideration in accordance with its reasons in *Okanagan, ibid*. On 6 June 2004, the British Columbia Supreme Court released its decision on the rehearing: [2004] B.C.J. No. 937, 2004 BCSC 610. Treating the remand order "as a rehearing of the original matter before me, taking into account the new material filed by the parties" (*ibid.* at para. 12), the court discounted events that had transpired since the original (2001) order and concluded that the case met all three of the criteria set out in *Okanagan, ibid.* (for which see next note). On that basis, it reaffirmed the original funding order.

[37] According to *Okanagan, ibid.* at para. 40, three criteria govern a party's eligibility for an award of costs in advance in public interest litigation: it must be impecunious and incapable of proceeding with the litigation by any other means; the claim must have sufficient *prima facie* merit; and the issues raised in the litigation must be of public importance and must not have been resolved in previous cases. Satisfying these three conditions is necessary, but may not be sufficient, to obtain costs in advance; the trial judge retains discretion even then to refuse such requests, and is to have regard in each case for the impact such an award would have on the other parties, especially private litigants: *ibid.* at para. 41.

[38] The interaction of Aboriginal title and provincial powers to issue licences is at the heart of much of the current litigation. The Crown has argued, *inter alia*, that Aboriginal title cannot be understood apart from the power of the Crown to infringe. See for example para. 43 of *Xeni Gwet'in First Nations v. British Columbia*, 2003 BCSC 249, which cites the province's contention (emerging from *Cheslatta Carrier Nation v. British Columbia* (2000), 80 D.L.R. (3d) 212 (B.C.C.A.)) that

> ... [Aboriginal] rights cannot be properly defined separately from the limitation of those rights. The latter are needed to refine and ultimately define the former: *R. v. Van der Peet*, [1996] 2 S.C.R. 507 at paras. 30–31.

[39] The Court in *Sparrow, supra* note 3, considered and rejected (at 1091–93) the possibility that existing Aboriginal rights might be delineated ("frozen") by the regulatory constraints imposed upon them at the time the *Constitution Act, 1982* came into force. Although one concern was with the creation at that point of a patchwork of variously regulated Aboriginal rights across Canada, the real concern was with a patchwork substantially based on "unreasonable" regulatory schemes in place in various jurisdictions across the country. Clearly the Court did not invalidate the notion of a patchwork, for it advocated a post-1982 case-by-case analysis of the infringement of Aboriginal rights by legislative enactment. Although principled analysis, we must assume, would impose some structure on the national scene, the regulatory schemes would vary by jurisdiction, so a patchwork is inevitable. The only difference would be that this new patchwork would not, presumably, incorporate unjustifiable legislative infringements on Aboriginal rights.

Elsewhere, the Court has considered whether the effect of legislative infringement is to define Aboriginal rights, or merely to regulate the *exercise* of underlying rights, which in their generality remain unchanged. For example, McLachlin J., in her dissent in *Van der Peet, supra* note 4 at para. 238, had this to say:

> Rights are generally cast in broad, general terms. They remain constant over the centuries. The exercise of rights, on the other hand, may take many forms and vary from place to place and from time to time.

Although the Court takes the position that rights themselves are general and constant, this can be little more than rhetoric, likely meant to assuage Aboriginal rights-holders. If a regulatory scheme substantially interferes with the exercise of an Aboriginal right, it matters little whether the underlying right remains unchanged, as the rights-holder has nothing but the exercise of the right. This is particularly (and perhaps uniquely) so in relation to Aboriginal rights, as complete control of the exercise of these rights is actually *held* by the fiduciary. Besides presuming a particular ontological vision of abstract rights (which, in some sense, the Court suggests, exist in the world distinct from their exercise), the picture obscures the true power of Canadian legislatures to define and delineate Aboriginal rights.

[40] Elsewhere I have argued that Aboriginal title is itself determined by the ability of the Crown to justify infringing it. In effect, the Court has conceptualized a form of title constructed in the very process of determining the power of the Crown to govern land and its use: in particular, land over which Aboriginal title is asserted. See "Justification of Crown Infringement of Aboriginal Title" (Paper presented to the *Delgamuukw National Review*, 2001) [unpublished].

[41] This is clear from the Crown's reluctance even to acknowledge that regulatory schemes might require reassessment in light of potential infringements of Aboriginal and treaty rights. In discussing *Marshall*, *supra* note 2, Thomas Isaac notes that the federal and provincial governments of Canada have been very slow to act in relation to their duties as spelled out by the Supreme Court: see "The Courts, Government and Public Policy: The Significance of *R. v. Marshall*" (2000) 63 Sask. L. Rev. 701 at 712 [Isaac, "The Significance of *R. v. Marshall*"].

[42] Showing *prima facie* infringement requires demonstration of an interference with, or diminution of, the established right. This has not been constructed as an especially difficult hurdle to get over. See *Sparrow*, *supra* note 3 at 1111–13.

[43] The overall test for determining the justification of legislative infringement emerges from *Sparrow*, *ibid*. This two-part test was then modified in *Gladstone*, *supra* note 5 at paras. 39–75. The Court in *Delgamuukw*, *supra* note 1, discusses (at paras. 160–69) the application of this modified test to Aboriginal title.

[44] In the words of Lamer C. J. in *Delgamuukw*, *ibid*. at para. 165:
> In my opinion, the development of agriculture, forestry, mining, and hydroelectric power, the general economic development of the interior of British Columbia, protection of the environment or endangered species, the building of infrastructure and the settlement of foreign populations to support these aims, are the kinds of objectives that . . . can justify the infringement of aboriginal title.

A number of commentators have criticized this list of "compelling and substantial objectives." Lisa Dufraimont goes so far as to point out that it is hard to see this as anything more than an attempt to legitimatize colonialism, and adds that it works in opposition to the stated aim of reconciliation: "From Regulation to Recolonization: Justifiable Infringement of Aboriginal Rights at the Supreme Court of Canada" (2000) 58 U.T. Fac. L. Rev. 1. See also Kent McNeil "Aboriginal Title and the Division of Powers: Rethinking Federal and Provincial Jurisdiction" (1998) 61 Sask. L. Rev. 431 at 453–55; McNeil, *Defining Aboriginal Title*, *supra* note 23.

[45] This is discussed in *Delgamuukw*, *supra* note 1 at paras. 162–69.

[46] Macklem and Lawrence consider the existence of a spectrum of consultative duties, and argue that courts have generally ignored this spectrum, choosing instead to focus on the minimal level of consultation mentioned by the high court: "From Consultation to Reconciliation," *supra* note 34 at 263–67.

[47] *Sparrow*, *supra* note 3 at 1113–19.

[48] *Ibid*. at 1115–16.

[49] *Ibid*. at 1116.

[50] *Gladstone*, *supra* note 5 at paras. 27–29.

[51] *Ibid*. at paras. 57–65.

[52] *Ibid*. at para. 63.

[53] *Delgamuukw*, *supra* note 1 at para. 168.

[54] *Ibid*.

[55] The duty to consult arising out of *Delgamuukw*, *ibid*., is discussed in Macklem & Lawrence, "From

Consultation to Reconciliation," *supra* note 34. There are many unanswered questions about the nature and scope of the duty to consult. Some of them will likely be addressed and resolved when the Supreme Court releases its decisions on appeal in *Taku River Tlingit First Nation v. Ringstad*, SCC Case No. 29146, and *Council of the Haida Nation v. Minister of Forests and Weyerhaeuser Co. Ltd.*, SCC Case No. 29419. Both appeals were heard on 24–25 March 2004. When such a duty arises (a major issue there is whether it could arise before the Aboriginal rights in question are established through negotiation or litigation), which parties are subject to it (the British Columbia Court of Appeal had held in the *Haida Nation* case that it could fall on the companies involved in the forestry dispute on land allegedly within Haida territory), and what particular actions it could require of those subject to it are just a few of the outstanding issues yet to be clarified and resolved.

56 Although the Court has said there is always a duty to consult, it meant this in the context of legislative infringement that required justificatory activities on the part of the Crown. In some circumstances, the original activity of the Crown could be so insignificant as not to count as legislative infringement. The onus is initially on the Aboriginal community alleging infringement to establish that the Crown activity *prima facie* infringes its Aboriginal or treaty rights. See *Sparrow, supra* note 3 at 1111–13, 1120–21. In such circumstances, one might say the fiduciary relationship rests in the background, but that no fiduciary duties befall the fiduciary.

57 The test for determining the existence of Aboriginal rights is found in *Van der Peet, supra* note 4 at paras. 44–75. The test for justifying legislative infringement is found in *Sparrow, ibid.* at 1113–19.

58 See *Delgamuukw, supra* note 1 at para. 167.

59 The different sorts of possible Aboriginal- and treaty-rights claims are categorized, and considered in their interaction with non-Aboriginal interests and rights, in Brian Slattery, "Making Sense of Aboriginal and Treaty Rights" (2000) 79 Can. Bar Rev. 196.

60 *Delgamuukw, supra* note 1 at para. 167.

61 *Ibid.* at para. 168. A requirement to seek consent will not arise, for this would give the titleholder the sort of exclusivity that the Court has found too threatening.

62 *Ibid.* at para. 169.

63 *Ibid.* at para. 167.

64 *Ibid.*

65 *Marshall, supra* note 2.

66 Rotman notes that "[i]ndeed, the *Marshall* . . . case was pointed to as being indicative of the worst of the excesses of judicial activism": "My Hovercraft is Full," *supra* note 11 at 631, para. 28.

67 In "The Significance of *R. v. Marshall*," *supra* note 41, Thomas Isaac notes at 705 that

> [o]n its face, a liberal interpretation by the Court of the historical evidence, albeit a progressive example, is not surprising considering the interpretative principles the Supreme Court of Canada has provided regarding treaty interpretation in this and other decisions.

Although Isaac goes on to note that "[w]hat is surprising . . . is the extent to which the Court was prepared to go to find a positive treaty right," the question he raises has to do with the proper role of an appeal court in relation to the interpretation of facts and evidence given at trial, not with the existence of a long list of "liberal and generous" principles of treaty interpretation that the Court could, and should, call upon in carrying out its task.

Leonard Rotman likewise argues that pre-existing principles of treaty interpretation inform the Court's reasoning in relation to the task of giving flesh to the treaty rights at issue. See "My Hovercraft is Full," *ibid.* at 623–24.

68 *Marshall, supra* note 2 at para. 5.

69 *Ibid.* at para. 56.

70 *Ibid.* See paras. 58–59 for the notion of a limit internal to the treaty right opening the way to regulation of the treaty to maintain this limit, and for the suggestion (at the end of para. 64) that further infringements could be justified under the test in *Badger, supra* note 10 (essentially the test in *Sparrow, supra* note 3, applied to treaty rights). The Court felt a need to revisit the question of Crown authority to infringe this treaty right to gather resources for trade in *R. v. Marshall*, [1999] 3 S.C.R. 533 [*Marshall II*].

[71] See, for example, Treaty No. 3:

> Her Majesty further agrees with Her said Indians that they, the said Indians, shall have [the] right to pursue their avocations of hunting, and fishing through-out the tract surrendered as hereinbefore described, subject to such regulations as may from time to time be made by Her Government of Her Dominion of Canada, and saving and excepting such tracts as may, from time to time, be required or taken up for settlement, mining, lumbering or other purposes by Her said Government of the Dominion of Canada, or by any of the subjects thereof duly authorized therefore by the said Government:

A. Morris, *The Treaties With the Indians of Manitoba and the North-West Territories, Including the Negotiations on Which They Were Based, and Other Information Relating Thereto* (Toronto: Belfords, Clarke, 1880) at 75.

[72] Quoted in full in *Badger, supra* note 10 at para. 31, discussed *ibid.* at paras. 49–68. The standard wording of such limitations can be seen in the excerpt from Treaty No. 3, *ibid.* Treaty No. 8 itself is available with surrounding documentation at <http://www.treaty8.org/t8fn_fullTexttreaty8.htm>, and from the government of Canada at <http://www.ainc-inac.gc.ca/pr/trts/trty8_e.html>.

[73] Quoted in full in *Badger, ibid.* at para. 31, discussed *ibid.* at paras. 69–73.

[74] *Marshall II, supra* note 70.

[75] Although some see *Marshall II, ibid.* as little more than a "useful clarification" (see *e.g.* Isaac, "The Significance of *R. v. Marshall,*" *supra* note 41 at 705), others run the gamut from charges that "these additional thoughts proffered by the Supreme Court created more confusion and resulted in additional media criticism" (Rotman, "My Hovercraft is Full," *supra* note 11 at 619, para. 4), to charges that the latter remarks create "an argument for bureaucratic supremacy" over Aboriginal treaty rights, an argument that "lacks any fidelity to constitutional supremacy or to the terms of the treaty" (James (Sákéj) Youngblood Henderson, "Constitutional Powers and Treaty Rights" (2000) 63 Sask. L. Rev. 719 at 739 [Henderson, "Constitutional Powers"]).

[76] Mere mention of future negotiations suggests a topic too vast for this paper. As the Mi'kmaq have asserted post-*Marshall*, why should there be a need to get into a quasi-treaty process when the Supreme Court has recognized their treaty right to gather resources to trade for necessaries? Suffice it to say that arguments can be made that the honour of the Crown is sullied by insisting on new negotiations, in light of the role that constitutional supremacy (as opposed to parliamentary supremacy) should play in this arena. See Henderson, "Constitutional Powers," *ibid.* at 731–32.

[77] For this, see for example Catherine Bell & Karin Buss, "The Promise of *Marshall* on the Prairies: A Framework for Analyzing Unfulfilled Treaty Promises" (2000) 63 Sask. L. Rev. 667.

[78] *Marshall, supra* note 2 at paras. 14 ("Certain assumptions are therefore made about the Crown's approach to treaty making (honourable), which the Court acts upon in its approach to treaty interpretation (flexible)"), 43 (". . . having regard to the honour of the Crown . . . the law cannot ask less of the honour and dignity of the Crown in its dealings with First Nations"), 44 (". . . I think the honour of the Crown requires nothing less in attempting to make sense of the result of these 1760 negotiations"), 49 ("This appeal puts to the test the principle, emphasized by this Court on several occasions, that the honour of the Crown is always at stake in its dealings with aboriginal people"), and 50–52 (reviewing the history of this principle in the common law, and concluding that "I do not think an interpretation of events that turns a positive Mi'kmaq trade demand into a negative Mi'kmaq covenant is consistent with the honour and integrity of the Crown"). Generally speaking, "[t]he trade arrangement must be interpreted in a manner which gives meaning and substance to the promises made by the Crown": *ibid.* at para. 52.

[79] *Ibid.*, at paras. 44, 50–52. Rotman argues that

> the majority's view of the honour of the Crown requires not only that the Crown be presumed to have acted honourably during its treaty negotiations with Aboriginal peoples, but also tints the interpretation of specific clauses of treaties to ensure that those clauses are meaningful when examined in the overall context of the treaty and the common intention of the parties in entering into it:

"My Hovercraft is Full," *supra* note 11 at 625.

[80] Although courts had considered before the question of incidental rights (see for example the

discussion in *Simon, supra* note 10 at 403, around the right to carry a firearm and ammunition to and from locations for treaty-protected hunting), the Court made a strong case for the inclusion of these sorts of rights under treaty protection, basing much of its argument on the principle of efficacy, which itself interacts with the fiduciary doctrine and the honour of the Crown to create a powerful argument for the protection of such implied rights as are necessary to make possible the exercise of the explicit treaty rights: *Marshall, supra* note 2 at para. 43.

[81] *Marshall, ibid.* considered expressly (at paras. 47–48) the relation between this treaty right and the common right of any British subject to gather from the land goods with which to trade for necessaries. The treaty offered some special protection against interference with its exercise, but only after 1982; before that, in the face of parliamentary supremacy, such promises really amounted to very little. With the advent of s. 35 of the *Constitution Act, 1982*, "special protection" is now in place. What this amounts to, however, we are exploring in this paper.

[82] *Badger, supra* note 10 at para. 39.

[83] Renegotiation may have particular appeal in relation to areas of the country not covered by land-cession treaties: areas where, for example, "peace and friendship" treaties have been acknowledged. Even land-cession treaties, however, could be ripe for renegotiation, when and as they guarantee continued hunting, fishing, and gathering. Given the new emphasis on, and strength accorded to, implied rights in *Marshall, supra* note 2, the Crown must now struggle to work out how previously ignored treaty rights (which could interfere seriously with contemporary land use and development) can be accommodated within the current legal and economic landscape.

[84] This is suggested as a strategy for those who might wish to use existing treaty rights as bargaining chips in the development of new treaties. Clearly the federal government would like to see this happen in relation to maritime resources, post-*Marshall*, where efforts are underway to achieve new agreements in respect of territories already subject to treaties.

[85] Patrick Macklem, *Indigenous Difference and the Constitution of Canada* (Toronto: University of Toronto Press, 2001) at 151–56; Brian Slattery, "The Hidden Constitution: Aboriginal Rights in Canada" (1984) 32 Am. J. Comp. L. 361; James (Sákéj) Youngblood Henderson, "Empowering Treaty Federalism" (1994) 58 Sask. L. Rev. 241; Gordon Christie, "Justifying Principles of Treaty Interpretation" (2000) 26 Queen's L.J. 143.

[86] It has to be borne in mind, however, that the claimant does not determine the nature of the claimed right; the Court takes the task of definition upon itself.

[87] The right might contain a power to control community members' own use of the resource. But once the community tried to assert control over the resource itself (not merely how its members used it), its claim would be more properly understood as a self-government right. As such, it would be certain to draw the attention of the Crown, for it would challenge the Crown's own authority to control the resource.

[88] For recent discussion, see *Mitchell, supra* note 30 at paras. 66–174, Binnie J., concurring.

[89] Section 35 (3) of the *Constitution Act, 1982* reads as follows:
> For greater certainty, in subsection (1) "treaty rights" includes rights that now exist by way of land claims agreements or may be so acquired.

[90] *Badger, supra* note 10.

[91] *Sparrow, supra* note 3.

[92] Two related questions arise: what such provisions would have to look like to isolate the agreement from the reach of the doctrine of justifiable legislative infringement, and how such stronger protections could be built into a modern agreement, given that s. 35 itself would seem to subject the agreement's terms to justifiable infringement. Whether the Crown could—assuming it would—agree to tie its hands in such protective provisions remains to be seen.

FIRST NATIONS–CROWN RELATIONS IN BRITISH COLUMBIA IN THE POST-*DELGAMUUKW* ERA

Gurston Dacks

In reviewing the legacy of *Delgamuukw v. British Columbia*,[1] history may judge it to have been more a political than a legal landmark. This paper will argue that a new form of First Nations–Crown relations is taking shape in British Columbia. This relationship is driven to a significant degree by the need to contain the stresses that the *Delgamuukw* decision added to the already problematic politics of Aboriginal rights and title in that province. *Delgamuukw* has exacerbated the problems of this politics in three ways. First, it has greatly increased the material value that the First Nations of the province attach to Aboriginal title, along with the level of compensation they expect for its surrender or transformation. The result has been to widen the gap between the financial positions of the First Nations and the federal and provincial governments as they attempt to negotiate land-claims settlements. Second, the Supreme Court in *Delgamuukw* did not, because it could not, dispel uncertainty concerning the actual location of First Nations title. This ongoing uncertainty has enabled both orders of government to retain their negotiating positions rather than accept the cost of altering them to meet the *Delgamuukw*-induced rise in First Nations expectations. Third, the Court's preference for negotiation over judicial fiat as the method for addressing First Nations claims intensifies the impasse in the claims negotiation process that its high valuation of Aboriginal title helped to create.

    The New Democratic government of British Columbia, which left office in 2001, responded to the political fallout from this impasse by establishing a set of policies that managed the frustrations of interested parties in the province while at the same time enabling it to pursue its economic priorities. The current government has continued these policies, which include an expanded process for consulting with First Nations concerning government-sponsored or -regulated projects, and a variety of "interim measures" relating to the First Nations' land-based interests. The government presents these policies as transitional to a time in British Columbia's future when most claims will have been settled. However, they can also be viewed as the foundation of a new Aboriginal–Crown relationship that could constitute a viable alternative for the future should the land-claims process fail. The focus of this relationship on the interests rather than the rights of the First Nations will make it easier to negotiate agreements that integrate First Nations more intimately into the mainstream of British Columbia life. Some will applaud the economic and social progress that this relationship promises. Others will condemn what they consider to be a process of manipulation in which government uses the stark urgency of the First Nations' economic situations to compel them to focus their energies on short-term economic benefits while their struggles for their rights—and, ultimately, their identities—languish. Whatever judgment one attaches to this outcome, it appears that the *Delgamuukw* decision may have had an effect opposite to that anticipated when it was delivered. Instead of fostering the settlement of claims, it may have rendered claims settlements so distant or unlikely as to help establish a new, non claims–based social contract in British Columbia.

THE HISTORICAL BACKGROUND

The political significance of the *Delgamuukw* decision arises from the fact that, with the exception of a small fraction of Vancouver Island and of the northeastern corner of the province, to which Treaty 8 applies, British Columbia is not covered by treaties ceding land to the Crown or addressing the Aboriginal rights of First Nations.[2] Until the 1970s, this situation did not hinder resource development in the province. It was generally presumed that colonial and subsequent provincial legislative acts had extinguished Aboriginal rights in the province.[3] However, a succession of judicial decisions, beginning with *Calder v. Attorney-General of B.C.* in 1973,[4] undermined this certainty. In its place there developed an understanding that Aboriginal rights could exist in areas of British Columbia. It became apparent that these rights could be asserted to prevent, or at least to subject to lengthy judicial delays, the resource-development projects upon which the health of the provincial economy relies. Section 35 of the *Constitution Act, 1982*[5] enhanced the stature of Aboriginal rights by according them constitutional recognition and protection, but failed to specify how they relate to the sovereignty of the Crown.

Faced with the prospect of resolving the uncertainties of this situation through lengthy and expensive litigation, the outcomes of which were unpredictable, the First Nations Summit of British Columbia and the provincial and federal governments preferred to pursue a process of negotiating First Nations rights. In 1993 they created the British Columbia Treaty Commission, whose role has been described as follows:

> It functions as an independent and impartial tripartite body, designed to assist in facilitating treaty negotiations by monitoring developments and by providing, when necessary, methods of dispute resolution.[6]

The British Columbia treaty process involves six stages: statement of intent to negotiate; readiness to negotiate; negotiation of a framework agreement; negotiation of an agreement in principle; negotiation to finalize a treaty; and implementation of the treaty. Fifty-five First Nations representing 122 of British Columbia's 198 bands and 6 Yukon bands have entered the negotiating process. Of these 55 First Nations, 40 are negotiating agreements in principle, 3 have negotiated agreements in principle that have not yet been ratified by the three parties, and 2 have reached the fifth stage of negotiating a treaty.[7]

In other words, after more than a decade, the British Columbia treaty process has not produced a single treaty. Viewed from the perspective that the Yukon and Nunavut land-claims settlements took approximately two decades to negotiate, the lack of output of the B.C. process does not definitively demonstrate its failure. However, the B.C. process is taking place with the benefit of the lessons learned from the modern land-claims settlements that have already been reached. Hence, it should be proceeding more swiftly than they did. Moreover, the problems with the process suggest that it will be a very protracted one.

First, and perhaps most fundamental, is the federal and provincial governments' insistence on putting a definitive end to the uncertainty that surrounds Aboriginal rights, including title, and the First Nations' reluctance to agree to this. Certainty is important for these governments for a very basic reason. Because the actual rights of the First Nations regarding specific pieces of land have not yet been determined, the legal obstacles faced by resource developers may deter them from proposing their projects. The result is to dampen economic activity, employment, and tax revenues in the province, thus frustrating critical goals for both orders of government. To eliminate this uncertainty, the two governments are proposing that the text of land-claims settlements define the totality of rights that First Nations will possess with regard to lands and resources upon the confirmation of the settlement. Aboriginal rights may persist, but their impact will be limited to the benefits that are defined in the claims settlement. Further, the governments insist that First Nations agree that they will not be able to litigate in order to expand their rights once they have signed their settlements, because such litigation would deny the governments the certainty that has been their major goal in pursuing land-claims settlements. Although this approach avoids the language of extinguishment of rights, most First Nations believe that it resembles extinguishment sufficiently closely to threaten their identity and their relationship to the land and the Creator, just as the blunter language of extinguishment did. Underlying their rejection of this approach is their rejection of its underlying assumption and purpose. They see governments as seeking to subsume Aboriginal rights under the larger body of Canadian law so as to bind them more tightly within Canadian society. In contrast, First Nations themselves view the treaty process as an opportunity to create an ongoing relationship between themselves and Canada, based on an equality of status. Although these two visions are not constantly on the negotiating table, their profound differences help explain the slowness of progress to date and, in all likelihood, in the future.

A second problem facing the claims process has been the provincial government's insistence that, at the end of the process, British Columbia's First Nations will possess no more than 5 percent of the total area of the province. For their part, the First Nations insist that the economic function of the treaty process is to ensure that they possess a sufficient economic base to provide for their future prosperity. They view the 5 percent rule as arbitrary and very unlikely to provide this base.

Third, the First Nations believe that the financial terms of claims settlements should compensate them for the value of the resources that were extracted from their lands in the past and for which they received no payment. The government's position is that the goal of the treaty process is to ensure the future financial strength of the First Nations, and that this should be the focus of negotiations. Focusing on compensation would not necessarily accomplish this goal. To the contrary, it would likely produce protracted conflict because a compensation process would have to establish, first, the areas on which each First Nation held title and then the quantity and dollar value (perhaps with interest calculated from the time of extraction to the present day) of the natural resources extracted on these pieces of land. Inevitably, fundamental disagreements would arise over these questions. These differences would have to be resolved by litigation, whereas the treaty process was created with the hope of sparing British Columbia the tribulations of claims-based litigation. There are thus sound reasons to avoid a compensation approach. However, to do so is to deny British Columbia's First Nations an argument that they believe can deliver to them huge sums of money that they view as rightfully theirs.

Fourth, the traditional lands of First Nations often overlap with those of their First Nations neighbours. To avoid pitting First Nations against one another in court, the competing interests that result from these overlaps need to be resolved by negotiation.

A fifth problem has been that the level of funding available for the treaty process has limited its progress. This funding is required to enable First Nations to research their claims. They also need it to assess the potential of government offers for achieving their goal of prosperity, to conduct negotiations, and to develop the capacity themselves to perform these functions or to retain others to perform them on their behalf. These are expensive functions, and are unavoidable if First Nations are to advance their legitimate interests properly. The funding initially established for the treaty process anticipated that about thirty First Nations would take part in it at any given moment. For the first half decade, this funding had to be divided among the more than fifty First Nations that actually entered the process. The result was that each received insufficient funding to develop and negotiate its claim expeditiously. In 1999, the federal government committed fifteen million dollars over three years to enhancing the capacity of First Nations to participate in the treaty process. This allocation, supplemented by provincial funding, strengthened the process to a degree. However, the lack of operational funding continues to limit what the process can accomplish.

THE IMPACT OF *DELGAMUUKW*

The *Delgamuukw* decision widened the gap separating the positions of the parties in the treaty process and encouraged First Nations to pursue their interests more resolutely. The Court's decision defined Aboriginal title as encompassing

> the right to exclusive use and occupation of the land held pursuant to that title for a variety of purposes, which need not be aspects of those aboriginal practices, customs and traditions which are integral to distinctive aboriginal cultures. . . .[8]

The fact that Aboriginal title permits First Nations to undertake a diverse (but not unlimited) range of forms of economic exploitation on their lands and confirms their right to be exclusive gives it a great economic value, as does their right to receive compensation if their rights are infringed. On the basis of this assessment, First Nations have expected the provincial and federal governments to increase the financial value of their settlement offers to compensate the First Nations for giving up their now more valuable rights to the lands whose ownership by the Crown the settlements would confirm.

They felt more comfortable expecting this revision of the governments' negotiating mandates because of the way that they expected the governments to interpret another element of the *Delgamuukw* decision. This was the Court's expansion of the significance of oral testimony. The Court observed that

> . . . the laws of evidence must be adapted in order that this [oral] type of evidence can be accommodated and placed on an equal footing with the types of historical evidence that courts are familiar with, which largely consists of historical documents.[9]

The First Nations believed that the governments would view this principle as weakening their cases in future litigation concerning Aboriginal rights because it would reduce the persuasive power of documentary evidence, which, reflecting non-Aboriginal views of historical events and relationships, tended to favour government rather than First Nations.

The federal and provincial governments certainly appreciate that the *Delgamuukw* decision increased the material value of Aboriginal title, where it can be proven to exist. They understand that a compensation-oriented model of claims settlements would require them to increase the level of compensation that they would have to pay First Nations to induce them to give up their now more valuable title. They are reluctant to contemplate spending additional sums of money for this purpose because of the fiscal burden and the political cost of alienating voters who are already reluctant about the cost of settling British Columbia's land claims.[10] Moreover, the Court's observation[11] that First Nations must be compensated for infringements of their title could prove very costly for the provincial government if it is required to share future resource rents with First Nations that have proven their title to lands on which resource extraction will take place.

In the face of what they consider the unacceptably high cost of dealing with First Nations on the basis of their proven title, the governments have drawn comfort from the fact that the Court did not actually confirm the title that the litigants sought. The Court affirmed the existence of title as a possibility, but for technical reasons associated with the pleadings could not attach it to any piece of territory. Instead, it set out a test for proving title in future cases. This test requires proof of exclusive First Nation occupation of the land in question before the assertion of Crown sovereignty (dated at 1846 for British Columbia) and, where this cannot be shown directly, proof of the maintenance of a continuous connection with the land from that time until the present day.[12] This is an onerous test for a number of reasons.

First, it may be difficult to provide evidence of a sufficient degree of occupation of the land over which a declaration of title is being sought. Physical evidence of occupation such as the remains of dwellings or enclosures around fields would probably prove sufficient. However, such evidence may not be present. Moreover, First Nations believe that they hold title over areas of land much larger than they can demonstrate through this type of evidence. To address such concerns, the Court indicated that evidence that a First Nation applied a system of laws to govern the use of the land would demonstrate occupation. However, despite the Supreme Court's assertions in *Delgamuukw* and *Van der Peet*[13] that the courts should give considerable weight to Aboriginal perspectives and oral testimony,[14] evidence of these legal systems may prove difficult to produce. This is particularly probable as Aboriginal practices may have effectively governed economic relations and land use a century and a half ago, yet not have had the clarity and history of consistent application that would make them recognizable as laws by a contemporary court. If pre-sovereignty occupation cannot be demonstrated in its own right, a First Nation may claim title by demonstrating an ongoing cultural attachment to the land in question. However, this may be difficult to demonstrate because First Nations have for several generations been removed from the vast majority of their traditional lands. Confined to reserves and, to varying degrees, denied access to their traditional lands, the attachment to these lands that First Nations can today demonstrate may not meet the test that the Court has set. In view of these considerations and despite the threat to the provincial government's authority posed by the *Taku River Tlingit*[15] and *Haida Nation*[16] court decisions, which will be discussed below, the federal and provincial governments have based their land-claims policies on the premise that First Nations will find it very difficult to obtain title to a significant amount of land through the courts. Therefore, and because of the cost of doing otherwise, the governments have not changed their negotiating approach in the British Columbia treaty process.

This response to *Delgamuukw* widened the already gaping divide between the parties at the treaty negotiating table. The positions of the parties on financial issues have become more distant. In addition, the tone of their relations have become more bitter; the First Nations found it perverse and offensive that the governments would not respect the validity and status that they felt the decision had accorded to their relationship to their lands.[17] The treaty process stalled.

The result was frustration all around. Obviously, the First Nations who were engaged in the treaty process were frustrated that a court decision that they had viewed as a victory had yielded them no advantage in their negotiations. Their leaders had invested a great deal of personal political capital in the decision to enter the treaty process, and this new disappointment called their judgment into question and weakened their credibility in comparison with those who had refused to enter the treaty process. Resource developers were frustrated because the treaty process had failed to provide them with certainty concerning the ownership of land and resources and the authority of the British Columbia government to manage those lands, certainty that they required in order to make their investment decisions. For their part, the two governments were frustrated that they had so little to show for their massive financial and political investment in the treaty process. Rather than receiving credit for their efforts, they faced ongoing pressure from both resource developers and First Nations as well as considerable dismay from the general population of the province.

In this way, the *Delgamuukw* decision exacerbated the problems of the treaty process to the point where it was not sustainable. In the short term, the heightened contradictions in the process certainly impaired it. However, viewed in a longer perspective, *Delgamuukw* has forced the participants in the process to find new ways of pursuing their overlapping interests. An often overlooked but very important feature of the British Columbia situation is that the interests of the major players in the politics of the treaty process do overlap. Indeed, they overlap sufficiently to bring into being a new regime to address some of the frustrations coming out of the treaty process and thus buy it some time. These interests can be described briefly.

The primary interest of the First Nations engaged in the process is to settle their claims on terms that they feel justly reflect the material value of their title, properly acknowledge their place in the Canadian Constitution—including their inherent right to self-government—and provide for an ongoing relationship with Canada. However, in the absence of such agreements, First Nations leaders who have committed to the treaty process need their decision to participate in it to be validated. The First Nations in the treaty process have borrowed $204 million from the federal government.[18] Any First Nation that withdraws from the process will be required to repay its share of that debt. The difficulty of making such a payment undoubtedly encourages many First Nations leaders to stay in the process, as does their unwillingness to risk their own legitimacy by abandoning the process that they had formerly endorsed. Immediate and tangible benefits from the treaty process would serve their interests by showing some return on their investment in the process and by assisting their people to begin building better lives for themselves.

For their part, resource developers have an interest in seeing development proceed. They thus are willing to contribute, within reasonable bounds of cost, to programs to improve intercultural relations in ways that hasten project approvals and discourage direct action or litigation by First Nations against their activities.

The interests of the provincial and federal governments lie in sustaining the negotiating process because it is a more attractive option than either civil disobedience or litigation on the part of First Nations. At the same time, they are reluctant to revise their claims policy because it rests on fundamental interests including cost containment, the avoidance of precedents that might have undesirable consequences elsewhere in Canada, and the desire of the provincial government to maintain full authority over the management of Crown lands.

This last concern has gained new prominence as a result of two judgments that the British Columbia Court of Appeal delivered in 2002. The first of these, *Taku River Tlingit*, questioned the authority of the provincial government where Aboriginal rights or title may exist:

> It is also possible that neither the Legislature nor Parliament has that power, in which case the many Indian bands of British Columbia, as to all resource development within lands claimed by them, have a right of veto, or at least have a right to have each proposed project considered by the courts on a case-by-case basis...[19]

In the *Haida Nation* case, the court suggested that it might be possible that "provincial laws of general application do not apply to aboriginal title . . . of their own force."[20] It also affirmed that "[i]f the claim to aboriginal title is supported by a good *prima facie* case, then anyone who violates the title will be liable when title is either conceded or proved."[21]

It will take time to discern the impact of these judgments on the First Nations–Crown relationship in British Columbia. Presumably, *Haida Nation* exposes resource developers themselves to potential liability in the future. Also, both judgments seem to raise the stakes for the provincial government, making it far more financially vulnerable for its promotion of resource development than it was when the courts did not recognize any obligation on its part to compensate First Nations until they had proven their title. The other comments in these judgments adverse to the provincial government would also seem to increase the government's desire to discourage litigation involving Aboriginal title.

THE POST-*DELGAMUUKW* RELATIONSHIP

The agendas of the First Nations, governments, and resource developers converge in that they necessitate a regime that advances their respective material interests without compromising the fundamental principles underlying each of their positions. The key components of this regime have been a greater emphasis on government consultation with First Nations and the growth of interim measures as a mechanism for managing First Nations–government relations.

The First Nations–British Columbia Consultation Process

The government of British Columbia formally got in the business of consulting with the province's First Nations in response to the Supreme Court's decision in *Sparrow*.[22] This decision[23] held that the federal government may infringe upon Aboriginal rights if the anticipated infringement meets a test of justification set out by the Court. Perhaps anticipating that future court decisions, such as *Delgamuukw*, would extend this obligation to provincial governments, the government of British Columbia established a process for assessing the extent to which its activities or those it regulates, such as mining, logging, oil and gas exploration, or pipeline construction, infringe on Aboriginal rights.

The first step in this process is for the relevant government agency to assess the potential that an anticipated activity infringes upon an Aboriginal right. If the likelihood is very low, the activity will be approved. However, if there is a potential that the activity will infringe upon an Aboriginal right, the government agency will ask the First Nation (or Nations) affected for evidence of any right or title it claims to possess and for its views on how the proposed activity might affect this right or title. The government agency will then assess the information that the First Nation supplies to determine the likelihood of Aboriginal rights or title existing on the land that would be affected by the activity. If this better-informed judgment is negative, the project is immediately approved. If an infringement will occur, the agency must decide whether the infringement is justifiable, keeping in mind the very broad range of purposes that the Supreme Court identified in *Delgamuukw* as legitimate grounds for infringing upon Aboriginal rights.[24] The project may be approved, denied, or, if approval is problematic, the agency can ask the project proponent to modify the proposed activity so as to avoid conflicts with such First Nations land uses as wildlife or plant harvesting or spiritual activities.

The *Delgamuukw* decision brought this process to the foreground for several reasons. The first is that it extended the application of the process beyond rights to include Aboriginal title, which involves a much more valuable interest in land and resources than other rights convey. Moreover, confirming the concept of Aboriginal title underscored the responsibilities of the provincial government. This title conflicts with provincial ownership of its lands and resources much more than does the subject matter of *Sparrow*, which involves only fishing, a matter of federal jurisdiction in any case.[25] Also noteworthy is the conclusion that provinces lack the authority to extinguish Aboriginal title.[26] As a result, the British Columbia government now devotes considerable resources to the consultation process and to supporting the many officials in the various departments of government who actually undertake consultations with First Nations. Because the consultation process is decentralized, often taking place in regional offices of departments such as Forestry, and Energy and Mines, it is difficult to count the number of actual consultations that occur. The frequency of these interactions can be appreciated from the 1999 observation of Marlie Beets, vice-president of Aboriginal Affairs of the Council of Forest Industries, that

> [n]early every action or decision made by a forester, whether working for industry or government, must include consideration of complex constitutional and legal issues relating to claims of aboriginal rights and or title. . . .[27]

If either a First Nation or a developer feels that the government has acted improperly in carrying out the consultation process, it has the right to litigate. The government, of course, attempts to avoid litigation, because litigation creates ill will between the litigants, reflects badly on the government's management of First Nations/non-Aboriginal relations, delays resource development, and, as in *Haida Nation* and *Taku River Tlingit*, exposes the province to a substantial risk of losing. Its desire to discourage litigation and to improve its own position should litigation arise is one reason for the vigour with which the government pursues the consultation process; it wants to be seen to be observing its obligations as set out in *Sparrow* and *Delgamuukw*. In addition, it attempts to bring business and First Nations interests together in individual cases for the benefit of the parties and to encourage them to stay out of court. For example, the Ministry of Forests negotiates with forestry companies where and how they will cut their annual allotments of trees so as to minimize the adverse impact of this logging on First Nation interests such as spiritual sites and traplines. Also, the criteria for obtaining tree-harvesting licences now provide for First Nations employment, either through joint ventures with First Nations or through hiring First Nations workers individually.[28] These types of arrangements not only keep the parties out of court, but also bring their respective interests more closely into alignment. Over the long term, it is reasonable to anticipate that they will make each side more comfortable in dealing with the other and with the rights the other claims to the lands and resources of the province.

Although the British Columbia consultation process is changing the way business is being done there, it is not universally embraced by all of the parties to it. Some First Nations reject the underlying premise of the process. Because they believe that they own the full extent of their traditional lands, they reject any process that starts with the assumption that the Crown owns the land. Other First Nations, particularly in oil- and gas-rich areas, are simply overwhelmed by the number of requests for information that they receive through the consultation process, the complexity of the analysis they must perform on proposed activities, and the speed with which they are sometimes asked to respond. First Nations also doubt the efficacy or sincerity of the consultation process because few projects are rejected and because the province does not award compensation for infringements of rights and asserts that it will not do so until these rights have been established in court. On the other hand, although some resource-development firms view the costs they bear as a result of potential Aboriginal rights and title to be a reasonable consequence of the legal situation, others complain about these costs, particularly in the face of difficult market conditions.

Interim Measures
Notwithstanding these concerns, it is clear that the consultation process is bringing resource-based businesses and First Nations into closer contact than they experienced before *Sparrow* and *Delgamuukw*. In doing so, it is reinforcing the impact of the second feature of the post-*Delgamuukw* era: the growing importance of interim measures.

"Interim measures" refers to a very broad array of government activities intended to improve relations with First Nations in the period preceding the settling of their land claims. From the perspective of First Nations, the fundamental purpose of interim measures is to protect their interests in the lands and resources that are the very subject of treaty negotiations. As the British Columbia Treaty Commission notes,

> [t]reaty negotiations ... take time. Meanwhile trees are still being cut, ore is being mined and fish are being caught. First Nations, who are taking on substantial debt to negotiate treaties, are increasingly frustrated that they are not sharing enough in the benefits of those resources in their traditional territories.[29]

The governments of Canada and British Columbia have responded to these concerns with what they term "treaty-related measures" (TRMs), which they view as a subcategory of interim measures, and which they describe as

> ... temporary arrangements negotiated within the context of the treaty process [that] may be formalized when a treaty takes effect. They are designed to accelerate treaty negotiations and bring certainty and economic development to local economies. TRMs will also help the province meet its legal obligations arising from *Delgamuukw* and other court decisions, and help resolve conflicts over land and resources use.
>
> Examples of treaty-related measures that negotiators can use to move specific issues forward at the negotiation table include: studies to generate information that will expedite treaty negotiations, protection of Crown land for treaty settlement, land acquisition for treaty settlement, First Nation participation in land, resource and park planning and management, and economic and cultural opportunities.[30]

Interim measures are a broader category of undertakings than treaty-related measures in that they are not necessarily negotiated in the process of treaty discussions. Although initially they were conceived of as supporting and facilitating the treaty process, their purpose has expanded greatly in recent years. A statement by the B.C. Ministry of Aboriginal Affairs describes them in these terms:

> We need to make sure that the business and economy of the province are able to run as smoothly as possible while treaties are being negotiated. . . . [Interim measures] encourage aboriginal and non-aboriginal interests to take cooperative approaches to identifying, conserving and enhancing natural resource interests in traditional territories. They can also ensure that First Nations have the opportunity to benefit from resource development in their area.[31]

As of 2003, the number of interim measures, including treaty-related measures, that had been signed exceeded 80.[32] As of May 2003, almost $25 million had been awarded to First Nations in 112 projects throughout British Columbia. These measures include: almost $1.9 million to assist the Treaty 8 First Nations in the development of B.C.'s northeastern oil-and-gas sector; $539,000 for the Skeetchestn Indian Band to conduct forestry research to determine the social and economic viability of alternative timber harvesting; $100,000 for the Campbell River Band to do a design and engineering study for a cruise-ship dock upgrade; $75,000 for the Esquimalt First Nation to pursue training that will build skills for the commercial development of reserve land; $530,000 for the Huu-ay-aht First Nation to revitalize the abalone shellfish aquaculture industry in Bamfield; $75,298 for a partnership between the Guide Outfitters Association of British Columbia and First Nations in northern B.C. to train six aboriginal students to work as assistant guides; and $230,000 for the Mount Currie and Douglas First Nations, involving independent power projects.[33]

The British Columbia government, supported by the government of Canada, has emphasized interim measures for several reasons. The first of these has been its desire to build support for the treaty process in the face of the frustrated expectations created by the *Delgamuukw* decision. The fact that treaty-related measures can be negotiated only by First Nations that have entered the B.C. treaty process strengthens the position of First Nations leaders who support the process; it encourages the First Nations already in the process to stay in it and those who are not to enter it. Moreover, it appears that interim measures, the broader type of undertaking, tend disproportionately to be negotiated by First Nations involved in the treaty process. This may reflect their greater level of comfort in dealing with government, as contrasted with First Nations that have adopted a more confrontational stance toward government. Regardless, this pattern emphasizes the material benefits that can flow from being a participant in the treaty process.

Second, interim measures integrate the First Nations people they affect into the mainstream British Columbia economy, give them an interest in the health of the larger economy, and in this way reduce the likelihood that direct action by First Nations will disrupt the logging and other resource-extraction industries upon which the B.C. economy so heavily depends. To the extent that interim measures provide employment-related skills to First Nations people and assist them to secure attractive work, these workers are likely to identify more with the provincial economy than would otherwise have been the case. Interim measures that fund collaborations between First Nations and private-sector firms will have the same effect. These jobs and collaborations will improve First Nations' understanding of resource-development firms, their professional practices, and their needs.

In emphasizing the economic over the spiritual aspects of Aboriginal lands, these outcomes may dismay First Nations traditionalists who see their peoples' cultures attenuating. However, interim measures make sense to many First Nations citizens and leaders. For their part, many resource-development firms are increasingly coming to welcome or at least to accept as good business practice their involvement with First Nations and their citizens. If this involvement can take root and flourish, it is reasonable to expect that it will improve corporate understandings of First Nations and their needs, and help to foster relations of trust. Interim measures that involve First Nations to whatever degree in land-use and resource-management policy (although always on an advisory basis concerning Crown lands) should have a similar effect of giving them more of a sense of ownership of policy decisions than they formerly had. Undoubtedly, conflict will occur, but it is less likely to occur as frequently or as destructively as in the past, particularly as interim measures have created entirely new channels of communication among First Nations, companies, and government.

Moreover, interim measures accomplish such integration without jeopardizing the provincial government's basic interests, which are to avoid validating First Nations' claims to rights or title and to maintain its full jurisdiction over the land

and resources of the province. Interim measures focus, not on rights, but on balancing the interests of British Columbia and various First Nations. Because interim measures are negotiated in a discourse about interests, not rights, they cannot be seen as incremental steps toward a de facto recognition of rights, nor argued by First Nations to be a recognition of their rights or title. Also, interim measures do not raise questions about jurisdiction. This leaves the jurisdiction of the government untouched—indeed, reaffirmed—because the implementation of interim measures requires government confirmation and funding.

The significance of interim measures should not be overstated. They have little effect, if any, on the many B.C. First Nations that have rejected the treaty process. Moreover, interim measures will have only the impacts (described above) that their scale makes possible; they will have to become much more numerous and well-funded to alter fundamentally First Nations–Crown relations in British Columbia. However, they are having an effect. To the extent that First Nations people find it in their interests to participate in the web of relationships spun by interim measures, they will be acting much more on the basis of their interests than their rights. In effect, their growing material dependence on the larger provincial economy may come to eclipse their commitment to a rights-based relationship and with it, the pressure their leaders feel to settle their Aboriginal claims. In the end, the *Delgamuukw* decision may have so increased the cost of settling claims, and so sensitized the provincial government and resource developers to the need to accommodate at least to some extent the expectations created by the decision, that it will produce a new economy. In this economy, First Nations and their members will participate effectively on the basis of special programs that reflect their interests, rather than their rights, and that are sufficiently generous to discourage them from taking direct action or litigating in pursuit of their rights.

CONCLUSION

It is possible that the future will see the settlement of a great many First Nations' claims in British Columbia. If so, the provincial government's policies of consultation and interim measures will have prepared B.C. First Nations to involve themselves effectively in resource-development activities. Indeed, these may form the basis of the ongoing post-settlement relationship that stands as one of the key goals in First Nations claims. However, also possible is a future in which unsettled claims form part of the legacy of the *Delgamuukw* decision, another part of which is an ongoing and sustainable economic and social process that expresses the interests rather than the rights of its First Nations and non-Aboriginal participants. Managing such a relationship while unsettled claims remain a source of grievance and uncertainty will not be easy. However, the consultation processes and interim measures that were, if not born, then at least brought to maturity to meet the post-*Delgamuukw* needs of British Columbia will be crucial to the success of such a future.

The 2001 election of a Liberal government in British Columbia has made this prospect all the more likely. The criticism that the Liberals had levelled at the claims process while they were in Opposition[34] translated, once they gained power, into a provincial referendum on the principles that ought to govern the land-claims process in the future. These principles confirmed already existing government positions or legitimized the provincial government offering less at the table than its predecessor. Particularly galling to the First Nations was the principle that their future governments would resemble municipal governments. Far from being the broadly and inherently empowered governments to which the First Nations believe the Constitution entitles them, these governments would exercise only delegated powers, and few of those. With many provincial voters boycotting the referendum and others spoiling their ballots, the eight principles proposed won 95 percent approval. However, the government followed this demonstration—however controversial—of support for an aggressive stance in claims negotiations with instructions to its claims negotiators to take a conciliatory stance in negotiations. Indeed, three agreements in principle were initialled in the first half of 2003.

The history of the current provincial government is contradictory. What is certain is that the First Nations experienced the referendum as a hugely alienating event, particularly as it involved the voters of the province, most of them non-Aboriginal, voting on the meaning of Aboriginal rights, which are supposed to be matters of law, not matters of majority opinion and self-interest. This alienation and the still-unresolved issues in the negotiations have increased the need to contain First Nations' frustration so as to discourage them from engaging in either litigation or direct action. In this context, the consultation processes and interim measures described above become all the more important.

To the extent that the current provincial government's policy is less supportive of First Nations in the treaty process than that of its predecessor, the already yawning post-*Delgamuukw* gap in expectations between government and First Nations will widen. In this most likely scenario, and especially if the Supreme Court affirms the lower court decisions in *Haida Nation* and *Taku River Tlingit*, the mechanisms of positive relationship-building may not be sufficient to prevent First Nations' anger from boiling over. However, given the delicacy of this situation, their potential for avoiding this outcome will be all the more important.

Two years have passed since the referendum, and the treaty process seems no more infirm today than it was before the vote. Perhaps—in view of the three new agreements in principle—it is even somewhat more successful than before. Taking a longer perspective, the Supreme Court of Canada has mandated consultation, and the *Taku River Tlingit* and *Haida* judgments have underscored that obligation. Moreover, the integration of First Nations into the resource economy of British Columbia is very much in the interests of B.C.'s resource-development sector, which will undoubtedly wield considerable influence with the provincial government. The likeliest result for the foreseeable future, therefore, will be one in which consultation and interim measures play an increasingly important role in rationalizing a situation in which land-claims settlements remain elusive in British Columbia.

NOTES

The author thanks the officials of First Nations organizations and the public servants of the governments of British Columbia and Canada who generously shared their time and insights during the interviews that form the basis of this paper. Many of the generalizations and the characterizations of positions of the various parties discussed here reflect recurring themes in these interviews, as well as in the documentary research on which this paper is based. Because these propositions represent widely held views that may, however, not have been definitively articulated by a single respondent or research document, some have not been referenced with specific citations.

[1] *Delgamuukw v. British Columbia*, [1997] 3 S.C.R. 1010 [*Delgamuukw*].
[2] Paul Tennant, *Aboriginal Peoples and Politics: The Indian Land Question in British Columbia, 1849–1989* (Vancouver: University of British Columbia Press, 1990) at 39–52.
[3] Patrick Macklem, *Indigenous Difference and the Constitution of Canada* (Toronto: University of Toronto Press, 2001) at 86-88; Michael Asch, *Home and Native Land: Aboriginal Rights and the Canadian Constitution* (Scarborough: Nelson, 1988) at 47.
[4] [1973] S.C.R. 313.
[5] Schedule B to the *Canada Act 1982* (U.K.), 1982, c. 11.
[6] Christopher McKee, *Treaty Talks in British Columbia: Negotiating a Mutually Beneficial Future*, 2nd ed. (Vancouver: University of British Columbia Press, 2000) at 33.
[7] British Columbia Treaty Commission, *Update, June 2004* at 12.
[8] *Delgamuukw, supra* note 1 at para. 117.
[9] *Ibid.* at para. 87.
[10] McKee, *supra* note 6 at 108.
[11] *Delgamuukw, supra* note 1 at para. 169.
[12] *Ibid.* at paras. 143–59.
[13] *R. v. Van der Peet*, [1996] 2 S.C.R. 507.
[14] It should be noted that, in *Mitchell v. Minister of National Revenue*, [2001] 1 S.C.R. 911 at paras 36–38, the Court qualified its earlier judgments about the weight to be attached to oral testimony. In contrast, see *Delgamuukw, supra* note 1 at paras. 80–82.
[15] *Taku River Tlingit First Nation v. Ringstad* (2002), 211 D.L.R. (4th) 89, 2002 BCCA 59 [*Taku River Tlingit*]. See next note.
[16] *Haida Nation v. B.C.* (2002), 216 D.L.R. (4th) 1, 2002 BCCA 462 [*Haida Nation*]. As of the summer of 2004, the Supreme Court of Canada had heard arguments and reserved judgments on appeal from this decision and the decision in *Taku River Tlingit, ibid.*
[17] "Rights Ignored—Leaders; Chiefs 'Offended' Gov't Has Failed to Heed Court Rulings" *Edmonton Journal* (28 February 2001) A2.
[18] British Columbia Treaty Commission, Financial, online: BC Treaty Commission <bctreaty.net/files_2/issues_financial.html>.
[19] *Taku River Tlingit, supra* note 15 at para. 96.
[20] *Haida Nation, supra* note 16 at para. 78.
[21] *Ibid.* at para. 76.

[22] British Columbia Treaty Negotiation Office, *Provincial Policy for Consultation with First Nations* (2002) at 8, online: British Columbia <www.gov.bc.ca/tno/down/consultation_policy_fn.pdf> 8.

[23] *R. v. Sparrow*, [1990] 1 S.C.R. 1075.

[24] *Delgamuukw, supra* note 1 at para. 165.

[25] Personal interview, British Columbia government official, 21 February 2001.

[26] *Delgamuukw, supra* note 1 at para. 175.

[27] Marlie Beets, "First Nations Logging" (Presentation to the Vancouver Section of the Canadian Institute of Forestry and the Vancouver Wood Forum, November 1999), online: Council of Forest Industries <http://www.cofi.org/whatwedo/aboriginalaffairs-1999nov9.htm>.

[28] Personal interview, Ministry of Forests official, 22 February 2001.

[29] British Columbia, Treaty Commission, *Annual Report, 1999* (Vancouver: 2000), online: B.C. Treaty Commission <http://www.bctreaty.net/annuals_2/99_index.html> at 37.

[30] British Columbia, Ministry of Aboriginal Affairs, News Release, "Treaty-related Measures" online: Indian and Northern Affairs Canada <http://www.ainc-inac.gc.ca/nr/prs/m-a2000/00153bk_e.html>.

[31] British Columbia, Ministry of Aboriginal Affairs, *Information About Interim Measures* (Victoria: 1995).

[32] British Columbia, Treaty Commission, *Annual Report 2003: Where Are We* (Vancouver: 2004) at 5.

[33] British Columbia, Treaty Negotiation Office and Ministry of Forestry, News Release, "Funds to Enhance First Nation's Forestry Opportunities" (21 May 2003), online: <http://www2.news.gov.bc.ca/nrm_news_releases/2003TNO0020-000511.htm#>.

[34] McKee, *supra* note 6 at 78.

CONCLUSION

Judicial Aesthetics and Aboriginal Claims

*Kerry Wilkins**

Rarely, if ever, since Europeans started teeming into what we now call Canada have the prospects for Aboriginal peoples here been especially auspicious. The present is most certainly no exception.

True, Aboriginal peoples no longer have to engage in treaty negotiations in a language they do not understand, but that is not because the newcomers have learned, as good guests would have, the languages of the peoples that welcomed them; it is because they themselves have had to learn the language of the intruders. And even today, they must deal with the fact that the courts on whom they must depend for enforcement of these solemn agreements look first to a form of memorialization—a written text—that was itself foreign and inconsequential to them, and that often differs from their own very often carefully preserved understandings of what those agreements had been.

True, federal authorities no longer gather up Aboriginal children and take them to residential schools to learn the ways of the settler culture and the teachings of the locally dominant church at the expense of their own intellectual, cultural, and spiritual traditions. Those who were so gathered, their communities and descendants, however, live today with the consequences of that separation and that fragmentation, and with the legacy of the deeply personal invasions many suffered while being raised by strangers.

And true, the rest of us no longer smile quite so indulgently when Aboriginal peoples today assert claims to traditional lands or resources. That, however, is so in significant part because the Nisga'a,[1] the Musqueam,[2] the Gitksan, and the Wet'suwet'en,[3] who had grown weary of being patronized, chose to take the risks and expend the resources required for litigation. Their efforts convinced the courts that they had interests worthy of legal protection, interests that the federal Crown had enforceable legal duties to honour and protect.

In short, there are now somewhat fewer overt threats to what remains of the Aboriginal patrimony here, but the damage wrought to that patrimony has been extensive. Today, the Aboriginal peoples have less of it to preserve and, in some important ways, less wherewithal with which to seek to preserve it. It is, nonetheless, a tribute to their courage, and to the richness and the integrity of their social, spiritual, and cultural traditions, that they have preserved as much as they have in the face of such concerted, ongoing pressures of colonization and settlement. One wonders how many European national cultural traditions could have survived as well under such unforgiving circumstances.

This book has offered perspectives, legal arguments, and critical and strategic analysis, all with a view to assisting Aboriginal peoples and those who support them to find their way through their current predicaments. Aboriginal communities themselves, and those within them responsible for their survival and integrity, are, of course, the ones to make the key decisions they face day by day; they will use (or not) what is offered here as they think best. They should do the same with the brief remarks that follow.

WHEN AND WHY LITIGATION MATTERS

I want here to offer some further perspective on the prospects for Aboriginal claims in litigation and on some possible ways of improving them. Others in this volume have called proper attention to the shortcomings of litigation and to the risks that Aboriginal peoples face when they resort to it.[4] I do not disagree with them. But hardly anyone disputes that Aboriginal peoples living in Canada today operate from a position of considerable material disadvantage. When power is the issue, settler governments are the ones with public permission to enforce, and, in exceptional cases, to use force. When wealth is the issue, others, almost always, can afford to outbid or outspend Aboriginal peoples or communities. Aboriginal peoples have only the powers of persuasion and moral rectitude—and the law, which today affords them at least some capacity to contain the reach of wealth and government power. I do not suggest that this is fair. It is not. But while the newcomers are in charge, it is likely nonetheless to remain the reality within which any solutions emerge. For the foreseeable future, therefore, Aboriginal peoples are going to have to resort, as prudently and as smartly as they can, to litigation to preserve what they have or to gain what they believe is theirs.

To say this is not to overlook the value, or the frequent utility, of negotiated arrangements. For all the reasons rehearsed elsewhere in this book,[5] it is indeed preferable for parties, where possible, to resolve their differences consensually and amicably than to resort to a process that is by nature adversarial. In the present dispensation, however, consensual arrangements that are successful from an Aboriginal standpoint are going to continue to depend on further successes in litigation. In this, I agree with Len Rotman.[6] I believe this to be so for at least three reasons.

First, as Rotman has argued, the Crown has shown little or no inclination to negotiate—or to take more generous positions in negotiations—with Aboriginal peoples except when compelled to do so by circumstances or by unacceptable risks.[7] There are several reasons why this is so that do not require resort to aspersions of prejudice or conspiracy. For one thing, the task of governing Canada is, at the best of times, extremely challenging and would be so even if there were not, and never had been, any Aboriginal presence here. Aboriginal issues and concerns compete with a host of other matters for the government's time, attention, and resources. And those who design political agendas may well have noticed that Aboriginal people so far have not chosen to vote in numbers sufficient to affect the outcomes of federal elections. For another, a government has no particular reason to enter into negotiations with anyone, or to improve its offers in negotiations already underway, if it has reason to believe that it can achieve its objectives without taking on that extra burden or making some gratuitous concession. Finally, governments, being large and composed of people who, like most of us, derive some security from continuing what they're used to, typically take a long time to change positions and approaches even when it's quite clear to them that the present course (whatever it is) is not working. It often takes something quite major—such as a court decision—to awaken those in government (and others) from their dogmatic slumbers.

Second, governments can respond to the pressure of adverse litigation results, once final, without much loss of face or credibility. When faced with threats of violence, meaningful economic pressure, or even civil disobedience, on the other hand, governments typically feel compelled to refuse to negotiate, lest they seem weak or encourage similar threats from others. Judicial decisions emanating from the Queen's own courts have sufficient public and institutional legitimacy not to trigger nearly so much political or bureaucratic defensiveness.

Third and finally, judicial decisions sometimes help clarify not only what the law requires of governments in respect of Aboriginal peoples, but what is possible for them in the way of consensual arrangements. At present, the relevant law may still be too unclear to support certain kinds of negotiated arrangements between Aboriginal peoples and governments. Here is one example. Aboriginal groups and communities asserting treaty or Aboriginal rights to hunt in a given province sometimes ask the provincial government to show respect for the rights they claim by refraining from enforcing general hunting regulations against their members. Such a request is not one to which a provincial government can easily accede on the basis of a mere claim of right, even if its policy is to accommodate Aboriginal hunting activity. As long as the rule of law remains a fundamental (albeit unwritten) principle helping constitute the Canadian legal order,[8] governments will not have the option of agreeing in advance to dispense with the enforcement of laws that otherwise would apply to a given group or individual; in the absence of defensible legal reasons for doing so, they may not make a practice of applying their statutes and regulations differently to some people than to others.[9] A community's bare assertion that it has a treaty or Aboriginal right to hunt within the province is most unlikely, on its own, to count as a defensible legal reason for dispensing with the application of provincial hunting law. And the province, acting on its own, almost certainly does not have the constitutional authority to confer such a right by treaty on the community.[10] Only if the province's own best legal advice supports the community's claim of treaty or Aboriginal right is there a trustworthy legal or constitutional basis for the dispensation requested by the community. And because the soundness of claims of Aboriginal right, in particular, depends on the careful consideration of historical, and sometimes anthropological and archaeological, evidence,[11] few provincial government lawyers are likely to opine with confidence that the right asserted exists without the benefit of a judicial decision to that effect. Armed with a judicial decision accrediting the community's right to hunt on the relevant lands, however, the community and a willing province would have the legal foundation required to come to terms on subsequent enforcement and game resource management practice.

For all these reasons, a prudent Aboriginal community will probably want to consider litigating certain of its claims of treaty or Aboriginal right, even if, in a perfect world, it would prefer to sort out its differences with the Crown by agreement. In litigation, there is a key strategic dimension. In what follows, I offer some brief thoughts meant to help inform strategic reflection, especially on the prosecution of claims of treaty and Aboriginal right.

THREE PROPOSITIONS

Three propositions, I believe, fairly summarize the Supreme Court of Canada's disposition so far—both what it has done and what it has said—toward section 35 of the *Constitution Act, 1982*[12] and the claims that Aboriginal peoples have brought pursuant to it.

Providing Meaningful Protection to Section 35 Rights

First, the Court remains firmly committed to the proposition that treaty and Aboriginal rights are entitled to, and will receive, extensive and meaningful protection—protection that the Court itself considers extensive and meaningful—from the effects of government interference. If you doubt this, please consider at least the following evidence.

To begin with, at the time the Supreme Court decided *Sparrow*[13] in 1990, there was still room for reasonable doubt about whether section 35 afforded *any* new protection to treaty or Aboriginal rights, or whether it, like section 36[14] (or, for that matter, the *Canadian Bill of Rights*)[15] might be nothing more than another unenforceable constitutional statement of good intentions. There is no such doubt any more.

Consider too that the Supreme Court had other options before it when it elected at the same time to impose on governments the burden of proving assertions that treaty or Aboriginal rights have been extinguished, and to adopt a very stringent test for proof of extinguishment.[16] It has since reaffirmed that standard in cases where extinguishment was in issue.[17] I know of no case since *Sparrow* in which a government, or anyone, has argued successfully that an authenticated treaty or Aboriginal right has been extinguished.[18] (This includes the three opportunities the Court has already had and declined to endorse blanket extinguishment of any inherent rights of Aboriginal self-government.)[19] In *Delgamuukw*, a case involving a claim of Aboriginal title to lands the size of Nova Scotia, the Court concluded unanimously that the provinces have had no power since Confederation to extinguish Aboriginal rights or title, where such rights exist.[20]

In addition, the Court has cleared new space and given new weight in the law of evidence to traditional Aboriginal forms of oral record keeping.[21] In several cases already, the Court has reversed lower court decisions that would have given government regulations priority over treaty or Aboriginal rights.[22] I cannot think of a case in which the Supreme Court has held that particular measures restricting the exercise of an authenticated treaty or Aboriginal right were justified. It has removed any lingering doubt that Métis are capable, as Métis, of having and exercising constitutionally protected Aboriginal rights.[23] Finally, and most recently, the Supreme Court, in *Okanagan*,[24] authorized trial judges, in appropriate circumstances, to award court costs before the trial against the Crown to impecunious Aboriginal parties bringing rights or title claims.

This is not the conduct of a court unconcerned about protecting Aboriginal peoples' treaty or Aboriginal rights. I see every reason to expect that the Supreme Court will continue to mandate protection for demonstrable Aboriginal and treaty rights from government measures or government conduct whose impact on such rights it considers unnecessary or excessive.

Respecting Benign Non-Aboriginal Interests
On the other hand, the Court is, if anything, even more firmly disposed to ensure that section 35 itself, and the judiciary's own interpretations of it, not interfere inappropriately[25] with the proper and necessary business of government generally or with the interests, concerns, and lives of private non-Aboriginal persons who played no part in the disadvantage that Aboriginal peoples in Canada have suffered. (If you doubt this, compare the number of times since *Marshall* that the Supreme Court has given an Aboriginal party leave to appeal an unfavourable decision involving a claim of section 35 right[26] with the number of occasions on which it has given leave to the Crown or a non-Aboriginal party from a lower court decision favourable to a section 35 right.[27] The disparity says something interesting about the Court's current view of "public importance."[28]) Many Aboriginal people may well find it outrageous that interests acquired at their expense by colonial settlers,

their governments, and their descendants should count today as sufficient reason to limit their own belatedly acquired constitutional protection from colonial interference. Fair enough. But like it or not, the fact of non-Aboriginal presence throughout Canada, and the *prima facie* innocence of that presence, are givens that suffuse the Supreme Court's approach to disputes involving Aboriginal claims of right; they are, from the Court's standpoint, something not to be mourned, but necessarily to be acknowledged. ("Let us face it," Chief Justice Lamer has famously said, "we are all here to stay.")[29] This is so, in my judgment, for at least three reasons.

One is that Supreme Court judges remain, to a person, upper middle-class non-Aboriginal individuals who are, by training, personal history, and perhaps inclination, more familiar and comfortable with mainstream rhythms and institutions than they are with the rhythms and ordering principles characteristic of Aboriginal communities. In closely contested disputes involving Aboriginal claims, they appreciate prereflectively much more clearly what is at stake for the broader non-Aboriginal community than what is at stake for the integrity of the Aboriginal community advancing the claim. Their intuitions about the authenticity (or lack thereof) of governments' and non-Aboriginal people's apprehensions are certain to be sharper and more accurate than their intuitions about the authenticity of Aboriginal peoples' representations about their own communities, or about the current efficacy of those communities' traditional patterns of social control and ordering, patterns capable, perhaps, of curbing the kinds of excesses about which non-Aboriginal people sometimes speculate. This discrepancy is a result, in large part, of the judges' probable personal unfamiliarity with the subtleties and the richness of the traditional Aboriginal teachings (in this, I agree with Sákéj Henderson):[30] an unfamiliarity it will be difficult for them, as appellate judges bound to the evidentiary record brought before them, to dispel all at once, or anytime soon. Greater familiarity with the rhythms and details of the traditions it is being asked to protect will no doubt ameliorate the Court's caution about the unknown, but such familiarity and trust can develop only gradually.

Another reason is that courts generally regard themselves (and many others also regard them) as the guardians of the entire Canadian legal and constitutional order—an order they perceive, rightly or wrongly, to include Canada's Aboriginal peoples and their institutions—and they take that responsibility extremely seriously.[31] Section 35 and the protection it affords is, of course, a part of that order, and the Court has said so.[32] But section 35, as drafted, is also unusually open-ended; as such, it has potential to countenance truly dramatic change.[33] This need not in itself be a bad thing, except perhaps where the change it engenders is inadvertent, unintended. The Supreme Court, I strongly suspect, understands itself to be charged with the task of ensuring that section 35 continues to address the backlog of Aboriginal exploitation, but in a way that harmonizes with, and does not jeopardize, the fundamental values and expectations that have given meaning and a sense of legitimacy to mainstream Canadian life.[34]

A final, related reason is that the Court may expect to find these duties of guardianship much more difficult in the absence of widespread public confidence in the soundness and judiciousness of its decisions. The public outcry that followed the Supreme Court's decision in *Marshall*[35] quite probably surprised, and very probably alarmed, the Court. (How else are we to understand its virtually unprecedented decision to issue reasons for judgment in *Marshall II*,[36] an intervener's (!) application for reconsideration of *Marshall* that ordinarily would have been dealt with summarily, and without reasons, from the bench?)[37] The intensely negative character of that public response may well have persuaded the Court that it could be jeopardizing its own institutional authority if its decisions, no matter how sound doctrinally, were perceived to ask too much all at once of non-Aboriginal peoples.

The tension should be obvious between these first two propositions that I believe inform the Supreme Court's approach to Aboriginal peoples' claims of constitutional right. On the one hand, the Court conscientiously intends to ensure that section 35 continues to afford meaningful and substantial protection to the commitments made to Aboriginal peoples in treaties and to the features essential to traditional Aboriginal societies. On the other hand, there is, in the Court's view, a critical residue of legitimate non-Aboriginal presence—an irreducible minimum of governmental authority and private rights, interests, and expectations—that it feels it must protect from the risk of displacement or dislocation, even at the expense of the rights section 35 protects. Different judges will explicate these competing imperatives differently; all seem committed to the view that it is possible to achieve some stable homeostasis between them.

Maintaining Ongoing Doctrinal Flexibility

The third proposition is that the Supreme Court seems concerned above all to keep its options open in dealing with the cases that come before it: to maximize its ongoing flexibility to do proper justice in each case individually. If very little, so far, is certain about the Canadian law of Aboriginal and treaty rights, that is because the Court's members seem to recognize that their intuitions about these matters are in many respects not yet refined enough or trustworthy enough to support general legal rules or firm doctrinal pronouncements—that, in respect of these matters at least, there are more things in heaven and earth than are dreamt of in its jurisprudence. Mindful of both the immense importance of these issues for all concerned and the immense variety of possible section 35 scenarios that might well arise for decision—of real and possible treaty provisions; of traditional practices or arrangements that might be integral to particular Aboriginal societies; of ways of affecting or constraining the use of treaty or Aboriginal rights; of policy objectives offered to justify such constraints; and of means of fulfilling those objectives with or without restricting (so much) the exercise of such rights—the Court has taken great care in its judgments to keep the ball in play: to keep from closing the door on rights claims or on justifications that might, on closer inspection and in proper context, seem to have merit.

This cautious pragmatism is evident in the Court's treatment of claims asserting rights of self-government—not yet saying "yes," but making a point of not saying "no"[38]—but not only there. There is still a provisional quality about much of what Supreme Court decisions have held about claims of section 35 right. When the test prescribed in *Van der Peet* for use in the identification of Aboriginal rights[39] seemed unsuited for claims of Aboriginal title and for Métis rights claims, the Court felt free, in *Delgamuukw* and *Powley* respectively, to depart from it and to offer different, somewhat more generous tests it considered better suited to those circumstances.[40] When the rigorous test for justification the Court had prescribed in *Sparrow*[41] appeared to have consequences it considered unacceptable for Aboriginal rights to engage in commercial activity and for Aboriginal title, the Court proceeded, in *Gladstone*[42] and in *Delgamuukw*,[43] respectively, to distinguish *Sparrow* and to prescribe a different, more generous justification standard, one that allowed for greater weight to be given to competing non-Aboriginal interests.[44] When the Court's pronouncements in *Delgamuukw* about the admissibility and weight of Aboriginal oral evidence[45] had consequences in *Mitchell* that the Court considered excessive, it revisited the earlier formulation and restated it more narrowly.[46] After rejecting, in *Van der Peet*, the suggestion that an Aboriginal right to engage in commercial activity could be characterized as a limited right to earn a moderate livelihood,[47] the Court, in *Marshall*, imported that very notion into an implied treaty right to harvest for sale.[48] Finally (my favourite example), the Court has held, in two decisions now, both that the provinces may infringe existing Aboriginal rights if they can justify the infringement in the usual way[49] and that Aboriginal rights and title are among the matters at the core of exclusive federal legislative authority under section 91(24) of the *Constitution Act, 1867*,[50] a conclusion that, on traditional principles, would have rendered such rights all but immune from the restrictive effects even of provincial measures that are valid and justifiable.[51]

An uncharitable commentator might characterize such jurisprudence as inconsistent, or even as unprincipled. This characterization has some legitimate appeal, especially to those (of whatever persuasion) who find planning much more difficult when the law is uncertain and unpredictable. (Lower courts, which must apply Supreme Court pronouncements as precedent even as the Supreme Court itself is refining its own intuitions and formulations, may find their predicament either frustrating, because this law still wants for coherence, or liberating, because it still offers such a rich array of conclusions that can claim anchorage in binding authority.) Be this as it may, it seems to me wise for those contemplating entering treaty or Aboriginal rights litigation to act, for the foreseeable future, as though that domain bears a sign that says "Under Construction; we apologize for any temporary inconvenience." And to be fair, there is something admirably conscientious about a court so concerned to avoid falling prey to the unexpected and untenable consequences of unreflective doctrinal consistency.

STRATEGIC LESSONS FROM THESE PROPOSITIONS

Three dispositions, then, appear to characterize the Supreme Court's approach to section 35 rights and jurisprudence: (1) a paramount disposition not to jeopardize the "skeleton of principle"[52] that holds the mainstream legal and constitutional order together and to leave enough room for both the usual functions of mainstream governance and the usual array of private enterprise and activity, where otherwise permissible; (2) a subordinate but resolute disposition to protect from unfair, unnecessary, or excessive interference the rights contained in the treaties and the truly essential traditional features of life in Aboriginal communities; and (3) a strong disposition to avoid doctrinal commitments that could compromise its capacity to reconcile the first two dispositions fairly and justly, case by case.

If this brief description of things is sound, what can prudent Aboriginal communities and their supporters do to maximize their likelihood of success in court in litigating claims of treaty or Aboriginal right? Several lessons—some obvious, some less so—seem to me to follow from it.

To begin with, it makes strategic sense for Aboriginal peoples making section 35 claims to take care to present themselves and their claims in ways, and in circumstances, that will maximize their attractiveness to mainstream Canadian judges.[53] In my experience, courts receive such claims most favourably when judges believe that outsiders—but especially governments—are taking unfair advantage of the claimant Aboriginal community. The most successful claims for constitutional protection, therefore, are those that seem to courts to be the most reasonable. Reasonableness here has several discrete components. Some pertain to the claim considered individually; others, to the larger setting in which the individual claims are perceived and appraised.

The Attractiveness of Individual Claims
One crucial indicator of the reasonableness of a claim for constitutional protection is proof of the importance to the claimant community of the interest, practice,

custom, or arrangement for which it is seeking protection. Where the interest is one that can be shown to be protected by treaty, this is not difficult. Courts now routinely accept that Aboriginal parties to treaties are entitled to expect the Crown to keep the treaty promises it made to them, as the Aboriginal parties might reasonably have understood those promises at the time the treaty was made.[54] In respect of Aboriginal rights, however, the issue is more complex, and more controversial. The Supreme Court's insistence in *Van der Peet* that Aboriginal rights (apart from Aboriginal title) include only that which has traditionally been "integral to the distinctive culture" of the claimant community[55] has come in for a good deal of astute and considered criticism,[56] but it does reflect, if perhaps too clumsily or overzealously, a strong sense that the constitution should not be understood to give Aboriginal peoples (or anyone else) licence to do just whatever they might want. If Aboriginal rights are unique to Aboriginal peoples, the sentiment is that such rights should protect only that which is unique to them as Aboriginal peoples.[57] This being so, it stands to reason that the courts will generally be most disposed to accord—and disposed to accord the most—constitutional protection to those features of life that they judge to be most important, and most particular, to the heritage and the integrity of the relevant Aboriginal community. Screening for matters integral to the cultures of such communities is an imperfect but serviceable way of making this appraisal.

It follows that the success of claims of section 35 right is going to depend in significant part on the depth and the soundness of their evidentiary foundation. The stronger a given claim's factual basis—the better the evidence demonstrating the nature and the importance of the candidate practice or arrangement to the heritage of the claimant community—when viewed from the standpoint of the traditional laws of evidence, the more difficult it will be for a court to reject it. It is true that the courts have approved admission and consideration in the adjudication of Aboriginal claims of forms of evidence that, from a judge's perspective, may seem unusual,[58] and that the Supreme Court has allowed appeals from decisions in which lower courts have declined to give such evidence sufficient faith and credit.[59] As *Mitchell* makes quite clear, however, the Supreme Court is still unsure about how to use and how much to trust such unfamiliar evidence and is exercising, and therefore encouraging, caution about claims whose authentication depends on acceptance of it.[60] The courts have much more experience, and therefore greater comfort, with the forms of factual proof to which they are accustomed. Reliance on forms of proof that judges still find unfamiliar introduces additional risk into the prosecution of an Aboriginal claim. In such situations, the likelihood that such evidence will suffice is apt to depend much more on how attractive—on how reasonable—the courts perceive the claim to be in other respects.

Apart from the inquiry into importance, a claim's attractiveness, from the standpoint of judicial aesthetics, is probably going to turn on at least three other kinds of considerations: considerations of proportionality, of discreteness, and of what one might call, with some irony, authenticity.

"Authenticity," in the ironic sense in which I use it here, measures how closely the right being claimed comports with judges' (often uninformed) preconceptions about what kinds of activity are "Aboriginal." A community claiming an Aboriginal right to hunt or fish for food[61] stands a better chance of success today than a community claiming an Aboriginal right to, say, raise funds by operating a public gambling venue[62] because non-Aboriginal Canadians conventionally associate hunting and fishing for subsistence, but not public gambling enterprises, with what they understand to be the "Aboriginal" lifestyle. Such preconceptions mean that the chain of inference required today to demonstrate that the candidate practice or arrangement is integral to the life of the claimant community is much shorter in the case of the subsistence harvesting. I do not mean to suggest that all judges harbour such stereotypes, or that those who do cannot be brought, given time, exposure, and experience, to abandon them, but only that some of them may very well and have not been, respectively. If true, this observation suggests that there may be prudence in tendering first for accreditation as section 35 rights those practices and arrangements most likely to strike non-Aboriginal Canadians as "authentically Aboriginal," reserving till later the claims whose acceptance may turn upon a better informed and more nuanced appreciation of the textures of historic and contemporary Aboriginal societies.

Proportionality, for its part, measures how the right being claimed is sized to fit the occasion that gives rise to the claim and the facts that are offered in its support. It means that the claim neither overreaches, seeking protection for vastly more than seems warranted by its evidentiary basis or by the circumstances giving rise to the litigation,[63] nor artificially understates the reach or the implications of the right for which accreditation is sought.[64]

Finally, discreteness measures the "containability" of a candidate right: the degree to which the court can plausibly circumscribe (to its own satisfaction) the boundaries of the right being claimed and limit its impact on life outside the community. The narrower the discernible scope of a candidate right, the more comfortable a court will be in accrediting it and the more attractive the claim of right will therefore be.

These propositions too suggest the prudence of an incremental approach: one that begins by establishing section 35 rights that are relatively narrow and tailored, then demonstrating, through experience of their responsible use, that they do not pose an unmanageable threat to the Canadian legal system or to the ordinary preoccupations of non-Aboriginal Canadians. After such a period of familiarization and relative comfort, the courts might very well be more receptive to some of the more ambitious claims of section 35 right, claims that today they might consider quite radical. The strategic challenge is to find the right pace at which to increase the mainstream system's tolerance for constitutionally protected Aboriginal difference. This prompts two more specific intuitions: one affirmative, the other cautionary.

Perhaps the most important way to enhance the attractiveness to judges of a particular claim of section 35 right is to demonstrate, on the evidence, that the candidate right is subject to, or even partly constituted by, effective, ascertainable community measures that govern, limit and can control engagement in it. The broader the prima facie scope of the right the community claims, the more its chances of judicial accreditation seem likely to turn on the presence or absence of such mechanisms of internal community discipline prescribing and preserving its boundaries. Demonstration of such constraints signals that the community has reasons and means of its own to protect and police the integrity of the practice or the arrangement in its own society, and affords the court criteria—procedural protocols, substantive standards, or both—that it can use from outside to distinguish protected from unprotected instances of the relevant activity. The protected ones are those observant of the community's own internal constraints.

Elucidating the network of responsibilities that situate a candidate right within the community's ordering rhythms can turn a scary looking claim of right whose reach seems potentially unlimited into something a court will consider more harmonious within the Canadian constitutional order. It will not, however, suffice for this purpose merely to assure the courts that they can "trust us" not to abuse the right as claimed. For one thing, the stakes in section 35 litigation are high. For another, non-Aboriginal judges are still too unfamiliar with the experience of Aboriginal ordering to feel sufficiently confident to take any such assurances on faith. They will need to be shown. Neither, as *Mitchell* indicates, will it suffice to affix strategically convenient constraints to the scope of a candidate right. Unless such constraints appear to emerge organically from the heritage and the collective mandate of the community, the court is apt to find them arbitrary and perhaps to suspect that it is being managed.[65] And there are few things courts like less than the perception that they are being managed.

The cautionary intuition is that phrasing a claim in terms of Aboriginal sovereignty is almost certain to jeopardize, perhaps fatally, its chances of success.[66] By this I do not mean either to suggest that Aboriginal peoples in North America are not sovereign or to deny the force of the arguments that one might use in support of their claims to sovereignty; those are completely separate inquiries. My point here is that Canadian courts are not, for the foreseeable future, a prudent place to be tendering such claims, whatever substantive merits such claims may have. It is in the very nature of claims of Aboriginal sovereignty to challenge the reach, the legitimacy—indeed, the very foundations—of mainstream Canadian governance and judicial authority, at least in respect of Aboriginal peoples. For this reason alone, non-Aboriginal judges are apt to find such claims lacking in both discreteness and proportionality, and therefore uncongenial.[67] But even if this were not the case, the courts would face compelling doctrinal pressure not to take it upon themselves to accredit such claims. In the first place, it is not open to them as judges to entertain doubts about the reality or the legitimacy of Crown sovereignty, because their own jurisdiction derives entirely from, and is coextensive with, Crown sovereignty.[68] They are, quite literally, the queen's courts, dispensing justice in her name and pursuant to her authority. Whether or not it is true to say that "there was from the outset never any doubt that sovereignty . . . vested in the Crown,"[69] Canadian courts, in exercising jurisdiction over a matter, proceed necessarily on the basis of the truth of that premise. Apart from it, they have no more jurisdiction than private individuals deliberating together about right and wrong. Second, questions about the sovereignty (or lack thereof) of other collectivities are understood to be matters for political, not legal, determination. ("[S]overeignty," the Supreme Court of Canada said recently, "is a political fact for which no purely legal authority can be constituted. . . .")[70] When such matters arise for decision in the course of domestic proceedings, our courts refer them to the federal executive and accept as dispositive the position communicated by the federal minister responsible.[71] Until, therefore, the federal government chooses on its own to affirm the sovereignty of Aboriginal nations occupying territory now considered Canadian, domestic courts have no obvious place to stand from which to do so themselves.

The Broader Context of Appraisal

The discussion so far has focused on the features of individual claims of section 35 right that operate to make them more or less attractive to the courts. But much can depend, as well, on the larger legal and constitutional context. It is within that larger context, not in abstraction from it, that the courts will be appraising the attractiveness—the reasonableness, by their lights—of the particular claims. Because the doctrinal foundations for section 35 jurisprudence are still in some respects malleable, Aboriginal litigants still have some real capacity to shape, even as they present their claims of section 35 right, the framework within which those claims will be measured. This fact gives rise to some very difficult strategic choices.

One example should serve to make the point. What power, if any, do provinces have to regulate, even through justified measures, the exercise of section 35 rights? Although we know that such rights are susceptible to constraint through justified federal measures, the status of justified provincial measures is still in dispute. Elsewhere, I (and others) have argued that the provinces have no power, except in a few very special circumstances, to regulate—even through justified measures—Indians' exercise of section 35 rights, because such rights lie at the core of exclusive federal authority over "Indians, and Lands reserved for the Indians."[72] Others maintain that the provinces may indeed regulate in justified ways the use of such rights.[73] As noted above, the Supreme Court decisions to date have supported both positions simultaneously.[74] They probably cannot continue to do so indefinitely.

In these circumstances, more than usual may depend on the arguments offered by Aboriginal litigants. Where do the interests of Aboriginal peoples lie in this controversy? Suppose, for example, that the provinces turn out to have no power to control either the exercise of Indians' section 35 rights or the lands that prove to be subject to Indians' Aboriginal title. From one standpoint, it is difficult to imagine a more substantial, or a more symbolically significant, victory for rights-bearing Aboriginal communities. Not only will they be able to exercise their constitutional rights irrespective of provincial displeasure and to assert those rights against future or proposed provincial measures that would limit or jeopardize their exercise; they will also have a basis in law on which to contest much that the provinces have done in previous years, especially in respect of lands that have been subject all along to Aboriginal title. Those who for years have acted on the assumption that their provincial Crown patents, licences, leases, and authorizations were valid and all they needed may find that they were mistaken: that their interests are subject to, and limited by, prior unextinguished section 35 rights or interests and that the province can do nothing about it.[75]

The problem is that these consequences (and the attendant risk, given federal inaction, of a regulatory vacuum here in mainstream law) are unlikely to escape the attention even of courts and judges that may feel bound by doctrinal consistency to endorse this result. And when this realization dawns, it is likely to prompt in them a profound disquiet. The stakes in the game of section 35 adjudication will abruptly have been raised dramatically. It would hardly be surprising if this outcome had what legal economists call a "substitution effect,"[76] prompting judges thereafter to scrutinize with extra special care the credentials of all subsequent claims of section 35 right. The risk, in other words, is that securing such robust protection for section 35 rights will mean, in practice if not in articulated judicial reasoning, that there will be substantially fewer of them, and that those few that do survive the more exacting scrutiny will receive protection through a much narrower range of activity. Existing tests for identification and definition of such rights leave the courts ample play for such retrenchment. The effect of success on this point, therefore, could very well be to create a climate in which all claims of section 35 right become a good deal less attractive. In comparison, the contrary approach—that such rights are subject to some provincial management where such management can, by the judges' standards, be justified—dilutes the constitutional protection that might otherwise have been available to existing treaty and Aboriginal rights. By doing so, however, it renders less heroic, and therefore more palatable, the enterprise of giving effect and giving scope to such rights in mainstream law.

It is hardly surprising, either, that different Aboriginal groups claiming section 35 rights and seeking constitutional protection from provincial measures have approached in different ways the issue of provincial regulatory capacity. Some have been content so far not to raise the generic issue of provincial capacity, preferring to argue only that the relevant provincial measures do not satisfy the Supreme Court's tests for justified infringement.[77] Others have featured the issue of division of powers infirmity prominently in their claims and legal arguments.[78] It may be worth acknowledging, though, that once the Supreme Court decides this issue—and it will decide this issue—the result will govern thereafter all "Indian"[79] collectivities that assert, or seek to rely on, existing treaty or Aboriginal rights. The same is true of other generic issues about such rights and their place within the Canadian constitutional framework.

This being so, it may well make good sense for the Aboriginal collectivities contemplating asserting such rights to deliberate together about how best to approach these generic "climatological" issues. The women's movement in Canada has achieved some considerable success in *Charter* litigation by deliberating, through the Women's Legal Education and Action Fund (LEAF), on the kinds of doctrinal developments that would optimize the options and the protection available to women within Canadian law, and by thinking strategically about how best to secure those outcomes in the longer term.[80] Such thinking comprises, among other things: reflection on the relative merits of litigation among other means of achieving particular ends from time to time; careful attention, case by case, to the risks and advantages of seeking big wins or incremental gains; and, by no means least, attunement to questions of timing and sequence in the presentation of legal issues to the courts for decision. The goal is to share resources to ensure, as much as possible, that courts not encounter women's issues except in circumstances in which the judges will already be disposed to welcome them and in which the facts and legal arguments can be presented attractively.

To the best of my knowledge, Aboriginal groups in Canada have no comparable mechanisms through which to reinforce one another and to coordinate efforts. (The Crown, provincial and federal, by contrast, does devote considerable time and resources to coordinating its Aboriginal litigation and to trying to reconcile its positions in litigation with its objectives, from time to time, in negotiation.) I have long thought that a nationwide Aboriginal body comparable to LEAF might have real value in helping develop and implement a strategy aimed at maximizing the breadth and depth of section 35's protection of Aboriginal ways of life. Such a body could contribute strategic discipline to current, more or less fragmented, efforts to litigate section 35 claims, in part by helping identify, at any given time, the claims that afford Aboriginal peoples the greatest prospect of collective cumulative success and that, from a strategic standpoint, therefore most deserve collective support. The want of such coordination and cooperation has probably left some Aboriginal groups without sufficient resources to substantiate promising claims as fully as those claims might deserve and require. It has definitely resulted, from the Aboriginal standpoint, in some truly frightening risks to the shape of section 35 jurisprudence. It was, for instance, nothing short of astonishing, from a strategic perspective, that the Supreme Court of Canada first encountered the notion of a constitutional right of self-government as a defence to prosecutions for high-stakes public gaming activities.[81] Say what you will about the importance of securing constitutional space for Aboriginal economic development, one can hardly imagine a less attractive setting than a monster bingo operation in which to introduce an audience of non-Aboriginal judges to Aboriginal peoples' inherent rights of self-government. Many of us held our breath when we heard of this in the mid-1990s, fearing that the very future of self-government jurisprudence in Canada hung in the balance. It speaks well of the Supreme Court that it exercised some restraint in its remarks there about self-government rights.

Finally, it would probably be unwise, from a strategic standpoint, to overlook entirely the impact of the relevant academic literature on the larger jurisprudential climate within which courts encounter section 35 claims. One must, of course, begin any such inquiry by acknowledging, first, that legal scholars have no obligation to be strategic and second, that it is far from clear what impact legal scholarship has on judicial deliberations, either generally or in respect of Aboriginal issues. On the other hand, it seems clear that many academics writing on Aboriginal issues in Canada do so in the hope, and with the intention, of making some affirmative practical difference on behalf of Aboriginal peoples in the developing mainstream jurisprudence. Insofar as this is true, it makes sense to consider the strategic impact of such material.

Imagine that you are counsel for an Aboriginal community that seeks the constitution's protection from certain government measures for some particular favoured arrangement or practice. You have assembled all the evidence available in support of the claim but now face the tasks of getting all that evidence before the court of first instance, of demonstrating that it entitles your client to an Aboriginal right—one with whose exercise the relevant government measures interfere—and of deflecting government efforts to justify any such interference. All this you must do within the framework of the existing Supreme Court jurisprudence on section 35. Suppose, finally, that no binding precedent clearly establishes your client's entitlement to the decision and the remedy it seeks: that your client's success or failure depends on the way in which your court applies the Supreme Court jurisprudence to your facts. You turn for assistance to the academic literature. What do you hope to find there?

About the last thing, surely, that you hope to find in the literature is a spate of critical writings that emphasize how unfavourable the Supreme Court's jurisprudence has been for Aboriginal peoples. If you need to have your court admit and consider certain unconventional forms of evidence, it will not help you to find and cite writings that elucidate how narrow the Supreme Court's approach to such evidence seems. If your chances of getting your client's claim of right accredited depend on persuading your judge to take an expansive view of the current rules for identification and proof, it will not help you to find authoritative, well-reasoned pieces that criticize the Supreme Court for having made it so difficult for Aboriginal peoples ever to establish such rights. And if you need to repel the government's efforts at justification, it will not help you to keep reading in the journals how generous the rules for justifying infringements of your client's rights have become. None of this is going to help you make and support the legal arguments that your client's position requires. What will help you are materials that emphasize and document the flexibility open to you, and to courts, within the existing law to tender and to entertain your relevant evidence and to give effect to your client's claims of Aboriginal right, and materials that identify and explicate the full gravity of the Supreme Court's justification requirements.

Unfortunately, in my experience, relatively little of the academic writing on section 35 rights is apt to assist you, as counsel, very much. A good deal of it may even inadvertently help the Crown or other non-Aboriginal interests oppose your client's claim, precisely because it features and accentuates the negative in the developing jurisprudence.

At issue here is not the substantive merit or the accuracy of such scholarly criticism of the section 35 jurisprudence. I often find myself in agreement with the negative critique; I too regret, for reasons often similar to those given in the journals, many of the choices the Supreme Court has made in giving effect to section 35. My concern here is only with the impact of such criticism on Aboriginal peoples' prospects for success with section 35 claims in the courts. And my point is only that scholars writing on these issues with a view to improving Aboriginal peoples' circumstances should reflect as they do so on the predicament in which their writings may leave Aboriginal litigants. When academics persist in characterizing the existing law as excessively unfavourable to Aboriginal peoples, the risk is that their characterizations may prove self-fulfilling.[82]

CONCLUSION

I want, in closing, to acknowledge a fair and obvious criticism of this entire discussion. My aim has been to offer Aboriginal peoples contemplating section 35 litigation some helpful generic observations about the perspectives and the propensities of the judges entrusted with their claims. In doing so, I have placed entirely to one side the needs, perspectives, problems, and exigencies of the actual Aboriginal communities that may be contemplating litigation.[83] In the real world, such communities do not themselves have that luxury. They do not, for example, always have as much control as they'd like over when and how their rights claims come before courts. One of their members may decide independently to assert a particular treaty or Aboriginal right in defence to a prosecution for some provincial or federal offence. Limitation periods sometimes require that a certain claim be brought now, or not at all. All too often, Aboriginal communities feel they must respond with section 35 litigation, whether or not they feel quite ready, when government or private activity threatens some interest, practice, or arrangement that they consider pivotal. And Aboriginal litigants generally must make do with the typically very limited resources available to them to pay for and conduct the litigation. Any or all of these circumstances may sometimes necessitate departures from the strategic desiderata that I have offered here.

So be it. My purpose has not been to criticize Aboriginal groups—who often proceed from within conditions more difficult than anything I have ever had to face—for conducting their section 35 litigation as best they can. My only purpose has been to invite such groups to take realistic and deliberate account, when and as they are able to do so in preparing their litigation, of the evident concerns and propensities of their non-Aboriginal judges. Doing so, in my judgment, will improve materially their chances of long-term success.

A more profound and related question is why Aboriginal peoples should feel reduced, in their efforts to obtain enforcement of the rights that have been theirs all along, to keep paying such solicitous attention to the sensitivities of the intruders who have displaced them and colonized their lands. The history of Canada, after all, is not replete with occasions on which the settlers and their descendants paid respectful, or really any, attention to the constitutive rhythms and understandings of their Aboriginal hosts. Quite the contrary. And the notion that Aboriginal peoples' best hope for justice today may lie in some exemplary attentiveness to their colonizers' fears is one that they may legitimately find galling. How convenient it must seem for someone in my position to be suggesting it.

I accept and respect this objection. There probably are irreducible tensions between the rhythms and currents that characterize litigation and those that constitute the various Aboriginal cultures and world views. Aboriginal peoples, left to their own devices, have always done justice somewhat differently from

Europeans and their descendants.[84] Even participating in mainstream judicial institutions is to some extent a compromise of traditional Aboriginal ways. The greater the sense of compromise, the better the reason for Aboriginal peoples to eschew litigation, where the option is theirs.

No one should pursue litigation unless already informed by a realistic ongoing sense of the limits of legal possibility and by an appreciation of the strain that litigation, by its nature, generates. Litigation is, in every sense, a trying business, not one to be undertaken without deliberation. Despite all this, there are times when Aboriginal peoples themselves conclude that litigation is a prudent and suitable means through which to try to achieve particular ends. (The fact that this seems to happen so often is still further proof that this is not an especially auspicious time to be an Aboriginal person in the territory now called Canada.) Once they have reached that conclusion, it makes some sense for them to approach that effort in a way that minimizes the risks of failure.

NOTES

* Special thanks to Eileen Hipfner for her careful reading of and judicious comments on an earlier version of this paper. Remaining mistakes and infelicities are, as usual, despite her best efforts.

[1] See *Calder v. British Columbia (A.G.)*, [1973] S.C.R. 313.

[2] See *Guerin v. Canada*, [1984] 2 S.C.R. 335; *R. v. Sparrow*, [1990] 1 S.C.R. 1075 [*Sparrow*].

[3] See *R. v. Nikal*, [1996] 1 S.C.R. 1013 [*Nikal*]; *Delgamuukw v. British Columbia*, [1997] 3 S.C.R. 1010 [*Delgamuukw*].

[4] See in particular the essays by Patricia Monture, Chris Manfredi, Len Rotman, Gordon Christie, and Gurston Dacks in this volume.

[5] See in particular Rotman, *ibid.,* and Dacks, *ibid.*

[6] See Rotman, *ibid.* at 203, 207, 214, 226–28.

[7] *Ibid.*

[8] See *Reference re Secession of Quebec*, [1998] 2 S.C.R. 217 at paras. 70–78 [*Quebec Secession Reference*].

[9] *Ibid.*; *R. v. Catagas* (1977), 38 C.C.C. (2d) 296 (Man. C.A.); A.V. Dicey, *Introduction to the Study of the Law of the Constitution*, 8th ed. (Indianapolis: Liberty Classics, 1982) at 114–15, 268–73.

[10] This is certainly true in respect of treaties that involve surrenders of Aboriginal interests in land; the Supreme Court has made it explicit that only the federal order of government has authority to accept such surrenders: see *Delgamuukw*, *supra* note 3 at para. 175. The court has also signalled clearly that rights set out in Indian treaties are within the core of exclusive federal authority under s. 91(24) of the *Constitution Act, 1867* (U.K.), 30 & 31 Vict., c. 3, reprinted in R.S.C. 1985, App. II, No. 5: see *e.g. R. v. Simon*, [1985] 2 S.C.R. 387 at 411 [*Simon*] ("It has been held to be within the exclusive power of Parliament under s. 91(24) of the *Constitution Act, 1867*, to derogate from rights recognized in a treaty agreement made with the Indians"); *R. v. White and Bob* (1964), 50 D.L.R. (2d) 613 (B.C.C.A.), aff'd [1965] S.C.R. vi, (1965), 52 D.L.R. (2d) 481 (S.C.C.). For very recent authority to similar effect, see *R. v. Morris and Olsen* (2004), 237 D.L.R. (4th) 693, 2004 BCCA 121 [*Morris and Olsen*] at paras. 16–25, Lambert J.A., and para. 200, Huddart J.A., leave to appeal to S.C.C. granted [2004] S.C.C. Bulletin 1680, [2004] S.C.C.A. No. 199 (QL).

[11] See *e.g. R. v. Van der Peet*, [1996] 2 S.C.4. 507 at paras. 44–75 [*Van der Peet*] (proof of Indian Aboriginal rights requires proof that a given custom, practice, or tradition was integral to the distinctive culture of the Aboriginal community asserting the right at its moment of first contact with Europeans); *Delgamuukw*, *ibid.* at paras. 143–59 (proof of Aboriginal title requires proof that

the claimant community had exclusive occupation of the relevant lands at the moment the Crown asserted sovereignty over those lands).

[12] *Constitution Act, 1982*, being Schedule B of the *Canada Act 1982* (U.K.), 1982, c. 11.

[13] *Supra* note 2.

[14] S. 36 of the *Constitution Act, 1982* declares that Parliament, the provincial legislatures, and the federal and provincial governments "are committed to" the principle of equalization payments and to the goal of reducing regional disparities in opportunity, economic development, and essential public services. I know of no decision that has held that s. 36 gives rise to justiciable obligations on the part of any government.

[15] S.C. 1960, c. 44, reprinted in R.S.C. 1985, App. III.

[16] See *Sparrow, supra* note 2 at 1095–99.

[17] See *e.g. R. v. Gladstone*, [1996] 2 S.C.R. 723 at paras. 31–38 [*Gladstone*]; *Delgamuukw, supra* note 3 at paras. 172–83. The Ontario Court of Appeal has cited with approval earlier authority to the effect that satisfaction of the test for proof of extinguishment requires "'clear evidence that [the government] actually considered the conflict between its intended action on the one hand and Indian treaty rights on the other, and chose to resolve that conflict by abrogating the treaty or right": *Chippewas of Sarnia Band v. Canada (A.G.)* (2000), 51 O.R. (3d) 641 (C.A.) at para. 240 [*Sarnia*].

[18] In *R. v. Horseman*, [1990] 1 S.C.R. 901 [*Horseman*], a decision issued about a month before *Sparrow, supra* note 2, a bare majority of the Supreme Court held (at 930–34) that s. 1 of the *Constitution Act, 1930* (U.K.), 20 & 21 Geo. V, c. 26, reprinted in R.S.C. 1970, App. II, No. 25, and para. 12 of the Alberta Natural Resources Transfer Agreement (NRTA), which is a schedule to that Act, operate to extinguish the right to hunt for commercial purposes that was preserved in Treaty No. 8. It is interesting to wonder whether the court would decide that issue in the same way today. In *R. v. Badger*, [1996] 1 S.C.R. 771 [*Badger*], which dealt with rights to hunt for subsistence under Treaty No. 8, the court worked hard (at paras. 41–48) to find room after *Horseman, ibid.,* to hold that para. 12 of the NRTA extinguished only the commercial aspect, not the subsistence or the social or ceremonial aspect, of the hunting right preserved in Treaty No. 8.

[19] In *R. v. Pamajewon*, [1996] 2 S.C.R. 821 [*Pamajewon*], the court rejected two First Nations' assertions of self-government rights but was prepared (at para. 24) to "[a]ssum[e] without deciding that s. 35(1) [of the *Constitution Act, 1982*] includes self-government claims," when and as such claims can meet the usual test for proof of Aboriginal rights. In *Delgamuukw, supra* note 3, the court (at paras. 170–71) sent back to trial the plaintiffs' claim for self-government rights, declining an obvious opportunity to affirm the conclusion of the majority of the court below (*Delgamuukw v. British Columbia*, [1993] 5 W.W.R. 97 (B.C.C.A.) at paras. 151–75, Macfarlane J.A., at paras. 479–84, Wallace J.A.) that all such rights were extinguished, at the latest, by Confederation. Most recently, in *Mitchell v. Canada (M.N.R.)*, [2001] 1 S.C.R. 911 [*Mitchell*], Binnie J., whose judgment concurred with that of the majority, argued at length (especially at paras. 149–54) that the constitution leaves no room for candidate Aboriginal rights that are deemed to be incompatible with the sovereignty of the Crown, but made a point of adding (*ibid.* at paras. 165–73) that this notion of "sovereign incompatibility" did not preclude accreditation, in some future case, of an Aboriginal right of internal self-government. The majority in *Mitchell, ibid.,* dealt with the appeal on a different basis.

[20] *Delgamuukw, ibid.* at paras. 172–83. In both *Van der Peet, supra* note 11 at para. 28, and *Mitchell, ibid.* at para. 11, the Supreme Court held that section 35(1) now precludes even the federal order of government from extinguishing Aboriginal rights.

[21] See *e.g. Van der Peet, ibid.* at para. 68, *Delgamuukw, ibid.* at paras. 78–108.

[22] See e.g. *R. v. Sioui*, [1990] 1 S.C.R. 1025 [*Sioui*]; *Sparrow, supra* note 2; *Badger, supra* note 18 (in part); *Nikal, supra* note 3; *Gladstone, supra* note 17; *R. v. Adams*, [1996] 3 S.C.R. 101 [*Adams*]; *R. v. Côté*, [1996] 3 S.C.R. 139 [*Côté*]; *Delgamuukw, supra* note 3; *R. v. Sundown*, [1999] 1 S.C.R. 393; *R. v. Marshall*, [1999] 3 S.C.R. 456 [*Marshall*].

[23] *R. v. Powley*, [2003] 2 S.C.R. 207, 2003 SCC 43 [*Powley*].

[24] *British Columbia (Minister of Forests) v. Okanagan Indian Band*, [2003] 3 S.C.R. 371, 2003 SCC 71.

[25] To be fair, the Court has made it quite clear that mere mainstream convenience will not be enough

to preclude accreditation or enforcement of s. 35 rights. It has expressly rejected—and, in my view, properly so—the proposition "that aboriginal and treaty rights should be recognized only to the extent that such recognition would not occasion disruption or inconvenience to non-aboriginal people. This," it added, "is not a legal principle. It is a political argument . . . that was expressly rejected by the political leadership when it decided to include s. 35 in the *Constitution Act, 1982*": *R. v. Marshall*, [1999] 3 S.C.R. 533 at para. 45 [*Marshall II*]. It has also said, however, that "limits placed on those rights" are "a necessary part" of their reconciliation "with the broader political community of which they are part, . . . where the objectives furthered by those limits are of sufficient importance to the broader community as a whole": *Gladstone, supra* note 17 at para. 73, and that s. 35 itself is the means by which the prior Aboriginal presence in North America "is reconciled with the assertion of Crown sovereignty over Canadian territory": *Van der Peet, supra* note 11 at paras. 31, 43.

[26] I know of only two, both quite recent: *Canada (Minister of Canadian Heritage) v. Mikisew Cree First Nation*, [2004] 2 C.N.L.R. 74 (F.C.A.), leave to appeal to S.C.C. granted, [2004] S.C.C. Bulletin 1191, [2004] S.C.C.A. 112 (QL), and *Morris and Olsen, supra* not 10.

[27] On 29 April 2004, for instance, the Supreme Court granted leave to appeal to the Crown in right of New Brunswick from *R. v. Bernard* (2003), 230 D.L.R. (4th) 57 (N.B.C.A.) [*Bernard*], and to the Crown in right of Nova Scotia from *R. v. Marshall* (2003), 218 N.S.R. (2d) 78, 2003 NSCA 105 [*Stephen Marshall*], both cases in which the courts of appeal reversed decisions below on Aboriginal title and on treaty rights to engage in commercial logging. That same day, the court refused, with costs, an Aboriginal plaintiff's application for leave to appeal the decision below in *Benoit v. Canada* (2003), 228 D.L.R. (4th) 1 (F.C.A.), a case in which the court of appeal reversed a trial decision that had awarded a blanket exemption from all taxation to Treaty No. 8 Indians. See [2004] S.C.C. Bulletin 710, 713 and 708, [2003] S.C.C.A. Nos. 467, 516, and 387, respectively.

[28] According to section 40(1) of the *Supreme Court Act*, R.S.C. 1985, c. S-26, the Supreme Court may grant leave to appeal from a court of appeal decision

> where, with respect to the particular case sought to be appealed, the Supreme Court is of the opinion that any question involved therein is, by reason of its public importance or the importance of any issue of law or any issue of mixed law and fact involved in that question, one that ought to be decided by the Supreme Court or is, for any other reason, of such a nature or significance as to warrant decision by it, . . .

[29] *Delgamuukw, supra* note 3 at para. 186.

[30] See his essay in this volume at 73, 76–77.

[31] See *e.g. Reference re: Manitoba Language Rights*, [1985] 1 S.C.R. 721; *Quebec Secession Reference, supra* note 8.

[32] See *e.g. Quebec Secession Reference, ibid.* at para. 82.

[33] Indications of the Supreme Court's attentiveness to this concern include its stipulation, in *Van der Peet, supra* note 11 at para. 49 and elsewhere, that definitions of Aboriginal rights "take into account the aboriginal perspective, yet do so in terms which are cognizable to the non-aboriginal legal system," its observation, also in *Van der Peet, ibid.* at para. 56, that Aboriginal rights cannot comprise "those aspects of the aboriginal society that are true of every human society," and its insistence, in *Pamajewon, supra* note 19 at para. 27, and *Delgamuukw, supra* note 3 at para. 170, that Aboriginal rights claims not be cast "at a level of excessive generality."

[34] I have argued this at greater length, with particular reference to inherent rights of self-government, in "Take Your Time and Do It Right: *Delgamuukw*, Self-Government Rights and the Pragmatics of Advocacy" (2000) 27 Man. L.J. 241, especially at 264–66. Compare W.I.C. Binnie, "The *Sparrow* Doctrine: Beginning of the End or End of the Beginning?" (1990) 15 Queen's L.J. 217.

[35] *Supra* note 22.

[36] Supra note 25.

[37] For further discussion of *Marshall II, ibid.*, see Manfredi, *supra* note 4. It may be interesting to compare *Marshall II* with *Cooper v. Aaron*, 358 U.S. 1 (1958), the United States Supreme Court's response to an Arkansas school board's request to delay by two years, on account of "extreme public hostility," implementation of the court's earlier decision, in *Brown v. Board of Education*, 347 U.S. 483 (1954), 349 U.S. 294 (1955), requiring desegregation of public schools.

³⁸ See *supra* note 19.
³⁹ See *Van der Peet, supra* note 11 at paras. 44–75.
⁴⁰ In *Van der Peet, ibid.*, for instance, the court held (at paras. 55–63) that nothing could be an Aboriginal right unless it were proved to have been of central and defining significance to the distinctive culture of the claimant Aboriginal society at the moment of that society's first contact with Europeans. In *Delgamuukw, supra* note 3, the court held (at paras. 144–45) that the moment the Crown asserted sovereignty over the relevant land, not the moment of first contact, was the appropriate time as of which to ascertain Aboriginal title, and (at paras. 150–51) that an Aboriginal community that had established occupation of its lands at the moment of sovereignty need not also demonstrate separately that those lands were of central significance to it at that time. In *Powley, supra* note 23, the court, mindful of the fact that there could not possibly have been a distinctive Métis culture at the moment of first European contact, concluded (at paras. 16–18, 36–40) that Métis claims of Aboriginal right should be ascertained instead as of the moment of effective European control in the relevant geographical area.
⁴¹ *Sparrow, supra* note 2 at 1113–19.
⁴² *Gladstone, supra* note 17 at paras. 54–75.
⁴³ *Delgamuukw, supra* note 3 at paras. 160–69.
⁴⁴ Even before that, in *Nikal, supra* note 3, the court had held (at para. 110) that "the concept of reasonableness forms an integral part of the *Sparrow* test for justification," despite having said in *Sparrow, supra* note 2 at 1118–19 that the reasonableness of regulatory measures "cannot suffice as constitutional recognition and affirmation of aboriginal rights."
⁴⁵ See *Delgamuukw, supra* note 319 at paras. 78–108.
⁴⁶ See *Mitchell, supra* note 19 at paras. 29–39.
⁴⁷ See *Van der Peet, supra* note 11 at paras. 11, 52. McLachlin J. (as she then was), who dissented in *Van der Peet, ibid.*, would have characterized such rights as limited to procurement of a moderate livelihood from resources on which the community had traditionally relied: see *ibid.* at para. 279.
⁴⁸ See *Marshall, supra* note 22 at paras. 57–61. McLachlin J., as it happened, dissented.
⁴⁹ See *Delgamuukw, supra* note 3 at para. 160 (section 35(1) "rights may be infringed, both by the federal . . . and provincial . . . governments. However, s. 35(1) requires that those infringements satisfy the test of justification"); *Paul v. British Columbia (Forest Appeals Commission)*, [2003] 2 S.C.R. 585, 2003 SCC 55 [*Paul*] at paras. 10, 24, 25 ("*Sparrow* stands for the proposition that government regulation, including provincial regulation, may, by legislation, infringe an aboriginal right if that infringement is justified").
⁵⁰ See *Delgamuukw, ibid.* at para. 178 ("The core of Indianness encompasses the whole range of aboriginal rights that are protected by s. 35(1). Those rights include rights in relation to land; that part of the core derives from s. 91(24)'s reference to 'Lands reserved for the Indians'") and para. 181; *Paul, ibid.* at para. 33 ("The 'core' of Indianness has not been exhaustively defined. It encompasses the whole range of aboriginal rights that are protected by s. 35(1)").
⁵¹ See *Delgamuukw, ibid.* at para. 181 ("s. 91(24) protects a core of federal jurisdiction even from provincial laws of general application, through the operation of the doctrine of interjurisdictional immunity"); *Paul, ibid.* at para. 15.
⁵² This phrase first appeared, as far as I know, in *Mabo v. Queensland [No. 2]* (1992), 175 C.L.R. 1 (H.C.A.) at 29 [*Mabo*], Brennan J. (for the plurality) ("In discharging its duty to declare the common law of Australia, this Court is not free to adopt rules that accord with contemporary notions of justice and human rights if their adoption would fracture the skeleton of principle which gives the body of our law its shape and internal consistency"). Somewhat comparable is the notion advanced in *Van der Peet, supra* note 11 at para. 49 that Aboriginal rights must be characterized "in terms which are cognizable to the non-aboriginal legal system."
⁵³ This is so, in my judgment, even where strong doctrinal arguments are available in support of a given Aboriginal claim or position. The following observations from Judge Richard A. Posner of the U.S. Circuit Court of Appeals, though offered in a context utterly unrelated to this one, seem apt and instructive here:

Judges are not easily fooled by a lawyer who argues for a change in the law on the basis that it would be no change at all but merely the logical entailment of existing law. The value of such argument is in giving the judges a professionally respectable ground for rationalizing the change, a ground that minimizes the appearance of novelty and so protects rule-of-law values. The judges must have reasons for wanting to make the change, however, and this is where a lawyer's brief, which furnishes the rationalization, the rhetoric, but rarely the reasons, falls down:

"Animal Rights: Legal, Philosophical, and Pragmatic Perspectives" in Cass R. Sunstein & Martha C. Nussbaum, eds., *Animal Rights: Current Debates and New Directions* (Oxford: Oxford University Press, 2004) 51 at 58.

[54] See *e.g. Marshall*, *supra* note 22 at para. 78, McLachlin J. (dissenting on other grounds); *Simon*, *supra* note 10 at 402; *Sioui*, *supra* note 22 at 1035.

[55] See *Van der Peet*, *supra* note 11 at paras. 45–46.

[56] See *e.g.* John Borrows, "Frozen Rights in Canada: Constitutional Interpretation and the Trickster" (1997) 22 Am. Indian L. Rev. 37; Bradford W. Morse, "Permafrost Rights: Aboriginal Self-Government and the Supreme Court in *R. v. Pamajewon*" (1997) 42 McGill L.J. 1011; Jonathan Rudin, "One Step Forward, Two Steps Back: The Political and Institutional Dynamics Behind the Supreme Court of Canada's Decisions in *R. v. Sparrow*, *R. v. Van der Peet* and *Delgamuukw v. British Columbia*" (1998) 13 J. L. & Soc. Pol'y 67; Leonard I. Rotman, "Hunting for Answers in a Strange Kettle of Fish: Unilateralism, Paternalism and Fiduciary Rhetoric in *Badger* and *Van der Peet*" (1997) 8 Const. Forum Const. 40; Russel Lawrence Barsh & James Youngblood Henderson, "The Supreme Court's *Van der Peet* Trilogy: Naive Imperialism and Ropes of Sand" (1997) 42 McGill L.J. 993; Kelly Gallagher-Mackay, "Interpreting Self-Government: Approaches to Building Cultural Authority" [1997] 4 C.N.L.R. 1.

[57] See *e.g. Van der Peet*, *supra* note 11 at para. 20.

[58] See *supra* note 21 and accompanying text.

[59] See *Delgamuukw*, *supra* note 3 at paras. 78–108.

[60] See *Mitchell*, *supra* note 19 at paras. 27–60.

[61] See *e.g. Sparrow*, *supra* note 2; *Nikal*, *supra* note 3; *Adams*, *supra* note 22; *Côté*, *supra* note 22.

[62] See *e.g. Pamajewon*, *supra* note 19.

[63] *Ibid.* at para. 27. This is so despite the Supreme Court's observation, in *Van der Peet*, *supra* note 11 at para. 54, that "the activities" that are subject to a claim of Aboriginal right "must be considered at a general rather than at a specific level."

[64] See especially *Mitchell*, *supra* note 19 at paras. 14–25.

[65] See *ibid.* especially at para. 20:
> It may be tempting for a claimant or a court to tailor the right claimed to the contours of the specific act at issue. In this case, for example, Chief Mitchell seeks to limit the scope of his claimed trading rights by designating specified trading partners. . . . These self-imposed limitations may represent part of Chief Mitchell's commendable strategy of negotiating with the government and minimizing the potential effects on its border control. However, narrowing the claim cannot narrow the aboriginal practice relied upon, which is what defines the right. . . . Moreover, it is difficult to imagine how limitations on trading partners would operate in practice. . . . Thus, the limitations placed on the trading right by Chief Mitchell and the courts below artificially narrow the claimed right and would, at any rate, prove illusory in practice.

Compare *ibid.* at paras. 120–24, Binnie J. (concurring).

[66] Recent failed attempts to assert sovereignty-type arguments in the courts include: *R. v. Williams*, [1995] 2 C.N.L.R. 229 (B.C.C.A.); *R. v. Chief*, [1997] 4 C.N.L.R. 212 (Sask. Q.B.); *R. v. Kahpeechoose*, [1997] 4 C.N.L.R. 215 (Sask. Prov. Ct.); *R. v. Ignace* (1998), 156 D.L.R. (4th) 713 (B.C.C.A.); *R. v. David*, [2000] O.J. No. 561 (QL) (Sup. Ct. J.); and *R. v. Janvier*, [2000] 9 W.W.R. 679 (Alta. Q.B.). (For Australian authority to similar effect, see *R. v. Buzzacott*, [2004] ACTSC 89 and the several Australian precedents cited there.) In *Martel v. Samson Band*, [2001] 1 C.N.L.R. 173 (F.C.T.D.), however, the Federal Court noted evidence that the United States had recognized, in a limited way, the sovereignty of the relevant tribe and refused, on that basis, to hold that such a sovereignty claim

could not possibly ground a cause of action in Canada. Jake Rupert, "Natives not bound by laws of Canada, lawyer argues" *Ottawa Citizen* (25 April 2004) A3, describes the current status of the most recent attempt to bring such a claim in Ontario.

[67] The Supreme Court does, after all, keep saying that section 35(1) of the *Constitution Act, 1982* is about "the reconciliation of the pre-existence of aboriginal societies with the sovereignty of the Crown": *Van der Peet*, *supra* note 11 at paras. 31, 43; *Gladstone*, *supra* note 17 at paras. 72–73; *Delgamuukw*, *supra* note 3 at para. 161; *Mitchell*, *supra* note 19 at para. 12.

[68] See *e.g. Sobhuza II v. Miller*, [1926] A.C. 518 (P.C.) at 525, 528; *Mabo*, *supra* note 52 at 31–32, 69, Brennan J., at 78, Deane and Gaudron JJ.

[69] See *Sparrow*, *supra* note 2 at 1103.

[70] *Quebec Secession Reference*, *supra* note 8 at para. 142, citing H.W.R. Wade, "The Basis of Legal Sovereignty" [1955] Cambridge L.J. 172 at 196.

[71] See *e.g.* Sir Kenneth Roberts-Wray, *Commonwealth and Colonial Law* (New York: Praeger, 1966) at 589–91; *Old HW-GW Ltd. v. Canada (M.N.R.)* (1993), 153 N.R. 136 (F.C.A.); *De la Penha v. Newfoundland* (1986), 63 Nfld. & P.E.I.R. 356 at 359 (Nfld. C.A.); *Chateau-Gai Wines Ltd. v. Canada (A.G.)*, [1970] Ex. C.R. 366 at 384; *Carl Zeiss Stiftung v. Rayner & Keeler Ltd.*, [1967] 1 A.C. 853 (H.L.) at 901–2; *Duff Development Co. v. Government of Kelantan*, [1924] A.C. 797 (H.L.) at 813, Viscount Finlay; at 830, Lord Carson; *Aksionairnoye Obschestvo A.M. Luther v. James Sagor & Co.*, [1921] 1 K.B. 456 at 474, aff'd on the point (but rev'd on other grounds), [1921] 3 K.B. 532 (C.A.). See also *State Immunity Act*, R.S.C. 1985, c. S-18, s. 14, as amended.

[72] See *e.g.* Kent McNeil, "Aboriginal Title and the Division of Powers: Rethinking Federal and Provincial Jurisdiction" (1998) 61 Sask. L. Rev. 431; Kent McNeil, *Defining Aboriginal Title in the 90's: Has the Supreme Court Finally Got It Right?* (Toronto: Robarts Centre for Canadian Studies, York University, 1998); Nigel Bankes, "*Delgamuukw*, Division of Powers and Provincial Land and Resource Laws: Some Implications for Provincial Resource Rights" Case Comment (1998) 32 U.B.C. L. Rev. 317; Kerry Wilkins, "Of Provinces and Section 35 Rights" (1999) 22 Dal. L.J. 185; Kerry Wilkins, "Negative Capability: Of Provinces and Lands Reserved for the Indians" (2002) 1 Indigenous L.J. 57 ["Negative Capability"].

[73] For one version of this argument, see Kenneth J. Tyler, "The Division of Powers and Aboriginal Water Rights Issues" (Paper presented at National Symposium on Water Law, Canadian Bar Association, Toronto, April 1999) [unpublished], especially at 4–9.

[74] See notes 49–51 *supra* and accompanying text. In *Haida Nation v. British Columbia (Minister of Forests)*, 2004 SCC 73 and *Taku River Tlingit First Nation v. British Columbia (Project Assessment Director)*, 2004 SCC 74, the Supreme Court dealt at length with the provinces' obligations, pending determination of the merits of First Nations' claims of Aboriginal right, to consult with First Nations about proposed measures that might adversely affect the rights claimed, but did not comment on the provinces' power (or lack thereof) to interfere with the exercise of the Aboriginal rights that First Nations turn out actually to have.

[75] See *e.g.* "Negative Capability," *supra* note 72 at 78–80, 102–6. In *Sarnia*, *supra* note 17, the Ontario Court of Appeal concluded (at paras. 243–310) that contests between downstream purchasers, whose root of title derives from the Crown, and Aboriginal communities holding unextinguished Aboriginal interests in the same land require determination case by case. In *Sarnia*, the Aboriginal plaintiffs were unsuccessful, but their claim was based on a technical defect, discovered over a century later, that voided a surrender of lands to which their leaders had agreed, in which the community acquiesced, and for which the community had been paid full and fair market value. All the equities in that case favored the downstream purchasers, who had purchased their lands with no knowledge, either actual or imputed, of the historic defect in the surrender.

[76] See *e.g.* Michael J. Trebilcock, "An Economic Approach to the Doctrine of Unconscionability" in Barry J. Reiter & John Swan, eds., *Studies in Contract Law* (Toronto: Butterworths, 1980) 379.

[77] See *e.g. Bernard* and *Stephen Marshall*, both *supra* note 27.

[78] See *e.g. Nemaiah Valley Indian Band v. Riverside Forest Products Ltd.*, 2003 BCSC 249, [2003] B.C.J. No. 361 (QL).

[79] This issue will not arise in respect of Métis Aboriginal rights unless it turns out that Métis, as such, are "Indians" for the purposes of s. 91(24) of the *Constitution Act, 1867*. The Supreme Court has yet to decide this issue. In *R. v. Blais*, [2003] 2 S.C.R. 236, 2003 SCC 44 [*Blais*], the court (at para. 36) expressly left that question "open for another day." Its reasoning in *Blais*, however, gives one reason to doubt that Métis are s. 91(24) Indians: see especially *ibid.* at paras. 27–31.

[80] For a helpful early overview of this general strategic approach, see Mary Eberts, "A Strategy for Equality Litigation under the Canadian Charter of Rights and Freedoms" in Joseph M. Weiler & Robin M. Elliot, eds., *Litigating the Values of a Nation: The Canadian Charter of Rights and Freedoms* (Toronto: Carswell, 1986) 411.

[81] See *Pamajewon, supra* note 19.

[82] A contrary view deserves acknowledgement here. Elsewhere in this article, I have argued, and offered documentation in support of my argument, that the Supreme Court's section 35 jurisprudence is still surprisingly fluid: see especially *supra* notes 35–51 and the accompanying text. Does it not make sense, one may well ask, for legal scholars to take the opportunity, while there is still some room for movement in the Supreme Court jurisprudence, to do what they can to show the court the shortcomings they perceive in its section 35 decisions? What better time could there be for thoughtful academics to make a difference?

I think this viewpoint deserves further thought. It may well be an issue upon which reasonable people disagree, even if their strategic objectives are compatible. My reluctance to embrace this contrary view stems at present from three concerns. First, I see little evidence that academic writings that criticize earlier Supreme Court decisions about section 35 are shaping the decisions the court makes subsequently. This in itself is hardly decisive; such influence could be subtle and unacknowledged. But second, and more important, the vast majority of section 35 adjudication takes place, and will continue to take place, in the lower courts, which have no choice except to work within the doctrinal framework the Supreme Court prescribes for them. Their task is to apply that framework, whether or not they happen individually to agree with it. Success before that audience depends much more on showing the court that the jurisprudence supports, or at least leaves room for, the result your client wants than on showing it how unfortunate that jurisprudence is. Finally, it has become, in recent years, increasingly rare for the Supreme Court to grant unsuccessful Aboriginal parties leave to appeal from section 35 decisions. (See *supra* notes 26–27 and accompanying text.) This fact intensifies the everyday practical importance of the work of the lower courts; it also suggests that the best way for an Aboriginal party to get a position or argument before the Supreme Court of Canada is to succeed with it in the court of appeal.

[83] Fortunately, other essays in this collection have done a commendable job of compensating for that deficit. See, in particular, the essays by Leroy Little Bear, Patricia Monture, Sákéj Henderson, Larry Chartrand, and Gordon Christie.

[84] See *e.g.* the Little Bear, Monture, Henderson, and Christie essays in this collection, and Associate Chief Judge Murray Sinclair (as he then was), "Aboriginal Peoples, Justice and the Law" in Richard Gosse, James Youngblood Henderson & Roger Carter, eds., *Continuing Poundmaker and Riel's Quest: Presentations Made at a Conference on Aboriginal Peoples and Justice* (Saskatoon, Sask.: Purich, 1994) 173.

INDEX

"act of state" doctrine 177
Aboriginal
    ceremonies 28, 30, 32, 33, 35, 36, 44, 45, 73, 242
    claims
        cost of 240
        funding 274–75
        litigation of 11, 12, 14, 15, 19, 20, 21, 23, 39, 41, 42, 51, 54, 76, 123, 145, 163, 174, 182, 191, 195, 197, 199, 202–40, 249, 250, 258, 264, 266, 268, 272, 273, 274, 275, 278, 279, 280, 285, 288–312
        negotiation of 19, 20, 21, 41, 68, 80, 195, 202–40, 265, 268, 271, 273, 274, 282, 302
    cultures 14, 15, 36, 43, 44, 50, 53, 78, 79, 80, 112, 149, 229, 275, 283, 297, 305
    Métis 160
    Elders 15, 73, 76, 77
    jurisprudences 15, 16, 70–73, 74, 75, 76–77, 79, 80, 81, 82, 83, 84, 85, 87, 89
    knowledge 15, 30, 35, 43, 44–46, 47, 61, 62, 71, 72, 77, 78, 82, 83
    languages 13, 15, 29, 30, 73, 78, 288
    law 67–89, 112
        "doctrine of continuity" 204
    medicine 30, 32, 33
    paradigms 26–38, 224

peoples
    Algonquin 30, 78, 264
    Anishnabe 61
    Assiniboine 36
    Blackfoot 26, 28, 29, 30, 36, 107
    Blood 28
    Cheyenne 30
    Cree 26, 30, 36, 44, 51, 59, 83, 182, 308
    Dakota 107
    Gitksan 35, 53, 64, 135, 178, 190, 288
    Gitxsan 135
    Gros Ventres 36
    Heiltsuk 130, 143, 212, 263
    Inuit 60, 116, 144, 148, 154, 163, 183, 185, 231
    Maliseet 59
    Mi'kmaq 19, 70, 82, 99, 124, 190, 193, 194, 195, 200, 213, 239, 256, 265, 269
    Mi'kmaw 70
    Micmac 30, 70, 145
    Mohawk 14, 23, 59, 60, 62, 130, 143, 184
    Musqueam 230, 235, 288
    Naskapi 30
    Navajo 31, 121
    Nisga'a 173, 174, 288
    Ojibway 30, 61, 156, 183
    Plains 13, 26, 29, 30, 31, 32, 33, 35, 36, 37, 51, 64
    Sioux 107, 121
    Sto:lo 52, 128, 142
    Tlingit 123
    Wet'suwet'en 53, 64, 135, 178, 190, 288
    philosophy 13, 27–30, 35, 37, 61, 72, 78
    rights 15, 17, 18
        to resources 19, 21, 22
    science 27
    title 12, 19, 20, 21, 22, 34, 35, 37, 50, 52, 53, 64, 69, 74, 78, 79, 81, 83, 84, 85, 86, 87, 89, 91, 101, 105, 107, 112, 123, 127, 128, 129, 131, 139, 140, 142, 144, 145, 146, 147, 148, 149, 150, 190, 199, 205, 206, 209, 210, 213, 224, 227, 232, 235, 236, 240, 241, 246–53, 253–56, 258, 259, 260, 261, 262, 264, 265, 266, 267, 271, 273, 274, 275, 276, 277, 278, 279, 280, 281, 283, 284, 292, 295, 297, 301, 306, 308, 309, 311
        and continuity of occupation 17, 111, 127–50, 204, 235, 247
        and Delgamuukw 18
        and exclusive occupation 17
        and present occupation of land 18
        infringement of 54
        Métis 12, 18, 151–88
    values 31, 35
    women 39–66
Aboriginal and treaty rights 20, 53, 246
    extinguishment

314   INDEX

"clear and plain" test 134, 135, 136, 146, 204–5, 230
   legal recognition of 204
   political trust doctrine 203–4
Aboriginal rights 84
   and provincial laws 79, 249–70, 290–91
   extinguishment of 88
   Métis
     independent nation theory 156
     trace theory 152, 155–57, 157–62
   sui generis nature of 68, 69, 71, 72, 73, 74, 75, 77, 78, 79, 80, 83, 86, 88, 89, 137, 138, 150, 224
   surrender of 145
Acadia 98, 99, 100
Africa 16, 92, 101, 102–5, 106, 108, 112, 114, 117, 119, 120, 123, 124, 125, 148
agriculture 45, 51, 53, 255, 267
Alberta 28, 145, 182, 190, 307
Alberta Task Force 27, 37
Americas 101
Annapolis Royal 99
Asia 92, 101, 105, 125
Askov v. The Queen 19, 24, 191–93, 195, 196, 197, 199, 200
Assembly of First Nations (AFN) 41–42, 222
Atlantic Canada 99
Australia 60, 85, 91–92, 108, 111, 131, 141, 142, 143, 175, 264, 309
Authorson v. Canada (A.G.) 223
Baker Lake v. Canada 171, 184, 188
Barbados 96–97, 115, 116
Barbary Powers 101, 118

Bastarache, Justice 20, 56, 65, 203, 215–16, 220, 221, 222, 223, 224, 225, 227, 229, 230, 239
Battle of Seven Oaks 151, 156
Bellegarde, Commissioner 234
Berlin General Act, 1885 107
Bernard 146, 265, 308, 311
Berwick 92, 117
Bill C-31 58, 65
Binnie, Justice Ian 20, 66, 70, 82, 85, 87, 88, 113, 145, 193, 194, 195, 196, 212, 215, 216–20, 221, 222, 223, 225, 227, 229, 230, 236, 237, 238, 239, 270, 307, 308, 310
Blankard v. Galdy 97, 98, 116
Bliss v. Canada 46
Brennan, Justice 86, 112, 129, 131, 142, 309, 311
British Columbia 22, 122, 124, 128, 130, 135, 165, 173, 174, 178, 190, 192, 216, 217, 237, 255, 267, 271–87
   Fishery (General) Regulations 199
   Ministry of Aboriginal Affairs 282, 287
   Treaty Commission 272, 281, 286, 287
   Treaty Negotiation Office 287
British Columbia Court of Appeal 80, 159, 163, 174, 198, 266, 268, 278
British Columbia Supreme Court 266
British Columbia v. Okanagan Indian Band 307
British Empire 93, 94, 99, 100, 101, 102, 103, 105, 107, 108, 113, 116, 119, 123, 124

British Settlements Act, 1887 107
buffalo 32, 33
Burma 118
Calder v. B.C.(A.G.) 20, 24, 34, 38, 80, 85, 87, 117, 173, 174, 177, 185, 187, 204, 205, 207, 215, 226, 227, 231, 272, 306
Calvin's Case 94, 95, 96, 97, 110, 114, 115, 116, 117
Campbell v. British Columbia 81, 83, 85, 87, 88
Campbell v. Hall 96, 99, 100, 101, 102, 105, 108, 109, 110, 117, 122, 125, 204, 237
Canada Act 1982 (U.K.) 112, 180, 199
Canada Jurisdiction Act, 1803 (U.K.) 172, 187
Canadian Bill of Rights 39, 40, 57, 291
Canadian Judicial Council 215, 221
Canadian Pacific Ltd. v. Paul 84, 137
Cape Colony 105, 116, 146, 237, 265
Caribbean 92, 96, 99
Cartwright, Justice 109
Channel Islands 93
Charter of Rights and Freedoms 19, 24, 39, 40, 41, 42, 56, 59, 60, 61, 62, 65, 67, 72, 85, 88, 120, 169, 170, 190, 191, 192, 197, 302, 312
Chippewas of Kettle and Stony Point v. Canada (A.G.) 234, 310
Chippewas of Sarnia Band v. Canada (A.G.) 148, 198, 201, 307, 311
claims strategies 258–62, 288–312
   government negotiation 289–90
Coke, Lord 93, 94, 95–96, 97, 115, 116

INDEX 315

colonialism 42, 45, 47, 64, 77, 267
colonial law 88
Colonial Laws Validity Act, 1863 87
Colonial Laws Validity Act, 1865 108
colonization 61, 84, 85, 166, 176, 183, 185, 186, 288
Committee for Justice and Liberty v. National Energy Board 221
common law 15, 54, 55, 69, 74, 75, 79, 81, 82, 83, 84, 86, 87, 88, 89, 92, 94, 97, 101, 103, 111, 112, 119, 120, 127, 133, 134, 135, 136, 137, 138, 140, 141, 142, 143, 144, 145, 146, 147, 149, 150, 168, 174, 175, 181, 186, 197, 204, 209, 248, 262, 265, 269, 309
Confederation 85, 204
Connolly v. Woolrich 171, 186, 231
conquest 14, 34, 87, 88, 93–94, 94–96, 97, 98, 100, 101, 103, 107, 116, 117, 121, 122, 167, 168, 170, 178, 213
Constitution 81, 82, 278, 285, 291
constitutionalism 69, 70, 81
constitutional supremacy 269
Constitution Act, 1867 81, 82, 87, 88, 110
  s. 109 122
  s. 91(24) 106, 145, 205, 207, 231, 295, 306, 312
Constitution Act, 1930 (U.K.) 182, 263, 307
  s. 1 307
Constitution Act, 1982 24, 39, 59, 78, 85, 87, 110,
123, 125, 203, 230, 266, 307
  s. 35 23, 24, 39, 50, 78, 79, 88, 91, 113, 119, 125, 133, 141, 146, 159, 160, 182, 183, 185, 190, 193, 195, 198, 206, 257, 270, 272, 291–96, 297, 298–305, 308, 311, 312
  and Aboriginal women 50–55, 61
  s. 35(1) 34, 39, 50, 60, 67, 69, 73, 74, 75, 78, 79, 80, 81, 83, 84, 85, 86, 87, 88, 89, 127, 128, 129, 136, 144, 145, 155, 160, 180, 185, 202, 206, 207, 212–13, 229, 231, 236, 239, 240, 307, 309, 311
  s. 35(1)(a) 234
  s. 35(1)(e) 234
  s. 35(2) 23, 153, 155, 181
  s. 35(3) 261, 270
  s. 35(4) 40, 41, 52, 60, 61
  s. 36 307
  s. 52(1) 81
Constitution of Canada 81
contact 17, 18, 19, 51, 63, 68, 70, 74, 80, 127–50, 151, 152, 154, 155, 156, 159, 160, 161, 163, 164, 165, 179, 181, 183, 184, 212, 260, 263, 265, 281, 306, 309
Cook v. Sprigg 105
Coon Come, Grand Chief Matthew 222
Corbiere v. Canada 55–58, 60, 62, 65, 66, 235
Coronation Oath Act, 1688 (U.K.) 84

Cory, Justice 143, 145, 191, 192, 193, 195, 199, 238
Countee de Derby's Case 94, 96, 99
Cover, Robert 72
Crevier v. Québec 88
Criminal Code of Canada 65
culture 13, 17, 26, 26–27, 32, 45, 50, 52, 57, 59, 60, 62, 63, 73, 74, 79, 80, 84, 85, 128, 129, 130, 134, 142, 143, 144, 146, 154, 183, 212, 241, 242, 262, 263, 264, 297, 306, 309
customs 27, 32
Delgamuukw v. B.C. 21, 23, 50, 52, 53, 54, 55, 64, 65, 68, 69, 74, 78, 79, 80, 81, 83, 84, 85, 86, 87, 89, 91, 105, 112, 127, 128, 135, 137, 138, 140, 141, 142, 143, 144, 145, 146, 147, 148, 151, 162, 163, 165, 173, 174, 175, 176, 177, 178, 179, 180, 183, 184, 186, 187, 188, 190, 199, 202, 205, 213, 214, 224, 228, 230, 231, 235, 236, 239, 240, 241, 245, 246, 252, 253, 256, 258, 260, 262, 264, 265, 267, 268, 271, 272, 275, 276, 277, 279, 280, 281, 282, 283, 284, 285, 286, 287, 292, 295, 306, 307, 308, 309, 310, 311
Denman, Lord 133
Denning, Lord 110, 117, 120, 124, 125, 134, 144, 145, 221
Department of Justice (DOJ) 208, 210–11, 217, 218–19, 234, 237, 238
de Grandpré, Justice 221
Dickson, Justice 84
Dumont v. Canada (A.G.) 153

316   INDEX

Dutton v. Howell 96, 98, 101, 116, 117
"effective control" doctrine 176–77
eagle 32
East African Court of Appeal 103
England 84, 92, 93, 94, 95, 97, 98, 99, 110, 115, 116, 117, 120, 133, 134, 135, 138, 139, 169, 171, 173, 175, 176, 183. *See also* Great Britain
Eurocentrism 83
European paradigms 12, 15
European Court on Human Rights 82
evidence 17, 21, 35, 82, 91, 130, 131, 136, 137, 138, 139, 142, 143, 148, 149, 165, 167, 170, 180, 182, 184, 192, 193, 194, 196, 197, 198, 199, 264, 265, 268, 275, 276, 279, 291, 292, 297, 299, 304, 307, 310
federalism 75, 77, 82, 122
Federal Court of Appeal 230, 240, 310
Federal Court of Australia 143, 148
feminism 46, 47, 48, 62, 63
fiduciary duty 54, 68, 80, 86, 166, 206, 207, 208, 209, 211, 214, 216, 227, 228, 230, 231, 232, 233, 234, 236, 250, 251–53, 255, 256, 258, 259, 264, 265, 267, 268, 270
Fisheries Act 128
fishing 14, 15, 19, 35, 51, 52, 54, 64, 70, 74, 82, 106, 114, 115, 130, 131, 145, 153, 162, 182, 190, 193, 194, 195, 198, 199, 208, 235, 242, 251, 253, 254, 256, 257, 258, 262, 263, 269, 270, 280, 298
   lobster 190, 194, 195

Foreign Jurisdiction Act, 1890 107, 108
forestry 194, 244, 249, 250, 251, 254, 255, 256, 259–62, 263, 267, 268, 280, 282
France 95, 100, 171, 176, 184, 186, 187
fur trade 130, 157, 169–72, 178, 187, 264
Fur Trade Act, 1821 (U.K.) 187
gambling 298
gas 279, 281, 282
gathering 14, 35, 51, 52, 53, 64, 70, 82, 193, 195, 197, 242, 247, 253, 270
gender 14, 39–66
Gonthier, Justice 66, 195
Goodswimmer v. Canada (Minister of Indian Affairs and Northern Development) 235
government regulation 21, 79, 109, 207, 231, 247, 268, 309
Great Britain 92–94, 94–96, 99, 100, 101, 102, 118, 166, 173, 176, 204
Gregoire, Judge 166, 184
Grenada 99, 100, 117
Guerin v. The Queen 34, 38, 54, 78, 84, 86, 117, 150, 206, 207, 212, 214, 226, 230, 236, 239, 240, 264, 306
Guernsey 92
Haida Nation v. British Columbia 23, 236, 268, 277, 278, 279, 280, 285, 286, 311
Halifax 99
Hall, Justice 85, 117, 177, 204
Henry I 114
Henry II 114
Henry VIII 93
Hewart, Lord 221
High Court of Australia 91,

92, 105, 124, 142
Hoffman, Lord 222
Holt, Lord 97, 98, 114
Hudson's Bay Company (HBC) 165, 167, 169–72, 178, 184, 186, 187
hunting 14, 15, 32, 33, 35, 51, 52, 54, 64, 70, 82, 105, 106, 109, 131, 142, 145, 153, 162, 171, 173, 182, 183, 190, 193, 194, 195, 208, 242, 246, 247, 249, 253, 254, 256, 257, 258, 262, 263, 269, 270, 290, 291, 298, 307
Iacobucci, Justice 66, 223, 239
imperial law 74, 75, 86, 91–126
India 16, 94, 101–2, 103, 108, 113, 117, 118, 119, 124
Indian
   non-status 61, 182
   status 57, 58, 59, 61, 158
Indian Act 23, 42, 54, 56, 57, 60, 65, 124, 125, 158, 182, 232, 236
   membership provisions 58
   s. 12(1)(b) 40, 58, 63, 64, 312
   s. 141 122
   s. 157 65
   s. 2(1) 59
   s. 77(1) 56
   s. 88 134, 141, 145
Indian Act, 1951
   s. 87 (now 88) 109, 124, 125
Indian Affairs 122, 123, 209, 228, 229, 232, 234, 240
Indian Association of Alberta 110, 120, 125
Indian Claims Commission (ICC) 207–11, 226, 232, 233, 234

INDEX   317

Indian Oil and Gas Act 264
International Court of
   Justice 86
international law 167, 168
Ireland 92, 93, 94, 95, 97,
   115, 116
Isle of Man 92, 93, 94, 97
Jamaica 97–99
James I 92, 95
James IV 93
Jersey 92
Johnson v. M'Intosh 122, 184
Johnstone v. Connolly 231
Judson, Justice 80, 85, 173,
   174
jurisdiction 69
jurisprudence 82, 203, 239
Kames, Lord 95
*Kitkatla Band v. British
   Columbia (Minister of
   Small Business, Tourism and
   Culture)* 235, 239
L'Heureux-Dubé, Justice
   56, 57, 58, 66, 74, 79, 80,
   81, 85, 87, 148, 149, 166,
   181, 200
Labrador 116
Lambert, Justice 82, 159,
   163, 174, 175, 183, 184,
   306
Lamer, Chief Justice 34, 35,
   52, 54, 67, 86, 87, 112,
   128, 129, 130, 131, 132,
   133, 134, 135, 136, 137,
   138, 139, 140, 142, 143,
   144, 145, 146, 147, 148,
   151, 154, 174, 176, 179,
   180, 181, 186, 195, 202,
   205, 213, 228, 231, 236,
   247, 264, 265, 267, 293
land 12, 13, 14, 16, 17, 18,
   19, 21, 22, 26, 28, 29,
   32–33, 33–35, 36, 37, 38,
   53, 54, 56, 59, 64, 69, 71,
   72, 74, 76, 78, 80, 81, 84,
   85, 86, 91, 94, 95, 103,
   104, 105, 106, 113, 116,
   117, 119, 120, 121, 122,
   127, 128, 129, 131, 135,
   136, 137, 138, 139, 140,
   141, 142, 145, 146, 147,
   148, 151, 152, 153, 154,
   159, 160, 161, 162, 166,
   167, 172, 173, 174, 175,
   178, 180, 181, 183, 185,
   198, 202, 209, 211, 213,
   224, 225, 229, 231, 232,
   234, 236, 237, 241–70,
   271–87, 306, 309, 311
   women's relationship
      with 65
land claims 20, 34, 65, 106,
   119, 205, 206, 271, 272,
   273, 277, 285, 286
Latin 78, 94, 95, 113, 115,
   186
Lavell and *Bedard* 39, 40,
   48, 57, 59, 65
law enforcement 15, 191,
   226, 288, 290–91
Law v. Canada 65
La Forest, Justice 86, 143,
   146, 179, 213
*La Société de Developpement
   de la Baie James* 171
Learned Hand, Justice 196,
   221, 223
legal pluralism 16, 76, 88,
   89, 92, 98, 110–11
legal positivism 68, 88, 144
Le Case de Tanistry 94, 122
logging 279, 280, 283, 308
lumber 190
Mabo v. Queensland 86, 91,
   112, 124, 129, 131, 142,
   143, 175, 309, 311
*Macauley v. P.C. Bongay (No.
   3)* 104
Macfarlane, J.A. 89, 174,
   307
Magna Carta 113, 137
Major, Justice 195
Malomo v. Olushola 103
Manitoba 182
Manitoba Act 153, 180, 185
Manitoba Court of Appeal
   187
Manitoba Provincial Court
   166
Mansfield, Lord 93, 98, 99,
   100, 101, 108, 114, 115,
   116, 117
Maori Land Court (New
   Zealand) 73, 85
Marshall, Chief Justice 85
McEachern, Chief Justice
   174
McLachlin, Chief Justice
   52, 56, 65, 74, 79, 80, 84,
   85, 86, 87, 89, 113, 132,
   143, 144, 148, 181, 191,
   199, 201, 213, 231, 239,
   265, 266, 309, 310
Meagher, Judge 166
Métis 27, 52, 60, 61, 142,
   151–88, 230, 292, 295,
   309, 312
   and Aboriginal rights and
      title 12, 18, 151–88
   and First Nations ances-
      try 18
   identity 180
*Migratory Birds Convention
   Act, 1917* 109
mining 247, 255, 257, 267,
   269, 279
Mitchell v. Canada (M.N.R.)
   78, 79, 84, 85, 86, 87,
   113, 143, 144, 148, 183,
   198, 201, 212, 213, 235,
   236, 239, 265, 270, 286,
   295, 297, 299, 307, 309,
   310, 311
Monk, Justice 171
Morrow, Justice 144
Mortmain Act 117
Mphumeya v. R. 104
Native Women's Association
   of Canada 41–42, 43,
   61, 63
*Native Women's Association
   of Canada (NWAC) v.
   Canada* 39, 59, 61

INDEX

Natural Resources Transfer Agreement (NRTA) 182, 187, 307
Nault, Robert 228
Navajo Nation Court of Appeal 121
Navajo Supreme Court 121
New Brunswick 146, 192, 196, 235, 265, 308
New Brunswick Court of Appeal 146
New Democratic Party 271
New France 87, 99
New Zealand 108, 111
Norman 92, 93, 113
Normandy 93, 115
North-West Mounted Police 165, 172
Northwest Territories Court of Appeal 148
North America 92, 94, 99
Norway House 172
Nova Scotia 70, 124, 146, 193, 194, 200, 265, 292, 308
Nova Scotia Court of Appeal 127
Nunavut 273
O'Neill, Justice 164, 180
Ohemeng v. Darkwa 104
oil 190, 279, 281, 282
Oke Lanipekun Laoye v. Amao Oyetunde 103
Ontario 61, 63, 122, 186, 191, 192, 311
Ontario (A.G.) v. Bear Island Foundation 147, 148, 223, 239
Ontario Boundaries 85, 169, 170, 171, 186, 187
Ontario Court of Appeal 160, 164, 234, 263, 307, 311
Ontario District Court 192
Ontario Superior Court 164
onus of proof 132, 133, 135, 137, 138, 205, 250, 264, 268

Opetchesaht Indian Band v. Canada 235
oral history 15, 45, 71, 73, 82, 135, 145, 190, 224, 275, 276, 286, 292, 295
Oregon Treaty 165, 173, 174
Pacific Islanders Protection Act 124
Parliament 75, 82, 84, 88, 93, 94, 96, 99, 100, 102, 108, 109, 111, 114, 125, 126, 134, 278, 306, 307
parliamentary supremacy 69, 82, 100, 108, 269, 270
plants 13, 27, 30, 32–33, 51
Pondoland 105
Privy Council 19, 85, 87, 96, 97, 98, 101, 103, 104, 105, 106, 107, 109, 112, 116, 117, 118, 120, 121, 122, 169, 171, 186, 187, 204
Québec 85, 99, 100, 106, 107, 130, 184, 190
  Fishery Regulations 199
Quebec Act (U.K.) 148
Quebec Court of Appeal 197
Quebec Superior Court 171
R.W.D.S.U. v. Dolphin Delivery Ltd. 88
R. v. Adams 78, 81, 87, 130, 131, 142, 143, 148, 149, 164, 184, 190, 199, 235, 263, 307, 310
R. v. Badger 79, 84, 141, 143, 145, 190, 199, 231, 235, 256, 257, 261, 263, 268, 269, 270, 307, 310
R. v. Blais 166, 182, 185, 187, 235, 312
R. v. Bow Street Metropolitan Stipendiary Magistrate and others ex parte Pinochet Ugarte 222, 223, 238, 239
R. v. Catagas 306
R. v. Chevrier 158, 182
R. v. Côté 75, 76, 78, 79, 86, 87, 89, 136, 142, 143, 144, 146, 148, 176, 186, 188, 190, 199, 235, 264, 307, 310
R. v. Desjarlais 182
R. v. Ferguson 182
R. v. George 109, 110, 125
R. v. Gladstone 61, 78, 80, 130, 131, 134, 138, 142, 143, 144, 149, 199, 205, 212, 235, 241, 251, 252, 253, 254, 256, 258, 259, 260, 262, 263, 267, 295, 307, 308, 309, 311
R. v. Gladue 55, 65, 235, 263
R. v. Horseman 263, 307
R. v. Lavallee 60
R. v. Lewis 120, 235
R. v. Marshall 19, 20, 24, 70, 82, 99, 113, 117, 124, 127, 141, 142, 143, 145, 146, 148, 170, 190–201, 213, 214, 215, 225, 226, 231, 235, 236, 239, 241, 245, 246, 256, 257, 258, 262, 263, 265, 267, 268, 269, 270, 292, 294, 295, 307, 308, 309, 310, 311
R. v. Morin 153, 166, 180, 184, 185, 191, 193, 199, 200
R. v. N.T.C. Smokehouse Ltd. 78, 148, 199, 235
R. v. Neil 220, 221
R. v. Nikal 78, 190, 199, 235, 306, 307, 309, 310
R. v. Pamajewon 78, 199, 235, 263, 307, 308, 310, 312
R. v. Powley 18, 23, 142, 151, 152, 155, 156, 157, 159, 160, 162, 163, 164, 165, 179, 180, 181, 182, 183, 184, 230, 235, 295, 307, 309
R. v. Secretary of State for Foreign and Commonwealth Affairs ex parte Indian Association of Alberta 117

INDEX 319

R. v. Sikyea 109, 125, 230
R. v. Simon 79, 117, 125, 141, 145, 197, 231, 246, 263, 264, 270, 306, 310
R. v. Sioui 79, 85, 88, 117, 134, 135, 141, 145, 212, 235, 307, 310
R. v. Sparrow 20, 24, 39, 60, 77, 78, 79, 80, 84, 86, 88, 125, 143, 144, 145, 150, 177, 184, 204, 206–7, 211, 212, 213, 214, 227, 231, 232, 235, 236, 239, 240, 241, 251, 252, 253, 257, 260, 261, 262, 263, 266, 267, 268, 270, 279, 280, 281, 287, 291, 292, 295, 306, 307, 308, 309, 310, 311
R. v. Sundown 78, 141, 235, 307
R. v. Van der Peet 18, 23, 34, 38, 52, 53, 60, 64, 67, 73, 74, 76, 77, 78, 79, 80, 81, 82, 83, 84, 85, 86, 87, 88, 89, 91, 105, 109, 112, 113, 127, 128, 130, 131, 132, 133, 134, 135, 136, 138, 139, 141, 142, 143, 144, 146, 148, 149, 151, 154, 155, 159, 160, 161, 163, 164, 165, 166, 177, 179, 180, 181, 183, 184, 199, 202, 212, 213, 229, 230, 231, 235, 240, 246, 253, 262, 263, 264, 265, 266, 268, 286, 295, 297, 306, 307, 308, 309, 310, 311
R. v. Vaughan 98, 116
racism 47
Red Crow 36
Red River 157, 180, 183, 185, 187
Reference re: Manitoba Language Rights 308
Reference re Secession of Québec 69, 79, 81, 82, 88, 111, 306, 308, 311

religion 33, 98, 101, 116, 145
reserves 41, 56, 61, 66, 106, 206, 216, 237, 276
residential schools 228, 288
resources 11, 12, 19, 21, 22, 23, 32, 48, 52, 66, 79, 124, 144, 190, 191, 194, 196, 212, 213, 234, 241–70, 273, 274, 277, 280, 281, 282, 284, 288, 290, 309
Re Eskimos 171
Re Labrador Boundary 171
Re Therrien 238
Richard I 139
rights
  customary 16, 17, 72, 86, 92, 94, 102, 103, 104, 105, 106, 107, 109, 110, 112, 113, 115, 118, 119, 120, 121, 122, 123, 133, 134, 135, 148, 205, 231
Roberts v. Canada 84, 85, 144
Robinson-Huron Treaty 204, 263
Roman
  empire 92, 119
  law 113, 115, 122
  treaties 113, 115
Royal Commission on Aboriginal Peoples (RCAP) 76, 83, 89, 156, 208, 209, 233
Royal Proclamation of 1763 34, 38, 65, 83, 85, 86, 87, 99, 100, 101, 110, 117, 138, 145, 148, 184, 213
rule of law 100
Saskatchewan 182, 184
Saskatchewan Court of Appea 182
Saskatchewan Court of Queen's Bench 180

Saskatchewan Provincial Court 166
Sault Ste. Marie 156, 164
Scales v. Key 133
Scotland 92, 93, 95–96, 115, 116, 117, 183
Scott, Chief Justice 186, 230, 238, 239
self-government 41, 43, 50, 53, 64, 65, 78, 81, 83, 88, 100, 106, 109, 123, 135, 149, 163, 260, 270, 278, 292, 295, 303, 307, 308, 310
Sharpe, Justice 160, 183
Simpson, Sir George 172
Sinclair, Associate Chief Judge 312
Sopinka, Justice 220, 223
South Africa 108, 121
sovereignty
  Aboriginal 83, 118, 184, 300
  British 70, 74, 79, 84, 85, 87, 204
  Canadian 88
  Crown 17, 18, 34, 68, 70, 74, 80, 81, 82, 84, 86, 87, 88, 91, 94, 95, 96, 101, 102, 103, 113, 114, 119, 122, 125, 135, 136, 137, 138, 139, 140, 143, 146, 148, 149, 151, 152, 153, 155, 180, 181, 184, 185, 186, 187, 188, 202, 212, 213, 228, 229, 231, 235, 236, 239, 247, 260, 265, 272, 276, 299, 300, 307, 308, 309, 310, 311
  and date of effective control 19, 175, 177
  assertion of 162–65, 165–78, 178–79
  European 127
  parliamentary 82, 126

320 INDEX

Specific Claims Resolution Act 208, 209–10, 229, 233, 234, 236

St. Ann's Island Shooting and Fishing Club Ltd. v. The King 230

St. Catherine's Milling and Lumber Co. 34, 35, 38, 106, 122, 203

St. Lawrence River 143, 176, 184

St. Mary's Indian Band v. Cranbrook (City) 84, 150, 235

Staples v. R. 169, 170, 171, 173, 186, 187

State Immunity Act 311

Statute of Westminster, 1931 108, 114

Supreme Court Act 200, 308

Supreme Court of Canada 11, 15, 18, 19, 20, 22, 34, 39, 40, 48, 52, 53, 54, 55, 56, 61, 63, 64, 66, 67, 68, 69, 70, 72, 73, 74, 75, 76, 78, 79, 80, 81, 82, 85, 86, 89, 91, 92, 99, 105, 109, 110, 111, 112, 113, 122, 123, 125, 127, 128, 130, 134, 135, 137, 141, 142, 143, 144, 145, 147, 149, 151, 152, 153, 154–55, 156, 159, 160, 161, 162, 163, 164, 165, 173, 175, 177, 178, 179, 180, 182, 183, 184, 187, 188, 190–201, 202, 203, 206, 207, 211–14, 215–23, 224, 225, 226, 227, 229, 230, 234, 235, 236, 237, 238, 241, 242, 246, 248, 249, 250, 251, 252, 253, 254, 256, 257, 262, 263, 264, 265, 266, 267, 268, 269, 270, 271, 275, 276, 277, 279, 285, 286, 291–96, 297, 300, 301, 302, 303, 304, 306, 307, 308, 310, 311, 312

Swail, Judge 166

Taku River Tlingit First Nation v. British Columbia 23, 236, 268, 277, 278, 280, 285, 286, 311

Taschereau, Justice 203, 204

terra nullius 86, 117, 167

The Kabaka's Government v. Kitonto 103

The King v. Sussex Justices 221, 238

title
  fee simple 34, 264
  trading 64, 70, 142, 145, 157, 169–72, 193, 194, 239, 243, 245, 256, 257, 263, 310
  trapping 33, 194, 256, 257, 258, 263

Treasury Board 209

treaties 13, 17, 29, 34, 52, 68, 70, 75, 79, 88, 96, 98, 99, 100, 101, 102, 104, 105, 107, 110, 113, 117, 118, 119, 122, 125, 134, 167, 172, 176, 177, 194, 204, 215, 230, 232, 239, 246, 256, 257, 258, 259, 261, 262, 269, 270, 281, 282, 294, 296, 297, 306
  Aboriginal view of 36–37
  British Columbia 22, 272
  Convention of Commerce 173

Treaties 1–7 107

Treaty 3 269

Treaty 8 257, 263, 269, 272, 282

Treaty of Albany, 1664 226, 240

Treaty of Paris 99, 176, 184

Treaty of Utrecht 176, 184

tribal courts 106

Truck house 70, 193, 194, 256

Twinn v. Canada 60

Two-Row Wampum 240

U.S. v. Wheeler 113

United Kingdom 81, 82, 84, 93, 94

United Nations 39, 83

United States 106, 109, 112, 113, 166, 173

United States Circuit Court of Appeals 309

United States Supreme Court 73, 113, 122, 184, 197, 199

United States v. Santa Fe Pacific R. 147, 231

Universal Declaration of Human Rights 39

Vancouver Island 272

Waitangi Tribunal 85

Wales 92, 93, 94, 115, 116

Watson, Lord 64, 106, 122, 203

Wewaykum v. Canada 20, 24, 203, 216–20, 221, 223, 224, 229, 230, 235, 236, 237, 238, 239

Wik Peoples and Thayorre People v. Queensland 91, 105, 112

Wildlife Act 199

William I (William the Conqueror) 93, 98, 114

Wilson, Justice 124, 144, 197, 214

Women's Legal Education and Action Fund (LEAF) 302

Worcester v. Georgia 73, 85, 112, 118, 122, 170, 173, 186

World Court 113

Wright, Justice 158

Wyld v. Silver 134, 145

Yorta Yorta Aboriginal Community v. Victoria 142, 143

Yukon 273

Zimbabwe 105